THIS INDIAN COUNTRY

American Indian Activists
and the Place They Made

FREDERICK E. HOXIE

PENGUIN BOOKS

PENGUIN BOOKS
Published by the Penguin Group
Penguin Group (USA) LLC
375 Hudson Street
New York, New York 10014

USA | Canada | UK | Ireland | Australia | New Zealand | India | South Africa | China
penguin.com
A Penguin Random House Company

First published in the United States of America by The Penguin Press,
a member of Penguin Group (USA) Inc., 2012
Published in Penguin Books 2013

Photograph credits appear on page 452.

Map illustrations by Tom Willockson

THE LIBRARY OF CONGRESS HAS CATALOGED THE HARDCOVER EDITION AS FOLLOWS:
Hoxie, Frederick E., 1947–
This Indian country : American Indian activists and the place they made / Frederick E. Hoxie.
p. cm. — (Penguin history of American life)
Includes bibliographical references and index.
ISBN 978-1-59420-365-7 (hc.)
ISBN 978-0-14-312402-3 (pbk.)
1. Indians of North America—Politics and government. 2. Indian activists—United States—
History. 3. Political activists—United States—History. 4. United States—Race relations.
5. United States—Politics and government. I. Title.
E98.T77H69 2012
323.1197—dc23
2012009287

Printed in the United States of America
1 3 5 7 9 10 8 6 4 2

DESIGNED BY NICOLE LAROCHE

Praise for *This Indian Country*

"Meticulous . . . enlightening." —*Booklist*

"*This Indian Country* is a proud . . . account of what it takes to get things done in the face of overwhelming resistance."
—*The Wichita Eagle*

"A capable, engaging work of history, important for students of official relations between the U.S. government and the Native peoples under its rule." —*Kirkus Reviews*

"This is an important, well-written, and thoroughly documented work about Native American leaders, who, while lesser known, are no less important." —*Publishers Weekly*

"Hoxie aims in a new book to tell how American Indians over two centuries persisted in claiming their rights in a country that once thought them irrelevant." —*Inside Illinois*

"A master historian at his very best, Frederick Hoxie deftly turns a series of evocative biographies into a compelling new synthesis of American Indian political resistance. In doing so, *This Indian Country* redefines the terrain of Native American historical memory, even as it centers Indian people in the full sweep of the history of the United States." —Philip J. Deloria, author of *Playing Indian* and *Indians in Unexpected Places*

"In this remarkable book, Frederick Hoxie portrays men and women whose weapons were words and whose battlegrounds were courtrooms, Congressional hearings, newspapers, and lecture halls. With ingenuity and tenacity, these Native American activists learned to navigate the corridors of U.S. power in Washington, D.C., a wilderness surely as daunting as any on the continent. Most remarkable of all, perhaps, these Natives didn't always lose in the ongoing contest for *This Indian Country*." —James H. Merrell, author of the Bancroft Prize–winning *The Indians' New World* and *Into the American Woods*

"This is a remarkable and absorbing book that shows why Indian peoples belong at the very center of American history. *This Indian Country* brings to life people who, unlike Crazy Horse or Tecumseh, would make terrible symbols and worse martyrs, but who made important history. These Indian lawyers, lobbyists, politicians, and writers were usually flawed and sometimes failures, but they drew on American ideas, emphasizing treaties and citizenship, to defend the tribalism and local control that American Indian policy attacked. Without them Indian country and the republic itself would be far different places."
—Richard White, author of *Railroaded* and *The Middle Ground*

"For five centuries, European nations and the United States levied all manner of assaults on the lives, land, governments, and cultures of American Indians. Yet Indianness never died out. Frederick Hoxie has brought his rare talents to bear on why this is so. Using well-selected political activists, he shows that these sustainers all kept Indian existence alive so that modern political activists like Vine Deloria Jr. could ignite and carry out a broad-based revival in modern times. This is as good a book as we will ever have to bring deep insight into the long arc of Indian history." —Charles Wilkinson, author of *Blood Struggle: The Rise of Modern Indian Nations*

"*This Indian Country* provides an invaluable exposition of the under-recognized political history of Native American intellectuals and activists. Judiciously framed and executed, it confirms Fred Hoxie's standing as the leading proponent and practitioner of contemporary American Indian history."
—Ned Blackhawk, author of *Violence Over the Land: Indians and Empires in the Early American West*

For My Sons, My Best Audience

Stephen

Philip

Silas

Charlie

At the particular time when these discoveries were made, the superiority of force happened to be so great on the side of the Europeans, that they were enabled to commit with impunity every sort of injustice in those remote countries. Hereafter, perhaps, the natives of those countries may grow stronger, or those of Europe may grow weaker, and the inhabitants of all the different quarters of the world may arrive at that equality of courage and force which, by inspiring mutual fear, can alone overawe the injustice of independent states into some sort of respect for the rights of one another.

Adam Smith, *An Inquiry into the Nature and Causes of the Wealth of Nations* (Oxford: Clarendon Press, 1976; originally published in 1776), Book 4, ch. 7, Part 3, 626

Contents

INTRODUCTION

For the past several years I have taught Native American history to college students in the Midwest. Since the subject is new to most of them, I usually begin each course with a simple exercise. I ask students to take out a sheet of paper and write down the names of three American Indians. Most who have responded to this question—bright young men and women in settings that have shifted with me over the years from a small liberal arts college to a large private university to the massive research institution where I now work—have grown up in middle-class suburbs or urban neighborhoods where they rarely have encountered Native people. "Everybody knows something about Indians," I tell them; "this exercise is a way of inventorying the extent of your knowledge as it exists today." I have conducted this exercise dozens of times, and the results seldom vary. Crazy Horse, Sitting Bull, and Geronimo are the Indians most frequently mentioned. (Following the release of Disney's *Pocahontas* in 1995, the Virginia "princess" frequently nudged one of the other three off the podium.)

After tabulating their answers, I ask the students to reflect on the result. If visiting Martians were to arrive suddenly and examine this outcome, what would they learn? The ensuing discussion always generates new insights, but the general conclusion is inescapable. Most Americans instinctively view Indians as people of the past who occupy a position outside the central narrative of American history. Three of the most frequently mentioned individuals were warriors, men who fought violently against American expansion, lost, and died. (Pocahontas was a "good Indian," remembered for assisting European expansion—and then dying.) The exercise suggests that Americans believe "real" Indians dwell in some distant time and place, apart from their own lives, and that Native history has no particular relationship to what is conventionally presented as the story of America. The images in my students' heads seem to underscore the idea that the United States is a "new" nation whose history stretches back to a founding moment that involved violent conflicts that "won" the land for "us" and left the Indians dispossessed. These images suggest Indians had a history too; but theirs was short and sad, and it ended a long time ago.

There is of course a great deal of truth in this conventional view. Native Americans were (and are) outsiders in America. Over the past two centuries most Indians resisted the rule of the United States and scoffed at the Americans' claim that their new nation embodied the triumph of human freedom. Native people had their own traditions which differed fundamentally from those the early explorers brought with them from Europe. At their first contact with Europeans, Indians were not Christians, nor were they preoccupied with private property. While consensual, their societies were not "democratic" in the European sense of the term. To Indians, iconic American frontiersmen like Daniel Boone or Andrew Jackson were hardly heroic or admirable; they were simply the latest intruders. They were not impressed that Jackson championed the "common man" because they understood the connection between his populist politics and his equally fervent campaign to expel the tribes from the eastern United States. Native people understood that opening new areas for "settlement" would mean the devastation of their ancient homelands.

The point of my first-day exercise is not to heap scorn on the nation's pioneers but to kindle curiosity about the real story of American Indians in the United States. If "real" Indians are warriors and the warriors were defeated and killed, how do we explain the Native people who survived the founding of the United States? What about the vast majority of Indians who were not warriors and who refused the Pocahontas role of assisting European settlement? Were they "real"? Do they have a history? And if the national myths tell only part of the story of the Native past, where do we look to find the rest? My informal quiz is intended to prod students to look beneath the surface of the popular beliefs that define Native people as exotic and irrelevant. I also ask students to consider why it is that Americans so easily accept the romantic stereotype of Indians as heroic warriors and princesses? Why don't we demand a richer, three-dimensional story? I pose a Native American version of the question the African American writer James Baldwin often asked white audiences a generation ago: "Why do you need a nigger?" My question is the same: Why do Americans need "Indians"—brave, exotic, and dead—as major figures in national culture?

My first-day questions are not unique. For many years historians, anthropologists, and literary scholars have repeated versions of my exercise in both their teachings and their writings about the Native American past. Confronting an earlier scholarly tradition that viewed Indian people as tethered to tradition and bound down by their exotic tribal cultures, proponents of a "New Indian History" have pierced through old stereotypes and distortions to portray Native Americans as three-dimensional actors, performing on the stage of history in accessible and comprehensible ways. This scholarship has uncovered the record of remarkable men and women who managed to survive the European invasion and participate actively in the creation of the modern world. While not denigrating nineteenth-century warriors like Tecumseh or Chief Joseph, the "New Indian History" has taught that since 1492 Native people spent far more time negotiating, lobbying, and debating than they spent tomahawking settlers or shooting at soldiers. This insight has inspired historians to tell stories of men and women who adapted ancient traditions to new circumstances or married new phenomena like Christianity or Western technology to the needs of their people. The "New Indian History" has recovered Native voices that allow students to hear previously ignored tribal perspectives on historical events. But even as we framed this new history, historians were confronted again and again by the public's enduring preference for warriors, feathers, and stories of Indian defeat.

This book counters that preference by presenting portraits of American Indians who neither physically resisted, nor surrendered to, the expanding continental empire that became the United States. The men and women portrayed here were born within the boundaries of the United States, rose to positions of community leadership, and decided to enter the nation's political arena—as lawyers, lobbyists, agitators, and writers—to defend their communities. They argued that Native people occupied a distinct place inside the borders of the United States and deserved special recognition from the central government. Undaunted by their adversary's military power, these activists employed legal reasoning, political pressure, and philosophical arguments to wage a continuous campaign on behalf of Indian autonomy, freedom, and survival. Some were homegrown activists whose focus was on protecting their local homelands; others had wider ambitions for the reform of national policies. All sought to overcome the predicament of political powerlessness and find peaceful resolutions for their complaints. They struggled to create a long-term relationship with the United States that would enable Native people to live as members of both particular indigenous communities and a large, democratic nation.

The story of these activists crosses several centuries. It opens in the waning days of the American Revolution, as negotiators in Paris set geographical boundaries for the new nation that ignored Indian nations that had fought in the conflict and had been recognized previously in international diplomacy. Native activists take center stage in the 1820s, when nationalistic U.S. leaders abandoned an earlier diplomatic tradition and pressed Indian leaders to surrender their homes to American settlers. The Choctaw James McDonald, the first Indian in the United States to be trained as a lawyer, is the protagonist of chapter two. McDonald became his tribe's legal adviser and drew on American political ideals to defend Indian rights, thereby laying the foundation for future claims against the United States.

A generation after McDonald, the Cherokee leader William Potter Ross developed and widened the young Choctaw's arguments. During the middle decades of the nineteenth century he traveled among Indian tribes in the West as well as to Washington, D.C., to recruit other Native leaders to defend tribal sovereignty. Among those who followed in Ross's wake were Sarah Winnemucca, a Nevada Paiute who in the 1880s became a nationally famous writer, lecturer, and lobbyist, and a group of remarkable Minnesota Ojibwe tribal leaders who battled both at home and in Washington, D.C., to preserve their tiny community on the shores of Mille Lacs Lake.

In the twentieth century the leading activists were often polished professionals like Thomas Sloan, an Omaha Indian who became an attorney and established a legal practice in Washington, D.C. The first Indian to argue a case before the U.S. Supreme Court, Sloan helped found the Society of American Indians in 1911 (serving as its first president) and encouraged other community leaders to create similar networks of support. In the 1930s, when Franklin Roosevelt's New Deal offered those leaders opportunities to speak out in defense of their tribes, these networks brought forth tribal advocates such as the Seneca Alice Jemison and the Crow leader Robert Yellowtail, as well as a new generation of intellectuals and thinkers, among them the Salish writer and reformer D'Arcy McNickle and the visionary scholar Vine Deloria, Jr., who by the time of his death in 2005 had become the leading proponent of indigenous cultures and tribal rights in the United States.

By the start of the twenty-first century the threads of activism developed by these individuals had woven themselves together so tightly that they produced the complex reality we observe today: a world where the descendants of indigenous societies and the children of the Americans who had dispossessed them can imagine living together as fellow citizens. The eight chapters that constitute this book focus on a dozen or so individuals who, at different times and places, took up the challenge of winning recognition for their communities within the political and institutional framework of the United States. While a great many other men and women were involved in this process, the stories of this small group of activists allow us to view the broad outlines of Indian America's long engagement with the power and political pretensions of the United States. They shared a common conviction that Native Americans, who had never consented to the establishment of the United States, nonetheless deserved recognition from its institutions and justice from its leaders.

The activists in this book were originals and innovators. Sarah Winnemucca, for example, had no more than a grammar school education, yet she forged alliances with humanitarian reformers across the country and argued forcefully that the trans-Mississippi West, which most non-Indians believed had already been "won" for civilization, was still a landscape of violence and brutality. Thomas Sloan, the Omaha lawyer, proposed that American citizenship would give Indian people the freedom they needed to claim their rights as members of tribal communities as well as the legal status to resist the dictatorial power of government bureaucrats and Indian agents. Similarly, the leaders of Minnesota's Mille Lacs band of Ojibwes, many of them illiterate in English, took the unprecedented step of hiring a team of prominent attorneys to press their claim for recognition and justice in U.S. courts.

These figures overlapped sufficiently with one another that through them we can follow an ongoing train of thought and action. This is not a simple story of linear progress and triumph in a climactic court case or legislative victory. Rather, it is a tale of continuous reflection, argumentation, and reform. The activists presented here were engaged in a grand conversation that produced a collective achievement beyond each one's imagination. James McDonald was a mentor and friend of Peter Pitchlynn, the Choctaw leader who later fought alongside William Potter Ross on behalf of autonomy for Indian Territory. Ross protested encroachments on Cherokee sovereignty in Washington, D.C., just as Sarah Winnemucca was speaking out against American national expansion in major cities across the country. Thomas Sloan established his Washington legal practice at the same time that the Mille Lacs Ojibwes were bringing their case into court. Sloan, in turn, was an ally of Robert Yellowtail, a successful Crow reservation politician who was promoted to agency superintendent by the same New Deal reformers who appointed D'Arcy McNickle to a senior post in the Indian Office. The latter two leaders worked together in the National Congress of American Indians (NCAI) during the 1940s, debating their views with the Seneca activist Alice Jemison, and joining with her to defend treaty rights and the power of tribal governments. Both Yellowtail and McNickle lived long enough to work alongside Vine Deloria, Jr., the author, lawyer, and activist who championed Native sovereignty in the 1970s, 1980s, and 1990s and who carried their struggle into the twenty-first century. The connections among these activists grew stronger over time, reflecting the rise of pan-Indian organizations such as the NCAI and the growing prominence of lobbyists who traveled to Washington, D.C.

The collective struggle of these men and women reveals the extent to which Native activists generated the ideas and constructed the legal and political doctrines that made it possible for Native American communities to survive in the United States. Taking place as it did in a nation founded on the presumption of Indian invisibility, theirs was a powerful humanistic achievement. Their lives teach us that Native survival was made possible by Indian people and their allies who had faith in their ideas and in nonviolent political activism. Their victories were triumphs earned by Native people who acted in accord with basic indigenous values: loyalty to one's homeland, mutual respect, and the central importance of human relationships.

This story of Native American activists should be a far more useful guide to the contemporary scene than tales of Geronimo's guerrilla warfare or Sitting Bull's stoic heroism. Most twenty-first-century Americans know that the old story of Indian defeat and disappearance makes no sense. There is too much evidence of Native survival surrounding us. People in the United States today easily recognize the artistic and cultural achievements of the continent's Native people and readily appreciate the contributions they have made to national life. Galleries and museums trumpet indigenous cultural achievements. And while popular tales of the Olympian Jim Thorpe or the World

War II Navajo code talkers may themselves be two-dimensional side-bars, they nevertheless directly contradict the old notion that Native people were always and everywhere the enemies of progress. Similarly, though Indian shamanism may be caricatured or dismissed by some, it is rarely labeled "paganism," as was the case only a few decades ago.

Outside the arena of popular culture, Americans are regularly reminded that Indian people are fellow members of our contentious democracy. In recent years tribes have been remarkably successful at asserting and defending their treaty rights to water and other resources. Likewise, instead of ignoring or denigrating tribal leaders, Congress and the White House regularly seek them out for consultation and negotiation. None of these aspects of politics and policy making exists without controversy, but it is unthinkable today that a Supreme Court justice could declare (as Justice Stanley Reed did in 1955) that "[e]very American schoolboy knows that the savage tribes of this continent were deprived of their ancestral ranges by force, and that . . . when the Indians ceded millions of acres by treaty in return for blankets, food and trinkets, it was not a sale but the conqueror's will that deprived them of their land."[1] Most Americans now know that Indian treaty councils involved more than the "conqueror's will" and that Native American history contained more elements than "savages" and "trinkets."

Within my lifetime American political institutions have come to appreciate that the words inscribed in long-ignored Indian treaties were actual agreements between sovereign powers that carved mutual promises into the edifice of the law. At the same time, religious organizations such as the National Council of Churches have come to accept the wisdom and integrity of ancient Native customs and beliefs. Many Native religious practices now enjoy legal protection, while Native veterans are honored, and tribal logging, fishing, and farming enterprises compete with their non-Indian neighbors for profits and market share. Closer to the nation's more densely populated areas, gleaming casinos now produce significant cash (and political clout) for Native groups. Poverty and the effects of past injustice remain in many places, but the simple, two-dimensional story of white progress and Indian suffering suggested sixty years ago by Justice Reed is clearly inadequate.

The people at the heart of this book provide an alternative to the old tale of conquest and victimization. Their story demonstrates that during the past two centuries Native people met the birth and territorial expansion of the United States with an array of strategies that ranged from direct and forceful opposition to flexible negotiation and accommodation. While striking different poses at different times and in different places, American Indians always insisted that for them, the United States did not embody human freedom. It was not, in Thomas Jefferson's phrase, a true "empire for liberty." These Native activists and the thousands of others who worked alongside them knew better, and they struggled both to be heard and to find settings where they too could enjoy American freedom. In a way, the story of their struggle is distinctly American, for it illustrates that the appreciation of tribal cultures and tribal governments we see today had its origins in the self-reliance and creativity of Native activists who engaged politically with a government that wanted them to disappear.

These activists rejected the idea that the worlds of Indians and non-Indians did not overlap and could not coexist, and their enterprise is part of the broad chain of events Adam Smith imagined in the pages of *The Wealth of Nations*: the struggle of "natives" from the "remote countries" to overcome the "injustice" visited upon them by Europeans in order to achieve an "equality of courage and force" in our own time. That larger story stretches across the globe and involves many others who refused to accept the colonizers' versions of events. The portion told here is a piece of that larger whole.

None of the figures in this book has ever made one of the lists generated by my opening-day exercise, but they all were recognized in their lifetimes as individuals unafraid to speak out on behalf of Indian rights and community survival. While many were of mixed ancestry, all were members of American Indian tribes. They exhibited extraordinary courage, though none confronted the United States on the battlefield. Their achievements occurred largely in legislative chambers, lecture halls, and courtrooms. They shouldered a common task: defining a place for American Indian communities within the boundaries and institutions of the United States. They also employed a common strategy: to use the invader's language, values, and institutions to create and defend that place. They believed that "Indian country" did not lie in the West or the North or the South, out beyond the borders of the nation but instead that it was located wherever Indians gathered together and resolved to live in accord with their ancient traditions and histories. This is their story and, through it, the story of this Indian country.

LAKE NIPIGON

Thunder
Bay

LAKE SUPERIOR

CANADA

Lake Nipissing

Ottawa R.

Montreal

Quebec

*Lake
Champlain*

Ft. Michilimackinac

*Georgian
Bay*

St. Lawrence R.

LAKE HURON

LAKE MICHIGAN

St. Croix R.

Fox R.

Wisconsin R.

Des Moines R.

Illinois R.

Missouri R.

St Louis

Mississippi R.

OZARK MTS.

OTTAWAS

POTAWATOMIS

MIAMIS

Detroit

Maumee R.

WYANDOTS

DELAWARES

SHAWNEES

Wabash R.

Ohio R.

LAKE ERIE

LAKE ONTARIO

Ft. Niagara

NEW YORK

MOHAWKS

ONEIDAS

SENECAS

PENNSYLVANIA

Pittsburgh

Mohawk R.

Hudson R.

VERMONT

NEW HAMPSHIRE

MASSACHUSETTS

Boston

CONN.

NEW
JERSEY

New York

Philadelphia

Delaware R.

DELAWARE

MARYLAND

Baltimore

APPALACHIAN MOUNTAINS

Monongahela R.

VIRGINIA

Richmond

James R.

KENTUCKY

Cumberland R.

Tennessee R.

CHEROKEES

CREEKS

NORTH
CAROLINA

Roanoke R.

Pee Dee R.

SOUTH
CAROLINA

Augusta

Charleston

ATLANTIC OCEAN

Disputed Spanish

American Border

CHOCTAWS

Ouachita R.

Red R.

GEORGIA

Alabama R.

Altamaha R.

Pensacola

St. Augustine

New Orleans

GULF OF MEXICO

Proposed Treaty Line 1782

Treaty Line 1783

Miles

0   50   100   150   200

CHAPTER ONE

ERASED FROM THE MAP

The American habit of disregarding living Indians is not founded in ignorance or prejudice; it is the product of history—of decisions made at the time of the nation's founding, then etched into policy and absorbed into popular belief. At the close of the American Revolution, when international statesmen and monarchs first recognized the existence of the United States, events and actors on both sides of the Atlantic conspired to erase Indians from the official life, and the official map, of the new nation. This erasure fulfilled the founders' desire to sever the diplomatic ties that had linked European powers to Native groups for centuries and confirmed the Americans' commitment to a "new order" on the continent. The young nation's leaders could then pretend that Indian people were irrelevant in international affairs as well as in much of U.S. public life. Their achievement created a new predicament for tribal activists who found themselves resident within America's boundaries but invisible to its leaders.

Despite the tradition of celebrating July 4, 1776, as the nation's birthday, the United States did not come into formal existence until September 3, 1783, when diplomats from America, Great Britain, France, and

Spain gathered in Paris to sign a series of agreements that both ended the conflicts among them and established the boundaries of a new country. It was those treaties, not the ringing words of the Declaration of Independence, that established the American nation-state.[1] Perhaps more surprising to modern readers is the fact that the expansive boundaries established for the United States in 1783, which extended to the Great Lakes in the north and the Mississippi River in the west, had little relationship to the places where the new nation's citizens actually lived. In 1783, 2.3 million settlers and their slaves lived within the new U.S. borders, nearly 98 percent of them in communities hugging the Atlantic seaboard. The 50,000 or so former colonists who had decamped for Kentucky during the 1770s represented the only sizable group of "Americans" living in the approximately 422,000 square miles of national territory that lay west of the Appalachians.[2]

In 1783 outposts such as Fort Pitt, on the Ohio River, or Detroit, on the western end of Lake Erie, contained only a few hundred residents. Beyond Fort Pitt, most of the Europeans living in the North American interior were descendants of the English, French, and Indian traders and soldiers who had activated the imperial claims to the region. Their interests were commercial; they felt no particular sympathy for the new American enterprise. Towns that later became part of the United States—St. Louis, Mobile, Pensacola, and New Orleans—stood outside the nation's borders and maintained a steady loyalty to Spain. The bulk of the country lying within the new nation's borders—the Ohio and Tennessee river valleys and the rivers flowing into the east bank of the Mississippi—was home to nearly 200,000 Native people, most of them living in agricultural villages tied to one another through trade, kinship, and military alliances. The inhabitants of this vast "Indian country" viewed the settlers' new nation with considerable unease.[3]

In the colonial era, European powers had asserted their control over the North American interior through diplomatic alliances with Native groups. The American rebels now in nominal control of the continent were prepared to break with that tradition. Not only did they claim that Indian lands were "empty," but in their negotiations with the European powers they refused to recognize the tribal nations in their territory. When the new national borders were announced, one American officer told an Indian gathering, "Your fathers the English have made peace with us for themselves, but [they] forgot you . . . and neglected you like bastards."[4]

Prominent among those ignored in the new treaties were Joseph Brant (Thayendanega), the charismatic Mohawk war captain who during the Revolutionary War had rallied tribes to attack Americans along the northern border with Canada, and Alexander McGillivray, the Creek merchant leader who had fought with the British in both Florida and Georgia. Both men were firmly committed to the British cause. Brant left his New York home early in the conflict to organize resistance to the "Savage Virginians" in the Ohio Valley.[5] McGillivray abandoned his family's prosperous trading post near Augusta at the start of the war, moving to his mother's Creek town along the Coosa River. When they were told of the territory granted to the Americans in Paris, Brant and McGillivray must have realized that they had, in fact, been treated "like bastards."

Soon after Brant and his Iroquois kinsmen learned of the provisional terms of peace in the spring of 1783, they gathered at the British post at Fort Niagara (soon to become "American" soil) to prepare a response. The Iroquois chiefs quickly concluded that the king "had no right whatever to grant away to the States of America their rights or properties." Brant shared their outrage, declaring: "England had sold the Indians to Congress." The assembly urged the Mohawk chief to travel to Quebec to meet with the British governor. They wanted reassurance that "they are not partakers of that peace with the King and the Bostonians."[6] The British commander at Niagara reported that the Indian chiefs with whom he had met found it "almost impossible to believe that the boundaries actually were run as reported. . . ."[7]

Forty years old in 1783, Joseph Brant was well prepared to make the case for the Indians' claim to their homelands. The Mohawk leader had grown up in the orbit of Sir William Johnson, the masterful superintendent of Indian trade in the eastern Great Lakes, whose close alliance with the Iroquois confederacy had sustained the crown's ties to the tribes in New York and Ohio for decades prior to the Revolution. Like many eighteenth-century frontier traders and diplomats, Johnson had brought a prominent Native woman into his home as his companion and diplomatic guide. Brant's older sister, Molly, was Johnson's consort during most of his career. As a member of a prominent family she provided him access to the Iroquois community. She served as hostess, interpreter, and adviser at countless conferences and diplomatic meetings and bore him eight children.

Brant came to live in Johnson's household as a teenager, and in 1761 he was sent to Eleazer Wheelock's Connecticut mission school to polish his English and learn European mores, manners, and customs. (An evangelist who came of age during the Great Awakening that swept through New England in the 1730s, Wheelock established a ministry that included Native Americans soon after he graduated from Yale College. He eventually used his success with young men like Brant to raise funds for ever more ambitious projects aimed at Indian education. The climax of these efforts was the founding of Dartmouth College in 1768.) After two years of instruction in English and the tenets of Christianity, Brant returned to Johnson's estate in central New York and took up life as a farmer and military servant of the crown. He moved easily among both Europeans and Native Americans. When he visited London just prior to the American war, the handsome young Mohawk met with cabinet officers and charmed the capital's grand dames with his perfect manners. He capped his visit by posing for the celebrated artist George Romney, whose portrait stripped away Brant's Christian manners and presented him holding a tomahawk and wearing a feather headdress.

As warfare with the colonists began in earnest in 1776, British officials turned to Brant to rally tribal leaders to attack the Americans on their western frontier. Paid at the rate of a captain and supplied with uniforms and arms, the Mohawk leader stitched together a regional coalition of Great Lakes tribes that fought with considerable success and continued even after George Washington had defeated the British forces under Lord Cornwallis at Yorktown in the fall of 1781. In 1782 war parties organized by Brant were victorious in battles at Sandusky in Ohio and Blue Licks in Kentucky. The following year, with the peace treaty still not concluded, the Mohawk leader urged the British command to launch a new offensive against the Americans. When Brant arrived in Quebec on May 21, he was eager to continue the fight. Baroness Frederika von Riedesel, the wife of a German officer whose troops were serving in Canada alongside the British, reported meeting the man who was considered "chief among the Indians." She noted in her diary that "his language was good, his manners the best." She added: "He was dressed half as a soldier and half as an Indian, and his countenance was manly and clever."[8]

Brant's host was Governor Frederick Haldimand, a Swiss-born mercenary who had served the British in North America since the Seven Years' War against the French in the 1760s. Haldimand was deeply embarrassed by the terms of the Paris treaty. When he first saw the peace terms in late April, he wrote a friend that his "soul [was] completely bowed down with grief. I am heartily ashamed," he added "and wish I was in the interior of Tartary."[9] As a military strategist who appreciated the power and territorial reach of Native military leaders like Brant, Haldimand understood that the king's Indian allies would continue to be important in postwar relations along the American border. He also understood that as experienced diplomats the Indians could sense that the Americans had changed the rules of diplomacy. Leaders like Brant had never before been so completely ignored. As Haldimand later explained to the Tory leader Frederick North, "they entertain no idea . . . that the King . . . had a right to cede their territories or hunting grounds to the United States of North America. These people . . . have as enlightened ideas of the nature and obligations of treaties as the most civilized nations have. . . ."[10]

The treaty terms announced in Paris confirmed Brant's deepest fears. During his 1775 visit to London he had met many of the Whig politicians who later negotiated the Treaty of Paris. He understood that their opposition to royal authority and their enthusiastic faith in the power of international trade led them to believe that abandoning the North American colonies could expand the market for British products and stimulate the national economy. From their perspective, the king's long-standing alliances with Native leaders were cumbersome and expensive artifacts of the past. Still, the Mohawk war captain made his case to Haldimand with extraordinary intensity. He demanded that the governor "[t]ell us the whole and real truth from your heart." Brant noted that nearly two hundred years earlier the Mohawks "were the first Indian nation that took you by the hand like friends and brothers and invited you to live amongst us." In return, he added, his tribe had always considered the British "a great nation bound to us by treaty and able to protect us against all the world."

When the Revolution erupted, Brant recalled that the Mohawks and their allies "were unalterably determined to stick to our ancient treaties with the Crown of England." Brant demanded that Haldimand fulfill his obligations as an ally: "Wherefore brother I am now sent on behalf of all the King's Indian allies to receive a decisive answer from you and to know whether they are included in this treaty with the Americans as faithful allies should be . . . and whether those lands which the great being above has pointed out for our ancestors . . . and where the bones of our forefathers are laid [are] secured to them." Knowing that the governor was well aware of the sacrifices his soldiers and their families had made during the long years of war—many, like Brant and his family, driven from their homes by rampaging colonial troops— the Mohawk captain closed by invoking his warriors' unbending loyalty. The Indians expected assistance, he declared, from "allies for whom we have so often [and] so freely bled."[11]

MORE THAN A THOUSAND MILES south of Quebec City, another Native leader who had fought for the British responded to the new American borders with a more aggressive strategy. Like Brant, Alexander McGillivray was the product of a prewar world of trade and imperial alliances. He was the son of Lachlan McGillivray, a Scottish trader, and Sehoy Marchand, the daughter of a French officer and a Creek woman from that tribe's prominent wind clan. Like William Johnson, Lachlan McGillivray was a newcomer to North America who gained access to the Indian trade by allying himself with a prominent Native family. Because the Creeks were matrilineal (tracing their ancestry through mothers) Lachlan's son Alexander was accepted as a member of the tribe and spent his early childhood among his mother's kinsmen along the Coosa River in modern Alabama. Lachlan McGillivray did not remain on the frontier, however, and in 1760—when he was ten—Alexander moved to Savannah with his family. There he was educated by tutors and introduced to the trading business by both Lachlan and his Creek relatives. When the American rebellion began, young McGillivray, like Brant, was eager to use his family and business connections to rally Indian leaders to the crown's defense.[12] Native war parties drawn from the Creeks and Cherokees were fiercely loyal. They helped secure Savannah for the British in the summer of 1779 and stayed on after their victory to repel a combined French and rebel assault on the city late the same year. When Charleston, the largest city in the southern colonies, fell to the British in 1780, McGillivray believed the region had been secured. He returned to his headquarters on the Coosa River. Unfortunately for the British, the Americans strengthened their resistance in the Carolina backcountry later in the year and the Spanish and French challenged the crown's defenses in East Florida and along the Mississippi. Creek warriors fought alongside the redcoats on both fronts, with McGillivray commanding a contingent that ultimately surrendered Pensacola to the Spanish in the spring of 1781.

By year's end Florida had fallen to Spain and the Americans had captured General Cornwallis's army at Yorktown. The situation grew increasingly desperate. American rebels seized the southern upcountry, and the Spanish occupied all the major trading posts in both East and West Florida. As in the North, Native forces nevertheless remained in command of most of the interior farmland and trade networks. Their leaders were no less incredulous about the outcome of the Paris negotiations than their counterparts at Fort Niagara. In a report on his meeting with "the chiefs of the nation" assembled at St. Augustine, the British commander reported that the Indians "lamented extremely" this unfortunate turn of events and had attacked their former allies for betraying their own standards of conduct. "Their fathers told them," he reported, "that an Englishman in the hour of misfortune or danger was a man who would die rather than forsake his friends."[13]

Like Brant, McGillivray had seen his family's prosperous prewar life torn apart by the American rebellion. He was forced to abandon his home, and his father surrendered much of his Georgia property to the rebels. Lachlan McGillivray returned to Scotland at war's end, while his son and other relatives remained in Upper Creek tribal towns along the Coosa River. As Alexander McGillivray and his supporters considered their next move, Lower Creek settlements situated near the Chattahoochee and Flint rivers decided to open talks with the former rebels now in charge in Georgia. At the end of 1783, seeing no alternative, this increasingly pro-American segment of the tribe signed a treaty ceding thousands of acres to the Americans.

McGillivray faced a crucial decision. Should he follow the Lower Creeks and make peace with the Americans, or should he seek a new alliance with the Spanish, ignoring their reputation for brutality and tightfistedness? McGillivray, who had recently been named "Head warrior of the Nation" by the Upper Creeks, barely hesitated. Charging that the British had "most shamefully deserted" his family, the Creek leader moved quickly to establish a relationship with the Spanish commander at Pensacola. Like the chiefs who had met with the British commander at St. Augustine, he believed his former allies had acted without honor, "unless," he wrote, "[s]pilling our blood in the Service of his Nation can be deemed so."[14]

In March 1783, at about the time Joseph Brant met with his fellow chiefs at Fort Niagara, McGillivray wrote to Arturo O'Neil, the Dublin-born Spanish commander at Pensacola, identifying himself as "Chief of the Creek Nations." He urged O'Neil to release a trader friendly to the Creeks who recently had been imprisoned on suspicion of spying. "'Tis without foundation," he wrote. Moreover, refusing to let the trader go would only endanger "the tranquility" that currently existed between their two communities. Six months later McGillivray appeared in person at the Spanish post to open talks. O'Neil later reported to his superiors in Havana that the Creek leader had told him that even though his former English allies would soon evacuate St. Augustine, they had urged McGillivray to "hold the Indians in readiness to recommence the war." Not only could the Creeks promise O'Neil a steady flow of deerskins, but, he reported, they would also "refuse" the peace overtures coming their way from Georgia. The commander was convinced that the Indians were "strongly opposed" to the Americans.[15]

BRANT AND McGILLIVRAY were puzzled by Britain's decision to abandon their Native allies. How could the crown's loyal auxiliaries, whose villages spread across every corner of King George's North American empire, have gone unmentioned in the international agreements that ended the American rebellion and created a new nation with a western border on the Mississippi River? How had a squabbling band of rebel leaders, who had almost no ability to project military power into the continent's interior, managed to win international recognition for a vast territory they could neither occupy nor rule? Why had the French and Spanish allowed this to occur? And most upsetting to them personally, how could sophisticated and loyal commanders like Brant and McGillivray, men treated as officers by the British, be so completely dismissed? Perhaps this was but a momentary aberration.

It was not. The 1783 Paris agreements changed how Mohawks, Creeks, and all other Native groups within the official boundaries of the United States would henceforth deal with outsiders. The accords accomplished the double trick of erasing Native people from the international diplomatic arena, while placing them under the authority of a nation that took no formal notice of their existence.[16] For major tribes, like the Iroquois and Creeks, who were accustomed to diplomacy, trade, and treaty making involving multiple European adversaries, a new world was coming dimly into view. A single power now claimed sovereignty over them but did not recognize their leaders or territorial borders. This predicament pitted tribal leaders like Brant and McGillivray against the deepest ambitions of a young nation intent on becoming a continental power. How had this happened?

THE AMERICAN REVOLUTION AND THE GREAT POWERS

From the outset, the American rebellion had required its leaders to wage a complex three-front struggle that was made all the more different by their ever-changing relationship with Indian tribes. Their most immediate concern was the imposing army of British and mercenary troops that swarmed across the Atlantic in the summer of 1776, but the Revolution's leaders also knew that popular support for their rebellion was thin. At least a third of their countrymen were either opposed or indifferent to the war for independence.[17] American leaders might condemn British Loyalists and malcontents as "cut throats and deserters," but they could not ignore their sizable presence.[18] Help from overseas was essential if the Americans had any chance of winning enough victories over the redcoats to rally their divided followers to the cause.

This calculation led the Americans to the court of Louis XVI, Britain's chief international rival. Members of the Continental Congress corresponded with French agents during the winter of 1775–76 and began debating a proposed model commercial treaty with the French within days of approving their Declaration of Independence. They counted on Paris's eagerness to avenge the loss of their North American colonies in 1763, and they were not disappointed. Shortly after July 4, 1776, Minister of Foreign Affairs Charles Gravier, comte de Vergennes, wrote that "providence [has] marked this moment for the humiliation of England . . . it is time to take revenge . . . for the evil it has done since the beginning of the century to those who had the misfortune to be its neighbors or its rivals."[19]

The French began supplying the Americans with covert aid, but the Continental Congress wanted a public commitment. With formal recognition from France the rebels believed they would be better able to cultivate additional military allies and financial supporters. To press their case, the rebel government dispatched its most experienced diplomat, Benjamin Franklin, to the French court. The seventy-year-old scientist was soon lobbying his hosts by holding receptions at his suburban residence and appearing regularly in Paris salons sporting a beaver hat, homespun clothes, and shoulder-length hair. The American victory at Saratoga, New York, in October 1777 (won by American troops firing French munitions) provided the reassurance the French required. A formal treaty was approved in early 1778. The agreement contained all the Americans had wished for with one caveat. Minister Vergennes had insisted that "the first and most essential" element in the new treaty "is that neither of the two parties shall make either peace or truce without the consent of the other."[20]

With Franklin now recognized as the ambassador of the United States to France, the Americans' attention shifted to Spain. The American diplomat Arthur Lee had visited Madrid in March 1777 to deliver a memorial warning the Spanish court that an English victory in

North America would allow King George to reign as "the irresistible though hated arbiter of Europe." Aid to the Americans could prevent that outcome. "This," he declared, "is the moment in which Spain and France may clip her wings and pinion her forever." The Spanish demurred, but the Americans persisted. Both the Americans and their French allies offered to help King Charles III retake Florida (lost in the Seven Years' War) and capture the British West Indies. They also hinted that a new alliance might enable the two Catholic powers to retake Gibraltar for Spain (the English had held that strategic spot for the past seventy years). The Spanish were receptive but noncommittal.[21]

The conclusion of the Seven Years' War in 1763 had coincided with the ascension of Charles III to the Spanish throne. A former ruler of Naples, Charles was a member of the house of Bourbon and thereby related to Louis XVI. Charles was a forceful administrator. He had promoted prosperity in Naples by adopting liberal trade policies and appointing competent ministers to regulate the kingdom. He came to power in Spain at a moment when the rise of urban merchant houses and the beginnings of industrialization had enabled Britain and France to expand the reach of their international trade. But the Spanish crown had continued to trudge along the old mercantilist path. It tightly controlled commerce between its colonies and the Iberian Peninsula and relied heavily on the extraction of mineral and agricultural wealth to enrich the mother country. As a consequence, as much as 80 percent of the goods shipped from Cádiz to the Americas in the 1760s were manufactured outside Spain. At the onset of the American rebellion the Spanish were therefore as eager to "clip" the wings of Great Britain's burgeoning economic juggernaut as they were to stymie its military ambitions.

The principal instrument of Spanish imperial policy during the American Revolution was José de Gálvez, a career bureaucrat who had risen from the post of inspector general in New Spain to become colonial secretary in 1775. Gálvez advocated loosening Spain's traditional restrictions on its American colonies. His most important achievement was persuading the king to increase the number of ports that were permitted to import and export goods between the Americas and the mother country. This reform produced a surge in traffic, particularly with Mexico City and the surrounding territories of New Spain.[22] Despite his willingness to innovate, Gálvez remained committed to the mercantile ideal of a self-contained empire. As Charles declared, "Only a free and protected commerce . . . can restore agriculture, industry and population in my dominions to their proper vigor."[23]

Spain, then, was of two minds. On the one hand, Spanish officials understood the power of free trade and manufacturing to produce new wealth. On the other, an alliance with the Americans could draw this collection of upstart traders (and smugglers) dangerously close to the empire's borders. In the end their fear of Britain prevailed over their fear of the unruly Americans. Following the French lead, Charles III declared war on Britain in the summer of 1779. Immediately after Spain had entered the war, Minister Gálvez wrote the governor of Louisiana to remind him of their objectives. The "principal object" of the king's American campaign during the coming war, he said, would be "to drive the [English] from the Mexican Gulf and the neighborhood of Louisiana."[24]

While the Americans were waging their international campaign for recognition in the royal courts of Europe, they were also acutely aware of the extent to which their rebellion had divided powerful political interests in Great Britain. The Tory prime minister Frederick North held firm to the goal of defeating the American insurrection, but the number of rivals within his own party, as well as the leaders of his Whig opposition, grew as the conflict wore on. John Adams reported from Paris in 1780, for example, that the Irish-born Lord Shelburne, one of North's fiercest critics, had recently declared in Parliament that "such is the situation in which we now find ourselves: not a single ally! . . . Such are the fruits of the prudence of our ministers," he added. "They have lost America, the most beautiful half of the empire, and against the half that remains to us they have excited all the powers of Europe."[25] Shelburne and others sympathized with the Americans' democratic ideals; many of them wanted to see similar electoral reforms enacted in Britain. Critics of the war also included a rising generation of free traders who insisted that once independent, the American colonies could become active trading partners and attractive customers for British manufacturers and banks.[26]

As the war stretched into its fifth year, a growing chorus of British politicians urged the government to cut its losses by recognizing American independence and negotiating a peace agreement with France and Spain. The king and his supporters in Parliament stuck to their guns, but when news of Lord Cornwallis's surrender at Yorktown reached London in November 1781, their support collapsed. Lord North exclaimed, "Oh God, Oh God, It's All Over." Though the king's advocates maneuvered for three more months, on March 20, 1782, North's cabinet, in power since 1770, finally resigned.[27]

In the wake of North's departure, George III reluctantly turned to the loyal opposition, inviting the aging Lord Rockingham, who had led the government during the Stamp Act crisis two decades earlier, to form a new cabinet. Rockingham managed to exclude the strongest antiwar voices from his government, but he served for less than four months; he died in July during an influenza epidemic. The king then turned to Rockingham's home secretary, Lord Shelburne, an idiosyncratic Anglo-Irishman who had served in the House of Commons for twenty years but who was selected primarily because the king detested his chief rival, Charles James Fox, an outspoken young advocate of American independence.

French and Spanish officials celebrated Britain's plummeting resolve. It seemed their diplomatic calculations had paid off. British power would now be reduced while the influence of the king's domestic critics would expand. But these celebrations were short-lived. The rebellion had united the Americans and their European allies, but once Cornwallis's sword had been handed to General Washington and the North government had fallen, the victors began to mistrust one another. The French and Spanish were eager to continue the alliance to ensure the "clipping" of Britain's wings, but the Americans, with a bankrupt treasury and a domestic population weary of war, were far less enthusiastic.

Acutely aware of their military weakness (the British, after all, continued to occupy New York and Charleston), the Americans could not survive without European arms and credit. On the other hand, France and Spain worried that Franklin and company might cut a quick conciliatory deal with their former rulers, ignore the interests of the continent's tribes, and sail for home. Spain's chief minister summarized those worries in early 1782, when he told the French ambassador in Madrid that "the Americans would always be English at heart. . . ."[28]

NEGOTIATING THE PEACE

The principal issue separating the rebels and their French and Spanish allies in the spring of 1782 was the size of the nation about to be created on the North American continent. The Americans sympathized with their partners' geographical concerns. They agreed, for example, that the French should be allowed to reclaim some portion of the rich North Atlantic fisheries they had harvested prior to 1763 and that the Spanish should be allowed to keep Louisiana and the Florida territories they had captured from the British in 1781. Franklin and his colleagues also sympathized with France's overseas ambitions in India and Africa. But the Americans had no interest in the Mohawks or Creeks or other tribes whose territories encroached on their own. From the first days of the war the Americans had declared their intention to claim all of Canada as part of their new country and to extend their western boundary to the Mississippi River. The French and Spanish quickly rejected those ambitious claims, but their opposition had been moot so long as British troops (and their Indian allies) occupied Detroit and Mackinac and dominated the North American interior from the Ohio Valley to New Orleans. In the spring of 1782, however, when the news from Yorktown and London reached Paris, the moment to resolve this disagreement had suddenly arrived.

Colonial Secretary Gálvez and the other Spanish ministers were committed to the reinvigoration of their colonial empire. They hoped New Orleans would become the hub of a trade network that would join the Spanish king's far-flung colonies in California, the Rio Grande Valley, and Texas to its new conquests in Florida. America's western ambitions would challenge this plan. The French ambassador in Philadelphia communicated Spain's opposition as early as January 1780. "It is the idea of the cabinet of Madrid," Chevalier de la Luzerne wrote, "that the United States extended to the westward no farther than settlements were permitted by the royal proclamation . . . of 1763."[29] The ambassador went on to note that since the lands between the Appalachians and the great river had been declared off-limits to American settlement by the British, they were "proper objects against which the arms of Spain may be employed for the purpose of making a permanent conquest for the Spanish crown. . . . Such conquest may," he added, "be made during the present war."[30]

The French agreed that the Indians' territory west of the Appalachians should be divided between Spain and the Americans. The French ambassador pointed out that his nation was "[u]nited . . . in treaties of alliance" with both Spain and the United States and was therefore "exceedingly desirous of conciliating" them. Luzerne reminded the Americans that Spanish support would be essential to an American victory. The revolution was not "past all danger of unfavorable events," he wrote, "until his Catholic Majesty [Spain] and the United States shall be established on . . . terms of confidence and amity."[31]

Though serious discussions among the diplomats in Paris began in early 1782, the situation remained fluid. American diplomats in Paris remained determined to press their demand for a western boundary on the Mississippi, but the leadership in Philadelphia appeared willing to accept something less. Robert Livingston, the rebels' secretary for foreign affairs in Philadelphia, warned Franklin that "our western and northwestern extent will probably be contested with some warmth" and suggested: "If the mediators should not incline to admit our claim, perhaps it would not be difficult to bring them to agree that the country . . . belongs to the nations that inhabit it [and] that it should enjoy its independence under the guarantee of France, Spain and Great Britain and America. . . ."[32] Similarly, while the British crown was also determined to defend the Appalachians as the Americans' western border, circumstances had brought Franklin's old friend Lord Shelburne into Rockingham's cabinet as home secretary. The two had worked closely together at the end of the Seven Years' War and perhaps would be able to strike a deal again. "I find myself returned nearly to the same situation which you remember me to have occupied nineteen years ago," the new minister wrote Franklin, "and I should be very glad to talk to you as I did then upon the means of promoting the happiness of mankind, a subject much more agreeable to my nature than . . . plans for spreading misery and devastation."[33]

The final source of uncertainty was the fact that despite their recent victory, the Americans remained militarily weak. They had been unable to dislodge the British from New York and Charleston or to challenge the king's navy on the high seas. The Americans had few weapons other than their resolve—and Franklin's pen. Tellingly, at a moment when he sought every possible advantage, America's most experienced international diplomat turned to the most scurrilous form of racist propaganda. In late April 1782, as serious negotiations with the Spanish and British were about to begin, the American ambassador in Paris sent a broadside titled "Supplement to the Boston Independent Chronicle," dated March 12, to the American ambassadors in Spain and the Netherlands and to several British newspapers. His goal was to undermine any claims Indian tribes may have had to recognition in Paris and to weaken the hand of his British adversaries.

Franklin's "Supplement" purported to be a special issue of the Boston newspaper that carried a letter from one Captain Gerrish of the New England militia. Gerrish's letter reported the interception of several packages of European scalps shipped from Britain's Indian allies to their commander, Governor Haldimand, in Quebec. A letter from a British officer was also reprinted in the broadside. His dispatch announced that there were nearly one thousand scalps in the shipment and included a request that his commanders "give farther encouragement" to the warriors who had collected them. The document was a complete fabrication and had been printed on Franklin's own press in Paris.[34]

In a letter accompanying the copy of the "Supplement" he sent to John Jay, the American representative at the Spanish court, Franklin noted that while he "suspected" that the document was false, "it is undoubtedly true as to substance . . . the English cannot deny such a number of murders having been really committed by their instigation."[35] While few were fooled by Franklin's ploy—it appeared in a few English papers but was widely dismissed—it provides a clear measure of the lengths the American ambassador would go to demonize the Native people occupying the lands the Americans coveted and encourage the Europeans to abandon their Indian allies.[36]

As treaty discussions got under way in Paris in May 1782, the Americans held to this anti-Indian theme while tiptoeing quietly away from their obligations to their European allies. French and Spanish commanders seemed hardly to notice because they were deeply engaged in planning the coming year's military offensives against the British. The French had already dispatched a fleet to India to challenge London's bases there, and the Spanish had begun planning for a massive September assault on the king's fortress at Gibraltar.[37] Meanwhile, in London, Shelburne and his colleagues were searching for a way to end the war honorably and at minimal cost. They rejected Franklin's initial offer of an immediate peace that would have added Canada to the new United States, but they made no counterproposal. As spring turned to summer, Franklin and his fellow Americans began to consider direct negotiations despite their treaty obligation to work solely in concert with Spain and France.[38]

Rockingham's death on July 1 and Shelburne's sudden appointment as prime minister produced the opportunity the Americans had been looking for. Hoping that Franklin and his colleagues could be persuaded to retain some link to Britain, the new prime minister pressed for a direct meeting with rebel envoys despite his refusal to agree to their precondition of a public recognition of their independence. While the Americans and the British sparred over these preliminaries,

John Jay (now acting alone in Paris because Franklin had fallen ill and Adams was away in Amsterdam) attempted to resolve the rebels' differences with Spain and France.

The New York lawyer insisted that his European allies recognize the U.S. claim to a western border at the Mississippi. As Jay, Spain's ambassador, the conde de Aranda, and the French minister, the comte de Vergennes, wrestled over the boundary issue, each began to realize that it was Britain that might resolve the conflict. Because it had been the imperial ruler of eastern North America, Britain could legally cede all of its territories to the Americans. At the same time, the Spanish minister knew that legal precedents would support Shelburne if he wished to set the new nation's border at the Appalachians. Aranda estimated that the Continental Congress (and the weary American electorate) would not continue the war simply to acquire the Ohio country and the Tennessee Valley.

Jay devoted much of August to exploring the boundary issue with Aranda. At their first meeting the Spanish ambassador confronted Jay with a large map of North America and, after reminding him that his country had been engaged in the region for more than two centuries, pointed out the obvious fact that regardless of the location of the future boundary, "that dividing line would have to run, in greater part, through the lands of the Indians. . . . All the territory we were looking at beyond the principal line of the boundaries of the colonies," the ambassador insisted, "was Indian land, to which both [the Spanish and the Americans] had equal rights, or equally unjust claims."39

Aranda did not mention his government's potential new allies in Florida and along the Gulf Coast. The Spanish understood that British authority in the Southeast had rested on the crown's ability to supply local traders like Lachlan McGillivray with sufficient protection and commercial support to maintain the alliances they had forged with the region's tribes. While Aranda was not yet aware of Alexander McGillivray's interest in forming an alliance with his government, he certainly knew that Creek warriors had fought alongside the British defenders of Pensacola in 1781 and that a program of local diplomacy could stitch this territory into Spain's North American empire.

Aranda told Jay that his government was ready to compromise, insisting that he and his colleagues "would not quibble over some leagues more or less in such a vast extent of territory."[40] When Jay remained adamant, Vergennes suggested bringing into the conversation Gérard de Rayneval, a member of the Council of State. Fluent in English and experienced in dealing with the American delegation (he had been among those who first welcomed Franklin and John Adams to Paris four years earlier), Rayneval convened a joint meeting at which he reviewed the international customs affecting imperial claims. He pointed out that by custom, establishing European jurisdiction over American territory required a nation either to conquer the local Native tribes or to negotiate treaties of alliance with them. He noted that the United States had not fulfilled either of these requirements. Much of the Ohio and Mississippi country, he noted, was occupied by Indians "not even as yet brought under control by anyone." He also reminded the Americans that when France ceded Canada to Great Britain in 1763, the diplomats at the peace conference had identified the Ohio River as the southern boundary of the former French colony. The new nation could not claim the Great Lakes, he reasoned, "not having taken possession of Canada." Similarly, the area south of the Ohio that lay "behind Georgia, the Carolinas and Virginia" was technically still part of British Florida and currently under the control of its latest conqueror, Spain.[41]

When Jay still refused to budge, the French offered the Spanish ambassador something new: an extensive legal memorandum that detailed the legal principles underlying their united opposition to the American land grab. Rayneval's memorandum reiterated European support for a compromise boundary and recognition of the Indians' right to be represented in future negotiations. It represented their strongest attempt to force their American partners to acknowledge the Indians' claims to sovereignty in the interior of North America. While falling short of accepting Native people as equal in status to themselves, the French and Spanish ministers pressed Jay to accept the reality that the continent contained a distinct group of independent political communities.[42]

In the end Ambassador Jay and his colleagues deflected Rayneval's arguments by immediately opening separate talks with the new Shelburne government in London. They quickly persuaded the prime minister to accept a western border at the Mississippi. Their efforts were assisted by a remarkable turn of events in the western Mediterranean. In late September the British learned that early in the month the long-anticipated French and Spanish assault on Gibraltar had been repulsed. This brilliant victory meant that King George's forces now faced no significant military threat outside North America. Whatever negotiating strength the French and Spanish may have had prior to their defeat had disappeared. The final negotiations were conducted by Franklin and the entire team of American ministers over the coming weeks. The Americans made several concessions to the British—granting them access to the Atlantic fisheries and recognizing the claims of Loyalists—but they would not retreat from their territorial demand. One British diplomat wrote that "these Americans are the greatest quibblers I ever knew." A draft treaty was initialed by both sides on November 30.[43]

Once the deal was struck, the Americans' European allies had no choice but to accept it. By concluding a separate peace, the Americans destroyed the diplomatic customs Aranda and Reyneval had struggled so hard to impose on them the previous summer, a world where Indians had a legal presence and an internationally recognized claim to their tribal homelands in the continental interior. Those customs had been erased by British opportunism and American greed. Over those lost customs the Americans laid the foundations of a new country that sought to ignore the Indian nations within its borders.

It took nearly a year for the British and American agreements to be translated into a finished document. It was not until September 1783 that the United States emerged as a recognized state. This document also erased, on paper, North America's indigenous people from international concern. While the reality of the Indians' military power and economic influence would require the Americans to continue dealing with Native communities through diplomacy and treaty making for decades to come, the Treaty of Paris eliminated the requirement that those interactions pass standards of international conduct or the scrutiny of foreign powers. From 1783 forward the struggle of Native peoples with the United States for recognition and accommodation took place within the boundaries of a nation that encompassed vast territories "unsettled" by its citizens. The American diplomats in Paris had achieved peace abroad but sparked new conflict within their new borders.

THE SHAPE OF THE FUTURE

Seasoned leaders like Joseph Brant and Alexander McGillivray could appreciate the political pressures that had caused their British patrons and American adversaries to betray them, but they continued to reject the settlers' claim, made on their government's new official seal, that the United States represented *Novus Ordo Seclorum,* a "new order of the ages." Indian communities outside American settlements tried to ignore the new boundaries. Some dismissed the Americans' growing presence by describing their expansion in religious terms, as prophets in the Great Lakes and the South preached that the Americans were sent by evil spirits. Others renewed their prewar military alliances with the British or Spanish. The Mohawks negotiated with Governor General Haldimand for a new Canadian homeland where Joseph Brant, his sister Molly, and other Iroquois leaders could settle in peace. After the war, Brant moved north to the Grand River in modern Ontario.

Even after he resettled on the Grand River reserve, Brant remained in contact with his tribal allies at Fort Niagara and in the Ohio country. He dreamed of reclaiming some part of the Mohawks' original homeland, but he did not hold out much hope for a new military offensive. In the summer of 1784 he attended a council with New York State officials, but he refused to recognize their authority. Brant returned to Montreal to press his British commanders to devise some strategy for countering the ambitions of the new government in Philadelphia. Haldimand welcomed the Mohawk chief's loyalty, but he remained powerless. "To this day I remain without any answers," the general reported to the crown's Indian agent for North America, adding that this "painful" fact forced him "to remain silent when called upon for advice by these unfortunate, deserving people."[44]

Joseph Brant traveled to London at the end of 1785 to explore the possibility of organizing military resistance to American expansion. He found the English receptive but wary. Shelburne's government had fallen, and public criticism of the Paris accords had stiffened the crown's resolve to block the young nation's ambitions. Citing the former rebels' refusal to pay damages to displaced Loyalists, the new prime minister, William Pitt, had announced that his forces would not vacate their posts at Niagara, Detroit, Mackinac, and Green Bay. His declaration effectively blocked American expansion across the Great Lakes. It also encouraged Brant and his Ohio allies to imagine that the western territories might yet be made an Indian homeland, protected from Americans by British power.

But Brant also discovered that his hosts were reluctant to commit themselves. The Mohawk leader had a long, private meeting with the home secretary, Lord Sydney. The government quickly arranged cash payments to him and his family to compensate for their losses in New York, but no one was interested in a new war. Whig politicians were quick to condemn Lord Shelburne's concessions to the Americans in the Paris treaty, but they fell silent when asked to explain how they might repair the damage that the peace agreement had done to their Native comrades. The best Brant could get was a letter from Lord Sydney urging the king's "Indian allies to continue united in their councils" in hopes that they might ultimately "secure to themselves the possession of those rights and privileges which their ancestors have . . . enjoyed." Words; nothing more.[45]

To the south, Spanish administrators preparing to take control of East and West Florida adopted a more confrontational approach. Continuing the effort to keep the Americans as far from New Orleans and the Mississippi River as possible, King Charles's first minister, Floridabianca, announced that because his country's peace agreement with Britain had granted the Spanish king the right to "retain" West Florida, it would recognize the northern border of that province at the mouth of the Yazoo River, a point more than one hundred miles north of the border claimed by the Americans. Extended east from the Mississippi, this expanded version of the Florida's boundaries would encompass large parts of modern Mississippi and Alabama and a generous portion of Alexander McGillivray's Creek homeland. In addition, Floridabianca announced that effective in June 1784 the Mississippi would be closed to American shipping.[46]

Charged with implementing his government's new policies, Vicente Manuel de Zespedes, the new governor of East Florida, encouraged Loyalists in Georgia and South Carolina to resettle in his province and cast their lot with Spain. At the same time, Alexander McGillivray (who was already negotiating with Arturo O'Neil in Pensacola) persuaded an old friend, William Panton, an Englishman who had planned to abandon his St. Augustine trading business once the Spanish took control, to stay on and continue the flow of European merchandise into the Creek homeland. Panton readily agreed, offering to seal the agreement by making the Creek leader a silent partner in his business. The two of them, soon joined by a second Englishman, John Leslie, persuaded Zespedes and his superiors to allow them to expand their business by establishing new trading houses at Pensacola, Mobile, and the Chickasaw Bluffs, a point on the Mississippi River near modern Memphis. The firm would be allowed to ship goods to and from Britain without paying the normally prohibitive Spanish tariffs. With encouragement from McGillivray and other local Native leaders, Zespedes in effect created an anti-American free trade zone along the Gulf.

The climax of McGillivray's diplomatic and commercial maneuvering in the immediate aftermath of the Paris negotiations was the treaty he signed with the Spanish at Pensacola on June 1, 1784. The Creek chief initiated the agreement with a forceful letter to Arturo O'Neil, the new governor of West Florida (based in Pensacola), in which he rejected the Paris agreements. He had just received a copy of the final text. He declared, "Britain . . . has no right to transfer us with their former possessions to any power." He went on to observe that "as a free Nation [we] have a right to choose our protector." McGillivray warned O'Neil that the Georgians were pressing against the borders of Upper Creek territory and that they would soon threaten Florida itself. An agreement with his tribe, together with the appointment of the Creek leader as Indian agent for "His Most Catholic Majesty," would "gain and secure a powerful barrier in these parts against the ambitious and encroaching Americans." O'Neil quickly accepted McGillivray's offer and invited him to come to Pensacola to sign a formal agreement.[47]

In late May McGillivray and the other principal chiefs of the Creeks traveled to Pensacola, where they celebrated their new alliance in the company of the Spanish governor of Louisiana, Estevan Miró, and Arturo O'Neil. The agreement did not immediately grant Panton and Leslie the right to trade at Pensacola (that would come later), but it did promise "permanent and unalterable commerce" with the Creeks and guaranteed the tribe's right of ownership in all their lands that lay within Spain's generous definition of Florida's borders. Finally, "to prove how different his way of thinking is from that of his Brittanick Majesty," the Spanish crown promised that if it were ever to lose its North American colony, it would grant its Indian allies other lands, "equivalent[,] . . . where they may establish themselves. . . ." A letter from Miró dated June 7 appointed McGillivray "commissary of the Creek nation" and granted him a monthly salary.[48]

The Paris treaty had left the Indian lands in the western two-thirds of the new United States an unorganized territory under the jurisdiction of a group of former English colonists whose headquarters lay hundreds of miles away in Philadelphia. In this uncertain setting, English, French, and Spanish officials could imagine countless scenarios for the future, scenarios that might possibly have restored some of their former North American empires and extended diplomatic recognition to indigenous communities. The Spanish, for example, could dream of a chain of North American provinces stretching from St. Augustine to San Diego. This domain could have been buttressed with alliances and trade agreements forged with men like McGillivray and his counterparts along the Mississippi and in the Southwest. These agreements in turn might have formed webs of protection for Spanish colonial agents and endorsement for the authority of their king. Such a network would have been perfectly consistent with the diplomatic practices followed by European powers over the previous two centuries.

The English harbored similar ambitions and seemed increasingly determined to retain their trading posts in the Great Lakes. They could imagine an inland commercial empire stretching west from the St. Lawrence and south from Hudson Bay to Detroit, Green Bay, and Lake Michigan. Furs, foodstuffs, and manufactured goods would flow back and forth through licensed centers scattered across the continental interior. French- and English-speaking settlements in the East would prosper under a symbiotic relationship in which their agricultural surpluses and commercial connections would facilitate the work of Native groups engaged in hunting, processing, and transportation.

While the French lacked a mainland base in North America, they retained rich Caribbean colonies and maintained the hope that they could serve as diplomatic arbiters between the major North American powers. This role would be buttressed by one of the legacies of France's former presence: a network of French-speaking traders and Native leaders who might yet implement Rayneval's and Aranda's notion that the continent's interior could be organized around a series of autonomous Indian protectorates.

It was possible in 1783 that such imperial dreams, fueled by international rivalries and encouraged by inventive Native leaders like Joseph

Brant and Alexander McGillivray, might have created a world where Indian communities could have regained recognition from European nations and forced a new relationship with the United States. If the boundaries and spheres of influence that existed in Paris had remained in place, a new equilibrium might well have emerged, protecting the ties that had been the basis of diplomatic and military stability on the continent during the previous two centuries. This was not to be.

The Paris agreements were signed on the eve of dramatic change in Europe and the Americas. Over the next twenty-five years, pressure on Indian landholding from settlers moving west into Kentucky, Georgia, and Ohio grew exponentially, triggering multiple confrontations with Native leaders and fueling the ambitions of countless local politicians.[49] At the same time, new states dominated by settlers began to form in Canada and Latin America, exerting similar pressures on Native communities living on the northern and southern borders of the United States. And in Europe a violent storm of revolution, war, and economic upheaval transformed the leadership of the major powers, separating them further from the eighteenth-century diplomatic world that had produced Brant, McGillivray, Aranda, and Rayneval. Placed in this context, the betrayal of England's Indian allies in 1783 was far more than a diplomatic rift; it heralded the emergence of an entirely new political landscape in North America, a landscape that was to evolve beyond the control of England, France, and Spain and eventually eradicate the diplomatic customs of the colonial era.

Frederick Haldimand, the governor of Quebec, remained distraught over his government's abandonment of Brant's Iroquois kinsmen and its other Native allies. He feared that in the future Indian people would find it impossible to win justice from the government of the United States. As he prepared to return to England in 1784, Haldimand worried over the Indians' future. In a letter to a colleague he grimly recalled that the chiefs had told him that the British "could cross the sea where we had other lands but that they must die on theirs rather than give it up. . . ."[50] The chiefs, he explained, believed that there would be no choices other than death or surrender. In the years ahead, their successors would struggle to find a path somewhere between those two tragic options.

CHAPTER TWO

THE FIRST INDIAN LAWYER

James McDonald, Choctaw

During the first years of American independence the dark choice tribal leaders had imagined before them—surrender or death— must have seemed somewhat overblown. Despite the ambitious designs of its ministers in Paris, the United States was clearly incapable of extending its authority into the continent's interior. No amount of rhetoric could sweep away the fact that Indian warriors, now equipped with English and Spanish guns, operated freely across their homelands, showing little fear of the patriots' impoverished government in Philadelphia. Tribal life in the Great Lakes region and the Ohio Valley continued much as it had during the years before the war.

In the decade following the Paris negotiations, the reality of Indian power would have been obvious to anyone who crossed the Appalachians. In 1790 and 1791 Native forces repulsed two American armies that ventured into northern Ohio from bases near modern Cincinnati. In these encounters, a coalition force comprised largely of tribes who

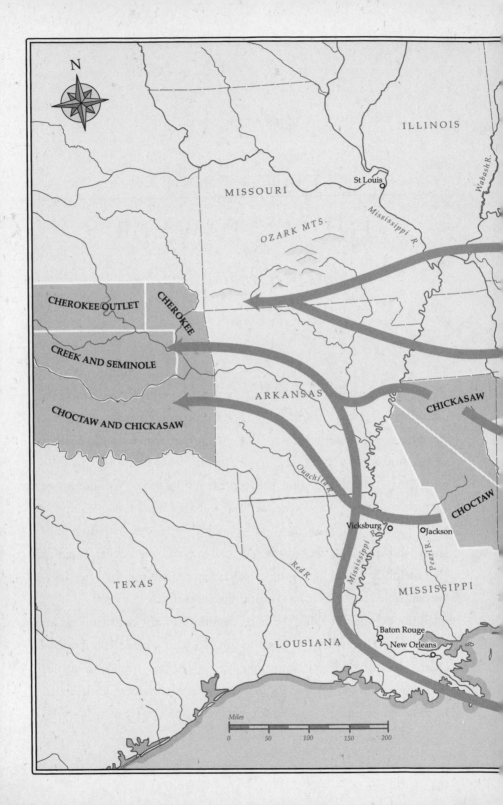

N

ILLINOIS

MISSOURI

St Louis

Mississippi R.

Wabash R.

OZARK MTS.

CHEROKEE OUTLET

CHEROKEE

CREEK AND SEMINOLE

ARKANSAS

CHICKASAW

CHOCTAW AND CHICKASAW

Ouachita R.

CHOCTAW

Vicksburg

Jackson

Pearl R.

Mississippi

Red R.

TEXAS

MISSISSIPPI

LOUSIANA

Baton Rouge
New Orleans

Miles

0   50   100   150   200

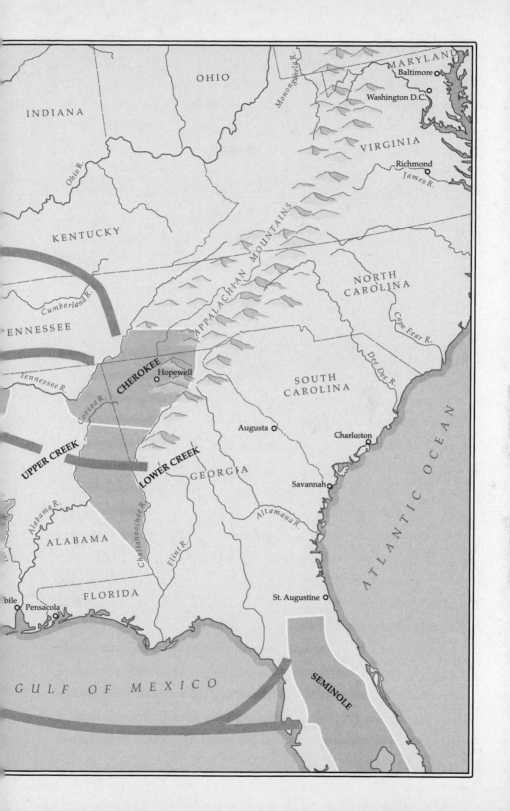

had fought in the Revolution under Joseph Brant (Shawnees, Delawares, Ojibwes, Miamis, and Kickapoos) killed nearly one thousand American soldiers and militiamen and chased the survivors out of their territory. The Indians effectively destroyed the young nation's military—twice.

President George Washington acknowledged the reality of Native power south of the Ohio when he invited the Creek leader (and Spanish ally) Alexander McGillivray to the nation's capital to sign a formal peace treaty. During the chief's 1790 visit, the president offered him an agreement sweetened with a brigadier's commission and a secret clause that granted him permission to import trade goods from his business partners in Spanish Pensacola into the United States without paying import fees.[1]

Tribal leaders like McGillivray could reasonably imagine that the long traditions of diplomacy and mutual accommodation that had guided relations with Europeans during the seventeenth and eighteenth centuries would continue despite the Americans' territorial ambitions.[2] They could hope that the generation of tribal leaders that succeeded McGillivray would grow up in a world where Native peoples and U.S. officials negotiated their differences in treaty councils and lived beside each other as neighbors and trading partners. Perhaps this rising generation of tribal leaders could find common ground with the new nation, fulfilling Thomas Jefferson's often stated hope that Indians and whites would eventually "blend together . . . intermix, and become one people."[3]

But rather than launch an era of mutual respect and ultimate amalgamation, the first decades of the nineteenth century were punctuated by violence, adversity, and the gradual separation of American and Indian interests. Tribal leaders had little opportunity to negotiate as equals with American politicians or to ally themselves with European diplomats. Instead, they faced repeated confrontations with land-hungry settlers and aggressive state governments that cared little for their rights or their homelands. By 1820 it was clear that the United States was prepared to compel eastern tribes to accept national expansion deep into the North American interior. Tribal leaders who came of age during at this historical moment were forced to give up the diplomatic approach of the last century and confront the Americans in the arena of national politics.

JAMES MCDONALD was an extraordinary representative of this new generation of leaders. Like Alexander McGillivray, he was the son of a European father and a Native mother. McDonald was a Choctaw, born in 1801 in his tribe's homeland in what is now Mississippi. His father is lost to the historical record, but his mother is not. She was a resourceful trader and landowner who was determined to promote her son as a bilingual tribal leader. Just as McGillivray's father sent him to Charleston to be taught English and business skills, so McDonald's mother enrolled her son in a Quaker-run mission school near their home. In 1813 she took the remarkable step of sending the twelve-year-old to Baltimore, Maryland, where the Yearly Meeting of Friends took charge of his upbringing. Within a decade he had been educated in the classics and was reading law in the office of John McLean, one of the most prominent attorneys of his day.[4] Equally striking, McDonald's return to Mississippi in 1823 after a decade's absence brought him to the center of a confrontation with white settlers who were demanding that the Choctaws and their neighbors abandon their homes and move beyond the settled borders of the United States. "The clouds appear to be gathering from every quarter and ready to burst over every fragment of the Indian race," McDonald wrote in 1826. "I see applications to congress from half the states in the union for the extinguishment of Indian titles to land—and to my mind it looks like a bitter and endless persecution."[5]

McDonald believed that it would be futile to use force to reverse this tide of "persecution." As a consequence, he became one of the first Native leaders to devise a political response to the new American national reality. He believed that political negotiations between the United States and educated Native leaders could establish the basis for long-term survival for groups like the Choctaws. Just as McGillivray, Brant, and other leaders of the Revolutionary Era hoped to negotiate sustainable diplomatic agreements with foreign powers, McDonald and many others of his generation expected they could forge with federal officials political agreements that would protect their homes and tribal institutions. Among those who shared McDonald's general outlook were John Ross, a trader's son who had grown up in the Cherokee homeland in northwestern Georgia; George Colbert, a Chickasaw planter and ferry owner in Mississippi; and Peter Pitchlynn, also the son of a Choctaw woman and a Scots trader. Pitchlynn was a childhood friend of McDonald's who remained a prominent planter and tribal leader through the end of the Civil War. Similar leaders emerged among tribes in the northeast, Ohio, and the Great Lakes.

James McDonald's life is particularly instructive because he was the first of these individuals to be trained in the American legal system. He also went on to act as an adviser to a group of traditional Choctaw chiefs who negotiated with American leaders in Washington, D.C. He was therefore the first Native activist to make the case for Indian "rights" directly to American political leaders and to negotiate for a recognition of those rights in a formal agreement. In his career, McDonald pointed out the contradiction between the Americans' public allegiance to the ideals of democracy and constitutionalism and their participation in extralegal assaults on the dignity and humanity of the continent's first people. Like his predecessors in the eighteenth century, McDonald sought recognition by the outside powers that intruded on the Choctaw homeland. Rather than defend the Choctaws as diplomatic actors on the international stage, however he made the case for a tribal presence, and tribal rights, within the boundaries and institutions of the United States.

With fifteen thousand members at the end of the eighteenth century, the Choctaws were among the largest southeastern tribes. Nevertheless, they were the first to abandon their Mississippi homeland in exchange for new lands in Indian Territory, the tribal refuge west of the Mississippi that eventually became the state of Oklahoma.[6] Surrounded and besieged in the East by aggressive frontiersmen, land speculators, and politicians, the Choctaws chose to leave the mounting chaos around them and move to a protected enclave federal officials had promised would become their permanent home. McDonald's tribe lacked the time or the allies to resist American expansionism. As a consequence, they were the first major group to see older, negotiated agreements replaced by new, coercive treaties. As McDonald and the Choctaws confronted the American officials who urged them to move west, they found they needed a new way of dealing with the United States.

James McDonald and his Choctaw kinsmen came to see that their tribe and the United States were no longer allies; they had instead become legal adversaries. In this altered atmosphere the tribe recognized that it needed something more to protect itself than military power or the blessing of its spiritual helpers. The Choctaws became convinced during the 1820s that they needed an advocate who could counter the Americans' logic, stall their ambitions, and blunt their threats. They no longer needed a charismatic chief; they needed a lawyer. In the decades to follow, other tribes reached the same conclusion.

For a brief moment in 1824 James McDonald became the Choctaws' lawyer. His short career marks the birth of a new approach to federal power and, by extension, the beginning of an American Indian political activism that was to inspire tribal leaders across the continent. Chief John Ross of the Cherokees rallied his community behind him and traveled repeatedly to Washington, D.C., to oppose the removal of his tribe from Georgia. In New England, William Apess, a Pequot who became a Methodist preacher, spoke out passionately on behalf of the rights of his and neighboring tribes and in opposition to the white settlers who surrounded and engulfed them. And Waubunsee, a Potawatomi chief who negotiated a series of treaties aimed at preserving his tribe's independence in the Midwest, sought to enforce those agreements on American officials even as his community was pushed west from Illinois into Kansas. Many followed the path that McDonald forged, but none traveled it as early or as eloquently as the Choctaw lawyer.

THE POSTWAR WORLD OF TREATIES

The conflicts McDonald would face in the 1820s were difficult to imagine in the years immediately following the Revolution. The Paris treaty had angered tribal leaders, but it soon became apparent that the new American government had little power in the North American interior and would have no choice but to continue the traditions of diplomacy and mutual accommodation that had marked relations with the Indians before the war. The United States was particularly accommodating in the southeastern interior, where Indians still outnumbered settlers and Spain and Great Britain occupied strategic outposts just across the national borders. In 1801, when James McDonald was born in Mississippi, the United States still treated the region's tribes as partners whose friendship rested on agreements ratified at formal treaty councils that strongly resembled the imperial gatherings of the eighteenth century.

In the Southeast the most important of these councils took place at Hopewell, the South Carolina estate of a backcountry trader and politician named Andrew Pickens. Negotiated in the closing days of 1785, the Hopewell agreements were intended to patch up relations with tribes, like the Creeks and Choctaws, who had opposed American independence and to establish diplomatic contact with groups whose primary allegiance was to Britain and Spain. The Choctaw delegation that traveled the five hundred miles to the Hopewell treaty grounds looked forward to the negotiations. They expected the Americans to welcome them as kinsmen and to shower them with traditional signs of peace: food and clothing.[7] The delegates wielded spiritual as well as temporal authority, for the tribe viewed their emissaries as powerful intermediaries who negotiated relations between their villages and the outer world of strangers, foreigners, and hostile spiritual beings, all of them with the potential to do them harm. From their perspective, they came to Hopewell prepared to restore the diplomatic world that had existed in the decades prior to the Revolution.

The Choctaw delegation was led by Taboca, a prominent warrior who represented a major town near the headwaters of the Pearl River. Taboca was viewed by his Choctaw kinsmen as a *fanimingo* (squirrel chief), a designated representative of the community charged with protecting its interests in encounters with outsiders.[8] His presence at the South Carolina treaty ground was a measure of his tribe's stability and his own diplomatic sophistication. When he met the American commissioners, Taboca could boast two decades of experience representing Choctaw interests at international gatherings. Over the previous generation French, Spanish, and British officials had recorded his presence in Mobile, St. Augustine, Savannah, and Charleston. Following the Hopewell conference he and his wife were to travel to Philadelphia and New York to meet with American leaders, including Secretary of War Henry Knox and Benjamin Franklin. Eight years later he led fifteen hundred Choctaws in a council where the Spanish governor of West Florida crowned him "King of the Choctaws" in an elaborate ceremony.[9]

Despite their high office, the Choctaw delegation arrived at Hopewell wearing only deer- and bearskins. In the tradition of frontier diplomacy, they expected the Americans would welcome them as kinsmen and supply them with clothing and food. Despite initial grumbling from the U.S. representatives, the delegates were soon wearing U.S. Army coats and sharing the Americans' supplies. The ensuing days were marked by additional detours into diplomatic ritual. Treaty sessions began with invocations of the power of the sun, a power the Choctaws associated both with creation and with the all-seeing eye of the Great Spirit. Like most Indian groups, the Choctaws imagined their communities as extended families. Foreigners could neither be trusted to keep their promises nor relied upon to be generous in times of hardship unless they could somehow be transformed into family members. The conference was therefore punctuated by numerous references to the importance of the family bonds that linked the Americans to their Native neighbors.

The Americans and Choctaws signed the Hopewell treaty on January 3, 1786. On that occasion the Americans appeared in their dress uniforms while Taboca and his fellow delegates performed an eagle tail dance before the entire assembly. Covered with white clay, the

Choctaws sang and waved eagle tails back and forth over their heads before approaching their counterparts and dancing before them. The Choctaws also carried white poles topped with white deerskins as symbols of peace and presented the U.S. officials with a white calumet. Taboca then kindled a sacred fire in the center of the treaty ground and made a special point of gathering up a few of its coals to take home with him as a record of the event. According to an American observer, Taboca brought the council to a close by touching the breasts of the government's commissioners with an eagle tail. He explained: "[T]hese feathers of the eagle tail we always hold when we make peace."[10]

The Hopewell treaty established peace between the Choctaws and the United States and announced the federal government's recognition of the tribe's control over its Mississippi homeland. According to the language of the agreement, American citizens were not welcome to settle in Choctaw territory. At the same time, the document noted that the Choctaws would give their allegiance to "no other sovereign" and would accept Congress's right to regulate their trade and "manage" their affairs. That last statement had little meaning when British traders still operated in the area, and Choctaw diplomats were negotiating similar agreements with the Spanish authorities in St. Augustine and New Orleans.[11]

The style and substance of the Hopewell treaty had counterparts in other parts of North America where American officials sought to establish peaceful relations with tribes on their inland borders. These treaties ended hostilities between the two groups and specified the boundaries between them. U.S. commissioners signed these agreements because they were aware of both their country's financial and military weakness and the steady threat posed to the young government by the British and Spanish troops stationed in a vast arc stretching from Niagara to Detroit, Green Bay, St. Louis, New Orleans, and

Pensacola. American officials were also concerned about the volatile atmosphere being created by western settlers who were constantly testing the limits of federal authority by trespassing on tribal land. Agreements separating settlers from powerful Native communities promised to bring peace to the border region while preempting military intervention from Britain or Spain.

The new Federal Constitution approved in 1787 stated that Congress would have the power to "regulate commerce . . . with the Indians" but said nothing about formal diplomacy or treaties. Nevertheless, soon after George Washington took office as the first president of the newly reorganized national government, he proposed that the Senate ratify previously negotiated agreements with western tribes in the same way that it would approve treaties with foreign powers. The president's secretary of war, Henry Knox, declared that the Indians "possess the right of the soil. It cannot be taken from them unless by their free consent, or by right of conquest in case of a just war. To dispossess them on any other principle would be a gross violation of the fundamental laws of nature. . . ."[12]

The most dramatic example of Washington's commitment to formal diplomacy was his decision in the summer of 1790 to invite Alexander McGillivray to the American capital of New York. Secretary of War Knox had urged the Creek leader to come north and instructed his subordinates to spare no expense in making arrangements for the delegation that arrived wearing feather plumes in their silk turbans, silver earrings, and gleaming gorgets of Spanish silver. The Americans hoped the treaty would set a fixed border between the Creeks and their Georgia neighbors and woo the tribe away from its alliance with the Spanish. The Americans punctuated their practical concerns with repeated pledges of friendship and peaceful intent. At the treaty signing, government officials showered their guests with strings of beads and ceremonial tobacco, and the Creeks responded with a "song of peace."[13]

Five years later a dozen Great Lakes tribes that had fought for more than a decade to stop the American invasion of their homeland met with General Anthony Wayne at Greenville in northern Ohio. They hoped to establish a permanent border with the United States and to set out the ground rules for future relations. The treaty they negotiated was approved by the "sachems, chiefs and warriors of the Wyandots, Delawares, Shawanoes, Ottawas, Chippewas, Potawatimes, Miamis, Eel-river, Weas, Kickapoos, Piankashaws, and Kaskaskias" and was designed to "put an end to a destructive war, to settle all controversies, and to restore harmony and a friendly intercourse between the said United States, and the Indian tribes." The Native representatives at Greenville accepted white settlers in southern and central Ohio in exchange for the United States' pledge to "relinquish their claims to all other Indian lands northward of the river Ohio, eastward of the Mississippi, and westward and southward of the Great Lakes and the waters uniting them. . . ." As had been true at the councils at Hopewell and in New York, the diplomats at Greenville sought to establish peace and stability with the methods they had inherited from the colonial era. Those methods would soon prove inadequate.[14]

COMING OF AGE IN
A SHIFTING LANDSCAPE

James McDonald was born into a world made secure by the Hopewell treaty, but he grew up in a world where American settlers and their political champions threatened the "mutual confidence" that had been celebrated at the South Carolina treaty ground. The first evidence of this threat appeared just as the new national constitution was being framed in Philadelphia. In 1787 Georgia's leaders refused to follow Virginia's and North Carolina's example and surrender the state's claim to the western territory described in its colonial charter. (The crown had granted Georgia's original proprietors the right to settle as far west as the Mississippi.) The issue lingered as a source of tension between state and federal officials until 1802, when Thomas Jefferson framed a compromise under which the state would give up its western claims in exchange for a federal pledge to extinguish all tribal land titles in its remaining territory. This unprecedented Georgia Compact had no immediate impact—state officials were content to allow the Indians to remain within their state in their relatively isolated villages—but underscored the federal government's commitment to the removal of all tribes from Georgia and, by implication, other areas in the Southeast where white settlers coveted tribal homelands.

Vocal opposition to Indian landholding in Mississippi began in 1803, after Napoleon had suddenly decided to sell the entire territory to the Americans. The French emperor's decision immediately transformed the Choctaw homeland from a distant border area to an inland province that boasted hundreds of miles of frontage on a river that was destined to become the nation's central highway.[15] Secure borders and the lure of plantation agriculture triggered a surge of settlement. The American population in the region doubled between 1810 and 1820 and then doubled again by 1830. New towns clustered along the east bank of the Mississippi as well as on the lower reaches of the Tombigbee River, two hundred miles to the east.

The American immigrants were soon calling for the creation of two territorial governments in the area. Congress had first organized Mississippi Territory in 1798 as a hundred-mile-wide swath of unsurveyed land hugging the east bank of the great river and then in 1803, had expanded its borders so that it stretched south from Tennessee to the Gulf. Finally, in 1817, the region took its modern shape when the Tombigbee settlements became the Alabama Territory, Mississippi's eastern neighbor.

Events on America's northwestern frontier echoed those along the Gulf. Secure borders, a surging settler population, and aggressive local leaders encouraged the rapid organization of Ohio, Indiana, and Illinois into territories and states during Jefferson's presidency. (Ohio became a state in 1803; Indiana in 1816; Illinois in 1818.) Jefferson championed both traditional Indian diplomacy and westward expansion. He understood the value of traditional diplomacy, but he also understood the rising power of western politicians and was far more likely to accommodate them.

In 1808 Jefferson supported a major purchase of Choctaw land. He noted that while it was "desirable that the United States should obtain from the native population the entire left (east) bank of the Mississippi," federal authorities were also determined "to obliterate from the Indian mind an impression . . . that we are constantly forming designs on their lands." The Choctaws' current debt of more than forty-six thousand dollars, he explained, provided a solution to this dilemma. Owing to "the pressure of their own convenience," Jefferson reported, the Choctaws themselves had initiated this sale of five million acres of their land. He wrote that he welcomed this "consolidation of the Mississippi Territory," and the Senate quickly ratified the agreement.[16] No longer playing the role of ally and kinsman, the president had become a facilitator of tribal debt relief and consolidated settlement in the former Choctaw homeland. Despite this purchase, however, the Choctaw borders established at Hopewell remained largely intact. When James McDonald left Mississippi for Baltimore in 1813, the Choctaws' homeland seemed secure. Choctaw farms lay scattered along the major river systems where tribal members raised both subsistence and cash crops. At the same time, prosperous trading families like McDonald's expanded their operations, investing in both large-scale agriculture and cattle ranching.

Unlike Joseph Brant and Alexander McGillivray, who were also sent away from their Native homelands to be educated, James McDonald traveled to an entirely new region when he left Mississippi in 1813. He spent a few years at a Quaker school in Baltimore, Maryland, before moving to Washington, D.C. Thomas L. McKenney, a Maryland merchant who served as the superintendent of the Office of Indian Trade from 1816 to 1822, and who later became the nation's first commissioner of Indian affairs, described the nature of McDonald's education in his memoirs. McKenney recalled that early in his tenure, Philip E. Thomas, a friend who was the secretary of the Baltimore Yearly Meeting of Friends, brought McDonald into his office in hopes of finding the young man a government post. Recalling their first encounter, McKenney wrote, "I soon discovered that there were qualities of both heart and head in this youth of rare excellence, and that nature had bestowed on him not only personal lineaments of uncommon beauty, but a manner and action altogether captivating."[17]

McDonald arrived in Washington in the spring of 1818, just as McKenney was attempting to persuade Congress to establish a "civilization" fund for Indians. The superintendent struck a Jeffersonian pose, arguing that federal subsidies for schools and model farms would hasten the tribes' assimilation into the American mainstream. Some of his critics did not believe Indians could be educated at all, while others argued that the proposal was simply a scheme for distributing federal dollars to the administration's missionary supporters. McDonald, articulate and "civilized," could appear as a human advertisement for what would be produced by the new program, the perfect rejoinder to

McKenney's critics. The War Department provided the superintendent with $330 annually for housing and feeding the young man and also provided a subsidy for a new suit of clothes. McDonald was soon hard at work in McKenney's office. In a few days the superintendent could scribble across a letter: "copied in haste by our little Indian."[18]

McKenney's lobbying (and perhaps McDonald's presence) paid off. In January 1819 Congress approved an annual appropriation of ten thousand dollars for "the civilization of the tribes adjoining the frontier settlements." McKenney's office was responsible for distributing the funds. The superintendent issued guidelines to missionary organizations stipulating that grants go to only those committed to putting up one-third of the cost of new schools and to offering instruction in the "mechanical and domestic arts." In addition, recipients of federal funds were required to "impress on the minds of the Indians the friendly and benevolent views of the government toward them and the advantage of . . . yielding to the policy of the government, and co-operating with it. . . ."[19] Jefferson's idea of compromise, in which Indians would "yield" to American expansion, was now being translated into legislation and government policy. As McKenney's superior, John C. Calhoun, wrote confidently a few months later about the tribal leaders who sometimes protested his actions, "our opinion, and not theirs, ought to prevail in measures intended for their civilization and happiness."[20] Sitting at his desk at the Indian Office, James McDonald appeared to be living proof of the wisdom of this viewpoint.

McDonald's skill and hard work impressed his superiors. "No young man in the District writes more or with more apparent pleasure," McKenney wrote at the time. Soon after the Civilization Fund was approved, the superintendent suggested educating the young man to prepare him for a profession. Dipping again into the War Department budget—perhaps into the new Civilization Fund itself—McKenney enrolled McDonald in a Georgetown academy run by Rev. James Carnahan. Again, the youth exceeded all expectations. "I soon discovered that McDonald was bent on distinguishing himself," McKenney later wrote. "His book was his constant companion." Carnahan agreed, noting that "he comes to school with his lessons all so well digested, and with more Latin, and Greek, and mathematics in one of them than the class . . . can get through in a week."[21]

McKenney witnessed the young Choctaw's academic triumphs for two years. As the Georgetown course reached its conclusion, the superintendent reported that he had raised McDonald's case with Secretary of War Calhoun. "Make a lawyer of him," Calhoun said. McKenney dutifully broached the subject with McDonald and eventually arranged for John McLean, an Ohio congressman who was returning to his home near Cincinnati to take a seat on the state's supreme court, to bring the young man into his law office. The Office of Indian Trade again subsidized McDonald's efforts, and again, the young Choctaw performed well. "Such was his capacity," McKenney later wrote, "that in about one-half the time ordinarily occupied by the most talented young men of our race, he had gone the rounds of his studies, and was qualified for the bar."[22]

Written twenty years after the events he described, McKenney's account of McDonald's education was obviously colored by the tragic events surrounding the campaign to force the tribe out of Mississippi. The former Indian commissioner claimed, for example, that McDonald responded to the prospect of pursuing a professional education by "pressing his hand against his forehead" and declaring, "Oh sir, it will be all lost on me." After a "deep sigh" McDonald was supposed to have added, "I am an Indian. . . . I am marked with a mark as deep and abiding as that which Cain bore. My race is degraded—trodden upon—despised."[23] The young man undoubtedly experienced moments of despair, but it is hard to imagine that someone who had exhibited such tenacity and talent for most of a decade would collapse into such a theatrical pose when offered an opportunity of this kind. His efforts on behalf of his tribe in the immediate aftermath of his legal education suggest that he was far more resilient and resourceful than McKenney knew.

In October 1823, McDonald reported to Secretary Calhoun that he had completed his legal training in Ohio but that he had been unable to secure a position with a local law firm. As a consequence, he wrote, "I now propose going to the state of Mississippi to visit my friends and relations." He added that "should the prospect of success in my profession be encouraging . . . I shall settle there and commence the practice of law."[24] McDonald soon moved south, taking up residence in Jackson, the new capital of the six-year-old state. He was as likely to have been struck as much by the continuities he found in his old homeland as by the changes. After all, many of his Choctaw kinsmen had participated in and supported the American settlement effort. As allies of the United States the Choctaws continued to farm and trade and maintain friendly ties to the government. In recent years they had resisted the anti-American entreaties of Tecumseh (who had traveled south from Indiana to recruit allies), joined forces with the Americans to beat back a nationalist Creek rebellion, and, most dramatically, fought alongside Andrew Jackson in his famous victory over the British at New Orleans.[25]

In addition to their military contributions, many Choctaws had encouraged the work of missionaries and embraced new businesses and new ways of life. Initially, the most accommodating were the descendants of traders like McDonald's father who had first entered the Choctaw country in the eighteenth century. The first of these traders, Nathaniel Folsom, John Pitchlynn (Peter Pitchlynn's father), Louis

LeFlore, Louis Durant, and Turner Brashears, quickly married into Indian families. Their wives' relatives helped them acquire supplies of deerskins and enjoy in return steady access to manufactured goods and luxury items they could use themselves or distribute among their relatives. In the process, they also produced new generations of mixed-heritage children like McDonald, whom the matrilineal Choctaws considered natural-born members of the tribe. Over time, these traders and their families took on a wide range of roles, and by the nineteenth century, one historian estimated, they constituted 10 percent of the tribe's population. John Pitchlynn served as the Choctaws' official interpreter at treaty gatherings from Hopewell onward, while Turner Brashears, an agent of the Florida-based British firm Panton and Leslie, opened a tavern on the Natchez Trace. Louis Durant is credited with introducing cattle ranching into Mississippi. Louis LeFlore operated west of the Pearl River, trading with Choctaws who crossed the Mississippi at Nogales (later Vicksburg) to hunt on the west side of the river.[26]

In the first decades of the nineteenth century these bicultural Choctaw trading families became increasingly involved in plantation agriculture and cattle ranching. They purchased African slaves, expanded their farming operations, and began operating ferries and taverns. Tribal land was owned communally, but wealthy individuals established their rights to agricultural acreage by clearing it and using it for cotton, cattle, and other crops, thereby accommodating themselves both to the advent of commercial agriculture and to the region's rigid social hierarchy. By 1830 Louis LeFlore's son Greenwood lived on a Yazoo River plantation with thirty-two slaves. Nathaniel Folsom's son David owned ten slaves, while among the tribe's woman slaveowners was Turner Brashears's daughter, Delila. Despite maintaining their tribal government and enforcing the borders to their homeland established at Hopewell, the Choctaws had come to accept dramatic changes in their culture: African American slavery, cattle ranching, square cabins, and enclosed farms and plantations devoted to cotton and other commercial crops.[27]

DESPITE THE CHOCTAWS' deep involvement in the region's economic growth, the tribe could not avoid the gaze of political leaders who viewed their presence as an obstacle to the region's development. The tribe confronted this reality in the spring of 1819, when the U.S. Indian agent John McKee notified their leaders that General Andrew Jackson had inquired "whether or not [the Choctaws] are disposed to treat" with the United States for the sale of the Mississippi lands and removal to a new territory west of the river. Jackson would conduct the treaty negotiations under a mandate from President James Monroe. The Tennessee war hero directed McKee to read his message to the chiefs "by way of preparing them for the cession." The general warned the agent that this proposed transaction would be the Choctaws' single opportunity to make a deal. "Now is the time and the only time the Government will have it in its power to make [the Choctaws] happy, by holding the land west of the Mississippi for them," he declared. "And this can only be done by their consent to an exchange, in whole or in part."[28]

The Choctaw leadership met later that summer and rejected Jackson's invitation. The tribe had long used the woods of modern Arkansas as a hunting ground, crossing regularly at Nogales and drawing on the territory's inventory of deerskins to supply their needs. Some, like Pushmataha, had also traveled farther west, visiting tribes as far away as the Spanish settlements on the Rio Grande.[29] As familiar as they were with the lands across the river, the Choctaw leaders had no interest in leaving Mississippi. "We wish to remain here," Pushma-taha, Jackson's former comrade-in-arms, told the agent. He did not consider the Choctaws who hunted and lived across the Mississippi members of his nation. "[T]hey are considered as strangers; they have no houses or places of residence; they are like wolves. I am well acquainted with the country contemplated for us," the chief told the American commissioners. "I have often had my feet sorely bruised there by the roughness of its surface." As for selling land in Missis-sippi, the chief was firm: "we have none to spare."³⁰

Monroe's insistence that the tribe meet with Jackson despite the leaders' unwillingness to discuss either removal or land sales reflected a shifting balance of power both in Washington, D.C., and along the Gulf. Acting on the president's instructions, Jackson traveled south from his home in Nashville for a face-to-face meeting with the Choc-taw chiefs.³¹ The tribe was to be represented by three men who had considerable experience with the Americans: Pushmataha, from the Six Towns District (Okla-hunnali); Mushulatubbe, from the center of the state (Haiyip Atukla); and Puckshenubbe, from the western divi-sion along the Mississippi River (Okla-Falaya).³² When they gathered at a forest clearing called Doak's Stand in October 1820, Jackson was blunt. Ignoring the tribe's prosperous farms, expanding plantations, and burgeoning cattle ranches, he announced: "You have more land than you can cultivate. . . . It is useless to yourselves." Continuing in the paternalistic manner that was becoming characteristic of govern-ment officials, he added that "the President expects no difficulty with his Choctaw children." Jackson offered a choice. Those who wished to travel west "can live in abundance, and acquire riches and indepen-dence." Those who chose to remain would be "protected by our laws. . . . As all parties are accommodated," he concluded "and the interest and happiness of all consulted, there cannot be any honest opposition made to the friendly proposals of your father the President." Refusing the government's proposal, he warned, would mean that the president "can no longer look upon you as friends and brothers, and as deserving his fatherly protection. . . . If you suffer any injury," he concluded darkly, "none but yourselves will be to blame."[33]

This was not a negotiation, and it was certainly not an occasion for celebrating the diplomatic kinship established a generation earlier at Hopewell or the military partnership that had been so effective in New Orleans five years earlier. The Choctaws, particularly leaders like Pushmataha and Mushulatubbe, who had worn American uniforms at the battle of New Orleans in 1815, must have listened to their former commander in shock. Their community was being presented with an ultimatum from the most powerful military leader of his age, delivered with the warning that the only alternative to immediate removal was to dissolve their tribal government and remain in Mississippi. Those who remained in the East would become state citizens, subject to local laws (which, among other things, barred Indians from testifying in court) and beyond the protection of federal officials. References to past diplomatic alliances or a brotherhood born of war were completely absent from Jackson's presentation. He demanded obedience. Sensing this dramatic shift in tone, Puckshenubbe calmly requested that all future statements be recorded. He also asked "that his half-breeds, who could read and write, might be permitted to perform this duty, to see that there were no mistakes and that everything was well done."[34]

The Choctaw chiefs and their advisers retreated to consider their reply. After a week they remained united in opposition. Jackson responded angrily, delivering a second blistering address before the council. He argued that the Treaty of Hopewell had granted Congress the "right to manage the affairs of this nation" and declared that if the chiefs refused his demands, the government would simply recognize whichever Choctaws assembled in the West as their government. This meeting "will be the last time a talk will ever be delivered by your father the President to his Choctaw children on this side of the Mississippi," he added. "You are advised to beware. . . . Your father the President will not be trifled with and put at defiance. . . . A heavy cloud may burst upon you and you may be without friends to counsel or protect you. . . . Your existence as a nation is in your hands," he told the chiefs. "Should you reject [the treaty] it will be a source of great regret, as it may be a measure fatal to your nation."[35]

The Choctaw leaders met again the following day, but they could not agree on a united course of action. Puckshenubbe, the group's senior leader, abruptly left the council grounds and announced that he would have no further contact with the Americans. The following day Jackson met with those who remained—"about forty or fifty headmen and warriors"—and made a deal. The tribe exchanged more than five million acres in Mississippi for a tract in western Arkansas and modern Oklahoma that the United States claimed contained thirteen million acres. The agreement also stipulated that the proceeds from the sale of some thirty-four thousand acres of ceded land would be used to support schools for Choctaw youth and a "light-horse" tribal police force to maintain order in their Mississippi homeland. Jackson's report on the treaty sessions also noted that he made "donations" ranging from five hundred to twenty-five dollars to twenty-three leaders in order to complete the transaction.[36]

For the Choctaws, the drama at Doak's Stand came not only from the experience of being browbeaten and bribed by their former military commander. More terrifying even than his threatening posture was Andrew Jackson's grasp of an aggressive rhetoric, which resonated with fellow westerners and was to fuel his presidential campaign. For those who accepted his premise, Old Hickory's logic was ironclad: Indians were backward hunters; they did not develop their land. Native tribes were therefore anachronistic vestiges of the past and should not exist within the boundaries of progressive American settlements.

Jackson's stance at Doak's Stand revealed the harsh new realities James McDonald and others of his generation would soon confront. Writing at the conclusion of his meeting with the Choctaws, Old Hickory predicted confidently (and without evidence) that "at least two-thirds of the nation here will remove to the country ceded to them" and "the remainder . . . will then be prepared to have the laws of the United States extended over them." He added ominously, "[W]e shall no longer witness the farce and absurdity of holding treaties with the Indians residing within our territorial limits."[37] Native leaders would soon meet others like the future president, men who would smoothly turn their backs on former allies and demand that tribal leaders choose between a "civilized" life as individual subjects or the "savage" life of tribes. The new generation of frontier politicians could imagine no place where Indian tribes might continue within the settled boundaries of their states.

Before Doak's Stand the Choctaws could rely on leaders like Taboca or Pushmataha to establish and sustain their diplomatic relationship with the United States. After Doak's Stand, Indians like the Choctaw chiefs were now cast by Jackson and his settler supporters as backward aliens, rather than partners in diplomacy. In this new environment the Choctaws would be best served by leaders who could confront the Americans' logic and challenge their authoritarian proposals. It was time to replace the diplomats with lawyers. It was time for a Choctaw like James McDonald.

THE INDIAN LAWYER

Andrew Jackson's prediction that people interested in learning to farm would soon move to the Choctaws' new Arkansas lands proved only half correct. Eager farmers soon arrived, but they were whites, not Indians. *Niles Weekly Register* reported in March 1821 that American squatters were invading the tribe's newly acquired western territory. Without prompting and with no evident sense of irony, several congressmen now called for the tribe's removal from Arkansas, the territory that General Jackson had promised would be their new homeland, but that they had yet to occupy.[38]

As the 1824 presidential election drew near, pressure mounted on American officials to resolve this Arkansas dispute as well as similar disputes in other southeastern states. Georgia continued to call for the removal of the Cherokees, while in Alabama officials focused their attention on the Creeks. Presidential candidate Jackson encouraged these pro-removal forces, but he was hardly alone. Secretary of War John C. Calhoun (also a presidential hopeful) issued a long report in the spring of 1824 that warned removal had been avoided thus far only because of the "humanity, kindness and justice" of federal authorities. The time was fast approaching, he warned, when the tribes would have no choice but to depart.[39] Even the retiring president, the Virginian James Monroe, sympathized with the removal advocates. Referring to Georgia, he wrote in early 1824 that he had long been "anxious . . . to meet the wishes of the state." Monroe cautioned against the use of force, but his sentiments largely echoed Jackson's. Referring to the southern tribes, he declared that "surrounded as they are . . . on every side by the white population, it will be difficult if not impossible for them with their kind of government to sustain order among them." The choice, Monroe argued, was simple: "wretched" chaos or removal.[40]

James McDonald returned to Mississippi in 1823, just as the presidential campaign was taking shape and the confrontation between "civilizing" tribes and southern states was coming into focus. That year the Choctaws sought redress on three matters: the status of their Arkansas lands (now occupied largely by whites), the government's failure to provide the funds for education promised in the 1820 treaty, and Mississippi's unrelenting demand for their removal. Calhoun had invited tribal leaders to a treaty council in 1822, but they rejected any further meetings with lower-level diplomats. They wanted to see the president. As the tribal leaders later wrote, "We had often met with commissioners [but] . . . they had uniformly stated . . . that their powers were limited. We, therefore . . . wished to visit the President of the United States (the fountainhead of power) and have a full understanding with him on all the points of difference between our white brothers and ourselves."[41] Calhoun approved bringing tribal leaders to Washington in 1823, but the project was delayed several times, and the Choctaw leaders did not arrive in the capital until October 1824. The delegation included all three "medal chiefs," including Pushmataha and Puckshenubbe, the man who had left the treaty grounds in 1820 rather than give in to Andrew Jackson's demands. In addition, the tribe sent along four recently elected district delegates to the tribal council and two interpreter-clerks who were the sons of white traders and Choctaw women: David Folsom and James McDonald.[42]

Despite frequent references to "white brothers" and bonds of friendship, the 1824 negotiations in Washington, D.C., were unlike any previous diplomatic encounter in Choctaw history. The somber tone of the meetings may have been set by the accidental death of eighty-five-year-old Puckshenubbe on the journey to Washington, but it was also clear from their first exchanges with government officials that the delegates were determined to keep the focus on a small set of issues. They had no interest in socializing or lobbying. "We have been here a fortnight," McDonald wrote his friend Peter Pitchlynn on November 6, "and yet we have transacted no business."[43] Initially, McDonald played a minor role in drafting communications between the two sides and sending reports back home, but as the conversations intensified, his command of English and his skill at framing issues in clear legal terms became indispensable.

Once formal talks began, the Choctaw delegation quickly seized the initiative. They rejected any discussion of further land sales in Mississippi. In a note in McDonald's handwriting sent to Calhoun during their first week in the city, the Choctaws expressed their "friendly disposition" toward the United States but insisted that the "wishes of our countrymen" precluded any additional sales of the tribe's eastern lands. The discussion then shifted to Arkansas, where the Choctaws insisted on receiving a good price from the white squatters who had invaded their territory. As the two sides negotiated price and method of compensation, Calhoun reminded Pushmataha that four years earlier he and the other chiefs had disparaged the quality of the Arkansas land. The chief replied crisply that he was simply "imitating the white man": in 1820 he had been buying land; now he was selling it.[44]

U.S. officials also proposed a variety of payment schemes involving different lump sums and annual payments. McDonald's former patron Thomas McKenney (now the commissioner of Indian affairs) communicated separately with the young lawyer, pleading with him to help the government close the deal. The Choctaws maintained that they deserved to be fully compensated for what they were giving up, and they insisted that gifts of trade goods, a part of the 1820 treaty, would no longer be acceptable. They wanted cash for their national treasury.

As the weeks wore on, the Choctaws pressed Calhoun and Monroe to make their best offer. Finally, on November 20, after several exchanges, they set their terms for the remainder of their stay. "Unless the Government can bring itself to the conclusion to make a more liberal offer," the delegates wrote, "the negotiation must come to an immediate close and the delegation [must] return to their homes."[45]

When Calhoun's answer arrived two days later, the Choctaw leaders composed a withering reply. While continuing to express affection for the South Carolina leader—the letter called him "our friend and brother"—the delegates pronounced the government's offer "altogether inadequate." They pointed out that the five-million-acre tract they were discussing was not as "remote," as the government claimed, but easily accessible to New Orleans by the Arkansas and Red rivers. The sale of only one-third the total would generate two million dollars for the government. "Is it not just and right," they asked, "that we should receive in annuity, a reasonable portion of that sum?" They expressed sympathy for the squatters who had made improvements to their homesteads, but they pointed out that those settlers were trespassers, acting "contrary to the laws of Congress. . . . The labor has not been ours," the delegates conceded, "but who can say that the property is not?"

The delegates closed their response with an outline of what they considered their last offer. They demanded the abolition of Article Four of the 1820 treaty, a provision that defined the Choctaws as no more than temporary residents of Mississippi; the immediate payment of the $6,000 annuity promised in 1820; the appropriation of a lump-sum payment for education; and educational annuities for twenty years that would bring them $450,000 for their western lands. (The proposed educational funds would be divided between "mechanical institutions" and colleges.) The delegates acknowledged that their price was beyond what the government had been prepared to pay, but "it is not more than what we think to be their just value." Besides, they added, "we wish our children educated." The delegates were clearly laying the groundwork for the long-term welfare of the tribe. Striking a conciliatory pose, but no doubt aware of the tenacious twenty-three year-old lawyer sitting beside them at the bargaining table, the chiefs ended by assuring their adversaries that they wanted the "rising generation" to "tread in those paths which have conducted your people . . . to their present summit of wealth and greatness."[46]

After conferring again with Monroe, Calhoun reported that the government could not meet the tribe's price. McKenney again pleaded privately with McDonald, urging him to persuade his colleagues to relent as a favor to their government "friends." The delegation held firm, and the commissioner's "little Indian," the eager student who had once copied letters in his outer office, appeared to stand with them, united in support of securing the tribe's Mississippi homeland and winning fair compensation for the territory taken from them by the Arkansas squatters. During the ensuing weeks, as McKenney urged the delegates to reconsider and the group discussed a number of smaller issues (including McDonald's desire to be compensated for the theft of slaves from his mother's Mississippi farm), Pushmataha, the tribe's eloquent spokesman, developed a virulent infection. He died on December 24. It is impossible to know the details of the Choctaws' deliberations after Pushmataha's death, but it seems evident that McDonald's knowledge of Washington, together with his ready pen, promoted him to a central role.

The delegation continued to drive a hard bargain. They refused a late-December offer from the government but agreed to reconsider if the administration would increase its price. After several more exchanges stretching into late January, the two sides agreed on $216,000 for the Arkansas lands. They signed a new treaty in Calhoun's office on January 22. The bulk of the federal payment would go toward education, and as proposed first by the Choctaws in November, Article Four of the 1820 treaty was altered to ensure that any change in the status of the tribe's remaining Mississippi landholdings would require the Indians' approval.[47]

The Choctaws could take great satisfaction from their tenacity and hard work. They had accomplished their principal mission of protecting their Mississippi homeland and of extracting the highest possible price for the Arkansas territory that had been forced on them five years earlier. They had also succeeded in winning a revision of the language of the 1820 treaty, a clear refutation of Jackson's bullying tactics at Doak's Stand, and in directing most of the tribe's new income to education. Moreover, the negotiations had been conducted in an unprecedented fashion. For the first time, written offers had been exchanged and revised and the delegates had worked systematically through an extended list of outstanding disputes, from the wording of Article Four of the 1820 treaty to compensation for military service performed by tribal members during the War of 1812.[48]

As THE CHOCTAW TEAM prepared to leave Washington, however, their pride in their achievement was mitigated by the realization that the predicament of Indian tribes in the American Southeast had, if anything, grown more dangerous. The 1824 presidential election had occurred just before the delegation arrived in the capital, and though Andrew Jackson had not prevailed in a contest where no one won a majority in the electoral college, he had proved himself to be the most popular candidate. The subsequent deal struck between Jackson's enemy Henry Clay and John Quincy Adams in the House of Representatives that put the New Englander in the White House outraged Old Hickory's followers. The general began working almost immediately on his 1828 campaign. Sensing the westerner's political influence, both President-elect Adams and his vice president, John C. Calhoun, made it clear that while they rejected Jackson's bellicose rhetoric, they supported Indian removal.

In the face of Jackson's rise, President Monroe seemed to retreat. In a January 1825 report to Congress, delivered just as the Choctaw negotiations were concluding, the departing chief executive recommended the appointment of new commissioners to "visit and explain to the several tribes the objects of the government," and he urged negotiations that would lead to "conveying to each tribe a good title to an adequate portion of land to which it may consent to remove." The bill Monroe proposed was no less coercive than the Removal Act Jackson rammed through Congress five years later. The Choctaws were also aware that the Creeks in neighboring Alabama were deeply divided over the Treaty of Indian Springs, signed a few weeks after the Choctaw agreement, which called for the group to leave Alabama for the West.[49] In mid-February 1825, perhaps with an eye to this uncertain landscape, the Choctaw delegation, led by McDonald, crafted an open letter to Congress.[50]

James McDonald was only one of seven signers of the Choctaw declaration, but its legal language and simple phrasing make it clear that he was its author. Thomas McKenney agreed and reprinted the document in his memoirs as evidence of the young man's intellect. The statement was a plea for sympathy and support, but it also articulated clearly and publicly ideas that were a central element in all subsequent Native American political activists' arguments. In their memorial, the Choctaws acknowledged first that the United States was expanding while their tribe was becoming weak. They admitted as well that this trajectory suggested that the "interposing hand" of God was telling them that "the time must come" when they would be "made to become like white men." But at the same time, the delegates wrote, the tribe's progress in education and Christianity "give us the consoling assurance that we are not doomed to extinction." They would become like white men, but they would not cease being Indians. Defined by their culture and history, the Choctaws would not disappear into the "civilized" population as so many American leaders assumed. The Choctaws pointed out that the "one great reason" for the Americans' success "has been the general diffusion of literature and the arts of civilized life among them." "Civilized" Americans should protect the Choctaws, not destroy them. McDonald explained: "You have institutions to promote and disseminate the knowledge of every branch of science; you have a government, and you have laws, all founded upon those principles of liberty and equality which have ever been dear to us. . . . The theory of your government is justice and good faith to all men. You will not submit to injury from one party because it is powerful, nor will you oppress another because it is weak. Impressed with that persuasion, we are confident that our rights will be preserved."[51]

The Choctaw memorial argued that the American state and the tribe shared a common set of political values: "those principles of liberty and equality which have ever been dear to us." As a consequence, the American government and American laws—the visible embodiments of the young nation's commitment to "liberty and equality"—should protect the tribe from greedy settlers and the politicians who pandered to them. The delegates argued that the nation's deepest political commitments would inspire its leaders to recognize the Choctaws' "rights."

The Choctaw statement created little notice. Its words were modest and, perhaps, naive. McDonald emphasized the values the two groups shared, confessing that if his white neighbors lived up to those values, he and his tribe would be willing to entrust their future to the "liberality of the South." Yet his central assertions—that Indians would not become extinct and that "law" and "rights," rather than race, should govern relations between tribes and the United States—marked a fundamental shift in political consciousness. The leaders of one of the most populous tribes in eastern North America, even as they acknowledged that their military power was slipping away, were staking their future not on force or ceremonial diplomacy but on the proposition that American "civilization" itself could underwrite their future. For the first time a political thinker had defined a space for Indians—and Indian tribes—within the boundaries of the U.S. nation-state.

"A BITTER AND ENDLESS PERSECUTION"

In April 1826, only fourteen months after publishing his remarkable memorial, the Choctaws' young lawyer slipped into a dark mood. James McDonald wrote his patron Thomas McKenney that his "exertions in behalf of the Choctaws at the last treaty . . . were persevering and zealous" but that they represented "the only incident within the last two or three years of my life to which I can look back with anything like unmingled satisfaction." He confessed that events over the past year had caused him to "regret that I ever accompanied the delegation to Washington."[52]

Across the United States there was an emerging consensus that Indian removal was inevitable. This was the cause of the dispiriting atmosphere McDonald noted. For the next five years he and his counterparts among the Cherokees, Creeks, and Chickasaws in the South, as well as the Potawatomis, Shawnees, Sauks, Miamis, and others in the North, heard from friend and foe alike that the demands of white settlers could not be quieted and that regardless of past promises, federal authorities were unlikely to uphold the Indians' "rights" to their treaty-protected homelands. McDonald was not the only Native writer to devise a defense of tribal rights, but he was certainly among the first and most eloquent. His unique training and intense, face-to-face engagement with adversaries in both Mississippi and Washington, D.C., produced a series of remarkably perceptive observations about the mounting crisis. His thinking reflected both the anguish of his time and the issues Indian leaders were to face in the decades to come.

In the immediate aftermath of his Washington sojourn, McDonald focused most of his attention on securing the subsidies for education that government officials had promised in the new treaty. The young lawyer was concerned not only that federal funds be used efficiently but also that white southerners recognize the Choctaws' potential for "civilization." "Every intelligent man with whom I have conversed is in favor of having a National Academy established in the nation," he wrote McKenney in 1826. "Some school of a superior order, and upon a plan something different from the missionary schools, is very much wanted in the nation." The lawyer envisioned an institution that was both "national" and "superior" and would therefore prepare young people to lead the development of the Choctaw nation. "I am sure," he wrote, "that money thus applied would give more satisfaction and produce better results than if disposed of in any other manner." McDonald opposed funneling educational appropriations through missionary organizations or the Adams administration's political allies. He was critical of the Choctaw Academy, opened with federal dollars at the Kentucky home of Richard Johnson, the tribal agent's brother-in-law, preferring a tribally run school that would prepare bilingual leaders who could interact with outsiders in a variety of arenas.[53]

It was at that time McDonald decided to return to Ohio to complete his legal studies. "I wish to apply myself closely to it for several months," he wrote from the North in early 1827. His goal was "to qualify myself for the practice."[54] He also urged his young friend Peter Pitchlynn, the son of the tribe's principal interpreter and a nephew of the district chief Mushulatubbe, to take advantage of the new government school. "Cheer up, look forward to brighter prospects, study hard and go back [home] with me in the fall," he wrote in 1827. "We shall rub through our difficulties and come off with flying colors in the end."[55] Other educated tribal members shared this optimistic view. George Harkins, an ambitious young politician from the western district (another nephew of a district leader), encouraged the homesick Pitchlynn, writing that "our country stands in need of smart men and therefore I hope and trust that you will improve your time in such a manner that it will fit and qualify you to tell our poor countrymen their rights. . . . I hope the time is not very far ahead," Harkins added, "when our nation will become one of the most enlightened nations upon the face of the earth."[56]

A number of McDonald's Native American contemporaries hoped to prepare the next generation of educated leaders who would be able to defend their tribes' place within the United States. Cherokee leaders in nearby Georgia had allowed Moravian and Presbyterian missionaries to settle in their homeland in the first decade of the nineteenth century principally because they wished to promote English literacy that could be deployed in politics and business; they had little interest in the Christian Gospel.[57] The Cherokees also sent a small number of young people—like McDonald, often the children of prominent mixed-heritage families—to distant boarding schools to prepare them for leadership. Several tribes in the North followed a similar pattern. For example, Black Hoof's Shawnees, a band in Wapakoneta, Ohio, who had rejected Tecumseh's call to fight with the British in the War of 1812, sent several young people away to be educated at the same time as they welcomed Quakers into their communities to improve their farming and stock raising practices.[58] In 1825 the Office of Indian Affairs reported that federal subsidies were going to thirty-eight schools (most east of the Mississippi) that together were educating more than one thousand Native young people from Pleasant Point, Maine, to Florissant, Missouri.[59]

As he worried over the organization of tribal schools, McDonald also expressed concern about the effectiveness of the Choctaw government. Proud of the 1824 delegation's performance in Washington, McDonald believed his tribe needed this type of efficient and unified leadership to sustain itself in an increasingly hostile political climate. He explained in an 1825 letter to McKenney that the Choctaws had historically functioned as three separate entities. In the eighteenth century the three districts had been united by language, clan, and cultural traditions and had formed a permanent alliance in order to deal effectively with outside powers. "Each district is politically independent of the other," the lawyer wrote. "They are bound together by no other than . . . kindred and common origin." This heritage caused the Choctaws "to be in a very unsettled condition." McDonald acknowledged that it was "painful as well as delicate" to address this topic, but it was unavoidable. The Choctaws needed a united leadership.[60]

According to McDonald, the absence of a unified tribal position on removal exposed the Choctaws to one of the government's oldest strategies: divide and conquer. Mushulatubbe, for example, who had interacted with federal authorities as a tribal spokesperson for decades, appeared receptive to pressure from pro-removal forces in Washington. Concerned for the well-being of his particular district and clan, the chief appeared not to share McDonald's commitment to the good of the "nation" (itself a new term).[61] In response, McDonald and other young men argued that an elected tribal council should replace the current system. The young lawyer joined forces with David Folsom, who had accompanied him to Washington in 1824, to unseat the older district chief. Arguing that the tribe needed leaders who could deal effectively and in English with powerful outsiders, Folsom deposed Mushulatubbe in the northeastern district in the spring of 1826. He followed up this victory with a campaign against Robert Cole, the traditional leader of the western district. Cole was soon replaced by his nephew, Greenwood LeFlore. For McDonald, what was even more important than this shift in leadership was the council's decision in August 1826 to write a national constitution and erect a meetinghouse that would form the center of a unified community. Folsom, LeFlore, and Tapenahomah, the chief of the southern district, produced this document nearly a year before the neighboring Cherokees announced a similar charter on July 4, 1827.

The 1826 Choctaw constitution established a general council made up of the three district chiefs and six other representatives, and it stipulated that the group would meet at least twice each year. The council would legislate on matters as diverse as prohibition and witchcraft over the next three years. Two chiefs acting together could veto legislation approved by the general council, but that veto could be overridden and the majority's will imposed on every district. The ideals of a centralized authority ruled by law rather than custom was now becoming part of tribal life.[62]

The Choctaws' reforms were echoed elsewhere in the region and beyond. The Cherokees' 1827 constitution was more elaborate than the Choctaws'. It established a three-part national government headed by a chief executive, a framework modeled roughly on the founding document of the United States. In 1828, the same year Andrew Jackson was elected to the presidency, John Ross became the head of the Cherokee

Nation and his fellow leaders took their places in the tribe's bicameral legislature and on the national supreme court. North of the Ohio River, tribes with long histories of decentralized leadership were less successful in the effort to create unified governments, in large part because federal authorities were quick to exploit their divisions to promote further land sales. (The infamous Black Hawk War in 1832, for example, in which one group of Sauks resisted removal from Illinois while another acquiesced, was a product of this government tactic.) Still, some tribes managed to create new systems of governance. Most notable of these were the Allegany and Cattaraugus Senecas, who replaced their hereditary chiefs with an elected council in 1848.[63]

The Choctaws soon had an opportunity to test their new political system. Just weeks before Old Hickory's election in 1828 a mass meeting in Montgomery, Alabama, called on the state legislature to extend its "exclusive jurisdiction" over all territory within its boundaries and condemned the federal government's "unconstitutional" protection of the local Creek tribe. The following month the Georgia legislature enacted similar legislation that declared all Cherokee laws null and void within the state. A month later Mississippi passed a parallel measure.[64] By the time he took office in March, Jackson could present himself as the champion of this expanding trend. Southern politicians had grown bolder, and Indians faced increased prosecution. The new president declared that the federal government would not act to "sustain those people in their pretensions." He assured his supporters that tribal governments operating within states "would not be countenanced."[65]

In the fall of Jackson's first year in office, his secretary of war, John Eaton, ordered William Ward, the Choctaw agent, to expel from the tribal territory all white men who did not have federal permits to reside there. Councilman David Folsom condemned the order as an unlawful intrusion into tribal affairs and a disruption of its long-standing trading and business practices. The Jackson administration ignored him. The Choctaws responded to the government's indifference by threatening a public campaign to win popular support for their right to regulate their own territory. The newly elected district chief Greenwood LeFlore traveled to Georgia, where he forged an alliance with the Cherokees (sealed by the Choctaw leader's marriage to the niece of their new principal chief, John Ross) and promised to take the Indians' case to Washington, D.C.[66] Unimpressed, the Jackson administration pressed forward with a removal bill authorizing the president to initiate the wholesale relocation of eastern tribes to the West. By early 1830, with Jackson's proposal moving toward passage, Folsom and LeFlore decided to take the initiative. They called a meeting of the tribe's general council for the purpose of defining a consensus position on removal. McDonald, who had returned to Mississippi from Ohio at the end of 1827, decided to attend.

When the Choctaw leaders gathered at their new tribal meeting-house on March 15, 1830, they decided that absolute resistance was impractical. The white population vastly outnumbered them, and worse, federal officials appeared indifferent to their plight. The council chose to draft a removal treaty of its own. Reviving negotiating tactics employed in 1824, the council offered a compromise: it would give up its tribal land and leave Mississippi, provided federal officials agreed to distribute generous tracts of Choctaw territory (640 acres for heads of families; 320 acres for every other "young man") to every tribal member who opted to remain in the state. In addition, the council's proposal called for financial compensation for Choctaws whose property would be abandoned when they moved west and generous material subsidies for tribal members who stayed in the East. In their view, the United States was obligated by its former treaty agreements to subsidize and support those who chose to remain in Mississippi as well as those who agreed to remove. The council also proposed naming a delegate to Congress who would represent the Choctaws in the House of Representatives. The leaders authorized Greenwood LeFlore to present the draft agreement to the administration in Washington, D.C.

The Choctaws hoped that their proposal would win Jackson's support. After all, the president's Removal Act had demanded only negotiations—it did not order immediate removal—and the statute's mild language had been approved by only slim margins in both houses of Congress. The president had repeatedly assured his growing ranks of critics that the planned expulsions would take place peacefully and that any Indians wishing to remain in the East and live apart from their tribes would be allowed to do so. If Jackson was being disingenuous, the draft treaty seemed perfectly suited to unmask him. The widely circulated *Niles Weekly Register* spoke for many when it noted in May that the Choctaws' draft treaty deserved support. "What they ask," the *Register* declared, "if it can be so managed as to inure to their benefit, and prevent them from being the prey of speculators and contractors, would be reasonable enough."[67]

McDonald had mixed feelings about these events. He applauded the tribe's conciliatory stance, but worried that it had acted in too great haste and conceded too much. On his journey home from the council, he wrote a remarkably candid letter to his old friend Peter Pitchlynn, a fellow supporter of the measure. "I have had more thoughts rushing thro' my head within the last few days than I could reduce to writing in a month," he declared. "I was at times on the point of losing all hope—but then my favorite motto would occur to my recollection—nil desperandum. Let us never despair." McDonald encouraged Pitchlynn to "follow with energy whatever your judgment dictates as the line of duty, and in time all will be well." He also wondered whether in the end he would join the tribe on its journey across the Mississippi. "I have a strong idea of embarking my fortunes with the Choctaw and going west with them. It would break in on many of my old schemes," he added, "but is not this the very crisis in which my services would be useful to my countrymen?"[68]

The next day McDonald remained uncertain. In a letter to McKenney, McDonald despaired that the tribe had placed too much trust in LeFlore. He had hoped that the council would appoint a small committee "to visit the President and to learn from him distinctly and fully what terms would be granted." He believed such a strategy could produce a better treaty drafted "with the utmost care" and "with provisions the most . . . explicit."[69] Clearly, McDonald was thinking of his experience with the Choctaw delegation headed by Pushmataha in 1824 and 1825. Over the next several months it became clear that LeFlore would not enlist him as an adviser and that the pro-removal Choctaws were largely acting out of a self-interested desire to secure property for themselves in Mississippi. It was apparent that LeFlore and other wealthy leaders cared little for the future of the tribe. "I am lying on my oars doing nothing," McDonald wrote Pitchlynn later that year. "I have no wish to go on a visit to the President . . . [unless] it is with ample authority and with the view of being really useful to the Choctaws." He feared that removal was "inevitable," but he still hoped for "a good treaty—a treaty that shall construct the permanent and lasting good of the whole. . . ."[70]

In the end the Choctaws' preemptive strategy didn't work. The majority of the tribe—small farmers who wished to continue living in the state—responded angrily to the concessions in the draft treaty, and several of the traditional leaders who had been ousted by Folsom and Leflore accused the young councillors of treason. At the same time,

Jackson's supporters in Congress dismissed the tribe's proposal as too conciliatory to the Indians' position and too expensive. Exploiting the widening divisions between rich and poor within the tribe, the administration quickly dispatched Secretary of War John Eaton and the president's old comrade-in-arms John Coffee to Mississippi to strike a deal with the tribe's general council.

When they arrived in Mississippi in September at a meeting place near Dancing Rabbit Creek, the U.S. treaty commissioners were confronted by near-unanimous opposition. At the center of the council grounds sat seven elder women, probably the matriarchs of the tribe's major towns, who represented the group's deep attachment to its homeland. The council began with speeches of welcome and friendship, but the situation rapidly deteriorated. While a young councillor delivered a speech on behalf of a compromise treaty, one of the elder women rose and waved a butcher knife under his nose, crying, "I could cut you open with this knife." Referring to his white father and Indian mother, she added, "You have two hearts."[71] Most of the six thousand Choctaws assembled for the negotiations voiced their approval. They insisted they remained loyal to the United States, but they would not accept removal.

Faced with such stiff opposition, the secretary of war and his colleague fell back on the tactics Jackson himself had used a decade earlier at Doak's Stand. They warned of impending chaos and violence, and they hinted that the president might dispatch federal troops to the area to force the tribe out. They also sought out the most moderate of the Choctaw leaders (beginning with LeFlore) and pressed them for an agreement. After several days of talk, supplemented with a steady supply of alcohol, they succeeded in exploiting the divisions within the tribe. Gradually several opposition leaders and town groups drifted away from the council grounds, leaving behind the American officials and the Choctaws willing to sign the agreement. On September 27 the members who remained present voted to approve the government's plan.[72]

McDonald was present at the treaty grounds throughout the proceedings. He even signed the agreement. He told Cyrus Kingsbury, a missionary with whom he spent several days immediately following the negotiations, that the U.S. commissioners had reacted angrily to the tribe's initial rejection of their demands. He reported that Eaton and Coffee had insisted that LeFlore and other elected tribal leaders bring their people into line. When it became clear that the assembled crowd could not be persuaded to accept the government's demands, the men who had framed the tribe's March proposal suggested forming a new committee consisting of McDonald and six other "young men" to draft yet another alternative treaty. McDonald reported that Coffee and Eaton at first accepted his group's proposal but then unexpectedly substituted a new government draft in a final meeting with the tribal leaders and demanded their acceptance.

McDonald reported that "a majority had left the ground before the treaty was signed . . . and most of those that signed it now regret it." Threats, bribery, and individual land grants to LeFlore and other leaders, including McDonald, had sealed the agreement. These would likely doom any effort by others to overturn the deal. LeFlore and his allies had been bought, and they would not now retreat. After speaking with McDonald, Kingsbury reported darkly that bribes and land grants had made the difference. "Those who could do anything," he wrote, "are too much interested in [the treaty's] provisions to oppose it."[73]

The Treaty of Dancing Rabbit Creek guaranteed the Choctaws a new homeland west of Fort Smith, Arkansas, in exchange for all the tribe's territory in Mississippi. The agreement, like the council that produced it, was a disaster. The tribe was now completely polarized.

New rounds of recrimination and accusations of treason undermined the credibility of the leaders who had accepted the agreement and shattered whatever unity might have been possible a few months earlier. Kingsbury passed on McDonald's pessimistic assessment: "[T]he nation is ruined. . . . The instability (some say 'duplicity') of LeFlore and Folsom have sunk all my hopes." The treaty retained a few fragments from the original March proposal—land grants were made to tribal leaders and to each head of family who wished to remain in Mississippi—but there was little hope that even these provisions would be enforced. The commissioners also promised to take up the tribe's proposal for a congressional delegate with the president, but it was unlikely that Jackson would be interested. Within months, emigration parties were beginning to leave for the Arkansas Territory.[74]

McDonald remained in Mississippi. He now owned, thanks to the treaty, nearly one thousand acres of land. But he left no explanation for his decision. Perhaps he was discouraged by the chaos surrounding the approval of the removal treaty, or perhaps, like other tribal leaders, he decided to cash in on the land he would receive under its provisions. He may also have wanted to pursue the dream of opening a law practice in Jackson. For more than a decade he had committed himself to working out a way of living with the Americans and playing the role of cosmopolitan community leader; perhaps that was still possible. He had been capable of remarkable optimism. In a speech to a mixed audience in Jackson, delivered a few weeks before the start of negotiations with Eaton and Coffee, he had urged white citizens of the state not to "inflict unnecessary suffering upon a weak and defenseless people. Do not oppress those who have . . . reposed in your magnanimity."[75] In the wake of the government's shameful conduct at Dancing Rabbit Creek, however, few would now agree with him. McDonald played no role in tribal affairs after 1830, and the tasks he identified as crucial—constructing a unified tribal authority, training a new generation of leaders, and negotiating a place for Choctaws within the United States—remained unfinished.

INTERNAL RIVALRIES AMONG Choctaws continued in the postremoval era, but unlike the Cherokees, who fought a guerrilla civil war among themselves for most of the decade following their departure from Georgia, the emigrants from Mississippi managed to achieve a measure of unity after resettling in their new homeland. This effort was no doubt aided by the absence from their midst of polarizing leaders from the removal era. Greenwood LeFlore, for example, widely condemned as a traitor to his tribe, remained in Mississippi, where he established himself on a prosperous plantation assembled from former Choctaw land. Mushulatubbe, Jackson's former comrade and a tenacious advocate of negotiation and peace, left Mississippi with his kinsmen, but he died soon afterward. It would be left to younger men, such as McDonald's comrade Peter Pitchlynn, to rally the tribe behind them and reorganize its government in the West.

As he faced the future in Mississippi, McDonald shifted his attention to new challenges. Choctaws who remained in the state would become subject to state law. What would it mean to be a citizen of the state—theoretically a part of the local community but without any guarantee of civil rights or liberties? His earliest reflections on citizenship were contained in a letter to Secretary of War Calhoun, written while McDonald was a member of the 1824 delegation to Washington, D.C. Noting that Mississippi did not recognize Indians as potential voters or allow them to testify in court, McDonald wrote that Choctaws were incapable of protecting their individual rights. "How hard the case of the Indian!" he declared. "How is he to go among a people with whose language he is unacquainted, and enter into a labyrinth of litigation in which his civilized white brothers are so frequently lost?" This situation, he declared, deprived Indians "of the privileges which are inseparable from the vindication of our rights. . . . How is a Choctaw to obtain redress," he asked his former boss, "when he is deterred by the statutes of Mississippi from giving his testimony in a court of justice?"[76]

McDonald understood that officials like Calhoun believed that the Choctaws had only two alternatives before them. Either they would become citizens of the state or they would remain members of their tribe. That conceptual separation of "civilized" polities and tribes lay at the heart of the expansionist logic that Andrew Jackson had presented so forcefully to the Choctaws at Doak's Stand: tribes were, by definition, "savage" and therefore incompatible with democratic states; they could exist only outside the settled boundaries of the United States. In his 1824 letter, McDonald traced the beginnings of a rejoinder to this reasoning. By pointing out the link between Indian "rights" and the "privileges" of citizenship, he asserted his own eligibility for recognition by American law. If American institutions recognized Indians as citizens (or perhaps dual citizens of both tribes and states), they would be able to "vindicate" their rights.[77]

McDonald's view that the Choctaws had rights as tribal citizens that could be recognized and protected in American courts set him apart from many other tribal leaders of his day as well as from most U.S. officials. He believed therefore that state and tribal citizenship could coexist. In his first annual message to Congress in December 1829, the message in which he called for a general removal bill, President Jackson attacked the idea that Indians could erect "an independent government" within a state. If such a proposition were allowed, he argued, it would diminish the state because Indians could not be at once citizens of tribes and citizens of a state. By allowing tribal governments to function, the president argued, federal officials would be "destroying the state which it was established to protect."[78]

The Cherokee leader John Ross held a similar view of the incompatibility of state and tribal citizenship. He argued, for example, that when they came in contact with American institutions, "the untutored Sons of nature became a prey; defrauded of their land, treated as inferior beings. . . . Such must be the fate of those tribes now in existence," he added, "should they be merged into the white population before they become completely civilized. . . ."[79] The Cherokees maintained this position throughout the removal debate, arguing that only a tribal government could protect the rights of Indians. "While he possesses a national character there is hope for an Indian," an editorial writer in the tribal newspaper wrote in 1829. But "introduce him to a new order of things . . . [and] he droops like the fading flower before the noonday sun." State citizenship would "cut a vital string in their national existence."[80]

The Choctaw lawyer made his position evident as a remarkable series of events during the removal debate in Mississippi reached a climax. In July 1828 McDonald wrote his friend Peter Pitchlynn that he had "thrown aside the idea of practicing law," presumably because as an Indian he would not have been able to testify in court.[81] Six months later, however, the situation unexpectedly changed. In January 1829 the unemployed lawyer reported that he was lobbying for the passage of a state statute that would extend Mississippi state citizenship to Indians.[82] McDonald noted that the bill had passed the state senate but was stalled in the house. "We must make an effort [in the] next session of the legislature," he wrote. "You and two or three others, decent and clever fellows, must come down and see me . . . and together we will deliver an address which cannot be disregarded." Perhaps recalling his stirring appeal to Congress four years earlier, he added, "should our case be presented in as strong and forcible a manner as I think it is susceptible of being, they must certainly become advocates of our cause."[83]

Perhaps because of McDonald's lobbying or because Mississippi's pro-removal politicians wanted to appear as benevolent as possible before their northern critics, the state legislature included a citizenship clause in an otherwise hostile statute passed in January 1830. While declaring that all tribal lands would immediately be subject to state taxation and that it would henceforth be illegal for anyone to exercise the authority of a chief, the new law extended "all the privileges and immunities" of citizenship to Indians living in Mississippi.[84] The draft removal treaty framed by the Choctaw council the following March also incorporated the idea that state and tribal citizenship could coexist. That language became part of the Treaty of Dancing Rabbit Creek. As naive as McDonald's idea may have appeared in hindsight, it is significant that he rejected the idea that it would be impossible for Choctaws to coexist with whites within a settled American state. As a lawyer he would have known that groups of Indians could form corporations or other associations within the state and that there were any number of legal entities they might create to define and protect themselves in the future. Despite the forces arrayed against him, he could still imagine a future in which Choctaws might enjoy "the vindication of our rights."

McDonald's faith in the benefits of state citizenship may have been a factor in his decision to remain in Mississippi, but that faith was quickly disappointed. In the immediate aftermath of the treaty signing, the Choctaw agent who had been assigned to register tribal members for land allotments in Mississippi refused to act, claiming that all the applications were the work of unscrupulous whites. At the same time, white settlers who refused to wait until the new treaty was formally ratified by the Senate poured into the tribal homeland. The fragile hope that the treaty might allow the growth of a new multiracial community that included Indian landowners, cattlemen, and even lawyers like McDonald disappeared amid a riot of speculation and lawlessness.

JAMES MCDONALD'S VISION of overlapping tribal and state citizenship remained controversial among Native activists for decades to come. Nevertheless, he may well have been the first to argue that membership in the American state could be an effective means of defending the rights of Native people. He also appeared willing to test the new state statute by putting himself forward as a candidate for public office. On March 28, 1831, just weeks after the ratification of the Treaty of Dancing Rabbit Creek, McDonald wrote that he was considering becoming a candidate for the state legislature. While he worried that his opposition to President Jackson would hurt his standing with white constituents, he announced that "If my friends wish me to run I will run."[85] McDonald imagined a community that would support his vision of the future and endorse him as a person who was both an Indian and a state citizen. A few days later he wrote the Choctaw agent, reporting his intention to run for the Mississippi legislature and his desire to "make a location as soon as possible" on the land granted him in the tribe's removal treaty.[86]

McDonald's March 30 letter is the last document we have in his hand. He died, apparently by suicide, six months later, in September 1831. His tragic death underscored the vast distance that separated the young lawyer's tentative and hopeful vision of the Indians' future from the racist and exploitive reality that quickly engulfed postremoval

Mississippi.[87] It is not difficult to imagine the despair a person of McDonald's genius would have felt as he watched his hopes for education, tribal government, and state citizenship evaporate before the forces of dispossession and white supremacy. The young attorney must have understood that he would never serve in the Mississippi legislature or represent his tribe again in negotiations with the United States. There were many rumors surrounding his death—a marriage suit was rejected by a white woman, an alcohol-induced depression—but whatever the truth, McDonald no doubt understood that the vague and mild protections he had helped write into the Dancing Rabbit Creek treaty would be treated with contempt by state and federal officials. The government would soon forget its past promises to his tribe.

During his brief career James McDonald sketched the initial outlines of a secular and self-conscious American Indian political culture that would eventually take root within the boundaries of the United States. His words and ideas suggested an entirely new way for Native communities to imagine themselves in the North American landscape. "By this accident," a friend wrote following the young lawyer's death, "talents and genius . . . are lost forever to the world which cannot easily supply the void." Henry Vose, the young Natchez journalist who wrote those lines, went on to declare his admiration for McDonald's "transcendent abilities" and to question the rumor that his friend had indeed taken his own life: "his aspirations were far too noble and his patriotism too fervent to deliberately abandon the stage of human action."[88]

Vose expressed his admiration for McDonald in a letter to their mutual friend Peter Pitchlynn, then preparing to move with the rest of his tribe across the Mississippi to Indian Territory. An admirer of both of these young Choctaw leaders, Vose could not help adding his estimation of what might have been possible had McDonald lived:

Poor McDonald! Could you and he have marched arm in arm in the efforts you are making to establish an undying fame, doubtless your task would be more cheering. But you have now all to do; for I fear you have none near, warm, ardent and enthusiastic as yourself, to promote the welfare of your nation. What a proud era it would be if the Choctaws would, one and all, devote themselves to the arts and sciences! . . . Why may they not become the manufacturers of the South and the carriers for the remote West? Unity is everything; without it, the proudest nations must fall, as Assyria, Babylon, Judea and others, to rise no more.[89]

EXPLORER AND *SYMBOL*

It is difficult to evaluate James McDonald's career as the first American Indian lawyer. While he managed one of the first and most effective negotiating sessions between an Indian tribe and its government adversaries in 1824 and wrote eloquently on behalf of elected tribal governments and programs of Indian education in the ensuing years, he did little to slow the forces that expelled his tribe from its Mississippi homeland. Thanks in part to McDonald, the Choctaws arrived in the West with the sense, expressed in Henry Vose's letter, that stable tribal leadership could be a powerful weapon against federal authority and that education in law, politics, and the English language would be critical to the community's survival. But the extension of citizenship to Choctaws in Mississippi triggered tremendous fraud that mocked young McDonald's idealistic hope that the privileges associated with citizenship could produce the "vindication" of their rights.

James McDonald was a Native explorer who searched American legal and political institutions for a means by which their democratic promise could be used to protect tribal communities. As he observed the processes of negotiation and political engagement, McDonald identified the tools tribes might employ to contend with the machinery of United States expansion: literacy, compromise, and new alliances with powerful non-Indians. The lessons he and the Choctaws learned in Mississippi in the 1820s were absorbed by other leaders of removed tribes. Each group applied these lessons in different ways. Some focused on education, others on political tactics and alliances, still others on economic innovation. Each of their innovations rested on the propositions James McDonald had written into the Choctaw memorial to Congress in February 1825. He had wrestled with these ideas as he speculated about the benefits of state citizenship for Mississippi Indians in the years that followed. Indians were a permanent presence within the boundaries of the United States, McDonald declared; they therefore could claim that American law and government should protect their rights, both as individuals and as tribal communities. He imagined that Native people could not be erased from the nation and he proposed that they therefore should participate in the nation's future.

Despite his early death, James McDonald symbolized the proposition that Native futures could be secured by the laws and institutions of the American state. His words and actions advanced the remarkable proposition that Indian tribes might reclaim some portion of their original homeland by invoking the laws and values of their dispossessors. McDonald's untimely disappearance from the historical stage underscored the futility of this vision in the cruel age of Andrew Jackson, but the persistence of his ideas in the "Indian Territory" that Jackson and his allies created west of Fort Smith suggests that Henry Vose was correct when he imagined that new tribal leaders like Peter Pitchlynn would not surrender. James McDonald offered an alternative to death or surrender. Produced by engagement rather than rejection and characterized by a search for vulnerabilities in the Americans' rhetoric, the young lawyer's ideas challenged the United States' claim to the continent as well as to sole ownership of the ideals of democracy, freedom, and justice. McDonald's "transcendent abilities" first identified this alternative pathway; his successors would explore and develop it.

CHAPTER THREE

THE MOUNTAINTOP PRINCIPALITY OF SAN MARINO

William Potter Ross, Cherokee

Nearly fifty years after James McDonald urged Congress to protect Indian rights, another Native activist from the Southeast voiced a similar appeal. In the dusty railroad town of Vinita, Indian Territory, near modern Tulsa, Oklahoma, the Cherokee chief William Potter Ross addressed a crowd of supporters. Like McDonald, Ross was a member of an elite group of Indians who had been educated by whites in an institution far from his tribal homeland. But unlike the Choctaw lawyer, Ross had spent his entire career in tribal politics. Born in the East, he had come west when his tribe was expelled from Georgia and in the ensuing decades had held a variety of offices. He had battled with political enemies within the tribe and traveled widely to lobby U.S. officials and others on behalf of the Cherokee Nation. In 1866, when his famous uncle Chief John Ross passed from the scene,

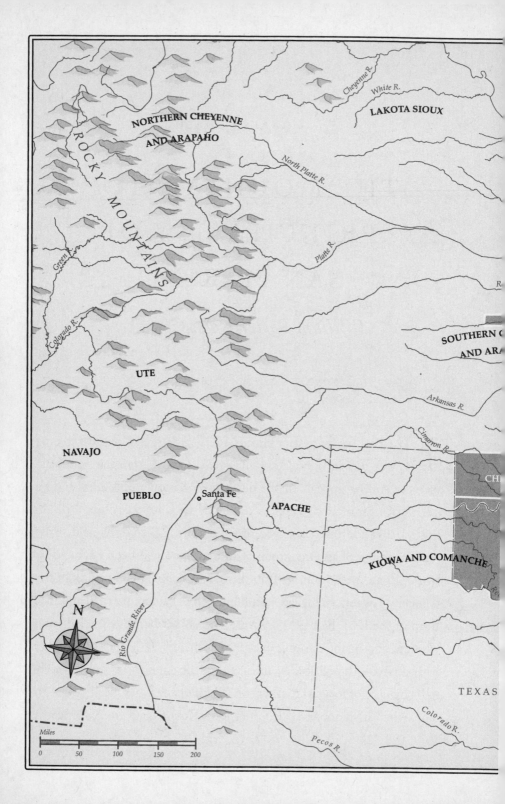

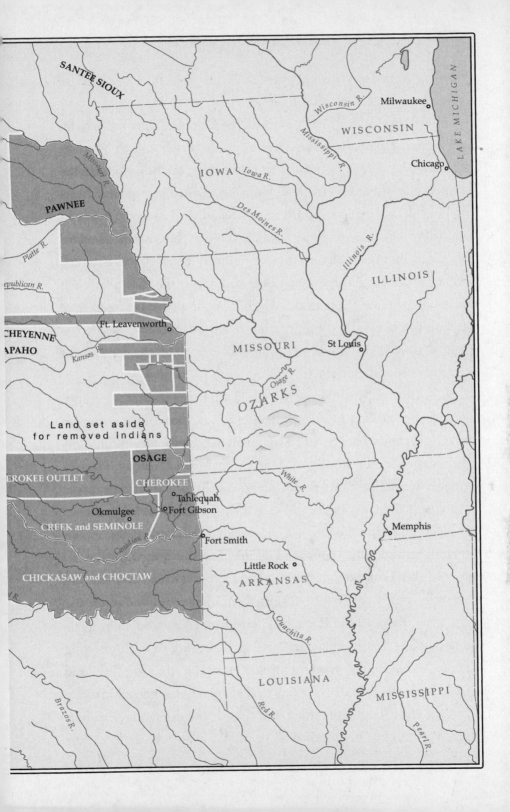

the tribe turned to William Potter to take his place. It seemed a proper reward for his years of faithful service.

In 1874, in that dusty railroad town, the Cherokee chief spoke to his supporters of a place in Europe where "justice" had been won by political action. A decade earlier and an ocean away, the tiny mountaintop principality of San Marino had peacefully resisted incorporation into the new Italian nation-state forming around it. Ross noted that this "little republic" had resolved its differences with the central authorities in Rome by negotiating a series of mutually beneficial treaties and trade agreements. The Sammarinese had acted, the Cherokee chief insisted, to honor "the centuries which have chronicled the freedom of [their] ancestors." They were not motivated by ignorance, but by "as pure a glow of patriotism and delight as ever animated the brow of ancient or modern citizen."[1]

In his speech Ross portrayed San Marino as a vigilant, protective eagle, perched high in its mountain eyrie and noted by comparison that "[no] Indian nation on this continent has shown a more conspicuous bearing in the history of America than the Cherokee." He reminded his audience that the Italian principality and their tribe shared common mountain origins. "The mountaineers of America have been overpowered but not destroyed," he declared. "Their defenses of their own rights and those common to all inhabitants of the [Indian] territory has been constant, unflagging and successful thus far despite the powerful influences arrayed against them." Just as an understanding national government in Rome had demonstrated its wisdom by guaranteeing San Marino's national survival, he argued, so the "protecting arm of the federal government" would be vital to the Cherokees and their neighbors in Indian Territory. The United States should imitate Italy by underwriting the tribes' institutions and defending their borders against the "heterogeneous" onslaught of unruly settlers. Ross warned that by failing to uphold the independence of the Cherokees and other Indian Territory tribes, American officials would be guilty of promoting "a revolution" on the western frontier that would surely trigger "wrong, fraud, deception, vice, immorality, insult, retaliation, blood, [and] extermination."[2]

While it is not particularly surprising that a well-educated member of the Cherokee elite would be so conversant with world events in 1874, it is significant that Chief Ross called on his audience to take a lesson from the practical world of European politics. A generation after the removal crises of the 1830s, Ross was still preoccupied with the issues arising from the enforcement of Cherokee treaty rights and the defense of tribal autonomy. Since arriving in Indian Territory thirty years earlier, he had written extensively and spoken frequently about the distinctive place Native nations could have within the United States. Not only was Ross aware of the process of national consolidation then taking place in Italy and other parts of Europe, but he had also observed the behavior of neighboring tribes and had witnessed the recent struggle of southern states to escape the authority of the federal government. Ross's assertion that there was space within America for an Indian San Marino was rooted in the search for ways to integrate small communities into modern nations, which was taking place both inside and outside the United States.

From Ross's perspective, it made perfect sense to view Indian Territory as another San Marino. Formed in the wake of the removal era, the area that eventually entered the Union as Oklahoma in 1907 had been established as a new homeland for relocated Indian tribes. Despite the fact that it was not administered by a presidentially appointed governor, as were other federal territories, the land often described as lying "west of Fort Smith" was now a common "home" for thousands of Indians. Some had traveled there voluntarily in the early years of the century, but most of the members of the large southeastern tribes—Cherokees, Choctaws, Creeks, Chickasaws, and Seminoles—arrived the 1830s. A second wave of settlement came after 1854, when the creation of the Kansas Territory triggered the relocation of several additional eastern and midwestern tribes (some moving for a second time). West of the resettled tribes were indigenous groups that lived primarily as hunters. Most prominent among these were the Kiowas, Kiowa-Apaches, Comanches, Cheyennes, and Arapahos. After the Civil War additional groups were resettled in the territory from as far away as California and Oregon. By the time of Chief Ross's speech in Vinita, Indian Territory contained nearly sixty thousand Native people living on dozens of reservations. While the cultures of these groups were wildly diverse, they shared a common desire to live autonomously within the United States.

William Potter Ross understood that common ambition. Recognizing that the ceremonial diplomacy of the eighteenth century was now an artifact of the past and that military resistance to American expansion was futile, Ross relied on practical political language to make his case. He rejected the conventional American assumption that Native communities were hopelessly backward, proposing instead that Indian social and economic progress would produce stability and lay the foundation for peaceful relations between Native groups and whites. After the Civil War, as a reunited American nation celebrated its industrial strength and continental power, William Potter Ross proclaimed his support for both "progress" and Indian nationhood. He believed the "pure glow of patriotism" could shine as brightly in his Indian Territory homeland as it had in San Marino.

BORN NEAR MODERN Chattanooga, Tennessee, in the summer of 1820, William Potter Ross belonged to an extended mixed-race family of traders, farmers, and political leaders. William's father, John Golden Ross, a trader, was born in Scotland. His mother, Eliza Ross, who shared the same last name as her husband but was not related to him, was the daughter of a storekeeper. Eliza's brother, John Ross, was the Cherokees' first principal chief.[3] Like many other children of elite families among southeastern tribes, William Potter was educated at boarding schools. He compiled a stellar academic record at a Presbyterian mission school in Will's Valley, Alabama, and at Greenville Academy in Tennessee, before being sent in 1837 to Hamil's Preparatory School in Lawrenceville, New Jersey. A year later he entered Princeton University, from which he was graduated in 1842. Ross was still in school in the East when the removal crisis reached its climax and his uncle became a national symbol of Indian resistance. He retraced his family's grueling journey west on the Trail of Tears the summer following his college graduation. Unlike his relatives who suffered and died on their way west, William Potter Ross made the journey safely by carriage.[4]

Despite his relatively comfortable journey, the young Cherokee scholar was soon plunged into the trauma and violence that accompanied arrival in Indian Territory. As a teacher in a rural school in the fall of 1842 he witnessed the tribe's efforts to make a living from its new lands. He also watched as his elders tried to reorganize their divided tribal government. He was not directly involved in the assassinations of Major Ridge and other leaders of the minority party who had agreed to sign the removal Treaty of New Echota, nor was he a target of the retaliatory violence organized by Ridge's relatives during the ensuing decade; but this civil conflict swirled around him and left a deep impression. After a year in the classroom, Ross moved to the Cherokee capital, Tahlequah. Through his uncle's patronage he secured a position as clerk of the national senate, and in 1844 the legislature appointed him editor of the tribe's national newspaper, *The Cherokee Advocate*.

Ross and his brother Daniel soon opened a sawmill and mercantile business in the commercial center that grew up around the U.S. Army base at nearby Fort Gibson. Through his political activity and business success, William Potter also became one of his uncle's most trusted advisers. When the Civil War began, Ross followed other members of the Cherokee planter class, many of them slaveowners like James McDonald and Peter Pitchlynn, into the Confederate cause. After the rebels' defeat at the battle of Pea Ridge in 1862, Ross was captured by advancing U.S. troops. When offered a parole the following year, Ross returned to his Fort Gibson wholesale business and temporarily abandoned tribal politics. He later joined the pro-Union Cherokee Home Guards, but avoided any further fighting. Instead, he urged his fellow Cherokees to avoid violence and refrain from participating in the raiding and revenge that destroyed many farms and plantations in the closing days of the war. He was remembered—appropriately for someone who wore both the gray and the blue uniform during the Civil War—as a man who "would rather have his people united than to see them fight each other."[5] At the conflict's end he served on the tribal delegation that negotiated a new peace treaty with the United States.

After the death of John Ross in October 1866, the Cherokee national council selected William Potter Ross to finish his uncle's term. As chief, he served on delegations that traveled to Washington, D.C., to represent the tribe and fielded the first challenges to the tribe's continued existence in Indian Territory. First as chief and then as a tribal senator and delegate, Ross was centrally involved in the struggle to maintain the autonomy of the Indian nations in the West. Throughout the 1870s and 1880s he remained an outspoken tribal leader while he edited two local newspapers and served on the tribe's board of education.[6] Ross witnessed the first land rush that brought non-Indian landowners into Indian Territory in 1889, but his death in 1891 saved him from being present either at the division of the Cherokee Nation into individual landholdings later that decade or at the dissolution of Indian Territory when Oklahoma became a state in 1907.

While many in Ross's Vinita audience lived to see Indian Territory erased from the nation's maps, the campaign the Cherokees and neighboring tribes waged against U.S. intrusion into their territory made clear that the new political culture an earlier generation of leaders had nurtured during the removal crisis survived to the end of the nineteenth century. William Potter Ross applied the political ideas that had sprouted first in the Southeast in the 1820s to new events unfolding in the West. In the process he elaborated and promoted an ideology of Indian autonomy and Native nationalism that could fuel other struggles in other regions across North America.

As they founded new governments in the West, the leaders of removed tribes held firmly to the positions they had articulated in their battle against Andrew Jackson. To avoid any future misunderstandings, they insisted that all removal treaties and all subsequent tribal charters and letters of understanding stipulate the Indians' perpetual right to their new homelands. The Choctaw removal treaty, for example, declared that the United States was "obliged to secure to the said Choctaw Nation of Red People the jurisdiction and government of all the persons and property that may be within their limits west, so that no Territory or state shall ever have a right to pass laws for the government of the Choctaw Nation . . . and . . . no part of the land granted them shall ever be embraced in any Territory or State."[7] The implication of these assurances was clear: there would be no repetition of the disputes between Georgia, Mississippi, and Alabama and the Choctaws, Cherokees, Chickasaws, and Creeks. Eager to secure the

Indians' removal as peacefully and quickly as possible, federal officials agreed to these demands, assuring the leaders of removed tribes that they would be undisturbed in their new homes.[8]

The legal guarantees embedded in their removal agreements defined the relocated tribes' unique status. The Cherokees, Choctaws, and other removed groups had no prior claim to their new homelands. As a consequence, in American eyes their sovereign authority in the West depended solely on the formal commitments made to them by the United States; it did not derive from long occupation or ancient tradition. Removal thus created an archipelago of Indian political entities scattered beyond the settled borders of the United States and led by literate, sophisticated politicians like Ross. In the second half of the nineteenth century the status of Indian Territory's removed tribes would rest on the legal guarantees promised them at the time of their relocation, while those in other parts of the country that continued to occupy their traditional homelands would trace their titles to the diplomatic recognition contained in treaties of friendship and alliance. This latter group included Navajos who had recently been living in a Mexican province west of the Rio Grande, Lakotas migrating into the Yellowstone Valley, Catholic Flatheads trading with Hudson Bay men in the northern Rockies, and Paiute bands adjusting to the ecological disruptions caused by Americans crossing the Great Basin to California. Despite these different circumstances, however, every tribe eventually became convinced that its future security depended on the explicit legal guarantees it had extracted from the United States in its treaties. William Potter Ross, an official of a tribe whose status rested on those guarantees alone, spent his career urging both his tribe and others to negotiate the best agreements possible and to hold the United States accountable for the promises it had made in those documents.

As he stood up to American politicians and white settlers who coveted his tribe's land, Ross argued that the Cherokee cause was the cause of all Native people. His interest in intertribal unity, for example, began as a political tactic (his tribe would be more likely to be heard if it had vocal support from neighboring groups), but by century's end the idea that all Native people shared common interests and that tribal governments together could represent Indian "civilization" had begun to resonate with a number of tribal leaders. Similarly, his rejection of the charge that "Indian" governments were inherently backward found echoes in the resistance of other tribes to U.S. intrusion into their affairs. At the time of Ross's death in 1891 the Cherokee leaders' prescriptions forged in the political turmoil of Indian Territory would be picked up and repeated by Native activists elsewhere. Building on the heritage of those who had endured removal early in the nineteenth century, Ross and his Indian Territory counterparts established a set of foundational ideas that other tribes began to adopt at the end of the century.

It is ironic that William Potter Ross, a member of a prominent Cherokee slaveowning family and a veteran of service in the Confederate cause, was a champion of indigenous nationalism and an enemy of white supremacy. His steady opposition to the American takeover of Indian Territory and his careful delineation of tribal rights, tribal citizenship, and native forms of modernity were framed in opposition to the government's desire to cancel its moral and legal commitments to Native people and to incorporate their homelands into a modern American nation-state. Cherokees like William Potter Ross rejected the ideal of a racially pure "white" nation because they were advocates of their tribes, not because they believed in racial equality. They advocated a political pluralism that could accommodate both tribes and binding treaties. Racial equality was less important to them than tribal autonomy.

A NEW POLITICAL CULTURE TAKES
HOLD IN THE WEST

The removal era was a time of multiple promises and intense suffering. The expulsion of the Choctaws, Cherokees, Creeks, Chickasaws, and Seminoles from the Southeast produced countless scenes of hardship and dislocation: frozen bodies buried alongside the gruesome Trail of Tears, confused families herded onto steamboats bound for unknown lands, terrified men and women hunted down by soldiers across the Appalachians and the swamps of Florida. Mixed with these horrors were repeated assurances from federal authorities that once their relocation was complete, Native people could look forward to a life of peace and quiet. Andrew Jackson himself had declared in his first inaugural address that the tribes agreeing to removal would live on lands "guaranteed" to them by federal power and that they would "be secured in the enjoyments of governments of their own choice, subject to no other control from the United States than such as may be necessary to preserve peace on the frontier."[9]

In 1838 William Potter Ross wrote that he wished the creator "may curse this people with some calamity for their cruelty . . . which will lower their *pride*," but as a Princeton undergraduate he did not witness any of the tragic events associated with the Cherokees' departure from Georgia.[10] He remained close to his uncle following graduation and, as editor of the tribe's newspaper, followed closely John Ross's negotiations with U.S. authorities over a new treaty to resolve the issues that had been left outstanding after removal. The Cherokees did not agree to a new treaty until the summer of 1846 when, pressured by President Polk, who was then preoccupied with the imminent war with Mexico. Chief Ross accepted an agreement that confirmed the legality of their hated removal treaty and authorized a five-million-dollar payment for their Georgia lands. Adding insult to injury, the costs incurred by the United States in its botched effort to transport the tribe to Oklahoma were deducted from this amount.

The 1846 treaty forced the Cherokees to accept the removal treaty, a document Ross and his allies had long abhorred, and it offered them far less financial support than they needed. But the treaty also assured that a secure patent would be issued to the Cherokees for their new territory, thereby giving it the status of a privately owned estate. The 1846 agreement also committed the United States to "forever secure and guarantee" their country.[11] On the surface, there was nothing directly objectionable in the terms of the 1846 agreement, but the delay in reaching it and the obvious enjoyment Indian Office personnel derived from undercutting and frustrating the powerful Cherokee leader made it clear to William Potter Ross that these federal promises could well prove as unreliable as the ones that had preceded them.

The Cherokees received another indication of federal intentions in 1846, when Chief Justice Roger Taney announced the Supreme Court's decision in *U.S. v. Rogers*. The case involved a white man, William Rogers, who had sought to overturn his murder conviction in federal court by asserting that as a citizen of the Cherokee Nation since 1836 he was beyond the jurisdiction of U.S. courts. Rogers seemed to have a solid argument. His victim, Jacob Nicholson, was also an adopted Cherokee. The Treaty of 1835 expressly recognized the tribe's right "to make and carry into effect all such laws as they may deem necessary for the government and protection of the persons and property within their own country . . . or such persons as have connected themselves with them."[12] Taney rejected that treaty pledge out of hand, however, noting that "from the very moment the general government came into existence . . . it has exercised its power over this unfortunate race in the spirit of humanity and justice and has endeavored . . . to enlighten their minds and . . . save them if possible from the consequences of their own vices." Because Indians were an "unfortunate" people defined by vice, Taney reasoned, all federal action was by definition both humanitarian and legal. Actions of the United States involving tribes were therefore not subject to judicial review. Taney's decision invited other federal officials to ignore any inconvenient promises they may have made to the tribes in the past.

Taney recognized that the criminal statutes governing federal territories specifically exempted crimes committed "by one Indian against the person or property of another Indian." Even so, the chief justice could not accept a political or constitutional definition of the Cherokee tribe. He insisted that the Cherokees were simply a racially distinct people. In his opinion "a white man who at mature age is adopted in an Indian tribe does not thereby become an Indian." Despite Andrew Jackson's pledge that tribes like the Cherokees would be "secure in the enjoyments of governments of their own choice," Taney declared William Rogers was simply a white sojourner in a racially defined community who could not change his race by connecting himself with the Cherokee Nation: "Whatever obligations the prisoner may have taken upon himself by becoming Cherokee by adoption, his responsibility to the laws of the United States remained unchanged and undiminished. He was still a white man, of the white race, and therefore not within the exception in the act of Congress."[13]

The shortcomings of the 1846 treaty and the explicit anti-Indian racism of Justice Taney's ruling underscored for young Cherokees like William Potter Ross the continuing uncertainty of the tribe's political status within the United States. Despite the promises that had been written into removal treaties across the East, federal officials rejected any challenges to their authority over Native communities. Tribal leaders responded to this harsh tone by redoubling their effort to become effective advocates for their cause. Aware that even powerful presidents like Andrew Jackson had powerful rivals and that representation in Washington could win them a sympathetic hearing before the American public, the removed tribes soon became a regular presence in the national capital. Delegations frequently appeared before congressional committees, tribal leaders routinely sought out the advice and support of Washington attorneys, and the Indian Territory tribes tried to make common cause with their Native neighbors.[14]

Leaders of the removed tribes were quick to promote the idea of multitribal "international councils" aimed at promoting peaceful relations among the tribes in Indian Territory and the surrounding region. These councils grew out of a tradition of peace conferences that U.S. officials had organized prior to removal to reduce tensions between western tribes (particularly the Osages, Pawnees, Kiowas, and Comanches) and the eastern Indians who had begun to migrate voluntarily to the West early in the century. Fort Gibson, erected in 1822 along the Arkansas River at a spot near the future site of the Cherokee capital of Tahlequah, had been the scene for several of these gatherings. One such meeting in 1834 involved more than a dozen tribes (including recently arrived Delawares and Senecas from the Midwest) that pledged friendship to one another and agreed to meet again to conclude a formal treaty. The 1835 Camp Holmes treaty, negotiated on the prairies west of Fort Gibson, fulfilled that goal. It established peaceful relations between the eastern tribes such as the Cherokees, Choctaws, and Creeks, and local groups such as the Wichitas and Osages. A second gathering the following year extended the Camp Holmes agreement to the Kiowas and Kiowa-Apaches.[15]

In the 1840s the Cherokee tribal government, along with the governments of neighboring groups, began hosting their own intertribal meetings. They took this step both because they were eager to maintain good relations with the powerful tribes that had previously occupied their new homelands—particularly the Osages, Kiowas, and Comanches—and because they were increasingly conscious of threats to their borders. To the south, the new Republic of Texas, dominated by slaveholders, seemed determined to remove its resident tribes and create a homogeneous, independent settler nation on the model of the United States. The Cherokees had little interest in antagonizing these aggressive neighbors, many of whom were recent arrivals from Georgia, Mississippi, and Tennessee. Tribal leaders in Tahlequah were also aware that Mexican officials to the west, still resentful of the Texans' recent success in their war of independence, were eager to form alliances with Comanches and other groups who had traditionally raided agricultural communities along the Arkansas River. To the north, resettled tribes from the American Midwest—particularly Delawares, Shawnees, Potawatomis, and Wyandots—were making new homes on the Missouri frontier. The disruptions accompanying their arrival triggered yet another round of retaliation and resentment among indigenous groups.[16]

Large intertribal gatherings began in 1843. In June of that year more than three thousand representatives of twenty-two tribes gathered at Tahlequah in response to invitations sent out by John Ross and Roly McIntosh, the chief of the Creeks. For four weeks the delegates made camp across a two-mile-wide prairie and participated in round dances, ball games, and parades. William Potter Ross, barely a year removed from his Princeton graduation, was among them.

When the formal sessions began, Chief John Ross reminded the delegates of the serious work before them. "Brothers," he cried, "it is for renewing in the West the ancient talk of our forefathers, and of perpetuating forever the old pipe of peace . . . and of adopting such international laws as may redress the wrongs done by the people of our respective tribes to each other that you have been invited to attend the present council." In addition to securing pledges of peace from all who attended, Ross won approval for eight written resolutions that established rules of conduct and included the declaration "No nation party to this compact shall without the consent of all the other parties, cede or in any manner alienate to the United States any part of their present territory."[17]

One white observer predicted that the 1843 gathering would "disperse without having done anything," but the resolution regarding land cessions was a clear signal that the men who had been victims of removal had a serious purpose. They wanted to forge an alliance that could hold their enemies at bay.[18] Often ignored by outsiders, these gatherings continued throughout the coming decade. The first extensive press coverage of an international council appeared in the spring of 1845 thanks to William Potter Ross, who traveled thirty-five miles southwest of Fort Gibson to a meeting site within the new Creek Nation. There he found more than seven hundred Creeks gathered to receive delegations from resettled southeastern tribes, including Choctaws, Chickasaws, and Seminoles, as well as other tribes that had been forced from the Midwest to Kansas, such as the Shawnees, Miamis, Delawares, Peorias, and Kickapoos, along with local groups, like the Osages, Caddos, and Quapaws. The Comanches, who had been specially invited in hopes of negotiating an end to their raids, refused to attend. Ross noted that it was "a source of great regret" that the Cherokees had not sent an official delegation but added that this was a consequence of a delay in notification and "by no means from any indifference on the part of this people to whatever relates to the peace and prosperity of the whole Indian population."[19]

"During the council," Ross reported, "the pipe of peace was smoked, the white paths cleared, the council fire lighted afresh and several speeches of interest delivered by the heads of the different representations present." The editor reprinted several of those speeches in *The Cherokee Advocate*. He also noted that "the nights were enlivened by the 'Terrapin Shell dance' of the Muscogees and the songs, drums, reeds and salutations (jumping and leaping) of the Osages." All the delegations confirmed the agreements made two years earlier at Tahlequah. The group even received a communication—and a pipe—from the Great Lakes. A group of "Winnebagoes, Chippeways, Tahwas and Menawallys [*sic*] sent a message expressing a desire to be "keep open the white path of peace that we may train up our children in it and teach them to be friendly with all men."[20]

The council's Creek hosts remained in the background for most of the 1845 gathering, but at its close, Tuckabatchemicco, the Upper Creek host of the event, offered a summary and a set of suggestions. He urged everyone to follow the example of the Osages and "bring in all the stolen horses" to the next general council. "Hereafter," he added, "quit stealing horses from one another." Tuckabatchemicco also noted that he would give the absent Cherokees "a talk" urging them to stop the "straggling men" in their country from stealing and committing murder. (This was a reference to the tribe's ongoing civil war.) Once the Indians succeeded in policing themselves, the Creek leader promised, the United States would have no reason to station troops in the territory. At that point, he suggested, this intertribal council could act as a general government: "When we shall all get at peace again with the different tribes, the troops may be recalled or dispensed with." Tuckabatchemicco and other leaders believed that a stable intertribal council could potentially evolve into a comprehensive system of governance for the entire Indian Territory.[21]

DESPITE HIS INVOLVEMENT with intertribal issues, Cherokee tribal politics remained William Potter Ross's principal preoccupation in the years before the Civil War. He represented the Tahlequah district in the national council government from 1849 to 1859, and in that position (as well as when he served as a member of tribal delegations to Washington in 1847, 1849, 1850, and 1855) the editor-activist lobbied for expanded federal funding for tribal schools and greater power for tribal institutions. In Washington he doggedly followed the process by which congressional committees debated the appropriation of funds promised to compensate the Cherokees for their losses during the removal process. "That Congress will much longer fail to make the appropriations . . . we cannot believe," he and another delegate wrote his uncle in 1850.[22] Still, action did not come until 1852 when $1.5 million was distributed to tribal members.[23] During the 1850s William Potter Ross also served as an officer of the Cherokee Temperance Society and the Cherokee Seminaries. He lived alongside other prosperous tribal leaders at Park Hill, a rich agricultural area near Tahlequah, and was an active figure in the social life of the Cherokees' planter elite.

Throughout his early career, Ross remained ambivalent about the institution of slavery. Like other members of the Cherokee leadership, he did not oppose operating agricultural plantations with slave labor. At the same time, he parted ways with his family's political rivals—the remnants of the Ridge/Boudinot group that had signed the hated 1835 removal treaty—who became outspoken defenders of slavery. These slaveowners challenged him in the 1855 district election, charging he was too sympathetic to northern abolitionists, but support from Chief Ross saved him from defeat.[24] Not surprisingly, then, Ross responded to the approaching prospect of secession and war by urging his fellow Cherokees to remain neutral in the dispute. Early in 1861, when federal forces abandoned nearby Fort Smith and its new southern commander demanded the Cherokees declare their loyalty to the South, William Potter Ross was among those who urged his uncle to "do nothing . . . keep quiet and comply with our treaties."[25]

John Ross held the Confederates and their sympathizers within his own tribe at bay for several weeks, but continued pressures from his rivals and the rapid retreat of federal troops soon forced him to negotiate an alliance with the South. Significantly, the treaty that the chief and his executive committee, which included William Potter Ross, negotiated with Albert Pike, the Confederate representative, read like a list of the issues the tribe had failed to resolve with U.S. officials over the previous two decades. The Cherokees would send a delegate to the Confederate Congress, the southern government promised to pay all outstanding claims related to the Cherokees' forced removal from Georgia, tribal officials would have the right to extradite and prosecute criminals who had fled to neighboring states after committing crimes in their territories, and—in a direct repudiation of the U.S. Supreme Court's ruling in *U.S. v. Rogers* fifteen years earlier—the Cherokee tribe was guaranteed the right to determine its own membership. Ironically (and incredibly) the treasonous Confederates, committed to the defense of racial slavery and white supremacy, were willing to recognize Indian tribes as autonomous political entities.[26]

As they signed their treaty with the Confederacy, Ross and his advisers issued a Declaration by the People of the Cherokee Nation, spelling out the reasons for the new alliance. In the document they explained that by casting their lot with the South, the tribe was exercising its "inalienable right of self defense" as well as its rights as "a free people, independent of the Northern States of America. . . ."[27] Their declaration neatly encapsulated the position that John and William Potter Ross had repeatedly defended over the past two decades. The pair had long rejected the American belief, posed during the removal crisis and by Justice Taney in *U.S. v. Rogers*, that tribes were nothing more than communities of backward and racially inferior people. They argued that their dramatic decision to ally with the South affirmed both their autonomy and their identity as a progressive national entity. Ross's declaration thus made it clear that the Cherokees' new partnership was as much a product of the past as a statement about the violent conflict that was about to erupt around them. Its terms affirmed how deeply the political culture that had first been articulated during the removal era had taken root in the alien territory that was now their home.

TREATIES DEFINE A NATION

The Civil War shattered the bonds that held Cherokee society together just as it destroyed national unity in the United States. In 1861, while William Potter Ross and others of his generation and class dutifully enlisted in the Confederate army, many loyal members of the tribe fled north to Kansas, where they settled until 1862, when Union forces began their return to Indian Territory. These "loyal" Cherokees quickly took control of Tahlequah, captured Chief Ross, and sent him east to negotiate a new agreement with the Union. But as often happened on the periphery of the Civil War's main battlegrounds, the American forces soon retreated again from the isolated Cherokee homeland, and Confederate sympathizers, led by Ross's old adversaries in the treaty party, organized a provisional, pro-Confederate tribal government and began taking revenge on the chief's supporters, whom they now labeled "traitors." The tide turned yet again in 1863, when U.S. forces captured Fort Smith and reestablished themselves at Fort Gibson. Determined to live out the war as a neutral civilian, William Potter Ross returned home.

The Union presence in the area remained slight, however, enabling southern sympathizers to burn Ross's store during a raid on Fort Gibson and to wreak havoc elsewhere in the nation. In 1863 and 1864 the surrounding countryside was a battleground where opposing guerrilla units attacked one another amid a backdrop of Confederate retreat and Union indifference. In this polarized environment, William Potter Ross joined the pro-Union Cherokee Home Guards as an act of self-defense. Writing to his uncle in Washington in January 1864, he noted that "the contrast between the past and the present [is] too overwhelming to be borne in silence. Then we were more than twenty thousand strong, with a government and laws of our own. . . . [N]ow all [is] changed." After describing the poverty and destruction around Fort Gibson, Ross concluded that the Cherokees now had "the forms but not the substance of freemen. . . ."[28] A year later, as Lee prepared to surrender to General Grant at Appomattox, the situation had not improved. "Everything has been changed by the destroying hand of war," William Potter Ross wrote his son, "We have not a horse, cow or hog left that I know of. . . ."[29]

In the aftermath of such wholesale destruction, John Ross was convinced that a new treaty with the United States was the only way the Cherokee tribal government could reclaim its authority over a suffering and divided populace. Only federal power could establish a structure that would both reconcile the factions within the tribe and protect its borders against settler onslaughts from Kansas and Arkansas. The Cherokee chief and other Indian Territory leaders made this argument at Fort Smith, Arkansas, in September 1865, when they met with President Andrew Johnson's skeptical commissioner of Indian affairs,

Dennis N. Cooley, at a large intertribal peace conference. The commissioner and his colleagues (who included General Grant's Seneca aide-de-camp, General Ely S. Parker) expected to dictate their terms to the defeated Indians. They rejected Ross's protestations of loyalty (happily embarrassing him by publishing his extensive correspondence with the former Confederate government) and demanded that the tribe sell part of its tribal estates in preparation for the creation of a new territorial government that would bring white homesteaders to live alongside the tribes.

Chief Ross and his supporters rejected each of these demands. They pointed out that despite their early alliance with the Confederacy, the tribe's constitutional leaders had returned early to the Union fold. (One of John Ross's sons had died wearing the uniform of the United States.) They also noted that the failure of U.S. forces to protect the loyal Cherokees after 1862 had prompted prosouthern groups in the tribe to unleash years of violence and bloodshed against them. The only reasonable response to the destruction now evident throughout the Cherokee Nation, Ross argued, was enhanced federal protection in the form of a new treaty and the rapid reconstitution of the Cherokee national authority.[30]

William Potter Ross underscored this connection between federal power and tribal authority a few years later, when he told a congressional committee that the "essence" of his tribe's relationship with the American government was embodied in the "pledges made to the Indians if they would but agree to a removal—pledges of protection from war, trespass, and intrusion from every quarter; pledges of self-government, pledges of ownership of their lands . . . These pledges exist today, and are as binding now upon all the departments of government and upon the people of the United States as they were when they were made."[31] This position became the Cherokees' mantra during their sessions with Commissioner Cooley. They refused to concede that Chief Ross had been a rebel, they rejected their prosouthern rivals' claim to a portion of the tribal homeland (Stand Watie and his followers wanted to create a separate Cherokee government of their own), and they insisted that a new treaty should be negotiated not in Arkansas but in Washington, D.C., a place they now knew well and where they could mobilize sympathetic white allies. Despite the Cherokees' weakened state and their leader's rapidly failing health, the Ross group's united intransigence persuaded Cooley to accept their demands and to suspend negotiations until all parties could reassemble in the nation's capital.

The Cherokee leadership's skillful evasion of Commissioner Cooley reminded William Potter Ross of another key element of the tribe's diplomatic strategy. While insisting that federal authorities enforce the "pledges" they had made in the past, the Cherokee leader also reminded his own followers that tribal unity was essential to their continued recognition by the United States. In a speech delivered to the Cherokee tribal council shortly after fighting ended in 1865, the younger Ross explained that he did not advocate reconciliation with his Cherokee adversaries for sentimental reasons. "Strife," he declared, "is fatal . . . it is the lever of ambition and cupidity and will be used for overturning our most precious rights. It has multiplied our difficulties in the past, increased the afflictions of the present and will present the greatest dangers in the future."[32] He urged the Cherokee public to embrace the tribe's institutions and elected leaders as a practical way of combating the divisions that undermined their standing before Congress and federal bureaucrats. He repeated this argument a year later in his first speech as Chief Ross's successor: "Our only hope," he told the tribal council in 1866, "is that unity of feeling and action that we have of interest and destiny." He pointed out the link between this unity and the "privileges" of tribal citizenship as he closed: "We are a community of men . . . as free as almost any on the continent. These are high and valuable privileges. Let us not despise or neglect them. . . ."[33]

TOO OFTEN HISTORIANS and other observers have been seduced by the nineteenth-century habit of dismissing tribal leaders like John and William P. Ross as "mixed-blood" Indians who cared for little beyond protecting their own privileges.[34] While technically correct—Ross and his peers were skilled political operatives who were proud of their cultural sophistication and tactical skills—this characterization runs the risk of replicating Andrew Jackson's and Roger Taney's racist view of Indians who, if sophisticated, must no longer be Native Americans. This view also obscures the differences between tribal advocates like William Potter Ross and their adversaries in the United States. Defining those differences, while assuring the Americans of their loyalty and "civilization," was the central challenge Cherokee leaders faced in the immediate postwar era. Throughout these years Ross insisted that strong treaties and a forceful national government offered a practical and equitable alternative to violence and chaos.

The Cherokees' political ambitions and tenacious tactics were on full display when the tribe's representatives met again with Commissioner Cooley in the spring of 1866 to continue their negotiations.[35] These delegates, including William Potter and his brother Daniel, met the American leaders in Washington, D.C., arriving just after representatives of Confederate loyalists, now called the Southern Party, finished their separate session with the U.S. government. The Southern Party Cherokees had quickly capitulated to all of the government's demands: admission of former slaves to citizenship, generous land grants to railroads, the sale of a large tract of tribal land to the United States, and the formation of a federally supervised territory to oversee all the area tribes. In exchange, the United States had tentatively agreed to a division of the Cherokee government and the assignment of a portion of its homeland to Stand Watie and the rest of Chief Ross's rivals. John Ross was very ill when he arrived in Washington—he conducted negotiations from a bed in his hotel room and died there four days after the finished treaty was ratified—but he understood that his delegation had no choice but to make significant concessions in order to persuade Cooley to set the southerners' agreement aside. The John Ross group labored through June and July to produce a document that, when ratified on July 27, accomplished their major goal: it ignored the Southern Party's demands and instead recognized Ross and his allies as the sole representatives of the Cherokee people. William Potter Ross later noted that even though many Cherokees considered the 1866 agreement "unjust, ungenerous and oppressive," its ratification meant that the tribe's "existence as a nation and the tenure by which they own and hold the lands reserved to them, [would] stand unimpaired."[36]

Nevertheless, the price exacted for the Cherokee Nation's "unimpaired" existence was steep. The tribe agreed to repeal all confiscation laws directed at Confederate Cherokees, to admit its former slaves to citizenship in the tribe, to grant two railroad rights-of-way through its territory, to create a territory-wide council of tribal representatives, and to convey to the United States all unoccupied tribal lands in Kansas and west of the ninety-sixth meridian (a prairie area commonly referred to as the Cherokee Outlet). At the same time, the tribe's careful negotiation exacted significant concessions from the Americans: the promised rights-of-way to the railroads were only two hundred feet wide (the companies would receive no additional land grants, as was customary in the West), the new territorial council for Indian Territory could operate only with the permission of each tribe's national government, and the Cherokee Outlet lands west of the ninety-sixth meridian would be purchased only to "settle friendly Indians" and thus would not be opened to non-Indian settlers, as had been proposed a year earlier at Fort Smith. Federal authorities also promised to pay back salaries and pensions to Cherokees who had served in the U.S. Army during the Civil War and to guarantee the tribe "the quiet and peaceable possession of their country" as well as "protection against domestic feuds . . . [and] interruptions and intrusion from all unauthorized citizens . . . who may attempt to settle on their lands or reside in their territory." Considering where Ross and his allies had begun a year earlier, the 1866 treaty was a remarkable achievement.[37]

During the years immediately following its ratification, Cherokee leaders pressed to expand concessions they had won in the 1866 treaty. They quickly resolved the debilitating political divisions that had nearly dissolved the nation during the war. During the summer of 1867 a group of John Ross's former supporters persuaded Stand Watie and his Southern Party to support Lewis Downing in that year's election for principal chief. Downing had been "second chief" during the elder Ross's last term but had been passed over as a successor in favor of the late chief's college-educated nephew. (Downing's inability to speak English was considered a liability at a time when the tribe required a forceful presence in Washington, D.C. In addition, as a matrilineal society the Cherokees were frequently inclined to favor sisters' sons in matters of inheritance and succession.) Following his victory over Ross in the November election, Downing made a series of bipartisan appointments that ensured stability within the tribe and helped him win reelection in 1871. But when Downing died unexpectedly early in his second term, the tribe asked William Potter Ross to take his place as chief.

Within weeks of his selection as chief, Ross assembled a committee to negotiate an agreement with officials from the Union Pacific

Railroad that would govern the rights-of-way stipulated in the 1866 treaty. Responding to a proposal submitted earlier to the tribe, the new chief invited company officials to Tahlequah to negotiate an agreement that in the twentieth century would be termed a joint venture. On October 31, 1866, tribal leaders and Union Pacific executives announced that the company would build a line from Kansas to Texas with a major station at Fort Gibson. In return the Union Pacific would accept tribal regulation of its rates within Cherokee territory, and the tribe would invest five hundred thousand dollars of the money it expected to receive for its Cherokee Outlet lands in company stock. The Cherokees were also guaranteed at least two seats on the company's eleven-person board of directors.[38] Because the 1866 treaty called for "congressional approval" for all future railroad construction, the tribe quickly moved to have the Union Pacific agreement ratified in Washington, D.C.

Disputes over land titles in the Cherokee Outlet and the tribe's authority to grant rights-of-way through land owned by other tribes delayed approval of the Union Pacific contract. In addition, the agreement became an issue in the following year's tribal elections. Charges that Ross and his political allies maintained a cozy relationship with the railroad caused the national council to void the contract shortly after Downing's election. Despite this outcome, the Cherokees' draft agreement with the Union Pacific was a clear indication of how eager tribal leaders were to control economic development in Indian Territory. And despite the decision to cancel the agreement, Ross's political enemies shared his ambition.

ONE OF ROSS'S CHIEF CRITICS was Elias Cornelius (E. C.) Boudinot, a prominent member of the Southern Party. Boudinot's father had been a signer of the New Echota treaty that had triggered the tribe's removal from Georgia, and he had been assassinated by Ross support-ers soon after the tribe arrived in the West. Only four years old when his father was murdered, Boudinot had been raised in New England by his mother's family but had returned to the Southeast on reaching adulthood. He took up residence in Arkansas, where he was admitted to the bar and later became active in state politics. During the Civil War Boudinot fought in a Confederate Cherokee regiment alongside his uncle Stand Watie, and he briefly represented the tribe in the Con-federate Congress. When the war ended, Boudinot was part of the southern faction's delegation to Washington, D.C., where he led the campaign to form a separate tribal government. After John Ross nego-tiated the 1866 treaty, however, E. C. relocated to the Cherokee Nation and became an active supporter of the new national party.

Boudinot was an ambitious entrepreneur who frequently placed his personal ambitions ahead of his loyalty to his tribe, but in the immedi-ate postwar years he, like William Potter Ross, concentrated on devis-ing ways for the tribal government to control the economic changes occurring around him. During the 1867 election season, when tribal members were debating Ross's proposed contract with the Union Pa-cific Railroad, Boudinot proposed an alternative, the construction of the Central Indian Railroad, an enterprise to be financed and governed entirely by the Indian Territory's major tribes. "My plan," he declared, "is to allow the Indians to build their own road and own it."[39]

The Central Indian Railroad never materialized, but Boudinot was rarely short of ideas. The following year he succeeded in persuading his prominent uncle to join him in founding the Watie and Boudinot Tobacco Company. The firm was organized to take advantage of a pro-vision in the Cherokees' 1866 treaty that allowed tribal members to market agricultural and manufactured products tax free inside Indian Territory and to distribute those products beyond their homelands "without restraint." In 1867 the partners erected a processing plant a few feet inside the Cherokee Nation, near Maysville, Arkansas, and in January 1868 they began producing chewing tobacco that could be sold throughout the Indian nations. In addition, because their new plant stood adjacent to productive tobacco fields in southern Missouri and western Arkansas, Boudinot and Watie hoped to compete for customers in the surrounding states of Kansas, Missouri, and Arkansas. In those markets the only chewing tobacco available came from processing plants in Louisville and St. Louis.

Missouri tobacco processors quickly responded to Boudinot's challenge by persuading Congress to revise the Internal Revenue Code so that taxes would be due on tobacco for all "articles produced anywhere within the exterior boundaries of the United States." As the Cherokee plant moved toward full production (it employed more than one hundred people in 1869), Boudinot denounced the new regulations and attempted to secure official approval for a system under which he would pay the tobacco tax only on the amount of his product sold outside Indian Territory. The Cherokee businessman seemed to be making progress until March 1869, when General Grant and the Republicans regained control of the White House, bringing with them a new level of hostility to tribal governments, particularly those headed by aggressive (and prosouthern) leaders.

In December 1869 the Bureau of Internal Revenue took control of the company's factory to prevent it from distributing tax-free tobacco to Indian clients and indicted E. C. Boudinot for violation of federal tax laws. Two Washington attorneys came to his defense: Robert Johnson and (in a remarkable show of resiliency) Albert Pike, the former Confederate general, who in 1861 had represented the southern government in its treaty negotiations with the Cherokees. When their client was found guilty of tax evasion in early 1870, Johnson and Pike appealed to the Supreme Court for a dismissal, claiming that the business privileges granted the Cherokees in the 1866 treaty should take precedence over U.S. revenue laws. If the tax laws were allowed to extend to Indian Territory, they argued, Indian treaties would be "as worthless as waste paper."[40]

When the Supreme Court's decision upholding Boudinout's conviction was announced in the spring of 1871, it was not only a blow to the concept of tribal political independence that the Cherokees had defended so forcefully over the previous three decades but also a clear indication that despite the inventive ideas of entrepreneurs like Boudinot and William Potter Ross, the justices were prepared to reject any suggestion that Indians might become autonomous economic actors. In his majority opinion, the Republican appointee Noah Swayne returned to the language Justice Taney had employed twenty-five years earlier in *U.S. v. Rogers*. It is "firmly and clearly established," Swayne declared, quoting the discredited former chief justice, "that the Indian tribes residing within the territorial limits of the United States are subject to their authority . . . where the country occupied by them is not within the limits of one of the states, Congress may by law punish any offense committed there." This proposition was so well settled, he added, that "it would be a waste of time" to discuss it.[41]

The tribe's defeat in the *Cherokee Tobacco* case greatly reduced its potential power while it underscored how strongly Ross, Boudinot, and other Cherokee leaders, despite the rivalries among them, had come to identify their community's national identity with the legal guarantees contained in its treaties. No longer symbols of a diplomatic alliance, these documents were now viewed as domestic charters that had a direct impact on daily life. Tribal governments were empowered by the privileges recognized in their treaties and constrained by areas where those powers were not spelled out. Whether granted by federal officials who were inclined to use generous language in an agreement, as the framers of the removal agreements had been, or dictated to the tribes in an atmosphere in which the tribes were defeated and weak (as had been the case in 1866), treaties spelled out the legal rights of Indian people.

INDIAN NATIONS UNDER ATTACK

William Potter Ross remained a prominent political figure in the Cherokee tribe despite his defeat by Lewis Downing in the 1867 election for principal chief. He was the most experienced diplomat in the nation, and as assaults on their independence multiplied, the tribal leadership relied increasingly on his knowledge of the American government. During the 1870s Ross served on the national council and in the Cherokee senate, represented the tribe regularly in Washington, D.C., and testified repeatedly before congressional committees. When Chief Downing died in 1872, Ross was called on for a second time to complete the term of a fallen leader. He remained an outspoken and active defender of American Indian nationalism until his death in 1891.

It is remarkable that Ross and his colleagues managed to hold off the settler onslaught for as long as they did. Federal officials began pressing for the extension of their authority over Indian Territory almost as soon as the fighting ended at Appomattox, yet no white settlers were allowed to purchase land within the reserve's borders until 1889, when the Oklahoma Territory was organized in a portion of the Cherokee Outlet. Even then Cherokee officials (and their counterparts among the Creeks, Choctaws, Chickasaws, and Seminoles) managed to hold their enemies at bay through legal challenges and tireless campaigns of lobbying and public protest. As a consequence, Congress did not formally strip the Indian Territory's tribal governments of their powers until 1898.

The efforts of leaders like Ross during the last decades of the nineteenth century created a common platform for tribal governments struggling to maintain their independence. Their speeches and declarations as well as their regular appearances in Washington, D.C., gave the cause of tribal autonomy attention enough to win the notice of sympathetic whites and tribes from other parts of the United States. As American settlers pressed against tribal territories across the West, other leaders called on the United States to stand by its treaties and protect the integrity of Indian communities, whether they were in New Mexico, Montana, or South Dakota. They too struggled to reconcile their nations'. futures with the future of the American state. They echoed the Cherokees' arguments and refused to be ignored.

High officials in the Indian Office had first called for the dissolution of Indian Territory during the 1866 treaty negotiations with the Cherokees, Choctaws, Creeks, and Seminoles, but a combination of tribal resistance and the press of other issues arising from the war had blunted that effort. The Cherokees were imaginative negotiators, but their inventive proposal to form an alliance with the Union Pacific provoked a backlash from rival lines. Their lobbyists proposed a congressional resolution, quickly passed in the summer of 1866, that committed the United States to making generous land grants along any future rights-of-way across Native lands "as soon as the Indian titles are abolished." In the wake of this new legislation (and the tribe's later abandonment of its contract with the Union Pacific) railroad executives and their lobbyists nimbly switched from being potential business partners of the tribe to taking up the goal of federal "territorialization."

When Congress first held out the promise of Indian Territory land grants to the railroads, it had also provided that the single north-south right-of-way called for in the 1866 Cherokee treaty would be awarded to the first branch line that could build its tracks across Kansas to the tribes' northern border. In March 1870 the Missouri, Kansas and Texas Railroad (a successor corporation to the Union Pacific, Southern Branch, and popularly known as the Katy line) accomplished this goal; it struck the Indian Territory border fifty miles ahead of its nearest rival. Drunken celebrations erupted in nearby Baxter Springs, Kansas, but the reaction in Tahlequah was far different. Understanding that a confrontation over the ownership of the Cherokee Outlet and other unoccupied areas within Indian Territory was about to escalate, Ross and colleagues from neighboring tribes gathered at Okmulgee, Creek Nation, and issued a collective declaration "in view of the perils which surround [our] people." Because Ross chaired the gathering, the resolution drafted at Okmulgee incorporated several themes he had developed earlier in his political career.

Ross and his colleagues insisted that they had no goals but peaceful coexistence and the "simple and honest administration" of the government's policies. At the heart of those policies, the Okmulgee delegates argued, was the "just and fair observance of existing treaty stipula-. tions." They urged federal officials to focus on these "stipulations" rather than accept the railroads' argument that restrictions on white settlement would limit the growth of civilization or the progress of the American nation. "We have been charged with opposition to progress and improvement," their declaration noted. "We are not opposed to progress; we are not opposed to improvements; we are not opposed to civilization; we are not opposed to the Christian religion." They insisted instead that their national histories ran parallel to the progressive trajectory of the United States. Their progress was steady, they assured the Indian Office, and could be disrupted only by intruders and "the cupidity of soulless corporations." The government owed them "protection and security," they argued. "You have promised them."[42]

It would be three years before the Katy line crossed Indian Territory to Texas, but its entrance into the tribes' domain triggered a flood of petitions from corporate lobbyists, regional politicians, and local boosters, urging action to extinguish tribal land titles along the railroad's right-of-way. Bills to dissolve unilaterally tribal governments and make Indian Territory part of the public domain quickly became a routine feature of the Washington landscape. The scene was darkly reminiscent of the clamor in Georgia and Mississippi fifty years earlier. The dispossession that federal officials in the age of Jackson had once promised the tribes would never come suddenly seemed imminent.

As he had done a few years earlier at Okmulgee, Ross responded to these new attacks by insisting that threats to federal authority in Indian Territory were also threats to the American nation's institutions and values. The fullest presentation of his views emerged at the end of 1870 from a meeting called initially by Ely Parker, President Grant's new commissioner of Indian affairs. Parker, a Seneca Indian who had been present when John Ross confronted Dennis Cooley in 1865, invited tribal delegates to gather once again at Okmulgee to frame a constitution for an all-Indian government for Indian Territory. When the delegates assembled, they selected William Potter Ross to chair the subcommittee charged with this task.[43]

Ross's committee proposed a government "for the country occupied and owned" by the territory's resident tribes. It declared that its purpose would be "the protection of their rights, the improvement of themselves, and the preservation of their race." Its draft charter recognized the authority of the separate treaties that defined the boundaries of each tribal homeland and reaffirmed the federal obligation to provide the subsidies promised each group in previous agreements, but it also created a two-house territorial legislature and provided for a governor elected at large. The governor would appoint judges whose courts would hear disputes appealed from individual tribal tribunals. The constitution also included a Declaration of Rights, which pledged to protect freedom of religion and free speech as well as to defend territorial citizens against arbitrary or cruel actions by their tribal governments. Ross proposed that the new territorial government initially extend its jurisdiction over only the large, relocated tribes represented at the Okmulgee Council, but he added that western tribes not present at the gathering—most prominently the Kiowas, Comanches, and Cheyennes—could join later to "secure our lands exclusively to ourselves and to transmit them to our children."[44]

The Okmulgee constitution was a remarkable attempt to bridge the legal and cultural differences between residents of Indian Territory tribes and the government of the United States. But its rapid demise suggests how vast the chasm separating these two entities had become. At the end of 1870 even the most sympathetic whites rejected the document's commitment to Indian autonomy.[45] Commissioner Parker was equally unenthusiastic. He altered the document to ensure the president's power to appoint the territory's governor and veto any of the legislature's statutes, and he redefined the territory's courts as federal, not tribal, institutions. Despite the appointment of a Native American Indian commissioner, the Grant administration was pursuing policies indistinguishable from those of local white settlers and the railroads.[46]

Congress subsidized four more Okmulgee conventions, but with no hope of winning congressional approval for their unique proposals, the gatherings deteriorated into annual occasions for venting frustration and denouncing visiting dignitaries. In June 1871, for example, Ross used the gathering to issue a rebuke to General William Tecumseh

Sherman after the Civil War hero had repeated the familiar claim that Indian Territory was lawless and filled with discontented tribesmen. Ross demanded the floor to explain that "what dissatisfaction existed" in the tribal homelands lived "in the minds of the whites." The Cherokee leader observed that it was "no more than justice that [Indians] should be allowed to elect their own way of enjoying the country that belonged to them by solemn treaties."[47] The Okmulgee gatherings were also an opportunity for leaders from eastern tribes to repeat their overtures to Kiowas, Comanches, and other western groups and urge them to join their coalition. While these invitations produced occasional meetings and tentative agreements, it was increasingly evident that federal officials had no interest in promoting pan-Indian solidarity.[48]

With the demise of the Okmulgee conventions, William Potter Ross turned to making his antiterritorial arguments to a national audience. Despite the fact that Ross did not belong to the ruling party within the Cherokee Nation, Chief Downing and his council often asked him to present their case to congressional committees considering legislation to allow white settlement in the territory. In 1872 he lectured the House Committee on Territories on the history of treaty making.[49] He reminded the legislators that this history had begun with the administration of George Washington and that to abandon the promises made by statesmen like him would betray a legacy of good faith and mutual respect. To abandon the tribes now, he added, "would be the wantonness of Hercules strangling an infant."[50]

On another occasion Ross relied on the principle of judicial precedent. He pointed out that John Marshall had written in 1810 that a state legislature could not cancel a land sale because a state could not "pronounce its own deed invalid" without violating the U.S. Constitution's prohibition against the sanctity of contracts. He argued the United States was now in a similar position with regard to Indian Territory. He noted that the Cherokees and their neighbors held their lands by treaty, but he added that removal treaties, because they did not apply to traditional homelands, were doubly binding on the United States. Because the Cherokees received their territory from the United States as a condition of their migration from the East, their removal agreements were, in effect, contracts comparable to the ones in dispute in Georgia in 1810. The Cherokees' title, he insisted, thus possessed "a sanctity which even Congress itself ought not to violate."[51]

Ross also appealed to the legislators' sense of moral obligation. Any action that violated the government's pledges of support and protection, he argued, would be "a repudiation of national obligations—[a] repudiation doubly infamous from the fact that the parties whose claims were thus annulled are too weak to enforce their just rights and were enjoying the . . . guardianship and protection of this government."[52] Ross argued that federal officials should fulfill the responsibilities expected of legal guardians. Such guardianship required the United States to recognize the rights and prerogatives of tribal governments. Ross explained: "The jurisdiction of the United States over the Cherokee Nation is a qualified one. It does not destroy her existence as a body politic in the rightful exercise of those attributes and franchises which have not been surrendered, but which have been guaranteed to her by treaties with the United States."[53]

Ross made dozens of speeches on behalf of the Cherokee Nation, but these fundamental principles remained central in all of them. His arguments were cast as ideal principles of national policy, but they grew out of his practical concerns as a tribal politician and rested on the foundation laid by his predecessors in the removal era.[54] His invocation of San Marino in his 1874 speech at Vinita occurred in the midst of this defense of tribal autonomy in Indian Territory. The image of the Italian principality, illuminated by the "pure glow of patriotism," enabled the Cherokee leader to set his tribe's appeal in the broadest possible context. Not only did he make the point that democracies could contain a variety of political units, but he also made it clear that the Cherokees had carefully studied the fate of other tribes. Wherever tribes or tiny nations lived, Ross observed, they should be allowed to choose their own form of government and their own system of land tenure. When systems were imposed upon them from the outside, whether from Washington or from Rome, the results were always disastrous: "Like the footprints of the exiles to Siberia or of those in the lion's den, [they] all point in one way."[55]

The compelling image of an autonomous San Marino and Ross's insistence on the prerogatives of tribes to choose their own forms of government emphasized the significance he and other leaders attached to the maintenance of firm borders to guard Indian Territory against an expanding American nation-state. During the 1870s, the maintenance of those borders became the Cherokees' central preoccupation. Referring to the various territorial bills before Congress, Ross noted that "the sum and substance, the alpha and omega of the whole matter, is to blot out all distinctions between this country and other portions of the United States. . . . I regard the whole of them," he concluded, "thoroughly unjust in their provisions towards the Indian people." He told his Vinita audience that destroying the tribal governments and dissolving the tribal homelands in Indian Territory would destroy the Indians' world, returning them to the very beginning of their history and forcing them to wander abroad, "as your fathers went forth from their native land, or as Milton sent forth Adam and Eve from Eden, when 'the world was all before them, where to choose their place of rest and providence their guide.'"[56]

Little occurred during the remainder of Ross's life to soften this desperate imagery. He was defeated by Oochalata (Charles Thompson) in the 1875 election for chief, and he failed to secure the National Party nomination for that office four years later, thereby ending his career as a Cherokee national leader. Nevertheless, he continued to represent the tribe in Washington—he was among a small group that met privately with President Grant in 1876—and spoke out frequently in the local press. Grant indicated later in 1876 that he intended to appoint William Potter Ross the federal agent for the five major tribes in the eastern half of Indian Territory, but the president never formally submitted the nomination.[57] In later years Ross served in the Cherokee senate and in other appointive offices, but he grew increasingly concerned about the deteriorating quality of life in the tribal homeland. Despite the railroads' failure to secure land grants in Indian Territory, their traffic brought hundreds of people into what had until recently been a restricted area. Texas cattlemen and their cowboy employees regularly crossed Indian landholdings as they drove herds north to Kansas, and prosperous Cherokees and other Indians used a loosely administered permit system to bring white sharecroppers and other laborers into the territory to work their farms and ranches. Crime, whiskey peddling, thefts of Indian timber and coal, and general lawlessness increased, while federal authorities did little to protect or assist the embattled tribal police.

By 1880 deteriorating conditions in Indian Territory and the increasing presence of non-Indians within the communities there had persuaded policy makers in Washington and among the tribes that creating a San Marino on the southern plains would require assertions of tribal and federal authority that they could not sustain. None of the territory's Indian governments had the financial resources or the organizational authority to mount major law-and-order campaigns against the gangs of criminals and unauthorized cattlemen that routinely circulated among them. For its part, the Indian Office was preoccupied with administering reservations across a vast western landscape while fending off congressional critics who argued that their support for Indian communities, as inadequate as it was, was misguided and too expensive. At the same time, budget cutters in Congress had little interest in sending federal troops to prevent squatters from trespassing on tribal land or subsidizing tribal courts seeking to bring white lawbreakers to justice. The Indians' "friends" in the missionary and reform communities were steadily retreating from Ross's view that treaties represented "pledges . . . [that] exist today, and are as binding now upon all the departments of government and upon the people of the United States as they were when they were made." They were being persuaded that dividing all Indian homelands into individual plots of land, assigning them to Indian families, and setting those families "free" to fend for themselves, a policy called allotment, made more sense as a national strategy. Allotment promised to be cheap, and the size of the Native population indicated that once the Indian estate was doled out to individual families, there would be millions of acres of surplus land left over to be claimed by white settlers.

SPEAKING TO THE INDIANS

In March 1874, *The Cherokee Advocate* carried a letter from a reader describing William Potter Ross's most recent appearance before the House Committee on Territories. The correspondent (who signed himself "the Raven") reported that Ross's presentation had occupied two hours and that it was "unquestionably unanswerable and clear." The correspondent then added: "There were present beside the Cherokee delegation, the Choctaw delegate, Col. P. Pitchlynn . . . Col. McIntosh and associates, and other Indians who happened to be in the city and who considered it to be a piece of very good fortune to be able to be one of the audience."[58] The image drawn by the Raven is intriguing. James McDonald's boyhood friend Peter Pitchlynn was now sixty-eight and had recently stepped down as the chief of the Choctaws in order to devote himself full-time to pursuing the Choctaws' legal claims against the United States for damages inflicted during the removal era. It is hard to imagine that he did not think, at least for a moment, about his old comrade as he listened to the testimony presented by the Cherokee chief. "McIntosh" was likely Colonel Daniel McIntosh, a former Confederate officer whose uncle Roly McIntosh had shared the chairmanship of the 1843 international council in Tahlequah with William Potter Ross's uncle John Ross. The younger McIntosh might have considered how Ross's words resonated with the elder Ross's invitation, issued thirty years earlier to tribal leaders to join him in reviving "the ancient talk of our forefathers."

William Potter Ross was certainly speaking in the spirit of that "ancient talk" as he addressed the legislators, but it was not clear that any of the city's powerful figures were willing to listen. The "other Indians who happened to be in the city" are of course impossible to identify. Nevertheless, the extension of rail lines across the West had generated a steady flow of Indian delegations to the nation's capital. Not knowing the "other Indians" present in the hearing room and lacking information about their command of English, we cannot know exactly which aspects of Ross's two-hour presentation his Native listeners would have understood. But we can be certain that the opportunity to hear a Princeton-educated Cherokee chief lecture white lawmakers about their legal and moral obligations to the Indians would likely have seemed an extraordinary piece of "very good fortune" for any visiting tribal leaders. His arguments were surely relevant to their own situations, regardless of where they lived.

The Raven did not mention non-Indians, but we can be reasonably certain that Chief Ross's audience also included lawyers working for the Cherokees, Choctaws, and Creeks. These tribes called on Washington attorneys to assist them at moments such as this as well as when they filed petitions with federal agencies or launched complaints before the U.S. Court of Claims. The Cherokees' attorneys were frequently members of Congress, such as the Indiana Democrat Daniel Voorhees, but they also included William Penn Adair, a tribal member who had practiced law in Indian Territory before the Civil War and who had since become a prominent tribal politician and frequent delegate to Washington. This group of Washington lawyers would have listened to Ross with rapt attention; a few of them may even have sacrificed some of their professional dignity and taken notes.

From the Raven's account we can know only a few members of the audience that listened to Ross's elegant 1874 testimony, but we know from subsequent events that in the decades following the Cherokee leader's appearance, Indian protests before Congress multiplied and intensified. The first wave of these emanated from Indian Territory, but they were soon joined by petitions and delegates from Native communities in every corner of the United States. Even without knowing the precise membership of Ross's audience, then, we can be confident that the community of tribal leaders, lawyers, and "Indians who happened to be in the city" grew significantly in the coming years. Despite the tragedy surrounding the eventual dissolution of Indian Territory in the 1890s and its forced absorption into the state of Oklahoma in 1907, the community of Indian activists drew on Ross's ideas and strategies. They expanded the arguments he had made on behalf of tribal autonomy and kept alive the idea of a Native San Marino existing peacefully within the boundaries of the United States.

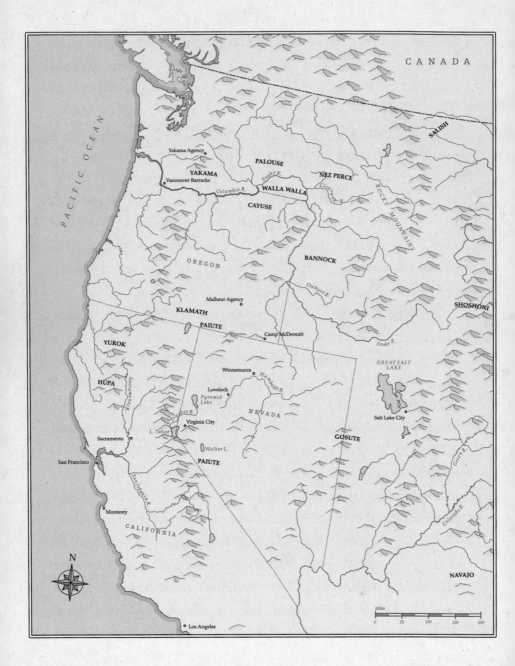

CANADA

PACIFIC OCEAN

SALISH

Yakama Agency

YAKAMA

PALOUSE

NEZ PERCE

Vancouver Barracks

Columbia R.

Snake R.

WALLA WALLA

Clearwater R.

ROCKY MOUNTAINS

CAYUSE

OREGON

BANNOCK

Owyhee R.

SHOSHONI

Malheur Agency

KLAMATH

PAIUTE

Camp McDermitt

Snake R.

YUROK

GREAT SALT LAKE

HUPA

Winnemucca

Humboldt R.

Lovelock

Pyramid Lake

Sacramento R.

Truckee R.

NEVADA

Salt Lake City

Virginia City

L. Tahoe

Sacramento

Walker L.

GOSUTE

Green R.

San Francisco

PAIUTE

San Joaquin R.

Monterey

CALIFORNIA

Colorado R.

N

NAVAJO

Los Angeles

Miles

0   50   100   150   200

CHAPTER FOUR

THE WINNEMUCCA RULES

Sarah Winnemucca, Paiute

In the decades following the American Civil War, many of the same actors who disrupted and undermined tribal governments in Indian Territory devastated Native communities across the West. Homesteaders, cattlemen, railroad promoters, real estate boosters, and political opportunists descended on territories that previously had been bypassed by American pioneers. They now "settled" these territories in a riot of violence and dispossession. The Paiute author and activist Sarah Winnemucca witnessed this devastation firsthand. During the 1870s and 1880s, she reported on the consequences of westward expansion into her tribal homeland on the eastern slope of the Sierra Nevada. Her lectures and writing described the proliferating crises this process created for Native communities like hers. She exposed the violence and injustice that accompanied the "winning" of the West and provided the public with a dramatic substitute for the white male voices that previously had dominated discussions of Indian policy making.

Her career formed a bridge connecting tribal politicians like William Potter Ross to Native activists who became involved in a national campaign for Indian rights at the end of the century. Winnemucca's slashing attacks focused attention on the unpleasant but inescapable fact that the Americans' rapid domination of the North American continent was achieved at an enormous human cost.

Winnemucca incorporated tales of local violence and individual suffering into a broad indictment of U.S. westward expansion. While she testified in some of the same Washington, D.C., committee rooms as Ross and his polished Indian Territory comrades, she also challenged U.S. officials with a fresh set of concerns. She not only demanded that the Americans live up to their own political ideals and promises, a theme her predecessors had often used, but also urged the nation's leaders to weigh their actions on the universal scales of justice and morality. Winnemucca challenged other Native leaders by presenting herself not as a lobbyist or politician but as an outspoken defender of her cultural values and tribal traditions. Instead of seeking a new treaty or statutory reform, she demanded that the Americans recognize her Indian identity and accept her humanity. Her candid disdain for the social hierarchies of her day disturbed many of her listeners in the worlds of humanitarian reform and tribal politics, but her career introduced a new, uncompromising tone to Indian critiques of the United States, establishing a style of attack others later emulated.

WHEN SARAH WINNEMUCCA was born, in 1844, California was a province of Mexico, Oregon was an integral part of the Hudson Bay Company trading empire, and her Great Basin homeland was a distant corner of an American West that was largely unknown to easterners. Over the previous two centuries her Paiute kinsmen had interacted occasionally with Spanish officials and individual American traders, but they had also managed to sustain a hunter-gatherer life rooted in the complex seasonal migration of small family-centered bands and the sophisticated exploitation of arid rangelands ringed by snow-capped mountains and crossed by glacial streams. By maintaining their traditional subsistence patterns, Winnemucca's kinsmen had also managed to sustain an elaborate set of social and religious rituals. Women played a vital role in Paiute life as food gatherers and processors, while men exercised authority over relationships with outsiders. Religious rituals led by men and women supported both the search for food and the ongoing desire for social harmony.

As she entered adulthood, Winnemucca witnessed the American conquest of the Southwest, the discovery of gold and silver in California and the nearby Sierra Nevada, and the ensuing tidal wave of American migration that all but destroyed her tribe's carefully sustained patterns of existence. For Winnemucca, the issues facing Indian people in the 1870s erupted from the violent invasion of her homeland and the continuous assaults the invaders had unleashed on both her individual dignity as a woman and her humanity as an Indian. As a consequence, Sarah Winnemucca's public career, while it crossed paths with contemporary struggles over treaty rights and government policy, exemplified her view that individual disputes should be understood in the broader context of America's continental conquest.

A LIFE OF TALKING BACK

Called Thocmetony (Shell Flower) by her family, Sarah Winnemucca spent her childhood in the arid country that lay astride the overland trail linking the midwestern United States and California. Thanks to the Mexican War and the onset of the gold rush, Thocmetony's band of Paiutes came into frequent contact with American travelers. Her grandfather Truckee and her father, Winnemucca, the chief's son-in-law, served regularly as guides to these groups. Most prominent among them was the explorer John C. Frémont. Truckee guided Frémont through the Sierras in 1846 and afterward remained with him in California. Truckee later joined in the American assault on the Mexican colony and became an advocate of friendship with the Americans.

Sarah Winnemucca's family belonged to a flexibly organized band that grew and contracted with the seasons and in response to the availability of food. During parts of the year large groups of Paiutes gathered to process pine nuts or hunt rabbits, while at other times small family bands separated and dispersed to exploit more scattered resources. Winnemucca and her relatives pursued this long-established pattern of hunting and gathering, but while still a child, she began to spend portions of each year in California. Her grandfather's association with Frémont and other Americans drew her into contact with the newcomers and earned her entrée into the homes of several white settlers.

Despite her family's friendly relations with the Americans, however, the young Paiute witnessed a number of violent encounters involving travelers, settlers, and her kinsmen. Two uncles were killed by whites during her childhood. As was frequently the case during periods of rapid migration, local government officials exercised little control over settlers and rarely enforced the boundaries separating Indian and public land. Because the tribe also lacked an effective central government, small incidents of theft or misunderstanding often triggered violent retaliation. During those early years of settlement she also saw the impact of cholera and other previously unknown diseases on her community, and she stood by as herds of cattle and horses trampled traditional tribal watering and gathering places into dust.[1]

Winnemucca's first sustained experience with whites occurred in 1857, when she entered the household of Major William Ormsby, a former gold prospector who had settled nearby in Genoa, Nevada. The thirteen-year-old Paiute girl was probably a servant in Ormsby's household, but during her two-year tenure she learned English and was introduced to books and modern conveniences by the major's wife, Margaret.[2] Following her return to her family, Winnemucca witnessed the onset of silver mining at the nearby Comstock Lode and the accompanying deterioration of relations between whites and Indians.

The disruption of the Paiutes' traditional hunting and gathering accelerated with the arrival of new groups of American prospectors and the subsequent appearance of new mining towns like Virginia City, founded in 1859. Areas of white settlement expanded, producing numerous disputes. Because the Paiutes did not farm, the extent of their territory was not obvious to the new settlers. Frequently prospectors traveled through an area and expressed outrage when local bands claimed it as their own. Tensions like these came to a head in 1860, when a series of murders and kidnappings prompted a settler assault on a Paiute band living on a reservation near Pyramid Lake. That assault was repulsed by the Indians, but the government responded to the incident by dispatching a detachment of 750 regulars to Nevada from the Presidio at San Francisco and subsequently establishing a permanent military post in what was now the Nevada Territory.[3]

Winnemucca's grandfather Truckee died soon after the Pyramid Lake War of 1860. His death, coupled with the establishment of American military authority in the area and the continued growth of white settlement, ushered in a new era in which the Paiutes were assigned to reservations and his granddaughter began to be called upon as an intermediary between government authorities and tribal leaders. The tribe had no single leader, but by the 1870s Winnemucca's father was frequently representing the group in dealings with outsiders. Thanks to his relative wealth, his relationship to his father-in-law, Truckee, and his English-speaking daughter, government officials believed they could communicate with the Paiutes by meeting with Winnemucca. The "chief" became better known among whites in 1864, when he took advantage of his prominence and began speaking before white audiences in lecture halls in both Nevada and California. At these events, which gradually evolved into performances of Indian customs and dancing, the chief would renew his plea for friendship, condemn frontier violence, and solicit money for his followers.[4] Such peaceful interludes were rare, however, as tensions with local whites continued and violence broke out at regular intervals.[5]

Sarah Winnemucca spent most of the 1860s living with her brother at Virginia City and at the nearby Pyramid Lake Reservation, but in 1868, amid continuing conflict with white settlers, the two agreed to move north and relocate with their father and other kinsmen at Camp McDermitt, a post that lay across the invisible territorial boundary with Oregon, but that was very much within the Paiutes' Great Basin homeland. It was at Camp McDermitt that Winnemucca first became a paid interpreter for the Indian Office and a prominent local figure who traveled easily among the American settlements, was married (briefly) to a white army officer, and assisted government agents and newspaper editors by providing them with information and advice. She was an effective aide to the local agent, persuading reluctant bands to relocate to the preserve and working closely with military commanders to protect the Indians' property and maintain the integrity of the reservation's boundaries. She even traveled to San Francisco to plead with military commanders for more generous supplies. She relished her prominent role, often appearing in local parades, riding sidesaddle and dressed in black. As one officer's wife later recalled, she rode "in perfect balance, her quirt hand lifted in a queenly salute."[6]

Winnemucca lived at Camp McDermitt until 1873, when she moved south to a village along the Central Pacific Railroad named for her father. Two years later she became an interpreter at a reservation that had recently been established along Oregon's Malheur River as a refuge for the region's Paiute-speaking Indians.[7] It was because of confrontations on the Malheur reserve that the young Paiute first emerged onto the national scene. In 1876 a popular agent was replaced by William Rinehart, a local merchant who insisted, upon taking office, that tribal leaders work under his direction rather than develop their own farms as they had been doing under his predecessor. When the chiefs protested—and Winnemucca forwarded their complaints to Washington—the agent accused his interpreter of disloyalty and fired her. Her dismissal incensed Winnmucca. In letters to local army commanders and the Indian Office, she accused Rinehart of colluding with local cattlemen and ignoring the well-being of the tribe.[8]

Two years after she left the Malheur agency, Winnemucca witnessed the outbreak of yet another border war between starving Indian bands and grasping settlers. In the course of this conflict, known as the Bannock War, she won praise from local commanders for her services as a messenger and interpreter. In the wake of these events, however, Winnemucca was shocked to learn that Indians such as her own peaceful group of Paiutes were to be moved arbitrarily to new agencies and assigned yet another political appointee as agent. Winnemucca's band was sent hundreds of miles north to the Yakama Reservation in the Washington Territory, where she was appointed agency interpreter. In 1879, sensing the start of yet another cycle of confinement and conflict, she resigned her post and traveled first to San Francisco and then on to Washington, D.C., to speak out on behalf of both the Paiutes and other neglected reservation Indians.[9]

For the next four years Sarah Winnemucca devoted herself to social activism. She lobbied army officers and government officials, lectured before women's organizations and reform groups, and developed her alliance with humanitarian reformers and women's rights activists. As she extended her network of supporters, she moved toward the center of a broader political arena; she also developed bold and wide-ranging critiques of both American expansion and the nation's rapidly proliferating reservation and "civilization" programs.

SARAH WINNEMUCCA'S MESSAGE

In 1883 Sarah Winnemucca published *Life Among the Piutes:* (Winnemucca did not use the modern spelling of the name of her tribe.) It was the culmination of her public efforts on behalf of Indian rights. It was also the very first book published in the United States by a Native American woman.

"I was a very small child when the first white man came into our country," Winnemucca wrote on page 1. "They came like a lion, yes, like a roaring lion, and have continued so ever since. . . ." The accusatory power of that opening line must have shocked her readers. Abandoning legalistic discussions of tribal rights, and setting aside any pretense that her story might offer a profile of native lifeways, Winnemucca's memoir focused on the theme of violence and betrayal. She described her grandfather's first attempt to welcome General Frémont to his homeland and noted how disappointed the old man had been in the American's frosty response. "I can imagine his feelings," she wrote, "for I have drunk deeply from the same cup."[10]

Winnemucca's manifesto was aimed at a wide audience. It was published with the assistance of two prominent woman reformers, Elizabeth Palmer Peabody and her sister Mary Peabody Mann, the widow of the educator Horace Mann. It was written during the activist's extended lecture tour in the East, probably while she was the sisters' houseguest at their home in Boston. The speed with which the book was produced suggests that it contained many of the stories Winnemucca had been presenting in public presentations over the previous two or three years. Some critics later charged that *Life Among the Piutes* was really the work of the Peabody sisters, but that is unlikely. Elizabeth Peabody had long experience with publishing and was a steady advocate of bringing women's voices before the public. She and Mary Mann likely inspired Sarah to publish her story, but neither sister had the knowledge or the inclination to write the manifesto herself. Mary Mann freely discussed correcting and editing the Paiute author's prose but insisted that she did little more than assist the young woman in her battle against what her friend called "her literary deficiencies."[11]

Beginning with her comparison of the Americans to a "roaring lion," Winnemucca employed vivid language to argue that the nation's conquest of the West, so celebrated by politicians and social theorists of the day, was brutal and violent. In addition to her bitter memory of General Frémont's disrespectful treatment of her grandfather, she recalled white travelers routinely burning the Paiutes' supplies of food, a tactic that prompted her kinsmen to flee to the mountains whenever wagon trains approached their territory. Commenting a few pages later on some of her first memories of whites, she added: "They are not people; they have no thought, no mind, no love. They are beasts. . . ."[12] Winnemucca never witnessed a major Indian rebellion or organized campaign to stop white settlement. Instead, she wrote, Nevada's history was characterized by unprovoked acts of violence and revenge. For her, this pattern of unrelenting hostility revealed the true nature of American expansion.

Winnemucca also charged that sexual violence was a fundamental aspect of expansion. Her speeches and writings were peppered with descriptions of rape and threats of rape. She recalled early in her memoir, for example, that while traveling as a child with her grandfather in California in the 1850s, she, her sister, and her mother were left in the care of one of Truckee's white patrons. She recalled: "The men whom my grandpa called his brothers would come into our camp and ask my mother to give our sister to them. They would come in at night and we would all scream and cry; but that would not stop them." Given the history of violence in the California goldfields (in which thousands of Native people were murdered by miners and settlers), her family could not resist. She wrote, "My uncles and brothers would not dare to say a word for fear they would be shot down."[13]

Winnemucca argued that Americans commonly exerted their authority over Indian women and men by violence. She explicitly rejected the common belief that Indian "backwardness" was simply doomed to give way to something better: American "progress." She reported, for example, that the Pyramid Lake War, which she witnessed in 1860, began when two white brothers kidnapped and raped a pair of young Paiute girls. "When my people saw their condition," she reported, "they at once killed both brothers and set fire to the house." Three days after the rape and the tribe's revenge, Winnemucca noted, the news was spread in typical frontier fashion: "The blood-thirsty savages had murdered two innocent, hard-working, industrious, kind-hearted settlers."[14] Similarly, the Bannock War, which began shortly after she had left Oregon's Malheur agency, was provoked when two white men attacked a girl who was gathering roots and "used her shamefully." The girl's relatives instantly retaliated. The rapists, a Bannock leader told Winnemucca, "are the cause of all our trouble. . . ." [15]

The new American regime, celebrated as an instrument of progress by officials in the Indian Office and in Congress, brought other hardships. Winnemucca described how as whites entered the delicate, arid environment of western Nevada, their horses and cattle destroyed many of the naturally occurring food sources that had long been staples of the Paiutes' subsistence cycle. In addition, she argued, ranching and mining enterprises fouled local streams and blocked the tribe's access to upland hunting grounds. Weakened by disruptions of their food supply, the Paiutes became increasingly susceptible to disease. Winnemucca described a cholera outbreak that occurred during her childhood. On her return from a trip to California she recalled being told "some very bad news . . . almost all the tribe had died off, and if one of a family got sick it was a sure thing that the whole family would die." [16]

The Paiute activist's list of expansion's damaging side effects included the suffering inflicted by the Christian bureaucrats dispatched to "uplift" her tribe. The reservations established in the Paiute homeland were staffed during Winnemucca's adult years by men and women appointed largely under President Ulysses Grant's Peace Policy, a program under which major Christian denominations nominated candidates for government posts. Winnemucca ridiculed this policy for introducing a wave of administrators who were publicly pious but who were personally corrupt or incompetent. She viewed these appointees with scorn, telling one Nevada agent that because the Paiutes were starving at their agency, he should be ashamed "that you talk three times a day to the Great Father in Spirit land." [17] At the Yakama Reservation, headed by the Methodist James Wilbur, Winnemucca derided the agent's converted Christian Indians by declaring that when they welcomed Winnemucca's group, they did not do so "because they loved us, or because they were Christians. No, they were like all civilized people; they came . . . because they were to be paid for it." [18]

Winnemucca's critique of American expansion in *Life Among the Piutes* was deeper and more threatening than the sum of its separate parts. By characterizing the U.S. onslaught as beastly, violent, and immoral, she attacked the idea that the extension of national power into the Great Basin was natural and benign. Americans entered the region by force and imposed their authority by terror. Christian benevolence simply provided a convenient cover for the enforcement of their rule. The Paiute would have been impatient with the legal parsing of William Potter Ross; she left no room in her narrative for the possibility of a humane government policy or for some legal reform that might correct the situation. According to her version of events, the suffering she witnessed was not rooted in political shortsightedness or administrative ignorance; it was the work of the "roaring lion" of violence, disease, and hypocrisy.

When she emerged onto the national stage in the 1880s, Winnemucca routinely contrasted the cruelty and immorality of American expansion with the humanity of the Paiute people and their traditions. In *Life Among the Piutes* she spelled out the civilized qualities of Native culture by pairing the activist's horrific account of the American "roaring lion" with poetic descriptions of traditional Northern Paiute life. Tellingly, Winnemucca titled her chapter on tribal life "Domestic and Social Moralities," another implicit criticism of the "morality" of the violent and irreligious invaders. Winnemucca described the affection that united all Paiute families. With the biblical injunction clearly in mind she noted: "We don't need to be taught to love our fathers and mothers. We love them without being told to." She emphasized the

tribe's devotion to chastity, education, modesty, hard work, and traditional gender roles. She noted that a father who does not provide
adequately for his children "is considered an outcast." She even
described the Paiute governance system as superior to the celebrated
U.S. Constitution. "We have a republic as well as you," Winnemucca
noted, where "anybody can speak who has anything to say, women
and all."[19]

Winnemucca's description celebrated Native values and rejected
the moral claims of U.S. nationalism. Not surprisingly, she did not
advocate a program of integration that would bring Indians into the
American mainstream. Instead, she envisioned an autonomous community of Indian people who could live in some secure portion of their
original homeland, apart from the disruptions caused by national
expansion.

In *Life Among the Piutes*, the reservation at Malheur where she had
lived in the 1870s was the model for Winnemucca's ideal Native community. Located in an isolated part of eastern Oregon, within the
radius of the traditional Paiute landscape, she recalled that the reservation had been both governed and protected by the agent Sam Parrish,
an idealistic pioneer who told the Paiutes: "I want you . . . to ask all
your people to come here to make homes for themselves. Send out your
men everywhere, and have them come to this place. This is the best
place for you all, and as soon as we get started, I will write to your
father in Washington, to send us a mill to grind our grain. We will
raise a little something this summer. We can plant some potatoes and
turnips and watermelons."[20] The tribe responded promptly to this invitation. Winnemucca reported that "we got along happily afterwards. . . .
We were all good friends, and our agent liked my people, and my people loved him." The only condition insisted upon by tribal leaders was
that the agent should keep white people away. "We do not want to

have white people near us," the leaders insisted. "We know what they are and what they would do to our women and our daughters."[21]

According to Sarah Winnemucca, the central element of this ideal reservation community was not its white agent or its emulation of "civilized" white behavior but its distance from American expansion. This distance protected aspects of tribal domestic life. In her view, the most effective counter to the conquest of her Nevada homeland would be the rehabilitation of traditional domestic life, not military action, religious revival, or a program of federal reform. She gave her version of that life a tribal name: Paiute. What in her childhood had been a label attached to a series of related hunting bands speaking the same language had become, in her version of events, the name of a coherent tribal community whose values and traditions could represent both a refuge from and an alternative to the American onslaught.

THE MOST POWERFUL PASSAGES of *Life Among the Piutes* and the most compelling feature of Winnemucca's lectures occurred when the activist turned directly to her audience and shifted her role from a witness of past events to a prosecutor acting in the present. Her judgment was fierce and unmistakable: she argued that it was her audience's society, not hers, that deserved the label "savage." One such moment occurred in the middle of Winnemucca's description of her tribe's confinement on the Yakama Reservation. Her kinsmen were forced to march north to the eastern Washington Territory despite the fact that they had refused to take up arms against the United States in the recent Bannock War. Stepping back from her firsthand account of events on the frontier, Winnemucca suddenly declared, "You who are educated by a Christian government in the art of war . . . you who call yourselves the great civilization; you who have knelt upon Plymouth

Rock . . . your so-called civilization sweeps inland from the ocean wave . . . I am crying out to you for justice. . . ."[22]

The effect of this tactic must have been even more jarring in a lecture hall when Winnemucca would shift in her Indian princess costume from meek self-pity to a voice that challenged her listeners to reimagine American expansion from the perspective of the private lives of Indian women like her. As a witness who could make the violence of conquest personal and testify to the cruel costs imposed upon Native families by continuous expansion, Winnemucca challenged her audience to reconsider the narratives of progress that justified the government's actions. Despite her genteel manner and her respectable white allies, she attacked the heart of America's ambition on the continent, the claim that the growth of the United States marked the natural evolution of human history from backwardness to modernity.

Sarah Winnemucca followed up the publication of *Life Among the Piutes* with a furious schedule of lecturing and lobbying. Elizabeth Peabody reported to a friend late in 1883 that the new author had made a private visit to the home of Senator Henry Dawes, the chairman of the Senate Committee on Indian Affairs, and "she has spoken in my hearing in Providence, Hartford, New York, Newburgh, Poughkeepsie, Dorset in Vermont, Salem, Cambridge, Boston again, and in Philadelphia."[23] In these presentations she no doubt repeated the charges in her book, but at the conclusion of all her speeches she asked her audience to add their signatures to a petition asking congress to restore the Malheur Reservation to the Paiutes. The petition asked for the grant of this land so that her kinsmen could "enjoy lands in severally [*sic*] without losing their tribal relations so essential to their happiness and good character and where their citizenship . . . will defend them from the encroachments of the white settlers, so detrimental to their interests and their virtues."[24] The appeal for a homeland that would preserve the "essential" relations among members of her tribe and prevent whites from any further "encroachment" was a fitting extension of Winnemucca's indictment of American expansion. She sought a future in which the Paiutes could survive as a community, apart from the violence and disruption that were sure to accompany any contact with American settlers. They would lead their own lives—both public and private—in their own community.

CHALLENGING "CIVILIZATION"

Sarah Winnemucca spoke out against the morality of American expansion just as federal officials were embarking on a national campaign to "civilize" all American Indians. Of course missionaries had striven to convert and "uplift" Indian people from the seventeenth century forward, but it was not until the middle of the nineteenth century, when the U.S. conquest of the continent became complete, that federal officials and the general public shifted the bulk of their attention from extending the nation's borders to creating a comprehensive system for incorporating indigenous communities into the nation. They hoped to integrate these individuals into the lower rungs of a modern industrial state.

It is difficult to identify the moment when the shift from public diplomacy to domestic reform first occurred. It probably began in 1849, five years after Winnemucca's birth, when, in the wake of the Mexican War and the settlement of the Oregon boundary dispute, Congress transferred the Indian Office from the Department of War to the newly created Department of the Interior. This transfer symbolized the American government's desire to move from an age of expansion, when Indians were external enemies to be defeated in war, to a period of consolidation, when civilian agents would oversee the national control in the interior. Under this new bureaucratic arrangement, the Indian Office set about creating federally protected enclaves for Indians within states and territories. These enclaves became known as reservations. The commissioner of Indian affairs promised in 1850 that these protected areas would be "supplied with stock, agricultural implements and useful materials for clothing," and he assured the public that the government would "encourage and assist [residents] in the erection of comfortable dwellings, and secure to them the means and facilities of education, intellectual, moral, and religious."[25]

The Indian Office's goal of making all the nation's Indian reservations places of "intellectual, moral, and religious" education was remarkably ambitious, but the program itself was implemented slowly and unevenly. In view of the many hardships surrounding the eastern removals, federal officials often found it difficult to persuade tribal leaders to lead their communities onto reservations or to accept the dramatic cultural changes required in these new "educational" settlements. Initially, a number of powerful Native groups, such as the Sioux and Cheyennes on the Plains, the Navajos in the Southwest, and the Yakamas in the Pacific Northwest, resisted this extension of American authority in their tribal homelands. This resistance, along with the many hardships that accompanied the transition to reservation life, triggered a number of violent conflicts with authorities. Fighting of this kind constituted the bulk of the Indian wars that captured public attention during the middle of the century. Crazy Horse and Geronimo, for example, were the objects of military campaigns precisely because they refused to live on reservations the government had created for their "education."[26]

It was not until after the reunification of the national government in 1865, when Sarah Winnemucca was in her twenties, that public support and federal authority seemed sufficient to launch a national campaign to transform Indian ways of life. The potential for this new effort became evident first in 1871, when Congress declared that it would no longer negotiate treaties with Indian tribes. In the future, congressional leaders announced, federal power alone would dictate the government's policy toward the tribes. In 1872, Commissioner of Indian Affairs Francis Walker, an economist who soon became the president of the Massachusetts Institute of Technology, explained this abandonment of negotiation by noting that national expansion had reduced Indians to powerlessness and widened the cultural gulf separating them from whites. "The westward course of population is neither to be denied nor delayed for the sake of the Indians," he declared. "They must yield or perish." The federal government's responsibility, Walker added, was not "to stay this tide (through the negotiation of treaties) . . . but to snatch the remnants of the Indian race from destruction. . . ." The commissioner advocated replacing treaties with a program of "directing these people to new pursuits which shall be consistent with the progress of civilization upon the continent."[27]

Commissioner Walker's observation that Indians must "yield or perish" and his sequential references to the "advance" of the frontier and the "wretchedness" of Indians underscored his conviction, shared by many in President Grant's administration, that the United States had an obligation to transform Native communities. For national leaders from the victorious North, the post–Civil War years seemed an era of triumph. "Every year's advance of our frontier takes in a territory as large as some of the Kingdoms of Europe," Commissioner Walker wrote in 1872. American success was assured and self-affirming. He added, "We are richer by hundreds of millions; the Indian is poorer by a large part of the little that he has. This growth is bringing imperial greatness to the nation; to the Indian it brings wretchedness, destitution, beggary."[28] Because American officials viewed themselves as people charged with promoting "imperial greatness," they felt unconstrained by previous treaties or informal understandings with the tribes.

The commissioner's self-confidence was reinforced by the nation's leading scientists. The Smithsonian Institution's John Wesley Powell, for example, the geologist who had led the first American expedition through the Grand Canyon and who later became the director of the U.S. Geological Survey, wrote in 1880 that enforcing treaties with Indians would fulfill only "a minor part of the debt" that the government owed Indians. "The major portion of that debt," Powell wrote, "can only be paid by giving to the Indians Anglo-Saxon civilization, that they may also have prosperity and happiness under the new civilization of this continent."[29] For Powell, Walker, and their generation of government officials, bestowing "civilization" on the tribes would not only add to the nation's "imperial greatness" but would also compensate the Indians for their dispossession. The stakes for people like Walker and Powell were very high. They believed that with one stroke, "civilizing" the Indians would eradicate Native identities, scrub clean the nation's guilty conscience, and burnish its global image.

DURING THE SAME DECADES when policy makers were turning their attention to Indian civilization, a parallel conversation was regarding the role of women in a rapidly expanding "civilized" nation was taking place. Fiction writers, political leaders, and social theorists such as the anthropologist Lewis Henry Morgan argued that only communities comprised of nuclear families would be capable of producing social harmony and economic prosperity across the continent. Families headed by male breadwinners and served by female spouses who maintained the household and instructed the family's children were viewed as the building blocks of a progressive and modern society. Monogamy and good housekeeping were essential ingredients of this imagined America.[30]

It was logical, then, that as the Indian Office and other agencies began to organize methods for "giving the Indians Anglo-Saxon civilization" and for "directing" tribes to programs of "intellectual, moral and religious" education, government officials turned to contemporary models of domesticity for their inspiration. When architects of the reservation system spoke of "comfortable dwellings," for example, or called for the distribution of tribal lands to individuals, they regularly conjured up a gendered image of civilized American families. They imagined Indian men would fence and farm small plots of land while their wives maintained households for themselves and their children. Government schools would teach men a trade or instruct them in efficient agricultural techniques, while Native girls and women learned cooking, sewing, and other domestic arts. Reformers viewed the inculcation of an array of American domestic habits as the central avenue by which Indian families would travel from wretchedness to modernity.[31] "Civilized" Native men and women would lay the foundation for new Indian communities that would transcend their backward traditions and ignore their recalcitrant traditional leaders.

The centrality of domestic reform to the Indian civilization effort had been apparent even in prewar proposals to establish reservations, but those ideas were given new life after the Civil War by reformers such as Lydia Maria Child, who sought to extend the promise of American civilization from newly freed slaves to Indians. A former abolitionist, Child declared in 1870 that "human nature is essentially the same in all races and classes of men," adding, "My faith never wavers that men can be made just by being treated justly, honest by being dealt with honestly, and kindly by becoming objects of kindly sympathy."[32] Women like Child and Amelia Stone Quinton, who had taught newly freed African Americans in the South immediately after the Civil War, were at the forefront of this effort. Their commitment to "all races and classes of men" inspired them to press for Indian schools and Indian citizenship. In 1879 Quinton founded the Women's National Indian Association, a forerunner of the later male-led Indian Rights Association. This activity inspired younger women, such as the anthropologist Alice Cunningham Fletcher and the popular author Helen Hunt Jackson, to join the effort.[33]

These women saw domestic reform aimed at civilization (education, traditional marriage, and individual landownership) as a solution for Native communities increasingly surrounded by land-hungry whites. Fletcher became an early advocate of replacing reservations with individual landownership and a firm supporter of the nation's growing network of boarding schools. Helen Hunt Jackson offered her prescriptions in the form of popular essays and stories. Her most famous effort was a romance set in the Mission Indian communities of southern California. Published in 1884, just a year after *Life Among the Piutes* appeared, *Ramona* portrayed the struggle of a Christian Indian woman striving to establish a household for her pious husband and son. Jackson's account of the heroine Ramona's homemaking in the face of racial hostility and rampant lawlessness echoed the domestic images in Harriet Beecher Stowe's more famous *Uncle Tom's Cabin* and other works that illustrated the nuclear family's ability to protect individuals from hostile outsiders. For Jackson, as for Fletcher and Stowe, a civilized home managed by a Christian matron could be both a refuge from lawlessness and a vehicle for transporting its members to a better place.[34]

Life Among the Piutes attacked the heart of this national campaign of uplift and domestic reform. Winnemucca's angry words were hurled at a uniform set of self-serving popular attitudes and a rapidly hardening government policy: Indians represented the past, treaties were obsolete, Native cultures must yield, and the incorporation of conventional American domestic behaviors was the surest recipe for civilization. Her speeches and writing, coming from an eloquent, self-confident woman, challenged that mind-set and proposed an alternative scenario in which Indian communities consolidated and progressed on their own within protected enclaves inside America's borders.

As early as 1870, Winnemucca had argued from her post at Camp McDermitt that the solution to Indian suffering was "a permanent *home* on [the Indians'] own native soil" and sufficient protection for that home so that "white neighbors can be kept from encroaching on our rights. . . ." This approach, she declared, would render "the savage (as he is called today) . . . a thrifty and law-abiding member of the community. . . ."[35] Thirteen years later, when she published *Life Among the Piutes*, she proposed the same solution, pleading in the closing pages of her narrative for the government to "give us homes to live in, for God's sake and for humanity's sake."[36] The common thread of her activist career was the dignity of Indian communities and the role within them of powerful Indian women who upheld the best standards of their tribal traditions.

Mary Peabody Mann promised *Life Among the Piutes* would tell "in detail to the mass of our people . . . the story of [Sarah Winnemucca's] trials."[37] Rooted in the story of herself and her family and aimed at establishing "homes to live in" for her community, the book was intended as a public testimonial that would provide a guide for Indian survival that challenged conventional non-Indian definitions of Native private life and civilization. Winnemucca's assault on the images outsiders held of Indian women and Native cultural life and her consequent assertion that Indians deserved a "home" within the conquered American continent were the central elements of her unique political agenda.

NON-INDIANS ATTACKED *Life Among the Piutes* almost from the moment of its publication. One group charged that Winnemucca's criticism of the Indian Office had been manufactured by senior military commanders who wanted to take control of the agency. "It is a great outrage on the respectable people of Boston," one critic charged, "to foist such a woman of any race upon us." Others saw her as the puppet of eastern elites. A reporter from her home state of Nevada, for example, dismissed the forty-year-old author as someone "who used to romp around in this country with an old blanket tied at the waist with a piece of clothesline. . . . It is probable," the journalist continued, "that she will never be appreciated in the West as she is in the East."[38]

In the years following the book's publication, Winnemucca's enemies became even more outspoken. The Indian Rights Association, an organization of white reformers founded in Philadelphia in 1882, dismissed her as a self-promoter. It declared that "nothing which has been done for her by her friends in the East or elsewhere has, so far, had any relation to her own or her people's progress." The association told its members that any support for Winnemucca would be "misplaced."[39] General O. O. Howard, a sympathetic army officer whom the activist had earlier counted as an ally during her campaign against Indian Office incompetence, dismissed her pleas as hysterical and baseless. The general noted in his own memoir published after the activist's death in 1891 that the Paiutes did not deserve any special consideration because they "were not yet far enough along the 'white man's road' to take advantage of [such] good fortune."[40] Even Winnemucca's tribe grew reluctant to endorse her. Her father's death in 1882 greatly reduced her political standing among the dispersed Paiute community, and her repeated trips away from Nevada to give lectures and raise money, compounded by her failure to deliver the assistance she had promised, fueled rumors that she was a self-serving fraud, an immoral woman, or, worse, a collaborator with the whites.[41]

Hostility to Winnemucca's political message remained the norm for most of the century following her death. The Paiute author has been remembered best by literary critics who discovered her in the 1980s but focused most of their attention on her relationship to her white sponsors and her support for the government's reservation system. Critics searching for an authentic Indian "voice" in Winnemucca's writings have expressed their doubts based on the author's collaboration with white editors and her apparent advocacy of "civilization." They accused her of pandering to her genteel audiences and presenting an "acculturated and Christianized viewpoint."[42] Even today few scholars look carefully at the significance of the political message she tried to deliver or at the reasons why she was so quickly forgotten by both reformers and the general public.

THE SARAH WINNEMUCCA RULES OF INDIAN PROTEST

The responses to Winnemucca's lectures and writing made it clear that her attacks had struck a nerve. Nevada newspapers had dismissed her as an immoral character as early as 1873, and the government agent she attacked in Oregon three years later cited her recent divorce and accused her of being a prostitute, "not a proper person to serve in any capacity at this or any other Indian agency."[43] James Wilbur, the Methodists' appointee at the Yakama Reservation, filed a similar report in 1881, noting that if Sarah Winnemucca's "influences could be removed, I have no doubt but the Piutes would cheerfully acquiesce in the desire of the Department. . . ."[44] Other agents echoed these charges, and stories of Sarah Winnemucca's troublemaking and immorality filled the correspondence files of the Indian Office. In the wake of the book's publication, officials in Washington rejected her plea that her kinsmen be allowed to return to Nevada or to reassemble at the Malheur Reservation. They recommended instead that the Malheur agency be closed.[45]

Sarah Winnemucca made no secret of her three marriages or her love for recreational gambling, which was common in her tribe where games of chance were an ancient tradition. Her enemies latched on to these facts to undermine Winnemucca's message. These negative portrayals illustrate the extent to which her contemporaries embraced the conventional view of domestic life and westward expansion. In Winnemucca's eyes, that expansion was neither natural nor benign, but to her critics, American "civilization" was marching bravely across the continent, disrupted only by an immoral "savage" woman who was incapable of accepting the nation's benign programs for uplift and improvement. She was not a violent rebel like Geronimo or Crazy Horse, but her resistance was no less threatening. From the perspective of the Indian Office and its defenders, the activist's outspoken manifesto simply disqualified her from participating in discussions of the Indian's place in the American future.

By the end of her eastern lecture tour in the spring of 1884, Sarah Winnemucca's personal life had become an embarrassment. Her third husband, a former army sergeant named Lewis Hopkins, whom she had married in 1881, had accompanied her to Boston and spent a considerable time there and elsewhere on her itinerary accumulating gambling debts. While she was in Washington, D.C., in April to lobby Congress and the Indian Office, Hopkins forged checks, using the names of some of his wife's supporters, and fled. Winnemucca was not involved in any of Hopkins's antics, but the scandal certainly confirmed the negative rumors that were already circulating regarding her virtue.[46]

Unable to win the release of her tribesmen from the Yakama reserve, Sarah Winnemucca returned to Nevada in the summer of 1884 and attempted to continue her campaign on the lecture circuit. Her efforts produced few results, and the embarrassment of her husband's desertion undermined her ability to lobby politicians and military leaders. Her failures also disappointed her supporters at home. The Virginia City newspapers reported on a lecture in the fall of 1884 that was "slimly attended," and even though the reporter approved of her impressive presentation, he (or she?) condescendingly described the now notorious author as more of a curiosity than a serious tribal representative. "The Paiutes regard her with suspicion," the article noted. "It is even suspected that she uses soap and a brush and a comb occasionally. To the genuine Paiutes these things are inconsistent with the traditions of the race. . . . She was regarded as a little queer by everybody."[47]

Winnemucca continued to speak in Nevada and California following her return to the West, but she had little success. She sought out audiences of sympathetic women. In San Francisco she lectured to an all-woman audience in the afternoon and a mixed audience in the evening. Winnemucca gradually shifted her appeal from an attack on the Indian Office to a more general plea for education and citizenship. She was also not above exploiting her audiences' racial prejudices to make her point. She told her female supporters in San Francisco, for example, that Indians should have the ballot "so they can stand on par with the gentleman with wool on the top of his head. . . ."[48]

Access to education had always been part of Winnemucca's general platform, but in the wake of her less than triumphant return to Nevada, the promotion of a tribal school became her central concern. Perhaps she had come to see this as an achievable goal. Disgusted with agency corruption and missionary hypocrisy, she now considered organizing a completely independent educational program. In the past she had promised lecture audiences that she would "educate my people and make them law abiding citizens," but because her goal had been efficient reservation administration, she had imagined accomplishing that task would be taken up by agents supported by the government. At another point she had thought of using white women as the principal instruments of reform. "You send white ladies into our midst to teach us instead of men," she had told one audience in 1879, "they would at least give us half [an effort] instead of none."[49] Now she concluded that Indians would do the work themselves.

IN THE SUMMER OF 1885 Sarah Winnemucca moved to her brother's small homestead on the outskirts of Lovelock, Nevada, and announced that she would open a school for local Paiute children. She proposed to teach her students to speak English and other basic skills but to introduce them to their lessons by using Paiute as the language of the classroom. Her school would not require children to leave their families or to wear military uniforms, as was common in the government's boarding schools. Moreover, she planned to include their parents in the enterprise by asking students to take their lessons in arithmetic and other useful skills home with them so that they could pass their knowledge on to their families. By the fall this small version of the Paiute "homeland" the activist had imagined in her lectures and petitions had become a reality.[50]

In the end even Sarah Winnemucca's most tangible success, a well-attended bilingual school operating outside the authority of the Indian Office, provided yet another example of how public intolerance and government rigidity marginalized and eventually defeated her. The ever-loyal Peabody sisters solicited funds for the school from friends in Boston and Washington, but few were interested in a project that had no relationship to the nation's missionary societies and no prospect of securing government funding.

In 1886 Elizabeth Peabody published a pamphlet that enthusiastically reported on the school's work and stressed its community roots. She wrote, "[I]t is a spontaneous movement, made by the Indian himself, *from himself*, in full consciousness of free agency, for the education that is to civilize him."[51] But such sentiments did not appeal to reformers committed to the conversion agenda of the major Christian denominations or to the government's authoritarian programs of domestic reform and moral uplift. From their perspective, Winnemucca's little enterprise seemed both inadequate and self-serving. Given the doubts already circulating about Winnemucca's personal life, some believed the school was simply a ruse to extract money from innocent easterners. The Indian Rights Association fanned these suspicions when it investigated the school in 1886. While praising the Peabody sisters' dedication, the IRA report dismissed them as "good, but strangely-infatuated ladies" who could not accept Winnemucca's "unreliable and bad character."[52] Despite praise from visitors and even the skeptical Nevada press, support for the school dwindled, and its doors closed after three years of operation.

IT IS NOT difficult to imagine the reasons that non-Indians would be reluctant to embrace Winnemucca's indictment of American expansion; the failure of other Native activists to come to her defense is more puzzling. A historian cannot draw any insights from negative evidence, so there is little that can be said about the Paiute tribe's silence in the wake of the public attacks on her virtue and honesty. Sarah Winnemucca's brother supported the school she founded on his Lovelock farm, but few other Paiutes came to her defense. It is also true that her cause elicited no noticeable support from other tribes in the region or from the few prominent tribal leaders who, by the time of her memoir's publication, had become familiar to the American public. Among these were the Lakota leaders Red Cloud and Spotted Tail and the Nez Perce chief Joseph, all men who lectured in the East in the 1870s, all silent. This silence also extended to the rising generation of educated Indian leaders.

Charles Eastman (Ohiyesa), a star pupil at the Presbyterian mission school for the Santee Sioux in the Dakota Territory, was a freshman at Dartmouth College the year *Life Among the Piutes* was published. Chief Joseph and Red Cloud had already pleaded their tribes' cases before eastern audiences, and Standing Bear, the Ponca chief who in 1879 had mounted a successful legal challenge to a government order confining him to his reservation, had recently completed a lecture tour of eastern cities.[53] None of these men ever mentioned Sarah Winnemucca in their speeches or their writings. In addition, each fall, beginning in the year *Life Among the Piutes* was published, the leaders of missionary and Indian rights groups would gather at a Catskill Mountain resort owned by a Quaker activist, Albert K. Smiley, to report on the progress of their efforts and to set future goals. Calling themselves the Friends of the Indian, the reformers met at Smiley's Mohonk Mountain House and soon became a powerful lobbying force that pressed for allotment, boarding schools, and citizenship. Beginning in 1889, the group also began inviting carefully selected educated Indians, such as Eastman, to address their meetings. They never invited Sarah Winnemucca to attend, and none of the invited Native speakers ever mentioned her name.[54]

Chastised by critics in both the East and West and ignored by the few Indians who managed to command some part of the American public's attention in the 1880s, Winnemucca fell from public view. She did not fit the government's narrative of Indian uplift or, apparently, the expectations of tribal leaders who preferred politically savvy—and male—spokespeople. But Sarah Winnemucca's contributions to Native activism, and to resistance against American expansion, are not impossible to discover. Her unique viewpoint was clearly evident in her assault on the smug assumptions of nineteenth-century American expansionism and in her rejection of the policies the American government had adopted to reform the domestic life of the tribes. Her uncompromising female voice and unapologetic public persona stand apart from the approach of practical Indian leaders like William Potter Ross or modern reformers like Charles Eastman. She refused to participate in either the language of political negotiation or the missionary-influenced agenda of cultural uplift. Her willingness to address the violence so endemic in westward expansion and her eagerness to defend the virtues of traditional Indian homes and families set her apart from all other Native activists of her time. Her outspokenness, and her marginalization, marked her as a new voice in the effort to ensure an autonomous Native presence within the boundaries of the American nation.

The persistence of Winnemucca's outlook is plain when one considers the American Indian intellectuals who came to prominence after her death in 1891. While none of these figures publicly praised the Paiute activist or her memoir, each of them expressed a version of her comprehensive critique. These individuals composed essays and memoirs that resembled the more strident approach of *Life Among the Piutes*. Winnemucca's successors were a diverse lot, but indictments of American expansion and colonial rule appear with growing frequency, if subtly, in their work.[55]

We cannot know what these activists understood about her career and the rapidity with which the reform community abandoned her, but we can observe that they followed what we might call the Winnemucca Rules. They shared her view of American expansion, but they did not discuss sexual violence, they did not attack missionaries, and they did not directly challenge a progressive view of America's destiny or the patriotic allegiances of their white audiences. Instead, they chose indirection.

Francis La Flesche was a model boarding school student like Charles Eastman. He went to work at the Smithsonian Institution in the 1880s and later published an outwardly entertaining childhood autobiography. His 1900 book was filled with tales of boarding school high jinks, but the author took several opportunities to insert his own commentary into the stories. When discussing the common practice of assigning students English translations of their given tribal names upon enrollment, for example, La Flesche wrote that "no native American can ever cease to regret that the utterances of his father have been constantly belittled when put into English, that their thoughts have frequently been travestied and their native dignity obscured."[56]

At another point, La Flesche described an impromptu quiz conducted by a visiting school inspector. "Who discovered America?" the bearded white man asked. "George Washington!" a star student replied. The irony and pathos in the scene were clear, but La Flesche made no direct comment, letting his joke do the work for him. His readers were left with the image of a Native student, forced to live apart from his own family, choosing one of the white man's pantheon of interchangeable heroes to satisfy his inquisitor. Winnemucca would never have been so subtle, but she certainly would have appreciated La Flesche's point.

Charles Eastman adopted a similarly humorous pose in a memoir published in 1916 following his years as a reservation physician and an organizer for the YMCA. The Santee author described a visit to a YMCA chapter on one reservation where he gave a public lecture urging local Indians to participate in the organization's Christian self-help programs. Eastman described an elderly man who responded to his speech: "After a long silence [the man] said: I have come to the conclusion that this Jesus was an Indian."[57] Like La Flesche and Winnemucca, Eastman was clearly aware of the destructive impact of American rule on traditional domestic life. Indians were not backward heathens, the old man had suggested, but were naturally inclined to Christian virtue. One of his Native kinsmen must have been the Messiah. Eastman made this point with his story; he did not need to turn dramatically to his audience, as Winnemucca had in her performances.

It is fascinating to consider whether any of these individuals read *Life Among the Piutes* or heard descriptions of Winnemucca's brief campaign to challenge the Indian Office and its ideology of progress. Eastman lived in Boston, the home of the activist's white sponsors, from 1887 to 1890 and was a frequent speaker at reform gatherings in the city. Perhaps he met Elizabeth Peabody or was given a copy of the controversial book. In the 1880s and 1890s, Francis La Flesche shared a house in Washington, D.C., with the reformer and anthropologist Alice Fletcher, who considered the young Omaha her adopted son. Formerly active in Boston's circle of abolitionists and women's rights activists, Fletcher became interested in Indian affairs at just the time when Sarah Winnemucca was lecturing and lobbying government officials. It is likely she heard the Paiute activist speak or owned a copy of her book.[58]

ANOTHER VOICE

Tracing the relationship among nineteenth-century American Indian thinkers and political leaders is a speculative and inexact enterprise. William Potter Ross testified in a congressional hearing room where a reference to Indians "who happened to be in the city" appeared by chance. Who were they? How did Ross's ideas about treaty rights and tribal unity circulate to other tribes and parts of the continent? Similarly, Sarah Winnemucca spoke to hundreds of eager gatherings and published a dramatic memoir, but no Indians spoke directly back to her, despite her fame and the passion of her words. At the same time, the themes she enunciated recur regularly (although in muted form) in the lectures and essays of the generation of Native authors who came immediately after her. How can we confirm the link?

Ely Parker, the Seneca brigadier general who became President Grant's commissioner of Indian affairs, provides yet another possible connection between Winnemucca and other Native writers who indicted American expansion for its violence and cruelty. In September 1865, as a military officer, Parker had accompanied the commissioner of Indian affairs when he summoned Cherokee leaders to

Fort Smith, Arkansas. There he watched as the victorious federal officials first dictated terms to tribal leaders and then retreated before the
cogent arguments and steely intransigence of the Cherokee leadership.
Later Parker served on the commission that investigated the massacre
at Sand Creek, Colorado. It was to Parker, now the head of the Indian
Office, that Sarah Winnemucca had written in the summer of 1870,
urging him to prevent white ranchers and prospectors from committing "acts of violence" against her community. "I know more about the
feeling and prejudices of these Indians than any other person," she had
told the commissioner; "therefore I hope this petition will be received
with favor."[59]

Ely Parker resigned from the Indian Office in 1871 amid unproved
accusations of financial mismanagement made against him by William
Welsh, an influential Philadelphia businessman and Christian
reformer. (William Welsh was the uncle of Herbert Welsh, the founder
of the Indian Rights Association.) After he left his post, Parker
returned to New York and tried his hand at business. Unsuccessful, he
became a clerk in the New York City Police Department, for which he
worked until his death in 1895. Sometime in the late 1880s, probably
while Sarah Winnemucca was struggling to keep her bilingual school
open in Lovelock, Nevada, Parker revealed in a letter to a friend how
disillusioned he had become with the culture and institutions of the
United States. "I have little or no faith in the American Christian civilization methods of treating the Indians of this country," he told Harriet Maxwell Converse (whom he addressed with the Seneca name
Gayaneshaoh).[60] "Black deception, damnable frauds and persistent
oppression have been its characteristics, and its religion today is that
the only good Indian is a dead one." Parker condemned the increasingly authoritarian nature of federal policy, revealed in an expanding

system of military-style boarding schools, and the rising popularity of proposals to impose allotment on tribes in every corner of the country. "All other methods of dispossessing the Indians of every vested and hereditary right having failed," he wrote, "compulsion must now be resorted to, a certain death to the poor Indians."

Parker's solution to this assault on Indian rights was "secular and industrial schools in abundance" and the recognition of Native claims to land. "There is land enough on this portion of God's footstool called America for the Indian and the white man to live upon side by side," he observed. Like Winnemucca, he didn't argue for the preservation of vast reservations or the negotiation of elaborate new treaties, but he was adamant that Native people deserved protected homelands in the United States, places where they could live without outside interference. "The Indian," the former army engineer declared, "wishes to be let alone in his wigwam."

Parker saved his harshest words for the reformers and missionaries who claimed to have Native interests foremost in their thoughts. He observed that reformers were urging the adoption of legislation that would divide tribal lands into individual allotments. Groups like the Indian Rights Association were claiming that Indians everywhere were eager to abandon their tradition of communal ownership. Parker disagreed: "The Indians, as a body, are deadly opposed to the scheme for they see in it too plainly the certain and speedy dissolution of their tribal and national organizations. It is very evident to my mind that all schemes to apparently serve the Indians are only plausible pleas put out to hoodwink the civilized world that everything possible has been done to save this race from annihilation and to wipe out the stain on the American name for its treatment of the aboriginal population." After unburdening himself, the former commissioner apologized to Converse for his "thesis on Indian rights and wrongs, an almost inexhaustible theme." He added, "I drop it since no good can result to continue it." The rest of his letter was devoted to Seneca folklore.

Questioning the ideology of American progress and equating the reform community's agenda with a plan to "hoodwink the civilized world" Parker too was observing the Winnemucca Rules of Indian Protest. He understood that his views were of little interest to the American public; he knew that "no good" would come from discussing them in public. Parker's angry private letter tells us nothing about his possible link to the Paiute author, but its tone and substance reinforce the impression that Winnemucca's public protests were not unique. They surfaced frequently in muted form among the activists who came after her. Indian leaders like Parker certainly would have understood the reasons for her disappearance from public view. While we cannot know for certain that the scattered Indian voices of Winnemucca, Parker, La Flesche, and Eastman spoke to one another a century ago, it is clear that they shared the former commissioner's conviction that the expanding American nation was intent on "dispossessing the Indians of every vested and hereditary right." Of all those voices, Sarah Winnemucca's was the loudest.

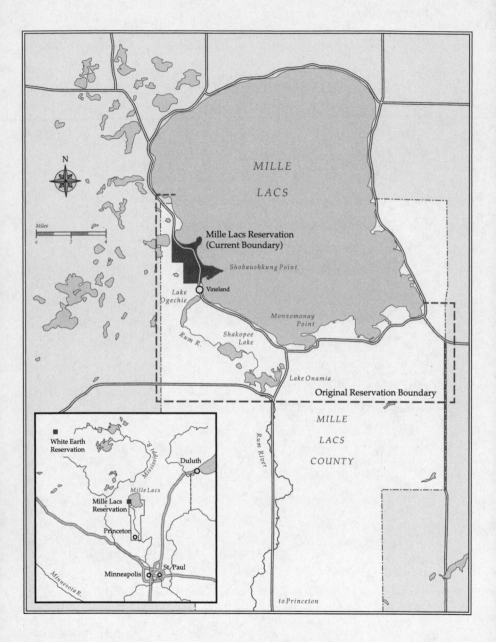

MILLE
LACS

Mille Lacs Reservation
(Current Boundary)

Shobaushkung Point

Lake
Ogechie ⊙ Vineland

Monzomonay
Point

Rum R.

Shakopee
Lake

Lake Onamia

Original Reservation Boundary

MILLE
LACS
COUNTY

Rum River

N

Miles
0   2   4

■ White Earth
Reservation

Mississippi R.

Duluth ⊙

Mille Lacs

Mille Lacs
Reservation

Princeton ○

Minneapolis ○ ○ St. Paul

Minnesota R.

to Princeton

CHAPTER FIVE

THE U.S. COURT
OF CLAIMS

The Mille Lacs Ojibwes

In the fall of 1880, Secretary of the Interior Carl Schurz proudly announced that the Indian Office was pursuing a "fixed line of conduct" that would "dissolve, by gradual steps, [the Indians'] tribal cohesion, and merge them in the body politic as independent and self-reliant men. . . ."[1] But as they set about "dissolving" the Indians' "tribal cohesion," the government's new programs instead stimulated a new round of Native activism. Officials like Schurz assumed they were managing the affairs of a conquered people who would ultimately do their bidding. They were wrong.

Across the continent, as tribal leaders confronted government initiatives aimed at disrupting and transforming their lives, they quickly grasped the connection between their local predicaments and the direction of national policy. Not all were successful, but many resisted the Indian Office's new initiatives and by century's end had generated an array of new arguments. They demanded, for example, that tribes should have a significant role in the development of their own lands and resources and insisted that tribal governments should continue to function as representatives of community interests. They pointed out that the promises written into past treaties, having never been repealed, should be enforced. They insisted on being heard.

As tribal leaders framed their opposition to the Indian Office, they grew comfortable using words like "democracy," "freedom," and "justice" to buttress their claims. They enjoyed tossing these American words back at government officials and became increasingly adept at finding forums where their arguments would carry special weight. While Indian activists shied away from Sarah Winnemucca's outspoken attacks on westward expansion, they understood that groups like the Indian Rights Association and other sympathetic individuals could be recruited to oppose cases of stark injustice and publicize their grievances. Similarly, while most American political leaders were reluctant to stand in the way of homesteaders or local boosters, incidents of lawlessness or violence frequently attracted the attention of outside authorities. Just as bloody massacres had often triggered public sympathy during the Indian wars of the 1860s and 1870s, so egregious cases of unfairness or mismanagement could now become the subject of reports issued by reform groups and religious leaders. Despite these gradual changes in white attitudes, the most famous Indian leaders of the era—Geronimo and Sitting Bull—continued to advocate military resistance even though both eventually surrendered to the American authorities.[2] Others sought escape, either directly, by crossing into Canada or Mexico, or indirectly, by joining one of the religious movements that emerged, as they had in previous moments of crisis, to offer their followers spiritual relief.[3] Most tribes rejected both of those options, however, choosing instead to remain at home and rally their communities to challenge the Americans with whatever political force they could muster. Outnumbered and outgunned, they pursued the tactics pioneered by earlier activists: they argued, they lobbied, and they searched the horizon for allies. In an age of upheaval they clung tenaciously to the belief that through political ideas and political actions, Indian people could survive the onslaught of white settlement and the government's campaign to "dissolve" their tribal communities.

The Mille Lacs Ojibwes were one such group. Occupying the shores of a central Minnesota lake, this tiny Ojibwe band insisted on its right to live undisturbed within the territory the government had guaranteed to it in treaties and other agreements. For decades the leaders at Mille Lacs turned aside the government's demand that they abandon their homeland and join other Ojibwe bands on the large, consolidated reservation at White Earth. Their impressive campaign began during contentious negotiations with the Indian Office, but over time it expanded to include appeals to the Indian Rights Association in Philadelphia, visits to elected officials in Minnesota and Washington, D.C., and, ultimately, a lawsuit in the U.S. Court of Claims. Despite the band's small size and lack of political assets, its leaders managed to stop the Indian Office in its tracks. They refused to comply with the government's orders, demanding instead that the United States honor its promises. The Mille Lacs leadership's campaign of resistance demonstrates how political tactics and legal arguments devised generations earlier in the Southeast and carried on to Indian Territory and beyond had created new avenues for activists across the continent.

FIGHTING REMOVAL AT MILLE LACS

The forced removal of Indians from their homelands did not end when the Cherokees were driven from Georgia in 1838. The Seminoles were pursued through the swamps of Florida during the 1840s, and in the 1850s local militiamen and regular army troops forced Indians in Oregon, Washington, and California away from their ancestral territories in order to accommodate American settlements. A decade later American bluecoats began a similar effort in Montana and the Dakota Territory. As late as 1903 Indian families living near San Diego were forced by federal officials onto the nearby Pala Reservation, while across the continent in Mississippi, Choctaws who had chosen to remain in the state a century earlier were forced to join their kinsmen in Indian Territory before Congress acted formally to dissolve the tribe.

This process of removal and relocation also took place throughout the vast Ojibwe homeland stretching across the inland watersheds of the Great Lakes and Lake Manitoba. These communities, which together formed the largest language group in North America, had first become known to Europeans in the early seventeenth century, when French and English traders discovered their hunting communities north of Lake Huron. Over the next two centuries the Ojibwes spread gradually westward as they learned to exploit their rich environment by combining gardening with seasonal rounds of gathering and hunting. Because their sophisticated knowledge of the region made them skilled partners in the hunt for animal furs, the Ojibwes also entered the orbit of trading companies based in the East. The group never recognized a single tribal leadership, but many gathered each summer for religious ceremonies or for communal rice harvesting, hunting, and fishing activities, and many of these groups came to see themselves as bands that shared a common habitat and history.

As they moved west along what became the border between the United States and Canada, the Ojibwes were most commonly identified through these bands, small multifamily groups that clustered in regular places that were rich in resources. They followed political and religious leaders and expanded and contracted with the seasons. As they migrated across the immense interior landscape of North America, band and family loyalty or ties to a particular location or hunting ground became a powerful source of identity. Over time non-Indian traders joined these bands, and the traders' mixed-heritage descendants came to dominate their business relationships with the outside world. Ojibwes avoided the first American removal campaigns because U.S. settlers were slow to reach the upper Great Lakes. The first railroad connecting Chicago to Lake Superior, for example, was not completed until 1883, fourteen years after trains had begun running between the east and west coasts. Limited by the region's short growing season and dense forests, homesteaders moved to Kansas and Nebraska before they considered migration to Minnesota. As a consequence, while they agreed to establish a half dozen scattered reservations in treaties signed in 1854 and 1855, nineteenth-century Ojibwes saw little reason why an alliance with the Americans should cause them to alter their way of life. They relied on the federal government's promise that they could continue to harvest the resources of lands they had formally ceded so long as they did not come into conflict with settlers. The specifics of landownership were largely immaterial until the 1860s, when the fur trade waned and the timber industry began to expand north and west of St. Paul.[4]

The first discussion of Ojibwe removal occurred in March 1867, when ten leaders of bands the government called the Chippewas of the Mississippi agreed to a new treaty that carved the White Earth Reservation, an eight-hundred-thousand-acre "suitable farming region," out of their traditional territory in northwestern Minnesota.[5] The United States proposed that all the Ojibwe people in the state eventually relocate to White Earth. This process soon lagged, however, and both local white settlers and Minnesota's congressional delegation grew impatient.

After several years of debate the state's Republican U.S. senator, Knute Nelson, proposed a solution. Nelson was a Norwegian immigrant who had recently moved to the state's western prairies to participate in the region's agricultural land boom. He submitted a bill that would give members of Ojibwe bands the option of resettling immediately at White Earth or taking individual homesteads (called allotments) on their current reservations. Passed in January 1889, the Nelson Act also provided for the sale of any remaining "surplus" tribal land following a band's allotment or removal to White Earth. The proceeds from those sales would be deposited in a Chippewa fund to benefit all Ojibwes in the state.

In the summer of 1889 a three-member Chippewa Commission toured the state's remaining Ojibwe reserves to negotiate the agreements that were to initiate the distribution of allotments and the transfer of bands to White Earth. When the commission reached the community living along the shores of Mille Lacs Lake, the easy scenario imagined by Senator Nelson came to a halt. Instead of finding people willing to give up their subsistence lifestyle and relocate to "a suitable farming region" two hundred miles away, they met band leaders who confronted them with demands that reflected both a clear sense of their own history and a keen awareness of the promises government men had made to them over the previous three decades.

Henry Rice, a former fur trader who had been one of the state's early U.S. senators, chaired the Chippewa Commission. He was joined by Bishop Martin Marty, a former Catholic missionary in the Dakota Territory, and Joseph Whiting, a Wisconsin businessman. The commission began its four-day encounter at Mille Lacs with a series of welcoming speeches and a formal reading of the Nelson Act.[6] With these formalities completed, Shobaushkung, a Mille Lacs band leader whose principal residence lay along the western edge of the lake, rose to speak. In traditional Ojibwe style, Shobaushkung emphasized that he spoke "from the feeling of the young men, from the old men and from myself. Whatever is said," he added, "will be said in the name of the whole tribe here. . . ."[7] The next day Manzomaunay, another band leader, whose village lay at the opposite end of the group's territory on the south shore of the lake, offered his greeting but added that the group had many concerns beyond the prospect of acquiring a homestead at White Earth. Referring to Commissioner Rice's long experience in Minnesota Indian affairs, the chief observed, "[Y]ou are not ignorant of the amount of money that has been taken from our annuities in the past."[8]

The leaders' opening statements alluded to a complex and contentious history they knew Rice and the other commissioners understood and were eager to avoid. In fact Rice had been present in 1855, when the Mille Lacs agency was created by a treaty with the United States. He well knew that the treaty reserved portions of four townships on the shores of Mille Lacs Lake, together with three nearby islands, "for the permanent homes of the said Indians."[9] He also knew that the bands occupying these lands had peacefully continued their traditional way of life over the ensuing thirty-five years.

Despite the fact that the commissioners were meeting with a group of Ojibwe men, they were aware that the community they represented contained dozens of families that sustained a stable and satisfying existence at Mille Lacs Lake. Operating in family groups, they gathered fish and wild rice from the lake each summer. Women maintained small gardens that supplemented their families' diet in summer and produced surpluses to keep them through the long winter. After camping near one another during the warm months, families dispersed to hunting camps in the surrounding woods once the frosts came. In spring they returned to the lake to reassemble in small villages, collect sugar, and reestablish their gardens and fishing camps. When possible, trapping and occasional wage labor supplemented their incomes. This cycle of gardening and gathering had been largely unaffected by the arrival of lumbermen who coveted the Indians' virgin pine or by the commission's program of removal to White Earth.

For the people at Mille Lacs, the most frightening event of the previous three decades had occurred in 1862, when Dakota Indians in southern Minnesota had attacked the Santee agency and neighboring white settlements in a desperate attempt to escape starvation on a barren, mismanaged reservation. Frustrated by the government ineptitude that had produced the revolt, several of the state's Ojibwe bands had considered joining forces with the Dakotas and clearing Minnesota of Americans. But the leaders at Mille Lacs Lake, frightened by the prospect of retaliation from nearby white settlers, refused to support the rebellion. Instead, Shobaushkung and the other chiefs warned the Americans of the impending danger and pledged publicly that they would remain loyal to the United States. As a consequence, when hostilities ended and a new treaty, punishing those who had participated in the fighting was written, a separate article declared that "owing to the heretofore good conduct of the Mille Lacs Indians, they shall not be compelled to remove so long as they shall not in any way interfere with or in any manner molest the persons or property of the whites."[10]

Because Shobaushkung was one of the signers of the 1863 agreement, he understood how important it would be to maintain a policy of strict nonviolence. He told Henry Rice at the outset of the 1889 conference that "the Indians do not wish to do anything that may hurt the feelings of the honorable commissioners or mar the peace and friendship that exists between us." He also reminded the Americans of his tribe's past service. "You know very well," he told the delegation, "that at the time the country was in difficulty and there was an outbreak what was the attitude of the Mille Lacs Indians. . . . The loyalty they showed [then] they still preserve." But Shobaushkung had more on his mind than reminding Henry Rice of his loyalty. He went on to describe the meager recompense his followers had received for their good behavior. "It now seems as if this reservation was shaking all the time, on account of the excitement and conflicting interests," he declared. "We wish you to quell that shaking. We wish to remain here, quiet and at peace."[11]

From Shobaushkung's perspective, the reservation was "shaking all the time" because timber speculators and white farmers were eager to take possession of the tribe's land. He was aware that almost immediately after he had signed the 1863 agreement, local settlers had begun accusing him and his kinsmen of violence and drunkenness. Squatters had appeared, claiming illegal homesteads on the reservation, and local government officials had ignored the Indians'—and the Indian Office's—protests. Shobaushkung and his colleagues had quickly mounted an opposition to these incursions. In 1875 they had returned to Washington to insist that the Indian Office uphold its commitments.

At a meeting with the commissioner of Indian affairs during that visit, Shobaushkung protested that "[w]e have clean hands and clean hearts." He assured the officials that the pledge of friendship he and his followers had made in 1863 was unchanged, and he reminded the commissioner that the band's title to its land flowed directly from personal encounters with American leaders. "The Secretary of the Interior and the President said that we should be considered good Indians and remain at Mille Lacs so long as we want to," Shobaushkung declared. When the commissioner cautioned him that the provision of the treaty he was relying upon was rather vague, Shobaushkung shot back: "I know what was on the paper." When the commissioner raised the possibility of moving to White Earth, Shobaushkung was equally explicit. He repeated that his community was united in its desire to remain where they were. "I do not know why it is that the Mille Lacs Indians, men, women and children, should feel so strong an attachment to the lake," he mused, "but if we should hear at any time that a removal was to be made, we should feel very bad."[12]

FOURTEEN YEARS LATER, when he faced Henry Rice and the Chippewa Commission, Shobaushkung's position was unchanged. The chief was willing to have the government divide the reserve into individual landholdings and issue land titles to his kinsmen (as the Nelson Act provided), but his followers would not remove to White Earth. His position was remarkably similar to the one Sarah Winnemucca had taken in her conversations with Carl Schurz a decade earlier. The Mille Lacs chief was indifferent to the legal particulars of his land title (whether property was to be individually or communally owned), but he remained adamantly loyal to his ancestral homeland. Shobaushkung assured the commissioners that the entire community agreed with him. "They say they wish to have their allotments made here and made solid under their seats," he declared. "Solider and solider every move of their bodies; that is what we want."

Commissioner Rice was reassuring but vague. He told the council: "You are entitled to select for your allotments the lands called farming lands . . . we do not ask you to dispose of a foot of that. And there will be nothing done with the lands until you have your allotments."[13] At the same time, because he appreciated the extent of the local demand for Mille Lacs land, Rice did not mention the thousands of acres of tribal land already claimed by squatters. He also avoided the issue of the government's unwillingness to remove those trespassers from Mille Lacs territory. When one leader pressed him to promise that "the whites will be removed immediately" from the reservation, the old trader retreated to the language of bureaucracy: "Your words are taken down," he said. "We cannot answer that question as it is a matter to be referred to Washington. . . . There is only one thing for you to be done; and that is for you to keep quiet and disturb no one. Wait until you hear from the Great Father," Rice added. "If there is anything wrong, he will correct it."[14]

Assured by these general statements and their long personal association with Rice, the assembled leaders agreed to sign an agreement that contained no specific description of the lands to be allotted at Mille Lacs. Indeed, it declared that they would "forever relinquish . . . the right of occupancy on the Mille Lacs Reservation."[15] Understanding that the reservation would be replaced with a block of individual allotments, the tribe's leaders believed the last phrase referred to surplus communal land remaining after all individuals had been assigned homesteads. The band was cooperative, as was its custom, but it insisted on one more pledge. As Rice presented a written document for the tribal members to sign, Wahweyaycumig, a younger chief, who later described himself as one of Shobaushkung's followers, demanded that the commissioners promise they would enforce the agreement. He asked for a personal pledge. "Let us raise our hands as a token of pure friendship," Wahweyacumig said. The council record notes that everyone, Indians and whites alike, then stood and raised his hands, "while the Indians shouted, 'Ho!'"[16]

The commissioners' promise was empty. Despite the pledges of friendship, nothing was done in the aftermath of the 1889 agreement to remove white squatters from the Mille Lacs Reservation or to allot any land to the tribal members who had raised their hands with Henry Rice.[17] To make matters worse, federal officials stood idly by as new intruders appeared and demanded that federal authorities ratify their illegal titles. Exploiting an obscure provision of the original Nelson Act that promised to recognize holders of "valid, pre-emption or homestead claims" when reservation lands came on the market, a small army of white settlers suddenly invaded the reservation, claiming they had been there for years. Nathan Richardson, a sympathetic local attorney in nearby Little Falls, Minnesota, reported in February 1890 that "at the present time according to the statements of these [Mille Lacs] Indians, nearly all of the lands of the reservation are claimed by squatters."[18] His statement came only three months after Commissioner Rice had pledged his good intentions.

Despite his position as a community leader in a white town near the reservation border, Richardson could not ignore the fact that the tribe was being treated unfairly. He reported his concerns to the Indian Rights Association. "I have heard for some time that there was an association formed for the purpose of seeing that the Indians were fairly dealt by," Richardson wrote the group's secretary, Herbert Welsh, in early 1890. He added, "I shall be pleased to assist you in any way I can to prevent . . . a great wrong and swindle from being perpetrated upon the Indians."[19] Richardson recalled that he had been present when Henry Rice assured the Mille Lacs chiefs that "if they chose to they could remain upon their reservation," and he had heard the commissioner urge the Indians to remain peaceful. "They have therefore been quiet and allowed the squatters to come and build shanties all over the reservation. Nearly every Indian garden has a shanty put up in it," he added, but the Indians continued to "rely on the promises made to them and submit to the indignities heaped upon them . . . believing that the government will deal justly with them and fulfill all the promises made to them."[20]

The IRA's Welsh forwarded Richardson's report to the Indian Office, but no action was taken. As had been the case in Georgia and Indian Territory earlier in the century, trespassing settlers were creating "facts on the ground" that their political representatives were loath to contradict. As in Georgia, the squatters at Mille Lacs stayed. After a year of lobbying by Minnesota's congressional delegation and the timber interests that supported them, Secretary of the Interior John Noble ruled that the territory reserved for the Mille Lacs Ojibwes in 1855 had ceased to be a reservation in 1863 despite that treaty's pledge that the band would not be displaced so long as it avoided conflicts with local whites. The 1863 treaty pledge only created an "interest, or easement or privilege" within the former reservation, Noble wrote, not a formal land title. He added that the band's "interest" in its homeland could now be set aside because the department had been "assured by the chairman of [the Chippewa] commission (Henry Rice) of the Indians' consent to remove from these lands to White Earth."[21]

Noble's decision injected new energy into the effort to move the Mille Lacs band to White Earth. Relying on his private reading of the 1863 treaty language and Henry Rice's bogus report that the band was willing to relocate, Noble concluded that the band had no more than an "interest" in their lakeside homeland. The secretary also seemed to share Rice's baseless predictions. "Renewed efforts were made for the removal of the Indians," the commissioner declared, "with gratifying results." During the year following the commission's visit, the local land office validated thousands of acres of squatters' claims.[22] By October 1891 another visiting member of the Chippewa Commission declared that the band's leaders had no alternative but to leave. "I told them they must go to White Earth," Darwin Hall reported. "I told them it was very doubtful about their receiving any more payments where they now are, at Mille Lacs." Hall urged the Mille Lacs people to leave, but at least he was honest enough to recognize the injustice in his demand. After studying the transcript of Rice's 1889 council with the tribe, he reported to his superiors: "These Indians were made promises which it is impossible for us to fulfill."[23]

This increasingly energetic campaign for Mille Lacs removal had little effect on the band. About one hundred tribal members agreed to leave for White Earth in 1891, but a large number of that group later returned home to resume their annual round of farming and gathering. When a new administration took office in Washington in 1893, the Mille Lacs leaders petitioned the Democratic president to take action where his Republican predecessor had not. Writing in October 1894, Waweacomsek and eleven other leaders (including Shobaush-kung's son Meegeesee) urged Grover Cleveland to ignore the "strangers who are here for the purpose of dispossessing us. As we have never consented to give up our lands," the leaders declared, "we believe our right to them is paramount to that of any other person or persons." Assisted, perhaps, by their local ally Nathan Richardson, the group also proposed placing the issue before "a court of competent jurisdiction" and requested that annuity payments again be made at Mille Lacs. A recent government order requiring the Mille Lacs to travel to

White Earth to receive the annuities owed them, they declared, was "outrageously wrong and unworthy of a civilized government."[24]

Within months of submitting their petition, it was clear to Waweacomsek and his colleagues that Democrats were no more interested in challenging white squatters than Republicans had been. Despite Richardson's encouragement and the sympathy of the IRA, they had not been able to win a hearing for their complaints. The Indian Office seemed prepared to ignore them until they accepted their fate and relocated to White Earth. At this point, exactly five years after their encounter with Henry Rice and the Chippewa Commission, the chiefs at Mille Lacs decided to take their fight to the American capital.

LOBBYING IN WASHINGTON, D.C.

As they considered how best to proceed, Shobaushkung and his colleagues recruited a new ally, Gustave H. Beaulieu. Gus Beaulieu was the grandson of Bazil Hudon dit Beaulieu, a North West Fur Company trader who had come to Lake Superior in the first decade of the nineteenth century and married into an Ojibwe family. Bazil's son Clement had also become a trader and had married an Ojibwe woman. Clement managed trading posts in Wisconsin and Minnesota and served frequently as an official translator at treaty councils. He had accompanied the Chippewa Commission to Mille Lacs in 1889.

Most Ojibwes had mixed feelings about the Beaulieus. Bazil and Clement had been important middlemen and advisers for both Indians and whites, but they were also commercially ambitious and frequently self-serving. Ojibwe leaders were also unsure of Gus. This third-generation Beaulieu had worked as a timber agent for the Northern

Pacific Railroad in the 1870s, helping the company acquire valuable real estate, and he had been an early settler at White Earth, operating a number of small businesses and a short-lived newspaper, the *Progress*. He eventually found work with the federal government, serving as a translator and clerk at the U.S. marshal's office and the office of the U.S. attorney. Familiar with the law but with no standing before the bar, Gus approached the beleaguered Mille Lacs leaders in 1895 and offered to represent them as their attorney. With few other prospects, the chiefs readily accepted.

In March 1895 Beaulieu prepared a new petition for the Interior Department that he hoped might spark formal negotiations with the authorities. Beaulieu's letter was a curious document. It repeated the Indians' charge that they had suffered "inhuman" treatment and declared "there is not a band of Indians . . . that is entitled to more consideration," but he also hinted that it still might be possible to move the group to White Earth. In fact, Beaulieu told the secretary of the interior that his father, Clement, had advised Henry Rice to use diplomacy with the band. He was sure persuasion and sympathy would produce results. "I know the nature of the Indians too well to believe that coercive measures will secure their removal to White Earth," Beaulieu wrote. "Conciliatory means alone should be used to secure this."[25]

While their attorney fished for a response from the Interior Department bureaucracy, his clients in central Minnesota restated their determination to stay. Three months after Beaulieu's letter, a group of chiefs, headed by Wahweyaycumig, who now described himself as Shobaushkung's successor, met with Nathan Richardson and asked him to forward a new petition to President Cleveland. In addition to asking for a return to the practice of disbursing annuities at Mille Lacs, the chiefs implored U.S. officials "to remove from among us the pale faces that are trying to take from us our lands" and "to give us what you in a most solemn manner promised us."[26]

The band maintained this two-pronged approach for most of the 1890s. Beaulieu sought a negotiated solution with officials in the Indian Office while the chiefs at Mille Lacs insisted that the federal government live up to its past commitments. They repeated this position in 1896, when the General Land Office announced that 4,833 acres of land within the reservation remained "unclaimed." Tribal leaders immediately demanded that these parcels be allotted to them.[27] Citing Secretary Noble's previous assertion that the band's reservation no longer existed, the Interior Department refused, and the stalemate continued.

When the McKinley administration took office in 1897, Gus Beaulieu, Wahweyaycumig, and Meegeesee traveled to Washington, D.C., to present their case to the new leadership of the Indian Office. "One of the objects of their visit," the local *Princeton Union* reported, "is to find out what right the white men have to go on their reservation."[28] The Mille Lacs lobbyists were facing an increasingly hostile political environment. The American settlers at Mille Lacs and their political allies across Minnesota were now offering their own version of recent events. They rejected the band's reliance on past treaties, substituting instead a rationale based on the language of race. Indians who insisted on staying at Mille Lacs were backward people, they argued, too ignorant to take advantage of the promising opportunities provided at White Earth. They were simply "old bucks" wishing to live out their days in the woods. This image of recalcitrant, ignorant Indians unwilling to embrace the government's progressive programs fitted neatly with the view of McKinley's commissioner of Indian affairs, a small-town Republican operative from Wisconsin named William Jones, who decreed that the Mille Lacs families would be better off at White

Earth, "where good lands are available for them and where they can better receive the care of the Government. Past experience demonstrates," Jones wrote, "that as long as the occupancy of the Mille Lacs lands is in dispute . . . the Indians will be slow to remove to the White Earth reservation where their condition could be greatly improved."[29]

This logic of removal took legal form in May 1898, when Congress passed a joint resolution that declared "all public lands" within the Mille Lacs Reservation to be "subject to entry by any bona fide qualified settler" and proclaimed that all previous homestead or preemption claims "shall be received and treated in all respects as if made upon any of the public lands of the United States."[30] The resolution had been proposed by the Duluth congressman Page Morris and supported by other members of the state's congressional delegation. Gus Beaulieu reported to the Interior Department that Chief Wahweyaycumig and other band leaders opposed Morris's bill, but Secretary Cornelius Bliss countered that the band had "parted with all their rights to the lands in this reservation" when it reached an agreement with Henry Rice and his commission in 1889. The protesting Indians were simply opponents of progress. Bliss did not mention the 1863 treaty or the promises made during the Chippewa Commission negotiations or the tribe's decade-long campaign to acquire allotments at Mille Lacs. With breathtaking duplicity the secretary noted that families at Mille Lacs "might have" claimed allotments there in 1889 but that their opportunity had passed. He continued, "[I]t is not apparent why the equities of settlers who have gone upon these lands . . . and made valuable improvements on them should not be recognized."[31]

Remarkably, the 1898 congressional resolution had no more effect on the band's determination to remain at Mille Lacs than any of the government's previous actions. The Indians refused to leave, and their "attorney," Gus Beaulieu, continued to look for a deal. He suggested that cash would persuade band members to leave their homes. In 1900 Beaulieu, now joined by the Washington claims attorney Daniel Henderson, convinced Minnesota Senator Knute Nelson that an appropriation of twenty-five thousand dollars would be enough to compensate the group for its losses and prompt it to decamp for White Earth. Nelson introduced his bill, but the Mille Lacs chiefs rejected it out of hand. A council meeting on the reservation instead approved a resolution condemning the white settlers who had "confiscated" their property and adding that they would "not accept or consider" any proposal that required their removal.[32]

Thus far during the Mille Lacs band's struggle the population of white settlers on the reservation had been sufficiently small that there had been few face-to-face conflicts between the Indians and their encroaching neighbors. Ojibwe families had maintained their traditional gathering traditions and had continued hunting, trapping, and gardening along the southern and western shores of Mille Lacs Lake. As the white population increased during the 1890s, several band members had also found occasional employment from local whites as day laborers and domestics. Despite more than a decade of legal and political wrangling, it appeared that Indians and whites were coexisting peacefully. A visiting government agent described the community in 1902 as "self supporting and well dressed." He noted as well that "their white neighbors speak very highly of them and say that they obtain credit readily from the neighboring merchants." Tribal members "meet their obligations with as much promptness as the white people in the community."[33]

In the new century, however, the press of white settlement began to move the two communities toward confrontation. Settlers and local landowners complained that Mille Lacs families were trespassing on their property, while Indians protested that the settlers' (who they insisted were squatters) were now interfering with their hunting, gardening, and gathering activities. The most visible conflict occurred on land claimed by Chief Shobaushkung's son Meegeesee at a site that encompassed his father's former lakeside village. Meegeesee had attempted to file a homestead entry on several lots adjacent to his father's previously recognized plot of land near Shobaushkung Point in 1891 but had been turned away by the local land office.

At the end of the decade a white settler, Olof Johnson, filed a homestead claim at Shobaushkung Point and initiated proceedings to evict Meegeesee for trespassing. When Meegeesee challenged the action, Johnson claimed his title had been guaranteed by the 1898 resolution confirming all homestead entries on the reservation. The chief and his supporters continued to protest Johnson's presence, and the case was forwarded to the secretary of the interior. In July 1900, just as the Nelson proposal to pay the Mille Lacs band twenty-five thousand dollars to remove to White Earth was scheduled for congressional approval, the Interior Department decided the case in Meegeesee's favor. Secretary Ethan Hitchcock ruled that Meegeesee and his family had lived on the land long before Johnson had arrived and that the chief "was driven from the land by the threats of the defendant, accompanied by a display of fire arms, followed by his arrest. . . ." Meegeesee had only been released, the secretary added, "upon his promise not to return to the land, except to gather his growing crop."[34]

Similar disputes surfaced in other parts of the reserve. In May 1901 the local sheriff evicted twenty-five families from land held by a white settler, marched them to the nearest highway, and burned their houses. The following month, another elder, GoGee, reported that a white settler named William Wallace had suddenly appeared at his home, claiming land on which he had been living for forty years. "I relied wholly upon promises made by the commission . . . of 1889," he declared. He asked the Indian Office "to render me such assistance as may secure from confiscation of my houses and other property. . . ." On June 7 a white businessman and notary public in nearby Vineland, Minnesota, forwarded a statement "the chiefs of the Mille Lacs Band" had asked him to record for them. They insisted that they were being "forced off" land they had occupied for fifty years. They also claimed that settlers had invaded the tribal burying ground that had been specifically set aside in the 1898 resolution.

These reports soon reached the Indian Rights Association in Philadelphia, and the group filed its own protests with the Indian Office. In October 1901 the IRA distributed a pamphlet to its national membership list, *The Urgent Case of the Mille Lacs Indians*. The association's report opened with the assertion that "probably no tribe of Indians in the United States has suffered to a greater extent by reason of unfulfilled promises and agreements on the part of the United States. . . ."[35] No longer an obscure case of bureaucratic confusion, the band's predicament was now being described publicly as an example of "unfulfilled promises." The chiefs had found at least one sympathetic forum.

Samuel Brosius, the Indian Rights Association's Washington lobbyist, wrote the Indian Office again in November, demanding that the commissioner come to the Indians' assistance. Brosius suggested that he consider temporarily suspending its prohibition against tribes hiring private lawyers to represent them. "Either the government is . . . duty bound to protect these wards of the Nation by bringing an action to dispossess the intruders," Brosius wrote, "or to allow the Indians authority to employ counsel to prosecute proceedings on their own account. . . . Justice calls for immediate action." Brosius pointed out that in light of Meegeesee's victory over Olof Johnson the previous year, it might be possible to ensure that every Indian with an improved homestead could be granted an allotment at Mille Lacs.[36]

The Indian Office rejected both of Brosius's alternatives. Instead of intervening to protect the band's land titles or encouraging a challenge to the local squatters in court, Commissioner Jones decided to take up Gus Beaulieu's idea of offering the chiefs cash in exchange for their promise to move to White Earth. The administration endorsed Senator Nelson's bill based on Beaulieu's idea and approved new language in the resolution that had been inserted at the urging of the Mille Lacs chiefs. It stipulated that Indians who had "leased or purchased" land on the reserve "shall not be required to remove. . . ." Thanks to the tribe's leaders, the House bill also declared that no money would be disbursed until "the Indians shall, by proper council proceedings," have accepted the measure and "declared the manner in which they wish the money disbursed." Sympathetic legislators also amended the bill to raise the proposed payment from twenty-five to forty thousand dollars.[37] When approved in May 1902, the bill seemed a fitting reward for the band's long campaign to remain at Mille Lacs.

But as had been true in the past, appearances were deceiving. When the "proper council proceedings" called for in the bill took place at Mille Lacs the following August, the Ojibwes gathered there were confronted by Inspector James McLaughlin, an imposing former blacksmith who was the Indian Office's chief enforcer. With a style that Andrew Jackson would have admired, McLaughlin was a blunt and aggressive negotiator who had the habit of lecturing and bullying tribal leaders until they agreed to his proposals. (He had first made a name for himself twelve years earlier at the Standing Rock agency in North Dakota, when he ordered the predawn arrest of Sitting Bull, a decision that triggered the chief's bloody death at the hands of tribal policemen.) At Mille Lacs, McLaughlin, who, like other Indian Office administrators, affected the title of major when dealing with Indians, came quickly to the point. "You have no claim to the lands upon this reservation," he told the assembly in their first session. Following the administrative line first articulated by Secretary Noble, he rejected the pledge contained in the 1863 treaty and dismissed the 1889 Nelson Act's promise that Indians gaining title to land at Mille Lacs need not leave for White Earth. "You will be protected," McLaughlin said of those who chose to remain, "but if any of you have such rights they are very few. There is no reason why you people should drift around this country and work for other people all the time." Echoing the sunny rhetoric of other Indian Office officials, he promised his audience that at White Earth, "[Y]ou can live happily and be independent in a very few years."[38]

The band's leaders were prepared for McLaughlin's pitch. Back in his community after his spring lobbying trip to Washington, Wahweyaycumig innocently pressed the government's representative to read and explain the 1902 statute's provision recognizing the rights of those who had acquired land on the reservation. The Mille Lacs headman recounted again the story of Henry Rice's public pledge in 1889. "I asked him to call the creator to witness that he was speaking the truth," Wahweyaycumig recalled. "I have not realized any of the promises that were made to me, neither do I recognize this act that you have read to me today as the one that was presented and ratified at the time Mr. Rice was here to treat with us." McLaughlin tried clumsily to steer the discussion back to removal but to no avail. As the gap between the speakers grew more apparent, GoGee, who had complained to the Indian Office a year earlier about squatters invading his home, voiced a question that must have occurred to many in this embattled group: "What is the reason why the white men wish my removal from these parts so much?"[39] McLaughlin had no answer.

After three days the council was deadlocked. Major McLaughlin insisted on removal; tribal leaders insisted on some acknowledgment of Henry Rice's 1889 pledge. Suddenly, as the sun began to set over the proceedings, Wahweyaycumig suggested something new. Since Congress had authorized forty thousand dollars to compensate tribal members for losses suffered at the hands of squatters, he observed, Mr. McLaughlin could demonstrate the government's good faith by surveying those damages and authorizing an immediate payment to the tribe. After the money was "placed in our hands," the chief suggested, "we will confer with you further. . . ." The government man was tempted. Why not? The money could be paid here, McLaughlin suggested, "provided you promise that you will remove after said payment." As if on cue, another chief, who had previously been silent, spoke up. Aindusogeeshig suggested that ten thousand of the forty-thousand-dollar payment authorized by Congress should be set aside for the purchase of land at Mille Lacs for those who wished to stay. He proposed using money appropriated for removal to buy land in the territory from which the government wished them removed! Not given to humor or irony, McLaughlin suddenly realized that he had been outmaneuvered. He instantly retreated. Setting aside money for land purchases, he assured the chief gruffly, "is something we cannot do under the appropriation act." The Mille Lacs leaders disagreed. After all, Wahweyaycumig and Meegeesee had lobbied on behalf of the bill and knew its language intimately. Aware that the new statute granted the chiefs the right to declare "the manner in which they wish the money disbursed," Aindusogeeshig matched McLaughlin's bluntness with his own. Referring to the conditions his chiefs had managed to insert into the most recent legislation, the chief declared, "These conditions as stated are the conditions upon which we are willing to accept the proposition."[40]

Gus Beaulieu, who had also participated in drafting the legislation in Washington, suddenly broke his silence and repeated the tribe's position. Five tracts of land at Mille Lacs were available, he noted, and they could be purchased with tribal funds. Following this purchase, anyone who wished to could remain to receive an individual portion. Anyone who preferred White Earth could move there. In addition, Beaulieu explained, those who removed to White Earth but who wished later to return to Mille Lacs could do that as well. GoGee quickly affirmed Beaulieu's statement. "These are our wishes," he declared. The assembly quickly adjourned. One can only imagine the color spreading across Major McLaughlin's face as the Indian leaders dispersed, leaving him alone at sunset beside Mille Lacs Lake.[41]

The next day McLaughlin accepted the council's offer and embarked on a weeklong appraisal of damages. His deputy, the White Earth agent Simon Michelet, while noting that he could not promise that the ten thousand dollars set aside would be approved by his superiors, was encouraging: "If you have got money enough you can buy all the land around this lake. . . ." While Michelet and McLaughlin compiled the roster of damages, the tribal council convened separately to draw up a proposal for the distribution of the promised forty thousand dollars. When the government representatives returned on August 30 to meet again with the chiefs, Wahweyaycumig and his colleagues were ready with a formal contract, presumably drawn up with the assistance of Beaulieu and, perhaps, his Washington colleague Daniel Henderson. The document committed the tribe to leave Mille Lacs, provided the government accepted the tribe's wishes regarding the disbursement of the $40,000 in compensation funds. Those wishes, spelled out in a second document presented at the meeting, included setting aside

$10,000 for land purchases, distributing $18,500 to individual tribal members at Mille Lacs, and paying Beaulieu and Henderson $6,500 for services rendered on their behalf since 1898.[42]

After some hesitation the Indian Office approved the 1902 agreement. The compensation funds were distributed, but Beaulieu never purchased the land, as he had promised. (He claimed obstruction from local landowners; his critics charged that he had given in to pressure from local whites or that he had simply pocketed the money.) Faced with yet another defeat, many tribal members began moving to White Earth, even though several families acquired land on the new reservation and then sold it in order to buy property back at Mille Lacs. By 1904 sixty-nine people (mostly families with young children) had relocated to White Earth, raising the refugee population there to approximately five hundred. By 1911 the Mille Lacs "removals" numbered approximately one thousand, among them Wahweyaycumig, the Shobaushkung protégé who had been acting as spokesman for the group.

But 284 of Wahweyaycumig's kinsmen, including Shobaushkung's son Meegeesee, refused to leave their Mille Lacs homeland.[43] This tiny group of families clung to small landholdings and clustered in shoreline villages around senior men like Meegeesee, GoGee, and Wadena, the son of Monzomaunay, one of the chiefs who had confronted Henry Rice in 1889. Many band members developed an itinerant pattern, moving back and forth between Mille Lacs and other Minnesota reservations.[44] The community's leaders had consistently defied the government's removal orders, but neither their tenacity nor their inventiveness had succeeded in forcing the United States to fulfill Henry Rice's pledge. It was in this atmosphere of struggle, eroding membership, and social fragmentation that the Mille Lacs Ojibwes turned to the courts.

AMERICAN INDIANS AND
THE U.S. COURT OF CLAIMS

At the end of the nineteenth century there was no clear avenue open to tribes, like the Mille Lacs Ojibwes, who wished to air their grievances in American courts. For most of the nation's history Indian leaders had aired their complaints against the United States at treaty councils. There U.S. officials compensated the tribes for past crimes while making a new round of promises regarding the future.[45] When formal treaty making ended in 1871, tribes no longer had a ready means of resolving their complaints against the federal government.

American citizens with grievances against the federal government could take their petitions to the U.S. Court of Claims, established in 1855, but a congressional resolution passed in 1863 barred Indians from the tribunal.[46] The only option for tribal leaders wishing to pursue claims against the federal government was to petition Congress for special jurisdictional legislation that would direct the court to hear their suits. Jurisdictional bills required a congressional sponsor, political allies who would argue on its behalf, and an administration willing to sign it into law once it was passed. Only then could litigation, itself an expensive and arduous process, begin. Because most decisions in the Court of Claims were later appealed to the U.S. Supreme Court, even a positive outcome of a case in its first hearing could be delayed for several years before an agreed-upon settlement figure could be authorized by Congress. All this legal activity would occur with the knowledge that the court would only make cash settlements. It had no power to return illegally taken land to plaintiffs.

Tribes exploring the use of the U.S. Court of Claims in the late nineteenth century battled the indifference of legislators and the hostility of an American public whose images of Native Americans had been shaped by lurid headlines that described Indian violence and rarely mentioned the government's broken promises.

The Choctaws were the first tribe to gain access to the Court of Claims. Their suit arose from damages suffered during the removal era. Interestingly, the tribe's chief lobbyist during the 1870s was Peter Pitchlynn, James McDonald's childhood friend, who had moved west with his kinsmen in 1831 and later served as a tribal chief. The Choctaw claim began in 1855, when the Choctaws and the United States signed a treaty that ordered the U.S. Senate to investigate the tribe's demand for compensation for improved lands lost during removal.[47] The case grew more complicated after the Civil War, as the tribe added new demands and groups of lawyers battled over their shares of the expected award.[48] After treaty making ended, Chief Pitchlynn moved permanently to Washington to lobby on behalf of a jurisdictional bill that was finally approved in 1881, two weeks after Pitchlynn's death. (Fittingly, the Choctaw leader was buried in Washington, D.C., in the same congressional cemetery where Chief Pushmataha, attended by James McDonald and other members of the Choctaw delegation, had been laid to rest in the fall of 1824.)

The Court of Claims issued its decision on the Choctaws' suit in January 1886, and in 1888 Congress appropriated more than $2.8 million to resolve the dispute. The tribe's victory quickly established a pathway other tribes proved eager to follow. In the forty-nine years following the passage of the Choctaws' tribal jurisdictional act (1881–1930), dozens of tribes petitioned Congress for similar legislation. Thirty-five cases were permitted to proceed to the court.[49] As the list of claims cases grew, the locations of tribes filing complaints spread gradually across the continent. The first ten Indian cases to be decided by the Court of Claims exclusively involved tribes that had been forced west to Indian Territory in the 1830s. The second ten cases, decided between 1895 and 1909, included two tribes from Minnesota and the Dakotas. By the time the court heard the third group of ten cases, only one involved an Indian Territory tribe (the Creeks), and none of them arose directly from the removal era. This third group (decided between 1910 and 1928) included cases originating in Colorado, Minnesota, the Dakotas, and Washington State.[50]

The growing list of tribes pursuing claims also revealed that Indian leaders were using the court to air general indictments of government incompetence and deception. In 1910, for example, the Otoe and Missouria tribe won approval for a jurisdictional act that directed the Court of Claims "to hear and determine all claims . . . of whatsoever nature which . . . said tribes of Indians may have or claim to have against the United States."[51] Similarly expansive claims were authorized for most of the tribes that were admitted to the Court of Claims over the next twenty years: the Omahas, the Pawnees, the Sisseton and Wahpeton Sioux, the Stockbridge of Wisconsin, the Creeks, the Yankton Sioux, and the Indians of Fort Berthold.[52]

The proliferation of complaints before the Court of Claims also triggered the growth of a small community of politically sophisticated Washington, D.C., lawyers who stood ready to be the Indians' advocates. In the early years of claims litigation, tribal attorneys were Washington claims agents, who specialized in winning financial settlements from the federal government. The lawyer who represented the Choctaws in 1881, for example, was Samuel Shellabarger, a former Ohio congressman, whose clients ranged from the Union Pacific Railroad to a group of unhappy stonecutters that complained about the pay they received for their work on the State, War, and Navy Building next door to the White House. The lawyers who represented tribal claims in the 1890s also included John J. Hemphill, a former congressman from South Carolina, and Marion Butler, North Carolina's Populist senator from 1895 to 1901. Butler, who opened his Washington law practice after he left the Senate, frequently worked in tandem with Josiah M. Vale, another Washington claims specialist.

In the twentieth century several individuals began to specialize in Indian claims litigation. Prominent among them was Daniel Henderson, who had worked with Marion Butler and Josiah Vale before taking on cases by himself. At the turn of the century Henderson represented the Eastern Cherokees before Congress and the Indian Office and had become a confidant of Minnesota senator Moses Clapp, the chairman of the upper house's Indian Affairs Committee. Henderson was also a frequent correspondent of Samuel Brosius, the Kansas attorney who had become the Indian Rights Association's Washington representative. It is likely that Brosius's correspondence with Nathan Richardson brought the Mille Lacs leaders and Gus Beaulieu to Henderson's door. Henderson assisted Beaulieu in securing passage of the forty-thousand-dollar appropriation in 1902 (earning twenty-five hundred dollars for his services), and in the aftermath of McLaughlin's failed attempt to resolve the conflicts on the reservation, he was no doubt interested in devising a new (and profitable) approach to resolving the tribe's predicament.[53]

THE MILLE LACS OJIBWES GO TO COURT

The Mille Lacs band's petition to the Court of Claims did not originate in central Minnesota, but in Washington, D.C., where two non-Indian actors—Daniel Henderson and Duluth congressman James Bede, linked by the shady presence of Gus Beaulieu—started the process. When they entered the court in 1909, the Mille Lacs band transferred the question of what Henry Rice had promised in 1889 from the political arena, where legislators, lobbyists, and Indian Office bureaucrats made the rules, to the legal world, where judges operated according to established procedures and precedents. Despite its distance from their Minnesota homeland, then, this new forum vastly enhanced the visibility of the Mille Lacs struggle. It would also enable the band's leaders to air their complaints in an institution charged with delivering justice to those who appeared before it. With conditions at home deteriorating and members drifting away to White Earth, imperfect justice in court would have been preferable to the indifference and hostility they had experienced elsewhere.

Henderson drafted a jurisdictional bill on behalf of the Mille Lacs band, which Congressman Bede filed in March 1906. No action was taken on the proposal until February 1908, when Senator Clapp's committee approved it and moved it to the Senate floor. It received final approval on February 15, 1909. The new statute, an Act for the Relief of the Mille Lac Band of Chippewa Indians, authorized the court "to hear and determine a suit or suits to be brought . . . on account of losses sustained . . . by reason of the opening of the Mille Lac Reservation. . . ." Barely ninety days following passage of the act, the band's attorneys filed a complaint that sought three million dollars in compensation for the government's negligence.[54]

An obscure sentence within the new law revealed its Washington pedigree. Unlike the 1902 bill, which had recognized the Mille Lacs band's authority over the allocation of the money Congress appropriated for its relief, the 1909 statute instructed the Court of Claims to determine the attorneys' fees that might ultimately be paid from the funds "due said band or to the Chippewa Indians of Minnesota." The

Mille Lacs chiefs were not consulted about the fees their lawyers would collect, and they certainly would have objected to the statute's vague language regarding the recipients of the financial award requested ("said band or to the Chippewa Indians of Minnesota"). Those provisions of the bill reflected an energetic lobbying campaign that had taken place behind the scenes while Bede's proposal worked its way through the House and Senate.

Work on the Mille Lacs jurisdictional act began in 1905, immediately following Gus Beaulieu's failure to purchase land as discussed with James McLaughlin. Furious with their "attorney," the chiefs declared that he was no longer authorized to represent them. Meegeesee and the other chiefs remaining at Mille Lacs also charged that Beaulieu had persuaded Wahweyaycumig and his family to accept an allotment at White Earth with the promise that the government agent at the reservation would recognize him as the headman of all his neighbors who agreed to relocate.[55] Despite the band chiefs' disapproval of their efforts, Beaulieu and Henderson had begun petitioning Congressman Bede to file a jurisdictional bill to recognize the tribe's mistreatment and provide a final settlement for the dispute. Chauncey Richardson, a Washington attorney who had represented White Earth Indians in separate proceedings, later reported that following the filing of Bede's bill, he had corresponded with Beaulieu and Daniel Henderson and accompanied Wahweyaycumig and two other "removed" Mille Lacs leaders when they testified before a House Indian Affairs panel in early 1908. (Beaulieu was also present, serving as translator.)[56]

As Bede's bill moved toward passage, Richardson also served as an emissary from Beaulieu to the Indian Office and proposed himself as one of the lawyers who would represent the Indians once the matter reached the Court of Claims. George B. Edgerton, the son of a former

Mohawk leader Joseph Brant, painted in London in 1776 by one of the city's leading portrait artists, George Romney.

The site of Fort Niagara, where numerous wartime conferences between British and Native military leaders took place. It was at Fort Niagara that Joseph Brant first denounced the borders granted to the United States in the Paris Peace Accords.

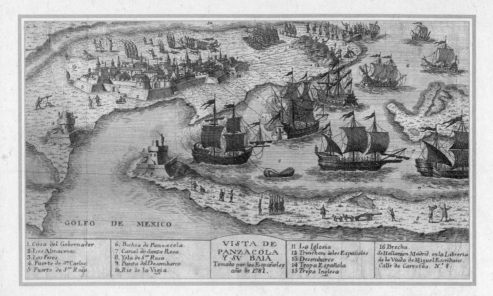

An engraving memorializing Spain's 1781 victory at Pensacola, Florida, over a combined British/Native force that included Alexander McGillivray and a group of Creek warriors.

Pushmataha, the Choctaw leader who fought with Andrew Jackson against the British in the War of 1812, negotiated for his tribe at Doaks Stand and headed a tribal delegation to Washington, D.C., in 1824. Pushmataha's sudden death during that journey propelled lawyer James McDonald into the leadership of the delegation.

Benjamin Franklin with the coonskin cap he wore while a diplomat in Paris in an effort to present himself to the French as a simple, rustic American.

Peter Pitchlynn, the son of a Scottish trader and a Choctaw woman and a close friend of James McDonald. Pitchlynn later emigrated to Indian Territory with his tribe and became its principal chief.

William Potter Ross (Cherokee)
in an engraving made in the 1870s.

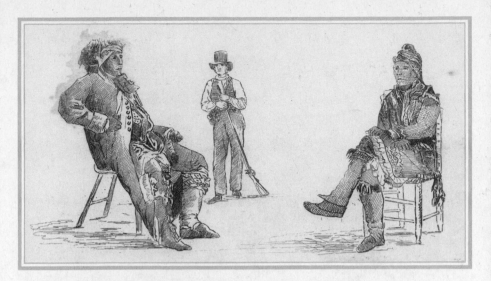

Chiefs of the Creek Nation and a Georgia Squatter, drawn from life with a camera lucida by Basil Hall during his tour of North America in 1827–28. Using a series of mirrors, the camera lucida allowed artists to trace a living image directly onto a drawing surface.

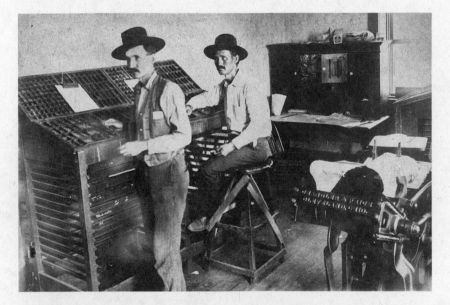

Typesetters at work in the offices of *The Cherokee Advocate* newspaper, Tahlequah, Indian Territory, c. 1880. William Potter Ross was an early editor of the tribal newspaper.

Delegates to an intertribal conference at Okmulgee, Creek Nation, Indian Territory in the 1870s. William Potter Ross presided over the first of these intertribal conferences in 1870.

Sarah Winnemucca (Paiute) in the Victorian attire she used for her formal appearances.

*S*arah Winnemucca in the "Indian costume" she used when speaking about Paiute culture.

As a U.S. military officer and the first Native Commissioner of Indian Affairs, Ely Parker (Seneca) negotiated with Cherokee leaders (including William Potter Ross) in 1865 and corresponded with Sarah Winnemucca. After leaving Washington, he held an obscure post in the New York Police Department and grew disillusioned with the government's Indian policy.

An Ojibwe village
at Mille Lacs Lake, Minnesota, 1885.

Mille Lacs Ojibwe tribal delegation, Washington, D.C., 1899. The tribe's unofficial lawyer, Gus Beaulieu, is on the right in the rear. Leaders in the first row are (left to right), O gee tub, Wahweyaycumig, Aindusogeeshig, and Nay tah waushence.

Leaders of the Mille Lacs resistance, c. 1910. Left to right: Wadena, Reverend Frank Paquette, Meegeesee.

Thomas Sloan (Omaha) at his desk in Washington, D. C., 1920.

Carlos Montezuma (Yavapai)
and his wife, Marie, c. 1920.

WASSAJA

INDIAN BUREAU

FREEDOM'S SIGNAL FOR THE INDIANS

Masthead of the first issue of Carlos Montezuma's
reform magazine, *Wassaja*, 1916.

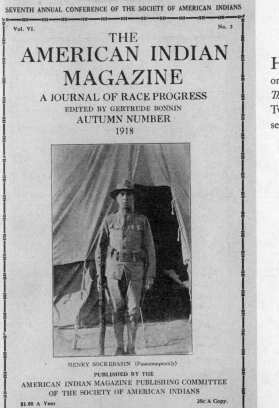

SEVENTH ANNUAL CONFERENCE OF THE SOCIETY OF AMERICAN INDIANS

Vol. VI.   No. 3

THE

AMERICAN INDIAN
MAGAZINE

A JOURNAL OF RACE PROGRESS

EDITED BY GERTRUDE BONNIN

AUTUMN NUMBER

1918

HENRY SOCKEBASIN (Passamaquoddy)

PUBLISHED BY THE

AMERICAN INDIAN MAGAZINE PUBLISHING COMMITTEE
OF THE SOCIETY OF AMERICAN INDIANS

$1.00 A Year   25c A Copy.

Henry Sockebasin (Pasmaquoddy)
on the cover of the Fall 1918 issue of
The American Indian Magazine.
Twelve thousand Native Americans
served in uniform during World War I.

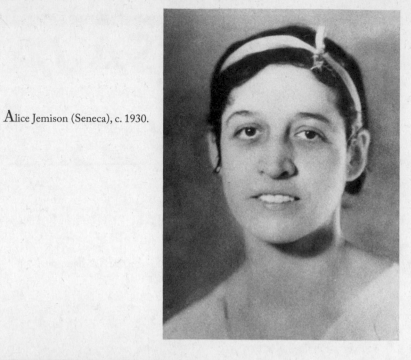

Alice Jemison (Seneca), c. 1930.

D'Arcy McNickle (Salish) during his early years at the Bureau of Indian Affairs.

Robert Yellowtail (Crow), left,
and Richard Sanderville (Blackfeet), 1930s.

National Congress of American Indian leaders, 1950s. D'Arcy McNickle, rear left. Front row (left to right) Helen Peterson (Sioux), Joe Garry (Coeur d'Alene), Ruth Bronson (Cherokee).

D'Arcy McNickle and Navajo elder, c. 1960.

John F. Kennedy, Jacqueline Kennedy, and Michigan Governor G. Mennen Williams greet NCAI leader Frank George (Nez Perce) in Hyannisport, Massachusetts, August 1960.

Robert F. Kennedy and Taos leaders, New York City, 1966.

Vine Deloria, Jr. (Sioux), 2005.

U.S. senator, a former Minnesota assistant attorney general, and a partner in the St. Paul law firm of Edgerton, Wickwire, and Rice, also joined the case.[57] Beaulieu, who referred to Edgerton at one point as "my lawyer," noted in 1908, as the jurisdictional bill moved toward passage, that he had conferred with Edgerton and drawn up an agreement with him respecting the Mille Lacs matter.[58]

A few weeks after finalizing his agreement with his very well-connected attorney, Beaulieu served as secretary and interpreter at a meeting of the Mille Lacs Indians who had resettled at White Earth. With Wahweyaycumig presiding, council members approved a resolution on December 15 authorizing George Selkirk to represent them in Congress and the courts for ten years. They promised Selkirk 15 percent of whatever "may be awarded, allowed, secured, invested or appropriated" as a result. Five weeks later, on January 23, 1909, a similar council convened at Mille Lacs. Beaulieu again served as interpreter. The council assented to the resolutions passed at White Earth. Two weeks after the second council meeting and one week before the final enactment of the Mille Lacs jurisdictional act George Selkirk signed over his rights as tribal attorney to George B. Edgerton.[59] The proposed statute did not contain the usual provision requiring tribal attorneys to submit their contracts to the Indian Office for prior approval. But the secretary of the interior forwarded the final legislation to the White House on February 15 nonetheless. He assured the president that he did not consider the missing provision "failure . . . as sufficient cause for the veto of the Act."[60]

The complaint filed by the Mille Lacs band on May 29, 1909, was signed by Edgerton and Chauncey Richardson, the latter listed as "of counsel." Despite its establishment origins and dubious provisions, the petition finally brought the Ojibwes' twenty-year struggle into a prominent public forum. The band's statement declared that all but

160 acres of the 62,000-acre Mille Lacs Reservation had been "wrong-fully and unlawfully opened to public settlement and entry" and requested three million dollars as compensation. Edgerton quickly began collecting depositions and assembling documents. He and his team, which grew to include the Milwaukee appeals attorney Frederick Houghton and Harvey Clapp, the son of the Minnesota senator who chaired the Indian Affairs Committee, also quickly prepared briefs to support their case. Houghton and Edgerton appeared before the court on behalf of the band when the case was argued in March 1911.[61]

The Mille Lacs leadership supported the suit despite the many compromises that had been made on the road to court. Beaulieu was untrustworthy, the band was divided, and the list of lawyers demanding compensation was growing steadily, but the chiefs were eager to be heard. All the major band leaders at both White Earth and Mille Lacs gave extensive depositions to document their complaints. Their testimony vividly underscored the extent of injustice that had been perpetrated against them. It created a solid archive of evidence that could not be disputed or denied.

The process of taking depositions began in July 1909 and continued well into the fall. The aging Mille Lacs headmen made compelling witnesses. Meegeesee, Wahweyaycumig, and others repeated the history of their band with consistency and the power of first-person narration. Many individuals described Henry Rice's 1889 pledge, and several pointed out the various deceitful tactics local settlers and government agents had used to prod them to leave their homes. But none was more eloquent than Naygwonabe, an elder who had not been prominent in earlier negotiations but who provided a compelling example of how Ojibwe people viewed the controversy over their land. Naygwonabe testified before the lawyers Edgerton, Clapp, and Henderson at Mille Lacs on August 4. He declared that he was ninety years old and lived "way off somewhere about the lake."

"Is your residence on the Mille Lac Reservation?" the lawyers asked.

"No, they drove me off where I used to live. . . ."

"How are you interested in this claim?"

"Because I was brought [up] and had my being from this lake; from this place."

Naygwonabe recounted how he had moved away to White Earth, as the government demanded, but that he had quickly sold his allotment there and returned home to Mille Lacs. When he returned, a white man was living on the land he had previously occupied.

"Did you know how he got it?" the lawyers asked.

"I asked him 'How do you come to own this land?' He says 'The big chief told me to come here and own the land.' . . . I told him 'I own this land because my old ancestors have owned this land and planted their gardens there.' And he asked me, 'Who gave it to you?' . . . I say 'The Great Spirit who owns us all gave me this land. That is why I am here.' And then he didn't say any more."[62]

The claims case encouraged the band's dispirited leaders to keep up the fight for their homeland. The Minnesota Chippewa commissioner Darwin Hall, for example, reported to his superiors just as the depositions were getting under way that the Indians believed the court would grant them "millions of dollars" and this prospect was "exciting them and making them less easy to control." Attorney Richardson confirmed this view a few weeks later, when he submitted a request on behalf of Waweyaycumig, the removed Mille Lacs chief at White Earth, who was now his client. Richardson reported that the old man demanded that all future allotments issued to members of his band at White Earth be concentrated near his allotment. Concentrated together near Wahweyaycumig at Elbow Lake, Richardson noted, they could fish and hunt as a group. He added that the band was "gregarious . . . intermarried . . . fond of each other, and have been fellow sufferers at the hands of the whites. . . ." The Indian Office rejected the request swiftly and firmly. The purpose of removal was individual landownership, the exasperated chief clerk wrote from his Washington office. The program was aimed at achieving "progress" and "uplift," not communal hunting. "The present policy is for segregation, not colonization," he added. "The consolidation of Indians in villages would be a return to tribal practices."[63]

Events over the next two years made it clear that neither the legal formalities surrounding the claims case nor the fact that the court's decision would be limited to money damages had quieted white opposition to the band's continued presence at Mille Lacs. While local residents continued to press for the band's removal, the Ojibwe families that remained at the lake were as determined as ever to stay. Congressman Bede reported to the Indian Office in 1908 that his constituents were "complaining about the conduct of the many Indians who are still living there. . . . Is it not possible," the congressman inquired, "to have these Indians sent to the reservation in the near future?"

The commissioner's office reminded Bede that every Indian who accepted an allotment became a U.S. citizen and was therefore "as free to come and go as they please the same as any citizen."[64] Hundreds of Ojibwe families exercised this right, occupying gardens, cultivating rice beds, and hunting grounds near the lake while pursuing their traditional subsistence activities. Families moved between the few spots where their title was secure and remote forested areas that remained unclaimed or unoccupied. Darwin Hall described the situation as it stood in the fall of 1910. "The land all around Mille Lacs Lake is owned by private individuals and is becoming valuable," he reported. "If the

Indians have any rights I am here to protect them, but they will be ejected from the land as the whites need it."[65]

A few weeks after Darwin Hall made this prediction the Mille Lacs Investment and Improvement Company purchased land at Monzomaunay Point on Mille Lacs Lake, a site occupied by an extended family headed by Chief Monzomaunay's son Wadena. Wadena's father had been one of the band leaders who had met with the Chippewa Commission in 1889 and later traveled to nearby Little Falls to seek the help of Nathan Richardson. His family had lived on the land for the last several decades. Eager to develop their lakefront real estate for vacation homes, the Mille Lacs Investment and Improvement Company immediately initiated eviction proceedings in county court. Its complaint charged Wadena and his kinsmen with "wrongfully withholding" the company's property. Wadena and his codefendants answered the charges with the assistance of two Duluth attorneys. Noting that they and their families had peacefully occupied Monzomaunay Point "by authority grant and acquiescence of the United States Government" for more than thirty years, they added what had become a familiar statement: "[N]one of said defendants have ever surrendered their rights to said lands or any portion thereof." Wadena and his family did not appear in nearby Princeton on April 5, 1911, when the dispute was aired in open court. As a consequence, the judge ruled in the plaintiff's favor, and a week later he ordered the local sheriff to remove Wadena from Monzomaunay Point.[66]

In early May, Sheriff Harry Shockley, a dozen deputies, and two wagons gathered at Mille Lacs to enforce the judge's order. The police detachment arrived early in the day, handcuffed Wadena, and, over his protests, removed forty people, described in the local press as "bucks and their squaws and families," from their village.[67] Some observers reported that the sheriff poured gasoline over the band's wigwams and cabins and set them ablaze after the group departed.[68] Similar conflicts had occurred elsewhere on the reservation, but the Ojibwe defendants usually just retreated to unoccupied spots along the lake and resumed their round of hunting, gardening, and gathering. Wadena was no exception. At the end of the news story describing his eviction, the local *Princeton Union* reporter noted that once the chief had left his homestead on the point, his manacles were removed, and he and his followers "moved silently down the trail until they found another tract of land which suited their fancy. There they settled down and will remain until such time as the paleface owner again drives them forth."[69]

Just weeks after his dramatic eviction from Monzomaunay Point, Chief Wadena and his fellow Mille Lacs Ojibwes learned that they had won a stunning victory in the Court of Claims. In its May 29 decision, the court did not mention the chief's recent difficulties, but it did praise the Ojibwe leaders' insistence on the right of their community to occupy their reservation under the provisions of the 1863 treaty. According to Judge Fenton Booth, that agreement "confirmed rather than extinguished their rights. . . . Their complete understanding of the treaty," he declared, "is manifested not only by their words spoken at council meetings, but by the dogged persistence with which they retained their residence on the Mille Lacs Reservation under the most discouraging circumstances. . . ." Nearly a century after James McDonald asserted that treaties conveyed rights to Indians that the nation's own values compelled the government to honor, the Court of Claims affirmed that the Mille Lacs leadership had been correct all along.[70]

Echoing the statements that Chiefs Shobaushkung and Monzomaunay had made to presidents and treaty commissioners nearly fifty years earlier, the Court of Claims declared that "the very term 'treaty' contemplates a series of mutual concessions and reservations to define explicitly the rights of the contracting parties." Indian treaties, the court added, "were no exception to the rule." The court concluded that despite repeated demands that they abandon their territory, the Ojibwes at Mille Lacs "remained as a band in open, notorious possession of the same, a lawful notice to the world of a claim of title. . . ." Judge Booth dismissed the government's argument that the group's title was somehow compromised by the encroachments of settlers and the neglect of Indian Office officials. Federal promises could not be eroded so easily. Calling the government's argument "repugnant," Booth added that minimizing the Indians' title "cannot be claimed as just," for it would undermine the goal of promoting "that permanent repose continually sought for in Indian treaties and acts of Congress." The court determined that an award of slightly more than $764,000 would bring about some measure of "permanent repose" for the tribe.[71]

Back in Mille Lacs County, the June 1, 1911, edition of the *Princeton Union* announced "Reds Get Large Reward," but of course Monzomaunay, Shobaushkung, Meegeesee, Wadena, and the other chiefs had never made cash their principal goal. Their objective remained protecting their lakeside homeland and winning recognition for their rights under the treaties of 1855 and 1863. Nevertheless, whatever hopes they may have had for new resources to support land acquisition at Mille Lacs were dashed when the court (acting under the provisions of Congressman Bede's original jurisdictional act) ordered that the government's compensation payments be paid directly to the general Minnesota Chippewa fund. This fund, created by Congress in 1889 to receive timber and land payments and administered by the Indian Office, would be completely beyond the reach of the community's leaders. In 1916, after two separate appeals to the U.S. Supreme Court and years of haggling among the band's attorneys over the size of their fees, the United States paid approximately $585,000 to the fund as compensation for the loss of the Mille Lacs' land and resources.[72]

The court's decision endorsed the Mille Lacs leaders' moral claims to their land and ratified both their legal arguments and their version of history. Fenton Booth and his colleagues on the Court of Claims affirmed that U.S. officials had failed to allot the Indians as Henry Rice had promised in 1889 and that Indian Office neglect and incompetence had enabled settlers to invade the reservation and deprive the Ojibwes of their land and resources. The Mille Lacs case had benefited from powerful legal and political advocates who, despite their obvious self-interest, forced an American court to hear and affirm the views of a tiny group of Indian leaders. In its deliberations, the Claims Court itself had enunciated an array of important principles: treaties created federal obligations to tribes, land tenure could not be dismissed at the whim of the Indian Office, and arbitrary actions by government officials could be reviewed if they were "repugnant."

But Wadena, Meegeesee, and the other Mille Lacs Ojibwes took little comfort from their victory. Like Sarah Winnemucca, the Ojibwes who continued to resist removal to White Earth understood that after years of conflict they were unlikely to reverse the power imbalance that had produced their predicament in the first place. Just as Winnemucca's white supporters were quick to sympathize with her plight and pity her for her suffering, lawyers, judges, and even members of the Minnesota political establishment acknowledged the suffering inflicted on the tiny Mille Lacs band. The parallel between their case and the Paiutes runs even deeper, for just as the charity extended to Sarah Winnemucca stopped short when she refused to endorse the virtues of American progress, so the justice delivered by the Court of Claims was limited to dollars deposited in a fund controlled by the Indian Office.

The victorious Mille Lacs band was forced to accept a symbolic payment that left them short of their central objective.

Orchestrated by white politicians and opportunistic figures like Gus Beaulieu and the cooperative chiefs who had already relocated to White Earth, the Mille Lacs case nevertheless reflected the remarkable utility of the American judicial system for embattled Indian communities. The Court of Claims had cast its spotlight on this obscure band and amplified the voices of GoGee, Meegeesee, and the now homeless Wadena. Their views had been affirmed by the court and recorded in the journal of its decisions. New precedents and principles had been established despite the fact that at least in the short run no one in the American government would recognize Naygwonabe's simple declaration that the "Great Spirit gave me this land."

INSISTING ON MILLE LACS

In the two decades following the Mille Lacs band's favorable judgment in the Court of Claims, its leaders continued to insist that local white settlers and government officials recognize their title to at least a portion of their original tribal homeland. During these years, several individuals, including the evicted Chief Wadena, were able to secure title to small homesteads within the boundaries of the original reservation. Some of those acquisitions were made possible by a 1914 congressional resolution allocating forty thousand dollars of the Minnesota Chippewa fund for land purchases. Nearly two thousand acres were purchased under this program, and another several hundred acres of that parcel were later allotted to band members under a second congressional appropriation approved in 1923.

During the 1920s, as hundreds of Mille Lacs band members

gathered on these small but secure homesteads, the Indian Office gradually accepted the fact that the band would never leave its lakeside home. As talk of removal ended, federal officials moved to deliver services to the group. The Indian Office opened a tribal school in 1924, and the new building in Vineland became a visible focus for community life. When Meegeesee died in 1927, the community used the memorial service held there to celebrate both his leadership and their survival. As a tribally commissioned history recently observed, the chief was a "self-reliant and courageous man" who "inspired these same qualities in his people. In death he left them physically. In spirit he lives on in the people."[73]

When federal policy changed dramatically during the 1930s, the Indian Office embarked on a program of encouraging the formation of modern tribal governments. The Mille Lacs community was ready to respond. In 1934 the band organized a local government as an autonomous unit of the Minnesota Chippewa tribe. In the ensuing decades the Mille Lacs band developed new political institutions (including a reservation business committee), its own educational and cultural organizations, and a thriving set of tribal businesses.

The band's remarkable victory in the Court of Claims was imperfect. It embarrassed and disrupted the government's civilization and removal campaign but did not restore the tribe's title to its reservation. Nevertheless, the court's endorsement of the Mille Lacs leadership's position affirmed a view of events that non-Indians ultimately found impossible to ignore. As the chiefs pressed their case, they encouraged other Native groups, along with reformers and sympathetic legislators across the country, to follow a similar course. (In fact between 1881 and World War II nearly two hundred petitions were filed before the U.S. Court of Claims.[74]) Over time this widespread resistance undermined the government's smug assumption that all Indians would obey its orders and conform to American-style "civilization."

In the last decades of the nineteenth century, as settlers across the United States surrounded and invaded the Indians' homelands, Native people like the Ojibwes at Mille Lacs grew comfortable defending their territories by reaching out to sympathetic reformers and seeking hearings before an array of governmental institutions. As this process unfolded, tribal leaders used those institutions—Congress, the federal courts, or the Indian Office itself—as forums where they could air their grievances and undermine the government's authoritarian "civilization" policies. In the years after 1900, rigid bureaucrats like Carl Schurz and James McLaughlin and ambitious local politicians like Knute Nelson and Henry Rice learned that it was ultimately impossible to orchestrate the lives of Indian people. At the same time, leaders of bands and tribes discovered that tenacious political resistance was not necessarily futile. The survival and ultimate revival of the Mille Lacs community demonstrated that the struggles of activists like Shobaushkung, Monzomaunay, Wadena, and Meegeesee would have a tangible impact on the Native—and the American—future.[75]

CHAPTER SIX

THE GOOD CITIZENSHIP GUN

Thomas Sloan, Omaha

In the spring of 1911, as the Court of Claims prepared to announce its decision in the Mille Lacs claims case and confrontations between Minnesota Indians and local policemen were attracting the attention of the press, a small group of activists gathered in Columbus, Ohio, to plan a national reform organization whose membership would be limited to Native Americans. A steering committee made up of the physicians Carlos Montezuma and Charles Eastman, the lawyer Thomas Sloan, the popular author Laura Cornelius, the actor and performer Henry Standing Bear, and Charles Dagenett, the highest-ranking Native American in the Indian Office, envisioned the Society of American Indians (SAI) as an organization where educated leaders could address the English-speaking public about indigenous issues.

Like the founders of the National Association for the Advancement of Colored People (the NAACP had met for the first time two years earlier) and other Progressive Era reformers, the founders of the SAI believed that securing U.S. citizenship for all Indians would empower their members to become forceful actors in the nation's democracy, for in 1911 only those Indians who had received individual land allotments under the Dawes Severalty Act were U.S. citizens. The new organization declared it had "no secret scheme to make money, to get legal cases and . . . to press claims." Instead, "The open plan is to develop race leaders, to give hope, to inspire, to lead outward and upward. . . . We ask every Indian to speak, to voice his wrongs, to tell of injustice. . . ."[1]

Soon after its initial meeting, the society steering committee shared its plans with the man who in 1911 was undoubtedly the most prominent American Indian advocate in the United States, Richard Henry Pratt, the former army officer who had founded the Carlisle Industrial Training School in 1879. As the nation's largest and best-known off-reservation boarding school, Carlisle symbolized the government's commitment to Indian uplift and educational advancement. Though Pratt's rigid program of cultural transformation would trouble modern multicultural sensibilities, his commitment to racial equality was unbending.[2] Removed from office by political enemies in 1904, Pratt was respected by the Native activists on the society's organizing committee for his integrity and outspoken contempt for Indian Office bureaucrats. Two members of the committee, Standing Bear and Dagenett, were Carlisle alumni, and two others, Eastman and Montezuma, were former school employees.[3] Sloan and Cornelius, who had been graduated from other similar schools, had become Pratt's correspondents in the years following his exile from government service.

The organizing committee wrote Pratt in hopes that he would publicly encourage their efforts, and they were not disappointed.[4] "Twenty-six years ago when the discussion was hot about lands-in-severalty for the Indians," the former headmaster replied, "the constant assertion" was that assigning Indians to individual plots of land "would make them citizens. This has been pretty much a fallacy. . . . To reach good citizenship is a long journey," Pratt observed. The new society should therefore "do no less than demand of the government of the United States the broadest and fullest training for that position."[5] He added, "Your good citizenship gun is the biggest and best you could have secured."[6]

The arresting image of a "good citizenship gun" signals the serious purpose of the new organization. The planning committee believed that focusing on the extension of American citizenship to all Native people would not only place them on an equal footing with the rest of society but would also empower Indians seeking to counter the Indian Office's authoritarian bureaucracy. Unlike European immigrants, who acquired U.S. citizenship simply by renouncing their home countries and taking up a new English-speaking identity, the men and women who gathered for the SAI's first convention believed their community had been swallowed up by the United States. While many remained intensely loyal to their tribes, the group acknowledged that Native Americans now constituted an invisible minority in a modern, continental nation.

"Justice" had always been a problem for Indians in the United States, the society's leaders declared in one of its earliest publications, but the Indian had "a greater problem, which when he solves it, will solve every other problem. It is that of *becoming a contributing, producing element, independent and self-sustaining. . . .*"[7] Unlike William Potter Ross, who had sought an autonomous independence for the Cherokee tribe, the founders of the Society of American Indians viewed the active engagement of individual citizens as the most effective means of carving out an "independent and self-sustaining" existence in the United States.

In 1911 most Americans assumed that once Indians became independent and self-sustaining, they would cease being Indians. The founders of the SAI disagreed. They knew from their own lives that a "contributing, producing" American citizen could also be part of an "independent and self-sustaining" minority community.[8] The group's first president, the Omaha attorney Thomas Sloan, summarized this perspective when he wrote during the SAI's founding year that the only proper response to the exploitation of Indians was a determination that Native people should "hammer hard" at their enemies. "Nothing can ever be done as long as we politely say that everything is all right," he declared.[9] Citizenship would place a political "hammer" in their hands.

As they argued for their right to campaign against exploitation, Sloan and his colleagues were participating in a broad, twentieth-century movement that was redefining the relationship between individuals and the American state. Viewed increasingly in the late nineteenth century as an institution capable of setting and implementing a collective agenda, the American nation was increasingly expected to deliver tangible benefits to its citizens: expansion into the West, prosperous industries, national standards for immigration, and, most ambitious, a uniform set of legal rights. While the Fourteenth Amendment (1868) had declared that all people "born or naturalized in the United States . . . are citizens of the United States," Congress and the courts in the late nineteenth century had retreated from enforcing those rights or spelling out exactly what they might be. Nevertheless, by the turn of the new century a steadily proliferating list of interest groups and lobbyists was seeking to define the meaning of U.S. citizenship in various arenas. The founding of the Society of American Indians was an example of this process at work, as was the organization of the American Federation of Labor (1886), the NAACP, the

Chamber of Commerce (1912), and the American Farm Bureau Federation (1919).[10]

Because the administration of Indian people and their territories was primarily a federal responsibility, the SAI's founders aimed their good citizenship gun at the Indian Office. From the perspective of the older members of the group—Montezuma, Eastman, and Sloan—the controls placed on individual Indians by reservation bureaucrats was demeaning and intolerable. Not only had they seen their independent tribal governments relentlessly attacked and dismembered, but critics of expansion (such as Sarah Winnemucca or even the leaders at Mille Lacs) had been ignored by public officials and white reformers, who urged the Indians to follow orders and remain silent. The moment had arrived, Thomas Sloan and his colleagues believed, for Indians to enter the political arena and wield the power of American citizenship.[11]

A NEW GENERATION OF ACTIVISTS

The founders of the Society of American Indians represented a remarkable generation of Native activists. Fluent in English and confident of their relationship with non-Indian reformers and educators, these men and women were prepared to "hammer" the authorities with their complaints. Thomas Sloan was among the most outspoken. Like most of the organizing committee, he had been born in the era of the Civil War, when his Omaha kinsmen still followed the ancient traditions of hunting and gardening that enabled them to exist apart from the Americans' industrial economy. Like them as well, Sloan witnessed the immense population shift that took place in the wake of the sectional conflict, burying Native communities beneath an avalanche of foreign immigration and internal migration that transformed the public's view of Indian affairs.

As military threats from Indians receded, tribes gradually became objects of nostalgia and pity. The band chiefs at Mille Lacs had benefited from this shifting viewpoint, as did other activists in recently "settled" states across the nation. Modern Native societies receded from public view, and in their place arose literary and artistic images, theatrical presentations, and cartoon caricatures. By World War I nearly all non-Indian Americans—from the Boy Scouts to the happy customers at Buffalo Bill's popular *Wild West Show*—had learned about Native people from actors and storybooks. Sloan and his colleagues understood that in the age of Indian-head nickels (first distributed in 1913) and James Earle Fraser's iconic statue *End of the Trail* (unveiled at the San Francisco World's Fair in 1915), the public would require extensive education if it were to grasp the difficulties Native people now faced in the United States.

Partial citizenship had been offered to Native people long before Sloan and his colleagues took up the cause. A century earlier many states had proffered citizenship to Indians who agreed to abandon their tribes and settle on individually owned plots of land. James McDonald and other removal-era leaders had found this offer intriguing, but the few who accepted it quickly learned that their new status had little meaning when it required them to give up federal protections for their treaties and lifeways. In Mississippi, for example, Choctaws like James McDonald who refused to head west detached themselves from their tribes and immediately were subjected to taxation schemes and economic pressures that rapidly separated them from their property. Those who tried to fight back were hampered by discriminatory state laws and the failure of federal officials to intervene on their behalf. Even when the Indian Office was willing to offer its assistance to individual

Indians, it had little legal basis for action. In California, for example, Indians subjected to arbitrary vagrancy laws, which relegated impoverished individuals to extended periods of servitude, were legally imprisoned and routinely exploited while federal officials sat idly by.

The Fourteenth Amendment's promise in 1868 to enforce "equal protection under the law" against the actions of state governments gave Indians some hope that as citizens of the United States they could call on federal officials or the courts for protection. Suddenly Natives, like African Americans, could imagine responding to racial discrimination by appealing to the authorities in Washington, D.C. While most tribal people preferred to remain within their traditional communities, the white reformers who had championed Reconstruction Era civil rights legislation increasingly suggested that citizenship rights could offer vital protection to American Indians. Despite the failure of national citizenship to protect African Americans from the systematic disfranchisement and the onset of Jim Crow laws in the 1890s, Indians, particularly young educated people like the founders of the SAI, believed this new legal status could enable them to live outside the control of the Indian Office and battle against hostile assaults from white neighbors.[12]

Because they came of age in the postwar era, Sloan and his society colleagues were prepared as no other Native generation before them had been to imagine a future lived outside the confines of a reservation. Montezuma, for example, a Yavapai from Arizona, had been educated in Illinois, graduating from the state's university in 1886 and the Chicago Medical College in 1889. Eastman had been taken from his relatives in Canada and enrolled in a Dakota Territory mission, then sent east to college and on to Boston University Medical School, from which he graduated in 1890. He never stopped identifying himself as Sioux. The same was true of Cornelius, educated at an Anglican boarding school, as well as Dagenett and Standing Bear, who had been taken to Carlisle from their homes west of the Mississippi. Nearly every tribe counted similar students among their members— individuals who had endured years of separation from their families but who continued to think of themselves as American Indians.

Because most of them had been separated from their tribes, the society's organizers were also aware of the cruel bargain most Americans imagined when they contemplated extending citizenship to Indians. Missionaries, schoolteachers, and reformers alike insisted that those who accepted membership in the American political community should forget their pasts while they shifted their allegiance to the United States. By doing so, these new Indian citizens were invited to serve as role models for others. On the surface at least, the members of the organizing committee appeared to have accepted this trade-off. Eastman, Montezuma, and Sloan, dressed in high-collared shirts and dark suits and married to white women, had settled far away from their tribal homelands. Eastman and his wife, a former reservation schoolteacher, lived in Amherst, Massachusetts. Montezuma married a European immigrant and settled on the South Side of Chicago.

But the surface of these activists' lives was deceiving. While seeming to accept the government's offer of civilization, they remained outspoken adversaries of the Indian Office. Their hostility to the national bureaucracy often confused government officials. After all, these "Red Progressives," with their Victorian manners and polished English, seemed perfect examples of "vanishing Indians," who would herald the final disappearance of Native cultures from the American scene. The SAI's founders could not forget their families, however, or deny the discrimination and slights they had endured during their lives. Most poignant in this regard was Carlos Montezuma, who lived most of his life in Illinois but who later sought out and took up residence with his Yavapai kinsmen at Fort McDowell, Arizona. Sloan once testified that he and his family "have always maintained their tribal relations with the Omahas."[13] For these activists, then, the good citizenship gun was not only an instrument for their own advancement but also a tool for protecting their families and communities.

THOMAS SLOAN'S LIFE fitted neatly with the biographies of his fellow committee members. He was born in St. Louis in 1863 to a white father and mixed-race mother, but he later testified that "during all of my life, I have been in contact with the Omaha Indians." Sloan spent his early childhood away from the Omaha Reservation, but in the 1870s he moved permanently to Nebraska, where he joined the household of his maternal grandmother, Margaret Berda Sloan. Margaret was the daughter of Michael Berda, a trader who also served as the Omaha's interpreter at treaty councils, and Taeglaha Haciendo, an Omaha woman who was the sister of a tribal chief.[14]

Sloan received a rudimentary education at a Nebraska mission school before going to work as a herder for white cattlemen who leased pastureland from the Omahas. Bright and inquisitive, the young man soon noticed that the local Indian agent and cattle company were cheating the tribe of its full income. When he complained, he later recalled, he was labeled a troublemaker. As he told a congressional committee in 1935, "My contacts have been those of an Indian and my experience of that kind. . . . [A]s a boy I had the same treatment that the full-blood Indians had."[15] That treatment included "being locked up, arrested by the police, abused and put in jail." Upon his release, the Omaha agent sent Sloan east to be educated at Virginia's Hampton Institute, a school founded to educate freed slaves but recently endowed with federal funds to also educate American Indian students.[16]

Like the other SAI founders, Sloan was a model student. He seemed a living embodiment of the prediction that education could raise Indians to a new, more sophisticated life. In 1887 Hampton's leaders took him to Washington, D.C., to attend the annual meeting of the U.S. Board of Indian Commissioners, a group of prominent reformers and missionaries that monitored the operations of the Indian Office. There "Lieutenant Sloan" proudly showed off his school uniform and good manners, lecturing the group about the lessons in "manliness" he had absorbed at Hampton. He praised Hampton's policy of putting Indian "officers" like him in charge of governing and maintaining their own dormitory, called the wigwam. He told of the Wigwam Council he had organized to ensure that the institution's rules against gambling and smoking would be obeyed. The future lawyer also informed the commissioners that the Indian students at Hampton had organized their own reading room and debating society. He declared that his ambition was "to get as thorough an education as possible," and he promised that he would soon return home to find employment and "be independent."[17]

When he returned to Nebraska, Sloan saw firsthand the hardships endured by traditional hunters and subsistence farmers after tribal lands had been divided into individual homesteads under the government's new program of allotment. He also witnessed the disruptions that occurred when non-Indian settlers began buying former tribal land on the reservation. They competed with Omaha families for water, timber, and other resources, while recoiling from the prospect of sharing their schools and churches with Indians. Many other SAI founders witnessed similar scenes, but Sloan's experience was perhaps more intense than most.

The Omahas were a particular subject of national interest. In 1879, when Sloan was sixteen, the Ponca leader Standing Bear, whose tribe previously had been removed to Indian Territory, escaped from the reservation there. He returned with his family to Nebraska and sought refuge on Sloan's reservation. The U.S. Army quickly captured Standing Bear, but instead of physically resisting the soldiers sent to arrest him, the chief, with the help of local reformers, filed a habeas corpus suit in federal district court demanding that the local judge release him. After a brief but widely reported hearing in which his captor, General George Crook, a veteran commander who had served alongside President Hayes in the Civil War, attested to Standing Bear's good behavior, the court granted the Ponca's request. Judge Elmer Dundy declared that the Indians "have the inalienable right to 'life, liberty and the pursuit of happiness' so long as they obey the laws. . . ."[18]

Once Standing Bear was freed, his local supporters organized an extended speaking tour for him. Their goal was to generate support for Indian education and citizenship by having the chief tell his story of imprisonment and freedom to audiences all along the eastern seaboard. "We are bound," Standing Bear would cry at the climax of his lectures. "We ask you to set us free."[19] At one of Standing Bear's appearances he met Alice Cunningham Fletcher, an aspiring student of the new discipline of anthropology, who quickly expressed a desire to visit his Nebraska reservation. Fletcher spent several months with the Omahas, learning not only about their hunting techniques and traditional ceremonies but also of their fear that they would soon share the Poncas' fate and be removed to Indian Territory.

An ardent supporter of individual landownership as a key instrument for promoting the tribe's civilization, Alice Fletcher began lobbying for passage of a special allotment bill that would divide the Omaha Reservation into homesteads and extend U.S. citizenship to the tribe. Under Fletcher's proposal, Indians would hold federally protected "trust" titles to their homesteads for twenty-five years. These titles would make their property tax exempt. At the end of the twenty-five years they would receive fee simple titles, and their land would be added to the local tax rolls. Her proposal received a warm welcome in Congress and became law in 1882. As Thomas Sloan completed his studies at Hampton, the Indian Office assigned the anthropologist to oversee the survey and division of the Omahas' homeland.[20]

Nebraska's Indians remained in the national spotlight in 1884, when the U.S. Supreme Court took up the case of John Elk, an Indian resident of the city of Omaha, who had attempted to vote in local elections. Elk argued that the Fifteenth Amendment's protection of the right to vote should extend to Indians like him who had chosen to live apart from their tribes. Despite enthusiastic support from Alice Fletcher and other reformers, the High Court denied Elk's claim, noting that because Congress had never defined the Indians' legal status, he was "no more 'born in the United States' . . . within the meaning of the . . . Fourteenth Amendment, than the children of subjects of any foreign government. . . ."[21] To correct this decision, Congress stipulated that the Omahas receiving allotments under Fletcher's bill would be recognized as U.S. citizens. In addition, when Congress passed a comprehensive law, the General Allotment Act, in 1887, it extended this citizenship provision to any Indian accepting an individual homestead. From the perspective of former Indian boarding school students like Thomas Sloan and his colleagues in the Society of American Indians, the prospect of a secure title to their own land, together with the protection of American citizenship and the enthusiastic backing of a network of non-Indian reformers like Fletcher, promised a future in which they would be able to fulfill a desire for a life of "manliness" and "independence."

Sloan returned from Hampton to Nebraska in 1889 amid this

atmosphere of official optimism. Under Fletcher's direction, the Omahas' Missouri River homeland was rapidly being divided into individual farms, transforming their pastures and hunting grounds into agricultural real estate. Tribal members were becoming citizens and registering to vote in local elections with the blessing of federal officials who seemed genuinely committed to supporting their entry into the American legal and political arena. Would this enthusiasm endure? According to the Indian Rights Association, allotment had "thrown wide open the door to Indian citizenship."[22] Fletcher called the new law "the Magna Carta of the Indians," but many Indians outside the circle of educated young English speakers worried that this new status would fail the Indians as quickly as it had the nation's former slaves.[23]

A series of unprecedented events soon forced U.S. authorities to define the meaning of Omaha citizenship. A rail line suddenly bisected the tribal homeland, bringing hundreds of white homesteaders to the area and spurring the growth of new towns along its tracks. The arriving settlers quickly set about buying up the tribe's "surplus lands" (reservation land left unassigned after allotments had been distributed to tribal members) and leasing Indian-owned trust property to expand their farms. Finally, in March 1889, the newcomers organized a new political entity, Thurston County, to govern their community. Named for a prominent railroad attorney who soon became a U.S. senator, the new county seemed barely viable; the bulk of its land base consisted of federally protected tax-exempt Omaha allotments.

In a few years a tribal homeland was transformed into a center of commercial agriculture whose economy was dominated by newcomers. Theoretically, Native citizens on the reservation would continue to enjoy federal protection for their tax-exempt land while also participating freely in the political life of Thurston County. But the extent of that protection and the nature of the freedom they would enjoy remained unclear. At first Sloan participated eagerly in the life of the new county. He worked as a census enumerator, a county surveyor, and an office clerk. He settled and voted in the new railroad town of Pender. Following the advice of his mentors at Hampton, the young graduate seemed eager to "travel the white man's road." Like many others who were drawn to the Society of American Indians, Sloan accepted the promise of citizenship. He understood that promise was vague and that he was taking a great deal on trust, but at least at the start of his career, the citizenship gun seemed to offer the means to a bright future.

EXPLORING THE POWER OF CITIZENSHIP

Sloan soon discovered the limits of U.S. citizenship. Immediately after his arrival in Nebraska, the young graduate learned that Alice Fletcher, the reformer who had been appointed special agent to oversee the allotment of the tribe's lands, had declared him ineligible for a homestead. She announced that both because of Sloan's Missouri birth and the fact that his grandmother Margaret had earlier received a homestead at the Nemaha Agency in southern Nebraska, the Indian Office no longer considered him a tribal member. The young graduate insisted that he had been a reservation resident at the time of the allotment law's passage and that he had no other family but his grandmother. Fletcher refused to hear Sloan's appeal, and the local agent declared the case closed. Sloan refused to remain silent. An Indian Office inspector named Arthur Tinker reported in December 1890 that Sloan had told him "he cannot be driven off the reservation." Tinker reported that Sloan "laughs at the order" from Washington, D.C., demanding that he leave the reservation. "This young man has some education," noted the inspector (apparently unaware of Sloan's stellar performance at Hampton), "and thinks, or seems to think, that he knows more than any one on the reservation. He is said to be a disturber, and should be moved off if he does not belong here."[24]

Hiram Chase, another educated young man of mixed ancestry, was a childhood friend of Sloan's who also had recently returned from the East. Like Sloan, Chase had been labeled a troublemaker, and he too had left the reservation in search of an education. Chase had not attended a government boarding school; with the support of his non-Indian relatives he had attended the University of Cincinnati, graduated from its law school, and been admitted to the Nebraska bar. Outraged by Fletcher's action and the Indian Office's intransigence, Sloan decided to read law with Chase. He was admitted to the bar in 1892.[25] This seemingly impulsive decision established Sloan's life-work. As he told a congressional committee in 1913, "I took up the study of law in order to enable myself to make fights against the agent [and] to protect myself and my people. . . ."[26] Throughout his career Sloan returned again and again to the federal courts, believing that only they could protect Indians from the arbitrary actions of the Indian Office.

Sloan challenged Fletcher's decision by filing a lawsuit against the United States. Seeking "the aid of the court for the protection of his rights," he demanded that the farm he and his grandmother had culti-vated since 1880 be deeded to him as an allotment. The Indian Office responded by seeking a dismissal of the suit, asserting, essentially, that individual Omahas had no right to challenge the government's author-ity. Its motion read in part that "the management of Indian affairs was entrusted to the Department of Interior" and "the court should not interfere" with the agency as it carried out its work. At the case's first hearing in federal district court in 1899, Judge Oliver Perry Shiras rejected this assertion of invulnerability, noting instead that the Omaha allotment act was fundamentally a contract between the tribe and the United States. Should Sloan be considered a member of the Omaha tribe, he wrote, "then it must be held that he comes within the class of persons entitled to allotments in severalty. . . . The complainant's right . . . to an allotment . . . is not inherited from his father or other ancestors," the judge added; "it is a personal right, conferred on him by reason of his being an Indian of the Omaha tribe."[27]

The Indian Office managed to reverse Sloan's victory on a technicality, but the young lawyer returned to court and won again. In its second ruling on the matter, the district court noted that federal officials had no authority to ignore a congressionally authorized procedure for challenging their actions, nor could they declare unilaterally that "children of free-born parents take the legal status of the father. . . ." Clearly irritated by the Indian Office's expansive view of its own power, Judge Shiras declared that there was "no good reason" to deny [Sloan] his property. Even though Thomas Sloan "is by habit, mode of life, and education a white man," the judge concluded, "that fact does not deprive him of the right to claim an allotment . . . as he was at the date of [the act's] adoption living on the reservation and is in fact of mixed blood."[28] The government appealed Shiras's decision, providing Thomas Sloan the opportunity to be the first American Indian to argue a case before the United States' highest court. The justices there upheld the district court's ruling, and Sloan received his land.[29]

As he prepared his allotment claim, Sloan also became embroiled in reservation politics. The Omahas were deeply divided over both the allotment process and their evolving relationship with the settlers migrating into their territory. At one extreme were tribal members who rejected the idea of becoming farmers, preferring to subsist by hunting and leasing their allotted land to cattlemen and large-scale farming operations. Opposing these traditionalists were people, like Sloan and Chase, who sought individual land titles and the elimination of the supervising presence of the Indian Office. The political battle lines between these groups shifted regularly as each side sought alliances with groups of competing cattlemen, farmers, railroad employees, and government agents. Membership in these rival groups was also fluid because it rested on family loyalties as much as on ideology or economic self-interest. Neither side had a monopoly on virtue. Those favoring the retention and leasing of trust lands, for example, often gravitated to wealthy ranchers, while those calling for allotment and individual independence allied themselves with enterprising small farmers. Because Sloan was an attorney with ties to both the tribe and businessmen in nearby Pender, he was frequently accused of wrongdoing. Sloan also served as the legal guardian of the estates of minor or elderly tribal members. These estates were typically leased to local non-Indian farmers, and guardians often attracted criticism. Given the unregulated, competitive atmosphere of the era, it is certainly possible that Sloan profited inappropriately from his work. Corrupt guardians of Indian real estate in Indian Territory attracted national attention in the early twentieth century, and the same practices could well have occurred in nearby eastern Nebraska. On the other hand, Sloan was never charged with being a central player in any of the reservation scandals. His actions over the more than four decades of his career suggest that he had little interest in personal wealth or corporate enterprise. He may well have been an opportunist, but he was probably not a crook.

It seems more likely that Thomas Sloan attributed the chaos and suffering at the agency as much to incompetent agents and patronizing reformers like Alice Fletcher as to the shady loan sharks and real estate speculators who were a growing feature of reservation life. His actions in the 1890s and the first years of the new century reveal an activist who believed that court-enforced rights were the Indians' best weapon against disruptive outsiders, be they government agents or unscrupulous swindlers. Just as Sloan had insisted on his personal right to an allotment of property, so he would argue in other settings that legal protections were the Indian community's most effective tool for preserving its property and autonomy. As a consequence, Sloan publicly supported causes that benefitted his own private economic interests as well as those that opposed government paternalism. He argued, for instance, that the Omahas had the right to sell and consume alcohol. Sloan insisted throughout his career that the rights derived from U.S. citizenship, not federal benevolence, provided the most effective protection for Indian people.

As was the case on other reservations in the allotment era, the federal agent assigned to the Omaha agency wielded enormous power in the administration of both tribal and individually assigned land. Outsiders wishing to lease trust property typically approached the local agent, regardless of which tribal member had been assigned to the land in question. Sloan had long criticized this practice, charging that agents, who were political appointees, were easily corrupted or susceptible to pressure from powerful local business interests. One Indian Office inspector confirmed this view when he reported in 1894 that "for several years . . . land companies and real estate brokers have by the connivance of the agent leased the most valuable portion" of both the Omaha and neighboring Winnebago agencies "for nominal sums."[30]

The occasion for this unusually candid comment was the arrival, in 1893, of a new agent, the cavalry officer William A. Beck. Initially assigned to the agency on a temporary basis, Captain Beck quickly learned that the Flournoy Livestock and Real Estate Company, headed by the Pender businessman William Peebles, had privately leased fifty thousand acres of allotted land that it was subletting to local settlers who were unaware that the practice was illegal. Beck was not opposed to leasing, but he sniffed the odor of collusion and insisted that all lease agreements between tribal members and outsiders be registered openly at the agency, as the law required. Acting on the eve of the fall harvest, the new agent ordered all unauthorized leaseholders to immediately vacate their farms. His actions triggered a three-year struggle that was fought out in federal courtrooms and the back corridors of the Indian Office.

In 1895, as his legal tussle with Flournoy was working its way to the Supreme Court, Agent Beck recruited Thomas Sloan to serve as the agency's leasing clerk. Beck hoped this educated young Omaha would oversee the public registration of the reservation's leases as required by law. Inspector James McLaughlin, the career official who fifteen years later tried to persuade Meegeesee and his fellow Mille Lacs Ojibwes to abandon their homeland, reported on Sloan's appointment. The young lawyer "gave up a lucrative practice in the town of Pender, 23 miles from the agency, to accept his present position," the inspector noted. McLaughlin added, "He is a young man of excellent morals . . . [whose] services are invaluable to the agency at the present time."[31] Sloan labored to formalize the reservation's leasing system, while Peebles and his political supporters in Pender charged him with corruption and fraud.[32]

The courts ultimately vindicated Beck's actions and rejected Flournoy's argument that by becoming citizens, the Omahas had surrendered the protection of the Indian Office. Judge Oliver Shiras, who had earlier ruled in favor of Sloan's application for an Omaha allotment, noted that tribal members "have the right to vote and to hold office" but that this status did "not necessarily show that the government of the United

States no longer owes them any duty of protection in regard to the reservation lands, and no longer possesses any power of control over them as a tribe."[33] Despite their victory, Beck and Sloan had little time to celebrate. With the arrival of a new administration in Washington in March 1897, the Omaha agent was replaced by someone who, one observer reported, had been recommended for the job by "[Nebraska] Senator Thurston and others."[34]

Thomas Sloan's encounters with Alice Fletcher and the Flournoy Livestock and Real Estate Company persuaded him that Native people should seek the shelter of the law and the protection of the courts rather than rely on politically vulnerable officials at the Indian Office. While continuing to assert that federal protections were not canceled by the acquisition of citizenship, in the first decade of the new century he took up a series of cases in which he called on the courts to defend the rights of Indian citizens against the arbitrary authority of the federal bureaucracy. He represented clients who challenged the tax-exempt status of Indian-owned bank accounts, defended men accused of violating federal prohibitions against "introducing liquor into Indian country," and questioned the power of the Indian Office's reservation police force to arrest individuals without filing formal charges against them. In each instance the young attorney questioned the Indian Office's power to assert its authority over Indian citizens. He came to believe that the unchecked power of federal officials, despite their often benevolent intent, diminished the citizenship rights of Indian citizens and led inevitably to corruption and exploitation.

Sloan's local reputation grew along with his legal practice. He was elected county surveyor and justice of the peace, and these offices further established his reputation and helped his business grow. In 1909 Samuel Brosius, the Washington agent of the Indian Rights

Association, referred to Sloan as "one of the brightest lawyers in [the] state."[35]

Sloan was also drawn into the county's business affairs. Because it had been organized to encompass the tax-exempt trust lands of the Omaha reservation, Thurston County, like many other similarly situated counties in the West, had a tax base too small to support public services for its non-Indian residents. As the county sought sources of revenue, the Indian Office warned that the Indians' trust land, the crops they produced, and the material assistance the government provided (such as farm implements and houses) could not be taxed. The courts agreed. The Supreme Court ruled in 1903, for example, that "Congress expected that the lands . . . allotted [on the Omaha reserve] would be improved and cultivated . . . that object would be defeated if the improvements could be assessed and sold for taxes."[36]

The court's bar on local taxation had seemed reasonable in the 1880s, when Alice Fletcher promised that allotment would trigger a rapid transition to individual landholding. Then, tax exemptions could be justified as a temporary protection for struggling Indian farmers. But as resistance to farming became more widespread, and abuses such as the Flournoy company's long-term leasing schemes placed the Indians' tax-exempt land under the control of cattlemen, what Richard Pratt had called the "fallacy" of allotment became obvious. The tax exemptions appeared now to be simply a loophole that both Indians and whites were happy to exploit for their own profit. Sloan's opposition to tax exemptions for Indian allotments seems to contradict his support for Native interests, but he viewed this protection like every other instance of federal intervention, as ultimately limiting the individual rights and freedoms of American Indians. Tax exemptions attracted large cattle interests that leased trust homesteads under the supervision of the Indian Office, leaving the allotments' owners perpetually indigent and on the sidelines. As a consequence, Omaha poverty would grow and the Indian Office would continue to oppress its incompetent wards. While he was certainly aware of the hardship local taxes would impose on allottees, Sloan argued that the only solution to agency corruption was for Indians to sever their ties to Washington.

In 1905, when Thurston County imposed a tax on the bank accounts of all its residents, local officials attempted to collect the tariff from Omaha Indians who had sold allotments left to them by deceased relatives. A 1902 statute had allowed for the sale of this trust property on the open market (provided the Indian Office approved) but had stipulated that any proceeds must be deposited in individual restricted accounts for the benefit of the Indian heirs. The Indian Office quickly challenged the county's new tax, arguing that even though the sale of these allotments conveyed a fee simple title to the land's new citizen-owners, the proceeds enjoyed the same trust status as the original allotment and could not be taxed. When the case reached federal district court in Omaha, Thomas Sloan argued the case for Thurston County.

It is likely that Thurston County had been inspired to impose its new tax by a recent U.S. Supreme Court decision that had offered an expansive definition of Indian citizenship rights. *In re Heff* had reached the courts when Albert Heff, a white man arrested for selling liquor to allotted citizen Indians in Kansas, filed a habeas corpus appeal charging that the Indian Office should have no authority to regulate the behavior of a racially defined group of American citizens. The government had responded with the unsubstantiated assertion that while they were citizens, Indians required special protection because they were not people "of full competence." The 1905 High Court would not accept this vague and explicitly racist argument. Writing for the majority, Justice David Brewer asked: "Can it be that because one has Indian, and only Indian blood in his veins, he is to be forever one of a special class. . . ?"[37]

When he appeared for Thurston County in its tax case, Thomas Sloan presented an argument intended to align himself with the justices who had ruled in *Heff.* He asked the district court to place a limit on the exercise of federal authority over Indian citizens residing on reservations. The alternative, he argued, was endless authoritarian control. In *Thurston County*, he argued that once the sale of an allotment had taken place and land had passed out of trust status, government supervision should end. The dollars generated by the sale became the property of the citizens who inherited them. Sloan was persuasive. In September 1905 Judge William H. Munger declared that "the mere fact" that the secretary of the interior had the authority to approve the sale of inherited trust land "does not vest in the United States a trust ownership of the income derived from it." Munger rejected the government's suggestion that the Indians' bank accounts should be considered the equivalent of perpetual trust allotments. That analogy, the court declared, "has no bearing upon the present case as Congress has given the Indian the unlimited ownership . . . of the proceeds of the sale. . . ."[38]

Sloan's victory in the Thurston County tax case came at a pivotal moment in the history of Indian allotment and of Indian policy generally. Over the previous two decades allotting agents like Alice Fletcher had fanned out across the United States, implementing the new allotment policy with groups as diverse as the Ojibwes at White Earth, Minnesota, the Nez Perces of Idaho, and the Cherokees in Indian Territory. The policy had spread so quickly and so extensively that many of its original boosters—Carlisle's Captain Pratt, the leaders of the Indian Rights Association, and even the allotment law's principal sponsor, the former Massachusetts senator Henry Dawes—had expressed uneasiness about the Indians' ability to adjust to the economic pressures they now faced as owners of commercial farms, even farms that were tax exempt.

Their unease became more pronounced in the wake of a highly publicized 1903 Supreme Court decision that had upheld Congress's authority to impose the allotment process unilaterally on tribes, even when its actions were barred by treaties. *Lone Wolf v. Hitchcock* had upheld the congressionally mandated allotment of the Kiowa Comanche reserve in Indian Territory despite the fact that its action took place over the tribe's objections and in violation of a ratified treaty. "The Supreme Court has virtually given Congress full power to take Indian lands," one prominent critic wrote in the aftermath of the *Lone Wolf* decision, adding darkly: "[A]ttempts will undoubtedly be made in all parts of the West to get possession of desirable Indian reservations."[39]

As the division of reservation lands accelerated in the first years of the new century, a growing number of reformers and policy makers concluded that earlier predictions that allotment alone would transform tribal peoples into prosperous farmers had been wrong. It now appeared that allotment could become a source of Indian poverty rather than its cure. But none of the policy's critics could agree on a politically practical response to this gloomy predicament. If the growing numbers of allotted Indians were failing to prosper, it would seem logical to conclude that the allotment law had been a mistake and should be repealed. Indians should be allowed to return to some form of tribal life, and reservations should perhaps be developed as corporate entities. Despite this logic, the support allotment enjoyed among non-Indians, particularly among major agricultural interests and potential settlers, made it unlikely that the program could be reversed.

Pressed to square the Indians' status as individual landowners and citizens with the obvious fact of continuing Indian poverty, the Indian Office and its supporters turned to a familiar explanation: Indians were backward people, incapable of attaining civilization in a single step. Government lawyers had used that argument to defend its special liquor regulations in the *Heff* case, claiming that Albert Heff's thirsty customers were not competent people, but their racial language had been explicitly rejected by the court. Undeterred, the Indian Office tried the identical tactic a year later, when it asked the court of appeals to reverse Thomas Sloan's successful defense of Thurston County's new tax on Indian bank accounts. This time it worked.

When the appeals court in *U.S. v. Thurston County* adopted the government's characterization of the modern Omaha Indians as racially inferior, Thomas Sloan, sitting in his Pender law office, next to his telephone and typewriter, must have been tempted to look in a mirror or check his calendar. Had he been transported to the buffalo hunting camps of his ancestors? When describing Indians, the judges clearly had not considered the Christian boarding school graduate and successful lawyer who had just argued the case before them. They announced to Sloan and his colleagues that federal supervision of citizen Indians was justified because these individuals "are still members of their tribes and of an inferior and dependent race." Restrictions on the Indians' property were necessary, they added, "to protect them from want and despair and the superior race from the inevitable attacks which these evils produce. . . ." Reasoning on from this invented image, the court could find no limit for the authority of the Indian Office. It declared, "Every instrumentality lawfully employed by the United States to execute its constitutional laws and to exercise its lawful governmental authority is necessarily exempt from state taxation and interference."[40]

Other courts and the entire federal bureaucracy quickly warmed to this racial theme. In the five years between the Supreme Court's decision in *Thurston County* and the founding of the Society of American Indians in 1911, Thomas Sloan heard racial justifications for extending federal authority over Indians with increasing frequency. In 1907 he challenged his own arrest by Winnebago agency policemen carrying out the local agent's order barring him from the reserve. The agent defended this preemptive action by charging that Sloan had been planning to engage in deceptive business activities. The Eighth Circuit Court of Appeals upheld the action on the grounds that despite their U.S. citizenship, the Winnebagos were "in a state of dependency and tutelage which entitles them to the care and protection of the federal government." The question of the limits of the Indian Office's protection was left open-ended. "When they shall be let out of that state," the judges added, "is for Congress alone to determine."[41]

AT THE SAME TIME that Sloan was challenging his arrest by agency policemen, he was also engaged in a long-running defense of Simeon Hallowell, a fellow Omaha Indian who had been arrested in 1905 for "introducing liquor into the Indian country." Like Sloan, Hallowell was an allotted member of the tribe, a U.S. citizen, and an active participant in Thurston County affairs. He had served as a local justice of the peace, an election official, a county assessor, and a member of the local school board. The arresting officers conceded that Hallowell was not a liquor dealer. He had transported the alcohol in question to his home "for the purpose of drinking and using the same himself" as well as providing it "to his friends or visitors." Despite his upstanding profile, Hallowell was convicted of violating federal liquor regulations in federal district court. When Sloan appealed the case to the Eighth Circuit in St. Louis, the justices there were unable to reach a decision. They wrote that Hallowell did not fit the court's image of the kind of

Indian who should be regulated by rules drawn up in Washington, D.C. The appeals court suggested that the Supreme Court clarify the situation by resolving this legal issue. They asked, "Is [Hallowell] liable to indictment and punishment" under federal law? The Supreme Court refused to rule and ordered a rehearing of the case.[42] Hallowell and Sloan returned to St. Louis for the reargument. In 1911, after Hallowell's conviction had been upheld yet again, Sloan turned to the Supreme Court for a definitive ruling.

This time the justices were prepared. In the six years since Hallowell and Sloan had first approached it, the Supreme Court had decided three cases involving the rights of citizen Indians. Two of these, *U.S. v. Sutton* and *U.S. v. Celestine*, were decided a week apart in December 1909. In both of them the Court upheld the federal prosecutions of citizen allottees accused of crimes on allotted reservations. (The accused had challenged their arrests, claiming that as citizens they were under the jurisdiction of state, not federal, authorities.) "It cannot be said to be clear," the Court declared in *Celestine*, "that Congress intended by the mere grant of citizenship to renounce entirely its jurisdiction over the individual members of this dependent race."[43]

The Court gave the "mere grant of citizenship" an even clearer definition two years later in *Marchie Tiger v. Western Investment Company*, a case argued two weeks before Sloan's second appearance before the justices on behalf of Hallowell. Marchie Tiger was a citizen allottee in Oklahoma who had asked the Court to cancel the deeds to two tracts of fee simple land she regretted having sold to non-Indians. The Justice Department lawyer arguing on Tiger's behalf explained the reasoning behind the government's extraordinary request that the Court set aside a private land sale involving adult citizens of the United States: "Minors and lunatics may be citizens and yet their property rights may be restricted," the Justice Department's Wade Ellis declared. "Full-blood

Indians of the Five Tribes are, as a class, incompetent. . . . [They are] unable to speak the English language and incompetent to guard their interests from designing persons."[44]

The Supreme Court announced its decisions in *Hallowell* and *Marchie Tiger* on the same day, May 15, 1911. *Tiger* was first. Agreeing with the Justice Department's characterization of Marchie Tiger as an incompetent, Justice William Day declared:

> It may be taken as the settled doctrine of this court that Congress, in pursuance of the long-established policy of the Government, has a right to determine for itself when the guardianship which has been maintained over the Indian shall cease. It is for that body, and not the courts, to determine when the true interests of the Indian require his release from such condition of tutelage. The privileges and immunities of Federal citizenship have never been held to prevent governmental authority from placing such restraints upon the conduct or property of citizens as is necessary for the general good. Incompetent persons, though citizens, may not have the full right to control their persons and property.[45]

After declaring Marchie Tiger incompetent and her land sale invalid, the Court turned to Hallowell. Citing the three cases that had been decided using racial justifications since Sloan had first brought Hallowell's complaint to them six years earlier (*Celestine*, *Sutton*, and *Tiger*) and noting that "[w]e . . . need not repeat what was there said," Justice Day disposed of Hallowell's appeal in a few paragraphs. "The mere fact that citizenship has been conferred upon Indians," he declared, "does not necessarily end the right or duty of the United States to pass laws in their interest as a dependent people."[46]

Without surviving diaries or personal correspondence, it is impossible to know Thomas Sloan's reaction to the *Tiger* and *Hallowell* decisions. At the very least it would have puzzled him to hear the nation's highest legal officials mouthing racial stereotypes that his teachers at Hampton had banished from their classrooms a generation earlier. He no doubt sympathized with efforts to protect troubled individuals like Marchie Tiger and to reduce the rates of alcoholism in Indian communities, but his lawyer's mind would surely have grasped the fact that Judge Day's decision opened the door to an immense expansion of federal power over Indians and, with it, a drastic reduction in the potential power of Native citizenship. If Indians as a legal class were incompetent, and their freedoms restricted as a matter of standard policy, then the Court could identify no constitutional or statutory limits to the power of the Indian Office. Of course Congress had acted—it had, after all, declared these allotted individuals to be U.S. citizens—but the Court's expansive definition of Indian incompetence trumped all opponents. As long as he was an Indian, Sloan himself would be subject to arbitrary decisions taken by officials acting according to their definition of his true interest. It is not surprising, then, that the good citizenship gun would have been an appealing slogan to Sloan and his SAI colleagues in the spring of 1911.

PURSUING CITIZENSHIP ON A NATIONAL STAGE

In the years immediately preceding the founding of the Society of American Indians, Thomas Sloan entered the orbit of an informal network of like-minded Native activists. Some of those who later became active in the society, such as Carlos Montezuma and Gertrude

Simmons Bonnin (Zitkala Sa), knew of each other as lecturers and popular writers. Others—the ministers Sherman Coolidge, Philip Joseph Deloria, and Charles Eastman's brother John—crossed paths while working as missionaries. Boarding school classmates frequently corresponded following their return to their home communities. These networks often overlapped with one another. The Eastman brothers, Coolidge, and Deloria, for example, all were active in the YMCA. Bonnin, a former Carlisle teacher, often met with former students and staff members. She and Montezuma were even engaged for a time.

Regional groups also appeared. These included the Black Hills Council in the Dakotas (1911), the Alaskan Native Brotherhood and Sisterhood (1912), and the Northwestern Federation of American Indians (1914). Since all these organizations became involved in lobbying, legal disputes, and claims cases, their leaders frequently encountered one another at the SAI's annual meeting or in Washington, D.C., as they called on law firms, legislators, and reform groups.

It is not clear when Sloan first corresponded with Charles Eastman, Richard Pratt, and Carlos Montezuma, but surviving letters indicate that the Omaha lawyer established a working relationship with each of these men around 1905, when he was working on appeals of the *Hallowell* and *Thurston County* cases. In a 1909 letter to Pratt, for example, Sloan referred to a meeting the previous winter in which eleven tribal representatives, counseled by the former Carlisle headmaster, had called on the secretary of the interior to urge greater funding for Indian schools. A press report from the same year noted that Sloan was also part of a delegation of boarding school graduates that called on President Taft a few days after his March 1909 inauguration. The group also included Alexander Upshaw, an Indian Office employee from the Montana Crow Reservation, the aspiring Pawnee writer and fellow

Hampton alumnus James Murie from Oklahoma, and the Reverend John Eastman.[47]

Sloan's deepest engagement with other activists in these early years occurred in June 1909, when he joined a group that gathered at Haskell Institute, the government boarding school in Lawrence, Kansas, to found the Indian Memorial Association. Among the organizers of this short-lived organization were Charles Kealear, a Yankton Sioux classmate of Sloan's from Hampton; Dennison Wheelock, a Wisconsin Oneida graduate of Carlisle who, like Sloan, had read law and been admitted to the state bar following his return from school; and Walter Battice, a Sac and Fox Indian from Oklahoma who had also attended Hampton before going to work for the Indian Office. The group elected Sloan president and adopted a series of resolutions critical of government paternalism. Removing the restrictions of guardianship, they argued, "is indispensable to . . . bringing the Indians into the full enjoyment of the rights and privileges to which they are entitled as men under the constitution and laws of this country."[48] The meeting provided an opportunity for Sloan to reestablish ties to former classmates and allies as well as to meet the Chicago-based Yavapai physician Carlos Montezuma.

By the time they began working together on the Indian Memorial Association, Dr. Montezuma had become an outspoken critic of the Indian Office. A powerfully built, dark-skinned figure who always appeared in formal attire, Montezuma was a walking refutation of the popular belief that Indians were backward people who could not adapt to life in modern society. His successful medical practice allowed him time for political activism; he rarely passed up an opportunity to speak out publicly against Indian Office arrogance and incompetence. He believed, as he once told the national convention of the Woman's

Christian Temperance Union, "The Indian . . . is entitled to the privilege of waging his contest for existence . . . just as much as other men are."[49]

Like other self-made men, Montezuma believed his own career should be a model for others. Adopted as a child by an itinerant Italian American photographer in Arizona, he was later placed with a foster family in Urbana, Illinois, the home of the state's new land grant university. Montezuma fully embraced his new home, learning English, earning a degree in chemistry, and then proceeding to the Chicago Medical College, where he earned his MD in 1889. His hostility to the Indian Office, like Sloan's, was based on personal experience. He spent four years as a reservation physician in the West and resigned in 1893 because of his disgust with the government's inadequate support for Indian health and his personal conflicts with the political appointees who ran the local agency. Montezuma moved on to Carlisle, where three years as school physician and a close association with Captain Pratt solidified his belief that education and citizenship would free Indians from government control.

Montezuma's return to Chicago in 1896 occurred just as Thomas Sloan's disputes with the government were producing congressional investigations and lawsuits. Both men witnessed firsthand the government's growing acceptance of racial incompetence as a justification for federal restrictions. While Sloan argued before judges who were growing comfortable with the view that Indians were incompetents, Montezuma spoke out against the increasingly popular view that the limits of the Native intellect were so severe that government schools should focus exclusively on vocational training. Native people, these experts declared, would require several generations to adapt to the modern world. Most prominent among these racial realists was Francis Leupp, Theodore Roosevelt's commissioner of Indian affairs, who declared on taking office that "the most common mistake . . . in dealing with the Indian is the assumption that he is simply a white man with a red skin." The government's goal, Leupp argued, should be the "improvement, not transformation," of Native people.[50] To Sloan and Montezuma, this "realism" was just another version of government paternalism.

The alliance between Sloan and Montezuma grew stronger in the immediate aftermath of the Society of American Indians' founding conference. The October 1911 convention in Columbus, Ohio, elected Sloan chairman and Charles Dagenett secretary-treasurer, presumably because Dagenett was based in Washington, D.C. The group also appointed an executive committee consisting of members of the original organizing group that had met in May. Standing Bear and Cornelius were included, plus Sloan's Omaha friend Hiram Chase and two newcomers: the Reverend Sherman Coolidge from Wind River, Wyoming, and the anthropologist Arthur C. Parker. Montezuma decided at the last minute not to attend the Ohio gathering.

Almost immediately, Montezuma, Sloan, and Cornelius complained to the executive committee that as a government employee Dagenett would have a conflict of interest in any disputes with the Indian Office. They insisted that he step down as secretary-treasurer. Doubts about Sloan were also raised from anonymous sources. Charges of unethical conduct first made against him years earlier at the Omaha agency were repeated, as was the charge that he approved the use of peyote in Indian religious rituals. The latter issue, which was particularly important among Christian Indian missionaries like Coolidge and John Eastman, would bedevil the organization for most of its history.[51]

When Sloan's critics suggested in November he be replaced by Coolidge, who lived in Wyoming, the chairman worried publicly that with the mild-mannered Anglican minister leading from his pulpit two thousand miles to the west, "the secretary would control."

Dagenett resigned in January 1912, and Sloan replaced him with Parker. The two seemed to communicate well, but opposition to Sloan continued, and Parker, inexperienced but ambitious, agreed with those who considered the Omaha lawyer a liability. Sloan wanted to continue. "We have waited too long to get together to do something," he wrote Parker. "I know that every day that we wait some Indian is losing some thing." Sloan argued that the situation was particularly critical in the West, where the allotment process was being extended to large, arid reservations that would quickly be overrun by settlers. As he explained, "Among the New York Indians a session of Congress or a year in time will not affect a material change, but among the Western Indians they and their property are in the way of an advancing and aggressive civilization. . . . We must be doing something," he wrote, "or I will resign."[52]

Sloan and Montezuma envisioned an aggressive organization that would provide legal assistance to tribes and lobby on their behalf before Congress. The Omaha attorney traveled to Washington in January 1912, rented an office, and threw himself into the legislative arena. "I have been busy at the Indian Office and with Congress," he reported on February 19. A month later he wrote that "there are many Indians here. . . . I have been able to get a number of them to come to the office." He added that the commissioner of Indian affairs had asked him "to meet at dinner to discuss the affairs of Indians generally."[53] The good citizenship gun seemed to be producing results on the national stage. Then suddenly, in late March, Sloan resigned and was replaced by Sherman Coolidge.

SURVIVING DOCUMENTS tell us little about Sloan's departure from the SAI, but his correspondence with Parker and the subsequent tone of the society's activities indicate that the founding leader's determination to take an aggressive stance toward the Indian Office worried others in the leadership group. Arthur Parker, uncomfortable with legal confrontations and western tribal rivalries, urged caution from the start. A nephew of General Ely Parker, who had served as Indian commissioner under President U.S. Grant, the thirty-year-old had not attended a government boarding school and had little experience with western tribes or reservation politics. His principal interest in 1911 was building a strong base of support among white reformers. Parker wrote Sloan immediately after the Columbus meeting to remind him that "we are a small disorganized body. . . . Unless we win the unhesitating confidence of all classes, we will surely fail as there is a sun in the heavens."[54] When Sloan refused to change his tactics, Parker argued even more strongly for caution. "If we can but demonstrate that we can run in harmony for even a little while and maintain an attitude of constructive criticism toward the government, not mere destructive criticism that suggests no remedy; if we can only demonstrate our sanity . . . and proceed cautiously, we will receive help from quarters that we little suspect."[55]

With the pious (and geographically distant) Reverend Coolidge installed as president, the society adopted a distinctly conciliatory stance. The first issue of the group's magazine assured its readers, who were both Native activists and non-Indian supporters, that it was not "a political or partisan organization." The issue emphasized the society's patriotism and support for the respectable Indian Rights Association. Writing to Pratt after the second SAI convention in Columbus in October 1912, Dennison Wheelock expressed the dissatisfaction of those who opposed this quiet tone. "I have not changed my opinion respecting the Society of American Indians which I told you at Columbus," Wheelock told his former headmaster. "I did not have very much faith in the society doing very much good for the Indians because of the limited experience of those who are the leaders." And Wheelock was not impressed with Parker. "The addresses and writings of the Secretary . . . are but the echo of the Indian Rights Association, Lake Mohonk, and such other paper shooters."⁵⁶

Agreeing that the society was now in the hands of "paper shooters," Sloan returned to his legal practice. He and Montezuma maintained their memberships in the SAI but passed up the group's annual meetings. Shuttling between Nebraska and Washington, D.C., the Omaha attorney became involved instead with an array of tribes and a number of congressional disputes over federal policy. His repeated confrontations with federal officials over the issue of Indian competence convinced him that Indian Office paternalism was the greatest threat to Indian rights. "Every Congress has before it legislation detrimental to the Indian," he told an audience of Indian students at Carlisle in 1912. "In nine cases out of ten the legislation is promoted by capitalists, speculators and railroad men who are more able than the Indian to reach their Congressmen, and through them the Indian Office. . . ." As a consequence, the arbitrary powers of this federal agency, charged with protecting Indians, were routinely used to exploit them. "The abolition of the Indian Office," he soon concluded, "is the only true solution of the Indian question." He wrote Arthur Parker, "We cannot be an Indian society and be neutral." He added, "It is time for action."⁵⁷

While Sloan aimed his attacks at the Indian Office, his real target remained the race-based guardianship restrictions federal authorities had established during the previous decade. Alluding to the restrictions placed on the property rights, civil liberties, and personal freedoms of dependent Indians, Sloan argued that Indian citizens were "the only persons who are denied the courts, the only persons who are deprived of liberty without due process of law, the only persons who are deprived of their property without due process of law. The only persons who are kept within Federal restraint and allowed to starve." The solution to this predicament was "citizenship and individual property rights." Indians had to rely on the courts, he insisted, because "the political powers may assert themselves over the Indian property and the political preferences are stronger than the Indian rights."[58]

Sloan's passion for the rights of citizen allottees was no doubt fueled by his growing list of frustrated and disillusioned Indian clients. The Omaha attorney, who by 1912 had permanently relocated to Washington, D.C., frequently represented plaintiffs who challenged the government's determination of heirs to individual allotments or who wished to appeal their exclusion from tribal membership rolls.[59] He carried yet another appeal of enrollment decisions at the Omaha agency to the Supreme Court in 1917.[60] He also joined forces with administration critics on Capitol Hill such as the Progressive senator Robert La Follette, a member of the Senate Indian Affairs Committee, who were willing to provide unhappy tribal leaders with a forum for their grievances. In 1913 one of La Follette's Senate allies, Joseph Robinson, from Arkansas, enlisted Sloan as a special agent for a Joint Commission to Investigate Indian Affairs. This assignment produced additional invitations from congressional Indian Affairs committees to travel to the Crow, Blackfeet, White Earth, and Yankton reservations to investigate charges of agency corruption and illegal leasing arrangements as well as charges that officials had arbitrarily classified tribal members as "incompetents."[61]

Sloan's travels widened the scope of his political contacts and allies. When he conducted his investigation at the Crow agency, for example, he reported: "I met there a number of Indians who I had met before at the schools, either at Hampton or Carlisle." As a result, he noted, "I did not meet any of the agency officials."[62] The attorney followed the same pattern in 1914 at the Blackfeet agency (where the agency police followed him throughout his visit). He avoided the local agent, spending his time instead with Robert Hamilton, a young Carlisle graduate who offered sensational testimony describing starvation and suffering among the tribe's traditionalists and widespread corruption among government employees.[63] Two years later Sloan used the testimony of some of these acquaintances at a Washington hearing. As he argued in support of a reform proposal, the attorney introduced the senators present to tribal delegates who had recently arrived from the Comanche and Klamath reserves, as well as to Hamilton, also in the city on behalf of his tribe.[64]

By the end of the decade Sloan had become a prominent figure in the world of Indian law and policy. When he appeared before the Senate Indian Affairs Committee in 1919, he introduced himself as a lawyer who practiced not only in the federal courts but also "before the Interior Department. I am a member of the Omaha tribe of Indians," he told the legislators, "and make a specialty of Indian work."[65] This specialty involved representing a number of tribes, either as attorney or informal adviser, and traveling regularly on their behalf. He reported meeting with the Sioux Black Hills Council in South Dakota, the Grand Council of the Chippewa Indian Tribe of Minnesota, and the leaders of the Osage tribe.[66] Throughout these encounters Sloan held firmly to the idea that collusion between the Indian Office and powerful non-Indian business interests was the principal reason why white officials insisted on defining Native people as "dependent" and "backward." "My idea of the situation is this," he told the Senate committee after a trip to a western reservation, "it seemed to me that [the Indians'] rights were made subservient to the cattlemen. . . . That instead of the tribes being the dominant owners of the soil and having the rights there, they were the fellows who were least considered, and through that treatment . . . they had become dependents."[67] "The grafter could not succeed in his graft," he declared in 1920, "if the Indian Bureau did not make it possible."[68]

By the end of World War I, Sloan and Montezuma were no longer isolated voices. Montezuma established his own network of supporters through *Wassaja*, a monthly newsletter he established in 1916 that carried the dramatic subhead "Let My People Go." His attacks on the Indian Office and on Arthur Parker's leadership of the Society of American Indians intensified during World War I, when the Chicago physician declared that Indians should not answer the military draft until they all were declared citizens. Eight months into the war, in December 1917, Montezuma announced the formation of a new organization, the League for the Extension of Democracy to the American Indians. Endorsed by a group that included Sloan, Charles Eastman, and Frank Beaulieu, son of the late Gus Beaulieu, the League declared its "chief aim" to be "the total abolition of the Indian Bureau as at present constituted." Adopting the language of patriotic groups that were supporting the war, Montezuma declared that he expected all Americans to support him. The elimination of the Indian Office, he wrote, should appeal to "staunch Americans, lovers of liberty and haters of Prussian methods of government. . . ."[69] As Montezuma intensified his attacks, the SAI grew less cautious. Arthur Parker stepped down as the editor of the group's magazine in 1918. He was replaced by the popular author Gertrude Bonnin, Montezuma's former fiancée, who, writing under the name Zitkala Sa, had published fiery critiques of government and missionary paternalism. Bonnin organized that year's annual meeting in Pierre, South Dakota, and invited Montezuma to address the gathering. Montezuma took the stage to deliver an address entitled "Abolish the Indian Bureau," and the assembly adopted resolutions endorsing citizenship and declaring that the Indian Office "was never intended to be a permanent part of the Interior Department."[70]

The idealism unleashed by the Allied victory in Europe reenergized Sloan's and Montezuma's attacks. Government paternalism represents "another Kaiser in America," the Yavapai physician wrote in November 1918; "we have done away with one, let the people of the United States do the same with the Indian Bureau."[71] Despite his opposition to the draft, Montezuma saw that Woodrow Wilson's idealistic framing of the conflict as a battle for democracy provided him an opening. He proposed including American Indians at the Paris Peace Conference. "Why? Because the Indians are a nation . . . [and] have never received justice from the United States. . . . You may speak about the abuses and mistreatments received by the Belgians, the Bohemians, Poles, Serbians, and other nations of the old country," he added; "their griefs [*sic*] . . . are no comparison to the treatment of the Indians."[72] Gertrude Bonnin agreed, writing a few months later in the society magazine that "the eyes of the world are upon . . . Paris. . . . Little peoples are to be granted the right of self determination." Bonnin noted that labor organizations, women's groups, African Americans, and the Irish all were to be represented at Versailles, but no American Indian. "Who shall represent his cause at the World's Peace Conference? The American Indian too made the supreme sacrifice for liberty's sake. He loves democratic ideals. What shall the world democracy mean to his race?"[73] Writing in the same issue, Charles Eastman, the society's new president, repeated the theme: "How can our nation pose as the champion of the 'little peoples' until it has been fair to its own?"[74]

The American Indians' impressive sacrifices during the war only added to the activists' argument. More than ten thousand Indians had served in uniform, most in integrated units. Choctaw code talkers won praise for their ability to maintain electronic contact between units on the battlefield while Sioux scouts were celebrated for their daring and bravery. Indian leaders supported bond drives and Red Cross campaigns, winning praise from both the Indian Office and their white neighbors. When the SAI gathered for its annual meeting in Minneapolis in October 1919, it seemed poised for a change in direction. Sloan and Montezuma were present, as were Eastman, Bonnin, Thomas Bishop, the leader of the Northwest Indian Organization, and a number of Ojibwe tribal members clamoring for greater control over their reservation resources. Also present were several of the men who had supported the League for the Extension of Democracy in the pages of *Wassaja* two years earlier: Theodore Beaulieu, the Reverend Philip Gordon, and John Carl. Carl, a lawyer, had also been present a decade earlier at the founding of the short-lived Indian Memorial Association.

According to an account later published in *Wassaja*, Sloan galvanized the Minneapolis meeting when he responded to a proposal from the floor that citizenship should be extended to only such "qualified" Indians as veterans or graduates of boarding schools. "The Indian is a native of this country," the attorney thundered, "and it is a universal rule of civilization that a person shall be a citizen of the country of which he is a native." Sloan acknowledged the sacrifice of Indian veterans but added, "The parents who furnished Indian boys for soldiers should be entitled to citizenship as well as their boys." Returning to a theme he had repeated before judges and congressmen for more than a decade, Sloan shouted, "The backward subject Indian needs citizenship more than the advanced Indian. He is the one who needs the protection of the laws of the country as much against dishonest or careless supervision as against the grafter who is permitted to assail his rights." After years on the fringes of the society's activities, Sloan seemed to be speaking for the entire membership as he ended on an idealistic Wilsonian theme: "It is time that the weak nations at home should receive some just consideration. . . . Let us apply the justice we are carrying to the weak nations abroad to the weak nations at home." According to *Wassaja,* "It was a speech never to be forgotten." When the balloting for president began, Sloan was elected with an overwhelming majority.[75]

THE LIMITS OF THE GOOD CITIZENSHIP GUN

Sloan entered office with a rush of enthusiasm. As Montezuma's newsletter exclaimed, "If there was ever a man who stood up for the Indian, it was Tommy Sloan." Referring indirectly to Sloan's light skin and gray hair, Montezuma added, "He has been rolled over, tested and found to be true to his race. Others would have given up in sticking to the Indians, but Tommy stuck."[76] Over his first months in office the new president redesigned the society's magazine in hopes that it would appeal to a wider audience and generate much-needed income. He also reached out to his contacts across the country. Richard Pratt was one of these who welcomed Sloan's election. "The large opportunities that come to you to aid the cause of the Indians," he wrote, "are now in abler hands than ever before."[77] And returning to the tactics he had proposed a decade earlier, Sloan began welcoming tribal delegations to Washington and orchestrating strategic meetings with government leaders. "I have taken a great many delegations to call on the President in the past two years," he wrote the secretary of the interior in 1923, "Indians from every part of the country." As he had in 1912, Sloan insisted that these encounters should produce more than pious expressions of sympathy. "The policies and treatment of Indians . . . must be changed by positive and prompt action," he continued. "If not, the words and actions of the President will be lost."[78]

Within months of Thomas Sloan's election, it became obvious that Montezuma's excitement and Pratt's optimism would be short-lived. The society's magazine claimed that the new president's "two hundred and twenty odd pounds of muscle, brain and energy seem tireless," but Sloan himself complained that Cato Sells, the commissioner of Indian affairs, and his chief deputy, Edgar Meritt, were "slandering" him with the Indian affairs committees of Congress. The relentless hostility of these outgoing Wilson appointees (and the Republicans' bright prospects for the coming election) may in turn have influenced Sloan's decision to call on the GOP's presidential candidate, Warren G. Harding, in the summer of 1920 and pledge his support. "I hope to arrange for the activity of Indians in those localities where their votes may be of effect," Sloan reported to Richard Pratt at the end of June, noting that Indians might well cast the deciding votes in Minnesota and Montana. It was time for politicians to look beyond their tribes, he added, and "stand for the Indians."[79] His blatant bid for political influence angered, and probably frightened, Sells and Meritt and reignited the resentment and internal feuding that had swirled around Sloan's tactics in the first months of the organization's existence. Sloan's old enemies were quick to renew their attacks on him. Arthur Parker resigned from the group's executive committee, while Charles Carter, a Choctaw and a Democratic congressman from Oklahoma, called Sloan's action "disgraceful." The educator Henry Roe Cloud suspended his membership to protest the actions of Sloan and other "extremists," while the former secretary-treasurer Gertrude Bonnin began circulating a petition attacking the new leadership.[80]

The society never recovered. Its 1920 conference, held in St. Louis, the city of Sloan's birth, was poorly attended and rancorous. The president was reelected, but he and the other leaders reported disappointing sales for their glossy new *American Indian Magazine*, and the gathering revealed continuing divisions over federal restrictions on peyote use and the organization's position regarding political endorsements. With declining membership and no white philanthropist or reform group coming forward to subsidize it or to support a redesign of its magazine, the society's budget problems multiplied. A year later only eight members appeared at an informal gathering in Detroit. The society held its final conference in Chicago in 1922. This meeting was not only poorly attended but obscured by a popular Indian encampment held in a forest preserve near the city. Hovering over the gathering as well was the absent Carlos Montezuma, afflicted with tuberculosis and living among his Yavapai relatives in Arizona. Montezuma died a few months after the Chicago gathering; the society never met again.[81]

THOMAS SLOAN HAD hoped that his support for Harding would win him the nomination to be commissioner of Indian affairs when the Republicans returned to power in 1921. Both he and his fellow attorney Dennison Wheelock of Wisconsin campaigned actively for the position (presumably so they could better abolish it), but they had little support beyond a few sympathetic congressmen and a narrow group of loyalists like Montezuma and Richard Pratt.[82] The two must have felt particularly chastened when Harding nominated South Dakota congressman Charles H. Burke, a former real estate developer and party loyalist who staunchly supported the Indian Office's paternalistic approach of "sympathy, patience and humanity." Burke claimed that paternalism had actually been a successful theme in both Republican and Democratic administrations. After all, he noted, the government had encountered "no hostile Indian uprisings such as marked . . . previous decades for three centuries." Burke could barely contain his contempt for the educated activists who had challenged the government's definitions of civilization. He preferred to focus on the Indian's "benighted" and "degraded" culture, whose existence provided perpetual justification for the government's high-handed actions.[83]

The intransigence of the national bureaucracy was revealed again to Sloan in 1923, when, following the resignation of Albert B. Fall as the secretary of the interior, disgraced by the Teapot Dome scandal, the administration invited a National Advisory Committee of One Hundred to gather in Washington for an "appraisal of national Indian policy." Announced in May, the list of invitees included Sloan and Wheelock and an array of their SAI rivals: Arthur Parker, Sherman Coolidge, and Henry Roe Cloud. The vast majority of the group, however, consisted of non-Indian experts: anthropologists, such as the Smithsonian's Frederick Hodge and the American Museum of Natural History curator Clark Wissler; reformers, including ninety-year-old Amelia Stone Quinton and the Indian Rights Association founder Herbert Welsh; the retired generals Nelson Miles, John J. Pershing, and Hugh Scott; and the prominent university presidents Nicholas Murray Butler (Columbia) and David Starr Jordan (Stanford). Among the other members of this diverse assembly were the popular writers Mary Roberts Rinehart and George Wharton James and the publishers William Randolph Hearst and Joseph Pulitzer.[84]

Sixty-six committee members gathered in Washington the following December to deliberate. Unfortunately for Sloan, the group elected Arthur Parker to chair the meeting, ensuring that the committee's pronouncements would be vague and conciliatory.[85] Among the fifteen resolutions adopted at the meeting were declarations of sympathy for the work of the Indian Office ("our benevolent desires have not been attained"), support for missionaries seeking to "bring religion into the thought and life of the Indians," and appreciation for the Harding administration's "great service in promoting and protecting the interests of the Indians. . . ." The group endorsed opening the Court of Claims to all tribes but did not mention Indian citizenship or suggest the need for a significant change in government policy.[86]

Sloan was disgusted. He wrote politely but pointedly to the secretary of the interior that "a group that seemed to have had prearranged . . . policies dominated the floor . . . using most of the time following out their program." The attorney was more direct when reporting to his old mentor Richard Pratt. Sloan declared that the Committee of One Hundred demonstrated clearly "how small and rotten the Indian Bureau may be." He charged that officials in the Interior Department had invited their allies to a preconference planning session and that Parker was "the Bureau's choice" to be chair: "He was a boob and every reference to the meeting marks him as incompetent at least." Sloan noted that all his own proposals "were seconded by Indians" but that none had been adopted. The gathering was "a great chance to expose the system," he wrote, but the possibilities had evaporated. "Hope you may see some changes in Indian affairs soon," he told Pratt, then added: "Just how it will come about, I do not know."[87]

Other critics of the Indian Office agreed with Sloan's negative assessment. The outspoken liberal reformer Oswald Garrison Villard of the *Nation* called Arthur Parker "the most incompetent and bemuddling chairman who ever presided over any such gathering," but he saved his strongest language for William Jennings Bryan, the three-time presidential candidate who in retirement had become "a professional religious zealot." Villard reported that the former secretary of state had hogged the spotlight at the committee meeting, demonstrating his desire "to shove the Christian religion down the throats of every Indian."[88]

The social worker John Collier was also present at the Washington meeting. The future New Deal commissioner of Indian affairs had been named to the Committee of One Hundred in the wake of his highly publicized attack on an administration-sanctioned scheme to deprive Pueblo Indians of their New Mexico lands. Like Sloan and Villard, he saw the heavy hand of the Indian Office throughout the proceedings. "It was amusing," Collier reported, "to watch how, as the meeting progressed, those who stood for the continuance of the existing order in Indian affairs gradually concentrated at the right of the hall, and the group standing for a new order concentrated to the left. . . . At the end," he noted, "the superb [Catholic] Bishop Lawler of South Dakota, was sitting with Thomas Sloane [sic] and Oswald Villard . . . plotting the means to circumvent the chairman, a reactionary."[89]

"There is so much to do that it seems hard to select the right move," Sloan wrote to Pratt in the wake of the Washington meeting. Nevertheless, he remained defiant—"there is no doubt I can do something," he added—but the optimistic spirit of the good citizenship gun exchange from a dozen years earlier had disappeared.[90] The society had disintegrated. Montezuma was gone, and other old allies were slipping away. Charles Eastman, now separated from his wife and living much of the year in a cabin near Lake Huron, had retreated from most public activity. Laura Cornelius Kellogg (she married Orrin J. Kellogg in 1912) was now focusing most of her energies on a campaign to reunite the widely dispersed members of the eighteenth-century Iroquois Confederacy. Other society founders, such as Dagenett and Standing Bear, had either retired or disappeared from the scene. The American public seemed more interested in the imaginary Indians favored by the

Boy Scouts and summer camps than in real people and their troubling complaints.[91]

Meanwhile, the relentless process of allotment had divided tribal lands, opened new tracts to real estate speculators, isolated struggling Indian farmers from one another, and gradually eliminated the barriers that had protected tribal enclaves from the destructive forces of the marketplace. Indians were losing their resources at an unprecedented rate. As a consequence, the *New Republic's* Elizabeth Shepley Sergeant wrote in early 1924, poverty had become the single dominant factor in Indian life: "Our Indian ward, in spite of his vast land reservations, in spite of the gigantic and expensive bureaucracy, and the innumerable missions and welfare societies created on his behalf[,] is immensely and incredibly poor."[92] In this darkening climate, Sloan returned to his legal practice and to his work as a lobbyist and congressional investigator.

FOR THE REMAINDER of the 1920s and through most of the following decade, Sloan continued to argue on behalf of Indian citizenship and in opposition to government paternalism. He represented tribes and individuals that had been treated arbitrarily and unfairly by federal authorities. He filed cases in federal court and appeared frequently before congressional committees. "Every time there is a hearing," the Indian Office's veteran assistant commissioner Edgar Meritt complained, Sloan "comes up and knocks the Indian Bureau and everybody else."[93] On most occasions, the lawyer appeared before congressional committees as counsel for visiting tribal delegates. His constant enemy was unchecked federal power. As he explained to a Senate panel in 1923, he had always been "impressed by the legislation in the past" that promised Indians citizenship while recognizing their claims on tribal property, but he had witnessed "a tendency to get away from that in the Indian Bureau."[94]

From Sloan's perspective, Commissioner Burke was a perfect illustration of the government's habit of concentrating authority in its own hands. The former South Dakota congressman's pliant response to the Interior Department scandals during the Harding administration, his manipulation of the Committee of One Hundred meetings, and his unbending public opposition to traditional native ceremonies and dances exemplified the worst aspects of Indian Office paternalism. Sloan believed not only that individual Indians deserved the right to question and appeal the government's actions but also that as corporate entities tribes should be treated with respect. "I feel that since they have been a treaty making power and recognized as that in the first instance," he told one congressional panel, "they ought to be fairly dealt with and be heard in everything that deals with and pertains to that tribe."[95]

Commissioner Burke's consolidation of Indian Office authority in the 1920s gradually shifted the context for discussions of Indian citizenship. Few activists now imagined that extending U.S. citizenship to Indians would empower Native people. The implementation of the Dawes allotment law over the previous three decades had extended citizenship to more than half the American Indian population, but the recipients of this new status were so hampered by poverty and overawed by the power of their federal supervisors that their lives had changed very little. Few of them gained political influence beyond their tribes, and all who lived on reservations remained under the administrative control of the Indian Office. Individual Indians could be jailed without trial, barred from performing religious rituals, and removed from participating in the disposition of trust property assigned to them. The conditions Sloan had witnessed as a young man on the Omaha reserve had hardly changed.

When a general citizenship bill was adopted in 1924, it stirred little interest. In January of that year the New York congressman Homer Snyder proposed that the secretary of the interior should issue a certificate of citizenship to any Native person who applied for one. Snyder's proposal passed the House, but when it was submitted to the Senate, Sloan's friends on the Indian Affairs Committee—particularly Wisconsin's Progressive Party standard-bearer Robert La Follette and his ally Burton K. Wheeler of Montana—rewrote the measure, expanding it into a unilateral declaration. Their revision said simply that "all non-citizen Indians born within the territorial limits of the United States . . . are hereby declared citizens of the United States." This revision formed the substance of the law both houses approved in May. The new measure stipulated that citizenship would not "impair" the right of anyone to share in tribal property, and Congressman Snyder assured his House colleagues on the eve of its passage that state restrictions on Indian voting, which remained on the books in Arizona, Utah, and New Mexico until after World War II, would be unaffected. The potential of the citizenship gun to transform the status and condition of Native Americans would remain unfulfilled.[96]

Despite his frustration with the federally sanctioned limits on Indian citizenship that had become commonplace in the 1920s, Thomas Sloan continued to work for an expanded understanding of Indian rights as he represented his clients in court and before Congress.[97] He never retreated from his opposition to the Indian Office. He opposed the federal government's effort to reorganize tribal governments during the 1930s, telling one congressional committee that the reformer John Collier's New Deal policies were simply another exercise in paternalism. "Is it necessary for [Indians] to give up their individuality as men," he asked, "to be segregated back into a condition out of which they were induced to make an effort to overcome?"[98]

"I am anxious to succeed and keep on with my work," Sloan wrote the Indian Rights Association in 1940, shortly before his death. He added, "I am not giving up, but I may be overcome . . . my clients . . . are harassed and threatened."[99] As he prepared an appeal to the Supreme Court on behalf of a group of California Indian allottees, the attorney must have been aware that his lifelong legal campaign had failed. While continuing to labor on behalf of the rights of Indian citizens, Sloan could see that without a shift in public attitudes and political climate, the judges and legislators hearing his appeals would not be sympathetic.

For activists like Sloan, the good citizenship gun had been an empowering idea. It promised legal equality and access to political power. The response of his adversaries in the Indian Office and elsewhere—that Indians are hopelessly backward and incompetent—had scuttled his efforts. The rising tide of Indian poverty only reinforced those racist views. Native people, many believed, were simply destined to suffer. Success would not come to activists like Sloan until such assumptions had been challenged and the concept of general racial equality had gained broad support. Only then could Native activists achieve the status that had been promised to Thomas Sloan and his colleagues in the boarding schools, churches, and meeting halls of their youth. For the moment the good citizenship gun lay dormant.

In 1968, more than forty years after Congress had extended citizenship to Native Americans, President Lyndon Johnson signed the American Indian Civil Rights Act, which, for the first time, spelled out what some of the rights of Indian people should be. Enacted after extensive hearings, in which Native witnesses described daily life in reservation communities, the law placed clear limits on the power of both tribal and federal authorities. The new law assured tribes and their members that they would be free from arbitrary authority and would have ready access to the courts. It is significant that the new law was passed in a different era and a generation after Thomas Sloan's death, for it reflected the transformation in racial attitudes that was occurring in the United States at the time of its adoption. In the end it was those racial attitudes, not the law, that had defeated the Omaha lawyer.[100]

————————————≺

Chapter Seven

THREE INDIANS WHO DIDN'T LIVE AT TAOS

Robert Yellowtail, Crow
Alice Jemison, Seneca
and D'Arcy McNickle, Salish

D uring the 1930s and 1940s Franklin Roosevelt introduced an unprecedented set of initiatives that saved the economy from economic catastrophe, united the nation in a global struggle against fascism, and in the process remade the relationship between the American people and their government. Empowered by the desperation born of multiple crises, his New Deal administration devised revolutionary new programs to regulate business, deliver assistance to impoverished citizens, and organize national resources for the common good. These efforts not only brought the federal government into the daily lives of Americans (in the form of Social Security payments, agricultural subsidies, and minimum wage laws) but also allowed the public to imagine for a time that its government could be a guarantor of prosperity, peace, and social progress.

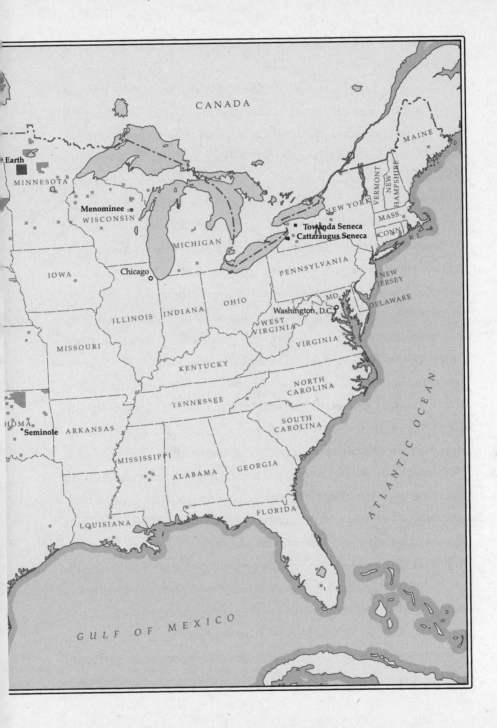

The Indian New Deal was a significant feature of the Roosevelt Revolution that swept through Washington, D.C. Between 1933 and 1945 Congress and the Indian Office collaborated to end the devastating policy of land allotment, enable the creation of modern tribal governments, improve Native education, and reverse the federal government's century-long campaign to replace tribal cultures and religious traditions with civilization. If James McDonald and William Potter Ross had miraculously reappeared in the national capital at the end of World War II, they would have found the official atmosphere completely unrecognizable. The United States seemed no longer dedicated to the Indians' disappearance from the American political landscape, and Indians were speaking out in unprecedented numbers.

Most accounts of this social and political transformation have logically focused on one man, John Collier, Roosevelt's commissioner of Indian affairs, who served for the entire twelve years of FDR's presidency and initiated most of the era's policy reforms. A former New York City social worker, Collier was (and remains) the longest-serving head of the Indian Office. Arriving on the scene at a moment when starvation and despair had infected tribal communities in every region, Collier worked furiously to send aid dollars to needy reservations while he created opportunities for Native Americans to participate in every new form of federal assistance, from highway construction subsidies to vocational training and conservation projects.

But measuring the achievements of the New Deal era through the career of John Collier would be a mistake. Not only was he given to overstating his personal contributions to the changes that occurred on his watch, but also focusing on legal and policy reforms obscures the period's most powerful event: the sudden emergence of an extraordinary generation of Native activists who seized the opportunities provided by the New Deal reforms to create a national leadership that by the 1950s was able to wield unprecedented influence over public discussions of the American Indian future. While this new generation of leaders appeared among many tribes and articulated a variety of concerns, three individuals can provide a shorthand summary of its origins and the diversity of viewpoints contained within it. Robert Yellowtail, a reservation leader from Montana, Alice Jemison, a Seneca activist from New York, and D'Arcy McNickle, a young writer who served the Indian Office in Washington, D.C., had different opinions of the New Deal, but they all jumped into the national political arena during those years of reform.

John Collier played an important role in creating the conditions for these individuals' rise to positions of influence, but despite his claims to the contrary, he neither created the three leaders nor shaped their— or their contemporaries'—political manifestos. McDonald and Ross might have been amazed by the scale of American Indian political activity in 1945 but they would not have been surprised by the positions Native activists were taking.

AT THE TIME of his appointment in 1933, John Collier was among the best-known Indian policy experts in the United States. He had spent most of the previous decade as the leader of the American Indian Defense Association rallying environmentalists, social reformers, and progressive politicians to the cause of protecting Indians from government corruption and abuse. His correspondents and supporters included the popular southwestern author Mary Austin; Roger Baldwin, the founder of the American Civil Liberties Union; the progressive reformers Arthur Morgan, Robert Ely, and Harold Ickes; and the

Progressive political insurgents Robert La Follette and William Borah. Collier's activities were generously supported by the General Federation of Women's Clubs and wealthy patrons in California and New York.[1] Significantly, the new commissioner had few ties to Native American activists outside the Southwest, where he had concentrated his efforts. As the Crow politician Robert Yellowtail wrote him from Montana in 1932, "At present your [*sic*] not known here."[2]

The major reason that John Collier was unknown to activists outside the Southwest was that his chief attachment was not to the reality of American Indians but to their image. The new commissioner was convinced that American Indians were modern embodiments of an ancient continental civilization. This idea first occurred to him in December 1920, but it remained with him for the rest of his life. The experience, which he called his "earth shaking discovery of American Indians," took place during a Christmas visit to New Mexico's Taos Pueblo.[3] Collier later recalled that as the costumed Native dancers emerged onto the Taos plaza, they "entered into myself and each one of my family as a new direction in life." They signaled, he added, "a new, even wildly new hope for the Race of Man." For him, these dancing Indians represented "face to face, primary social groups"; they were living proof that "deep community yet lived on in the embattled Red Indians." He decided on the spot that the campaign to protect the Indians "must not fail."[4]

These were powerful words, but they did not acknowledge that in 1920 most Indians did not live at Taos, and few shared Collier's romantic view of Native culture. He believed from that year onward that the nation's indigenous communities had become stagnant in the twentieth century and were waiting to be saved. That faith inspired him to bring Indian issues to national attention, but it also blinded him to the efforts and perspectives of the Native activists who rallied to his side during the New Deal. Collier believed to the end of his life that he had reawakened the Indians during his years of activism, but the tribal advocates who emerged during the New Deal and carried the Indian cause forward into the 1950s were not his creations; they were the heirs of decades of advocacy by predecessors in every corner of the nation. The modern tribal activists' demands—that Native cultures be respected, that treaties be enforced, and that the Indians' citizenship rights be respected—were not initiated by John Collier or Franklin Roosevelt. These national figures did, however, create dozens of new avenues that enabled Natives to bring their demands before the public and hundreds of new forums where those demands could be heard and amplified.

THREE ACTIVISTS

If John Collier had sought out Indian leaders beyond the plaza at Taos in 1920, he would have discovered that the vast majority of the prominent Native men and women was preoccupied with practical needs; they had little interest in saving the "Race of Man." They understood that the violence and dislocation visited on their people during the previous half century had divided, not united, their communities. While drawn to Collier's idealism, they were more likely to be skeptical that the omnipotent spirit he had sensed at Taos would come to them through the revival of deep community. Three individuals— Robert Yellowtail, Alice Jemison, and D'Arcy McNickle—typified the young leaders Collier overlooked.

Collier's Montana correspondent Robert Yellowtail was a remarkable tribal politician.[5] He was born in 1889 on the Montana reservation that had been carved out of the Crows' ancestral hunting grounds in the shadow of the Bighorn Mountains. Despite the trauma of being forcibly removed from his family at the age of four and confined to the local agency boarding school, Yellowtail had been an eager and accomplished student—so eager, in fact, that as a teenager he asked the local authorities to send him to Sherman Institute in Southern California to further his education. He excelled there. He even dreamed of becoming a lawyer. He returned to the reservation in the first decade of the new century. While dismissed by the local agent as "nervous, highstrung [and] bad tempered," he became active in tribal affairs.[6]

Reservation leaders—men who had hunted buffalo as young men—quickly recruited the articulate young Yellowtail to serve as their translator and adviser. He helped the chiefs negotiate grazing leases with local cattlemen and accompanied a group of them to New York and Washington, D.C., in 1913. But his potential was not made plain until two years later, when he appeared before a special tribal council meeting to discuss the opening of the reservation to white homesteaders. The Montana senator Henry Myers and Wyoming governor Benjamin Kendrick chaired the gathering, but the local *Hardin Herald* noted that Robert Yellowtail delivered "an extended speech" that attacked the sale of tribal land to outsiders. At the time Yellowtail held no position in the tribe, but his speech garnered enthusiastic praise from the audience. Montana papers were usually dismissive of local tribal leaders, but the *Herald* reporter noted that this young man was "quite an orator."[7]

Yellowtail quickly became a fixture on the reservation, serving as a confidant of tribal elders, an elected council member, and, increasingly, an advocate for tribal rights. He learned to defer to aging warriors such as Chief Plenty Coups and to support their claims with incisive modern arguments. In 1919 his stirring use of Woodrow Wilson's language of self-determination at one congressional hearing turned heads in Congress and among other tribal leaders. The senators sat in silence as Yellowtail quoted the president's call for self-determination and exclaimed that "our lands . . . were, to begin with, ours . . . not given to us by anybody."[8]

During the 1920s Yellowtail took up the role of a political boss. He assembled majorities in tribal council meetings and made life difficult for local ranchers and farmers during negotiations over the leasing of tribal land and resources. He was unafraid to call for the removal of unresponsive federal agents, and in 1926 he jumped eagerly into the effort to win approval for a jurisdictional act that opened the way for the tribe to file a suit in the U.S. Court of Claims. Yellowtail's activism won him an invitation to participate in the Committee of One Hundred, assembled in 1923 by the Interior Department and where he likely met both Thomas Sloan and John Collier. A lifelong Teddy Roosevelt Republican, the Crow politician attended the national GOP convention in 1928 and announced a plan to run for state senator in 1932.

Yellowtail was representative of the Indian leaders who had been pressured for decades to sell off tribal grazing land and open other resources up to outsiders. Following in the footsteps of William Potter Ross, the young Crow leader argued that reservations should be viewed as autonomous enclaves that deserved federal protection. This outlook emerged not from a mystical faith in community but from practical experience and was shared by other leaders who had followed similar paths. Despite Yellowtail's correspondence with John Collier, he exhibited little interest in the reformer's vision of Indian contributions to "the Race of Man." Instead, Yellowtail proposed that the major parties adopt identical platforms endorsing the proposition that the "principles of representative government" should apply to "all of the inhabitants of the United States, including the many Indian tribes now denominated as 'wards.'"[9] He believed tribes should organize their own governments, review federal budgets, and oversee the appointment of Indian Office personnel at their agencies.

Robert Yellowtail reasoned in broad strokes. He believed, for example, that individual Indians like him should seek elective office in county and state governments and be engaged in the local economy, even while he called on the Indian Office to protect his tribe's special tax exemptions and federal subsidies. He encouraged the national government to support the Crows financially, but he rejected outside interference in tribal affairs. In short, he supported goals that seemed often to contradict one another: citizenship, individual rights, treaty rights for Indian groups, federal assistance, individual entrepreneurship, and tribal autonomy. In 1932 neither Yellowtail nor his fellow tribal leaders worried much over these conflicts. His philosophy was pragmatic: press for whatever seemed attainable, and manage the choices that arose. As he wrote in a circular to Montana tribal leaders in the spring of 1932, "The game in the final analysis is played politically: we . . . should play it . . . to get results."[10]

YELLOWTAIL REPRESENTED only one set of Native activists whose concerns did not conform to the new commissioner's romantic vision. Another group, represented by the Seneca activist Alice Jemison, were the heirs of Carlos Montezuma's campaign to abolish the Indian Office, an institution they believed was hopelessly committed to paternalism. In 1933, a decade after Montezuma's death, a number of his former colleagues carried on his fight. Thomas Sloan, now relocated to California, was one of them. The Omaha attorney's most prominent clients during the New Deal were Coahuilla band members in the burgeoning resort town of Palm Springs, California, who petitioned federal authorities to grant them clear titles to their increasingly valuable real estate. They believed the government's protections were preventing them from enjoying the full benefit of their properties.[11]

This link of opposition to Indian Office paternalism with support for land rights was also evident among the New York Senecas and other Iroquois groups whose long-standing call for the enforcement of their treaties often erupted into public view.

The six Iroquois tribes that lived in New York State and the province of Ontario occupied several scattered reserves, most created in the aftermath of the American Revolution. Consequently, disputes over land titles and treaty rights had a long and complex history. By the early twentieth century these local disputes had begun to emerge on the regional stage. In 1920 a New York State federal appeals court ruled in *U.S. v. Boylan*, a case surrounding the sale of land held by a group of Oneidas. The court declared that the sale could be reviewed by the federal courts because the area remained part of "Indian country." It ruled that the Oneidas, one of the six Iroquois communities in New York, "exist as a separate band or tribe," despite the fact that their official tribal government had long since moved west to Wisconsin. They deserved protection as "a separate nation."[12]

The verdict in *U.S. v. Boylan* vindicated the activists who had first brought the suit to court and coincided with the work of a special commission established by the state legislature to review the entire subject of Iroquois land titles. In 1922 the Everett Commission issued its report, which confirmed the charges tribal leaders had been making for decades about New York's illegal role in the loss of tribal land. The state legislature ignored Everett's recommendations, but the commission's findings encouraged local Native leaders and their white allies to continue to press their claims in federal court.[13]

But the most dramatic event related to Iroquois treaty rights during the 1920s originated across the border in Ontario, when the traditional leadership at the Six Nations reserve, originally established by the British crown as a home for Joseph Brant and his followers, sent a tribal representative, Levi General, to the League of Nations in Geneva, Switzerland, to protest its treatment by the Canadian government. Accompanied by George Palmer Decker, a Buffalo lawyer active in the land claims litigation taking place on the American side of the border, General charged that Ottawa's attempt to impose an elected council at Six Nations violated formal commitments made to Brant and other Indian allies more than a century earlier. After being rebuffed by the League, General turned for help to the Iroquois communities in New York. There he enlisted Clinton Rickard, a young Tuscarora activist, and representatives from other Iroquois communities to support him. Levi General's international campaign awakened broad interest in Iroquois treaty rights, inspiring Rickard and his allies to redouble their efforts.[14]

Rickard formed the Indian Defense League of America in 1926 to rally supporters of treaty rights. He encouraged other Iroquois leaders to expand his campaign against state intrusion into their communities.[15] Soon a new and younger party of Seneca activists came to power at the Seneca reserve at Cattaraugus, near Buffalo. Reflecting the same aggressiveness as Levi General and Clinton Rickard, these activists launched a court case that by 1931 had affirmed the tribe's right to resolve heirship disputes on tribal land. Their attorney was George Decker, the man who had accompanied General to Geneva.[16]

IT WAS OUT OF THIS heady mix of litigation and renewed political activism that Alice Lee Jemison emerged into the arena of Seneca politics. While still in her twenties, Jemison became the personal secretary to the Senecas' elected leader, Raymond Jimerson. She served as the leadership's interpreter, speechwriter, public relations coordinator, and legal adviser, playing a role similar to Robert Yellowtail's with Crow elders in Montana. Like that of Yellowtail, Jemison's facility with English and her ready grasp of the link between local issues and national Indian policy debates soon propelled her onto the national stage.

Jemison was born in 1901 at Silver Creek, New York, near the Cattauraugus Seneca reserve. Both her parents had attended Hampton Institute at about the same time as Thomas Sloan. Her father, Daniel Lee, was a cabinetmaker from the Eastern Cherokee community in North Carolina, and her mother, Elnora Seneca, was a member of a local family prominent in tribal affairs. The Senecas traced family affiliations through female ancestors, so Alice's community recognized her as a member of her mother's Seneca clan.

Alice excelled at writing and debate and dreamed of becoming a lawyer, but she married soon after graduating from Silver Creek High School and quickly had two children. Soon after, Alice's marriage to La Verne Jemison foundered, and she spent most of the 1920s working at a variety of short-term jobs in Silver Creek and nearby Buffalo. By 1930 she had been a nurse, a factory worker, a clerk, a peddler, a dressmaker, and a secretary.[17]

Alice Jemison's personal struggles coincided with both Levi General's appeal to the League of Nations and Clinton Rickard's decision to found the Indian Defense League. Through her family's position at Cattaraugus she also witnessed rising tension between Seneca tribal leaders and local politicians in Buffalo and Albany. She became familiar with George Decker and other lawyers who were willing to support the tribe's claims to land as well as to legal jurisdiction over its territories. During the 1920s Jemison also met Joseph W. Latimer, an attorney who had worked closely with Carlos Montezuma in Chicago in the early years of the century. Latimer had moved his law practice to New York in 1918, but he continued to publicize Montezuma's positions, although like the man himself, he became less an enemy of tribal governments than of the Indian Office. During the 1920s Latimer served as an adviser to tribal leaders in Arizona, Montana, and Oregon, and he advertised his views in a series of self-published essays and newsletters. His polemical pamphlet *Our Indian Bureau System*, which appeared in 1923, accused federal authorities of maintaining an "autocratic dominance" over "the Indian's entire existence." So long as this control remained, he argued, "Indian citizenship is a name only."[18] Jemison, an avid reader of Latimer's pamphlets, quickly adapted his attacks on Washington to her defense of the Seneca tribe and its treaties.

Jemison first became personally involved in a major controversy in 1930, when two Seneca women were accused of murdering Clothilde Marchand, the wife of a prominent Buffalo artist and museum designer. The case unleashed a torrent of anti-Indian rhetoric in the city. Jemison soon moved to Buffalo to serve as spokesperson for tribal leaders. She protested the lurid portrayals of the two women that appeared in the local press and called on federal officials to intervene on their behalf. She wrote letters and press releases on behalf of the accused. While her appeals were not successful—the two women were found guilty—her columns won her the attention of the local press as well as the admiration of the Seneca community. At the end of the case the *Buffalo Evening News* invited Jemison to write a column on Indian affairs. Both the Seneca leadership and the attorneys who represented the accused women urged her to accept; they had come to rely on her ready pen and her ability to link local disputes to the cause of tribal autonomy and Indian rights.

JEMISON'S COLUMN WAS SOON syndicated to a national audience by the National Newspaper Alliance, and she used her newfound influence to comment on important issues facing the Indian community. Following Franklin Roosevelt's election to the presidency, Iroquois leaders from across New York decided to nominate Joseph Latimer to be commissioner of Indian affairs. Jemison made the case for the lawyer's appointment in her column. She insisted that the Indian Office had failed the state's indigenous people. Conditions among New York's Indians were terrible. Tuberculosis was rampant, tribal schools were almost completely unfunded, and unemployment in the third year of the Depression was worse than even in nearby industrial cities. The Indian Office, she argued, rested on principles of "slavery, greed and oppression." Missionaries and other well-intentioned outsiders did nothing more than "work hand in hand" with federal authorities.[19] "We are weary unto death of the propaganda for a continuance of the bureau to further 'protect' the Indian," she wrote. Calls for action from groups like John Collier's American Indian Defense Association were "sponsored by wealthy people . . . many of whom have never seen an Indian . . . [but] who think they know what is best for the Indians." Jemison argued that Latimer was not a romantic; he was "a man who will give an understanding ear to our expressions, and who, having heard, can and will sponsor legislation to promote our welfare, not as wards but as free men and women."[20]

Jemison, like Robert Yellowtail, was immersed in local politics. Not surprisingly, when the administration announced Collier's appointment in April 1933, the Senecas were deeply disappointed. How, Jemison wondered, could the president claim to represent a new deal? No one in the incoming administration had consulted tribal leaders. The appointment, she wrote in a letter to the *New York Times*, was simply another sad chapter in the tired tale of "government by a bureau in which Indians have no voice. We . . . dared to raise our voice regarding the man whom we considered best qualified to be our guardian," she added, but to no avail. "An open council of all Indians might easily have been called and everyone given an opportunity to speak." Instead, she noted, "Mr. Collier and the new administration have placed themselves in the same position occupied by the officials of the bureau since its inception 100 years ago, the position of totally ignoring the Indians and their wishes regarding their own affairs."[21]

A THIRD GROUP of Indians that emerged in the 1930s was made up of men and women who, like Thomas Sloan and many early members of the Society of American Indians, had chosen to pursue careers away from their traditional homelands. They were ambitious to succeed in the larger society, but they harbored mixed feelings about leaving their Native traditions behind. They included educators, writers, church workers of various kinds, and independent businesspeople. Representative of this group was an aspiring young author writing fiction about the American West from an unlikely address on West Fourth Street in Greenwich Village. Three years younger than Alice Jemison, D'Arcy Dahlberg had grown up on Montana's Flathead Reservation. His mother, Philomene Parenteau, had come to Montana as a child with her parents, Isidore and Judith, Canadian Métis/Cree Indians and followers of Louis Riel, the Métis visionary who in 1885 had attempted an overthrow of Ottawa's authority on the western plains. Following Riel's capture and execution, the Parenteaus fled south to Montana, where they were offered refuge by the Salish community living on the Flathead reserve in the northwestern corner of the state. Dahlberg's father was William McNickle, an Irish American handyman who came to the Mission Valley at about the same time as the Parenteaus. William McNickle married Philomene in 1899; D'Arcy, their third child, was born in 1904.[22]

The young boy's life took an unexpected turn in 1913, when in the aftermath of his parents' bitter divorce the reservation agent ordered him enrolled in a federal boarding school for Indians in Chemawa, Oregon. There he witnessed the regimentation and discipline of the Indian Office's assimilation policy firsthand. Nine-year-old McNickle wore a stiff wool uniform, slept in a large dormitory with dozens of other children, and absorbed a curriculum that mixed basic skills and vocational training. He remained in Oregon for three years and returned to his mother's home only after her marriage to a laborer named Gus Dahlberg. Despite this traumatic separation from his family, young D'Arcy (like Yellowtail, Sloan, and others) took comfort in his studies. He loved to read and to imagine the world beyond Montana. He dreamed of becoming a writer. "It was a strange business, this going to school," one of his fictional characters muses in a short story Dahlberg published at the end of the 1920s. "He sat in his classroom and swallowed everything greedily. His head was full of things that had happened thousands of miles away and hundreds of years ago. But he knew better than to talk about them when he got home."[23] Back in the Mission Valley, Dahlberg attended the local high school, then enrolled at the University of Montana in nearby Missoula.

In 1925, D'Arcy Dahlberg left Montana without graduating from college in order to travel and study in Europe. He later settled in New York, where he enrolled in night classes and supported himself with freelance writing and short-term editorial jobs. He labored over his first novel, an upbeat story of an Indian schoolboy's successful return to his reservation, which darkened and grew more pessimistic as he revised. By 1932 Dahlberg had come to realize that his unique upbringing and Native heritage had left an indelible mark on him. He reclaimed his boyhood name, McNickle, and reflected in his writing on the lessons he had absorbed as a child from his grandfather

Isidore. By the time his novel was published as *The Surrounded* in 1935, McNickle's tale had evolved into a portrait of the cramped lives young Indians faced as they struggled to make their way in a hostile and racist society.

McNickle's years in New York had given him perspective on his boarding school education. He came to see American society as obsessed with material wealth and willfully ignorant of its frontier past. His rethinking of frontier encounters and American expansion was revealed in "Meat for God," a short story published in *Esquire* magazine in 1935. The story is narrated by an ancient French fur trader who settled years earlier with the Salish Indians in northern Montana. He condemns the ignorance of modern white settlers—"fence-diggers, land-plowers, and house-builders"—and despairs over the popular belief that "the old ways were completely gone." After impulsively killing a deer out of season, the old hunter (speaking perhaps in the voice of McNickle's grandfather) realizes that he has broken the white man's law. "They would all come after him," the old man concedes, "the sheriff, the judge, the soldiers." The aging trapper eludes their judgment by destroying the animal carcass in an immense bonfire. "That night there was no meat for supper," McNickle wrote at the story's end. "But that was nothing new."[24]

In 1934 McNickle's precarious circumstances and deepening engagement with the reality of American Indian poverty and despair prompted him to write to John Collier. He hoped to join the reformer's staff in Washington, D.C. In his application letter the struggling author described himself as someone "interested in writing about the West, not in the romantic vein in which it has been dealt with in the past, but with the object of revealing in fiction . . . the character which was formed by the impact of the Frontier upon the lives of the people who settled it. . . . [A]t the risk of appearing to court your interest," he added, "it would be a real privilege to take part in the work of reconstruction you are carrying forward."[25] Collier replied positively, but nothing came of the exchange until a year later. In late 1935 the commissioner apparently decided he could use the help of an articulate Native American who shared his enthusiasm for reconstructing Indian life. He invited the young author to become an administrative assistant in his office.

While hardly large enough to constitute a politically significant interest group, several other young, educated Indians shared McNickle's admiration for Collier and joined the commissioner's team. Like the struggling young author from the Flathead, they had not been involved in the controversies of policy debates of the 1920s; they had lived away from their home communities and had had little or no previous contact with the new commissioner. Despite the fact that they had not been part of Collier's epiphany at Taos, they shared his admiration for traditional Native culture. The Indians farthest removed from their Native traditions proved in many instances to be enthusiastic supporters of the commissioner. They viewed him as the champion of the old ways.

While Iroquois leaders remained cool to Collier, most Native activists in the 1930s welcomed the new commissioner's promise to move away from the authoritarian policies of the past. His promotion of Indian causes seemed to open an arena where pragmatic tribal leaders like Yellowtail, critics like Jemison, and intellectuals like McNickle could interact with one another and find an audience for their views. Whether in support or opposition to the New Deal, however, Native activists like these three became increasingly vocal and visible during Collier's twelve-year tenure in office.

COLLIER'S REFORMS

John Collier's chief legislative achievement was the Indian Reorganization Act, which ended allotment and fostered the establishment of modern tribal governments. His original proposal, submitted in February 1934, was written by a government legal team headed by a twenty-four-year-old lawyer named Felix Cohen. The brilliant son of the philosopher Morris Cohen, Felix Cohen knew the Ivy League far better than the world of American Indians. He had earned his law degree at Columbia and a PhD in philosophy from Harvard. He and Collier believed the most effective method for protecting Native cultures was to emulate Great Britain's imperial practice of ruling its overseas colonies "through the native chiefs." The reorganization bill then sent to Congress proposed establishing federally sanctioned tribal governments on reservations that would consolidate individual landholdings into a single entity that would develop and manage cooperative enterprises.

When congressional leaders registered a lukewarm response to the commissioner's bill, Collier tried to rally support for it by hurriedly organizing nine congresses of tribal leaders. However, these gatherings, held in March and April 1934, at agencies and government schools across the nation, generated more questions than enthusiasm. Nevertheless, Collier struggled to incorporate many of the Indian leaders' concerns into a revised bill that he sent to the Indian affairs committees of Congress in late May. The legislators remained unmoved.

As summer approached, Collier finally sat down with the committee chairmen who oversaw Indian legislation, Montana Senator Burton Wheeler and Nebraska Congressman Edgar Howard. By early June these negotiations had produced a vastly revised bill that quickly came to a vote. One congressman commented later that his colleagues had changed "every provision [of Collier's original bill] except the title."[26] The statute signed into law in June by President Roosevelt was written in Washington, D.C.; it contained nothing of what had been suggested by tribal leaders or Indian activists.

Throughout the negotiations Collier retained his basic commitment to ending allotment and creating federally recognized tribal councils that would empower native chiefs to govern their reservations. The commissioner made numerous concessions, but Wheeler and Howard continued to resist so dramatic a shift in policy. The negotiations with Collier received a crucial boost, however, when President Roosevelt (in a letter written at the behest of Interior Secretary Harold Ickes) pushed the parties to a resolution. The president warned that if there were no action, the nation would soon witness the "extinction of the race." In the end it was this image of vanishing Indians, not the voices of living ones, that made the difference.

Wheeler, the Indian Affairs Committee chairman in the Senate, assured the president that "something can be worked out," and over the next few weeks he and his colleagues produced the final bill. As passed, the Indian Reorganization Act was less than half the length of the commissioner's original draft. It ended allotment and accepted home rule for tribes by establishing procedures for organizing tribal governments and chartered business corporations. Wheeler and Howard rejected Collier's suggestion that the new councils have the power to acquire individual allotments for community use, and they eliminated a series of clauses that declared federal support for tribal cultures. The new law also would not apply to Native communities in Alaska and Oklahoma.[27]

The Indian Reorganization Act (IRA) fell far short of Collier's original vision. While it ended allotment, it made no provision for restoring any of the millions of acres of Indian land that had passed to whites because of this policy over the previous half century. The law empowered tribes to manage their remaining common lands but did almost nothing to reduce the power of the Indian Office over reservation life. Officials in Washington, D.C., continued to manage tribal schools, hospitals, and other community institutions. Despite its limitations, however, the IRA created an unprecedented platform for tribal leaders. The elected heads of reservation governments were no longer viewed as backward enemies of progress; they were now legitimate local officials. As such, tribal leaders could expect to be consulted over policy initiatives and to be involved in government programs affecting their homelands. When special programs within the Civilian Conservation Corps and the Works Progress Administration were organized to benefit Indians, for example, tribal officials had the opportunity to help distribute new jobs to their constituents. When other agencies provided funding for reservation schools, medical facilities, and roads, community leaders were present to coordinate their efforts. As federal spending rose on reservations during the New Deal (the Indian Office budget increased 30 percent), the prominence and prestige of community leaders rose along with it.

THE INDIAN DEBATE

Collier once wrote that during his term in office he "told the Indians: you are of the world. . . . Draw now on your own deep powers; come out of your silence." He believed that the Indian Reorganization Act and other New Deal initiatives brought the nation's Native people to "a rediscovered realization of their place in human history."[28] An appealing image, but of course the Indians had never been silent.

Alice Jemison, for example, was among the most vocal Native leaders during Collier's first months in office as she moved from attacks on the new commissioner to criticism of his new reorganization act. She and the Seneca leadership resented Collier's presentation of himself as the Indians' spokesman. "We consider that we are in a better position than anyone else to know what we need," she wrote. "We have an equal right . . . to voice our desire."[29]

When Jemison first read the proposed reorganization bill, she declared, "We are tired of experiments. Try this out on someone else."[30] From her Seneca perspective, Collier was simply the latest self-appointed friend of the Indian who, while claiming to end the group's "silence," insisted on speaking loudly for it. The new commissioner was a man who spent his time "soliciting money at the expense of Indians," Jemison testified before a congressional committee in 1935, "spreading propaganda to the effect that these Indians should be kept as wards, poor savages that they are."[31]

Because Jemison equated federal guardianship with inferiority, she saw no value in programs that would extend the Indian Office's authority over Native communities. She preferred to base her tribe's relationship with the United States on treaties. "Our situation in New York State is entirely different from any other Indians in the United States," she argued. The Iroquois Confederacy's visible presence during the American Revolution, together with the fact that no provision was made for them in the Treaty of Paris ending the conflict, prompted the United States to sign a treaty with the Senecas in 1794 that secured their land titles and guaranteed their free passage across the international border. Despite their having lost much of their land in the ensuing 140 years, Jemison argued, "We have been free and have made progress because we have been a self-governing people. . . ."[32]

For Jemison and the Seneca leadership, the Indian Reorganization

Act's strategy of "ruling through native chiefs" made little sense. Many tribes agreed. Not only did the new law seem redundant—the Senecas, Crows, and many other tribes already had reservation governments—but it had been written by legislators who had not consulted the Indians of New York State. "Before you take our vested rights and liberties away by law," the tribe's president wrote to Senator Wheeler in April 1934, "we are entitled to a hearing." Using phrases that likely were drafted for him by his young aide, the Seneca president Ray Jimerson added: "It is un-American to do otherwise. We rely on the principles of government by the governed, and equality before the law the same as other Americans."[33]

Once the IRA went into effect, Jemison repeated this charge whenever she found a congressional forum that would hear her. In the spring of 1935, for example, she declared her tribe was "fighting for the sacred right of freedom. . . . Indians that are suffering under that [Indian] Bureau," she added, "are our brothers, and we are here to assist them."[34] Despite his benign image, she observed, Collier was simply reinforcing the authority of Indian Office bureaucrats. She dismissed the Indian Reorganization Act as "a very devastating step toward reviving the life of an already overdeveloped, antiquated, autocratic, un-American bureaucracy."[35]

Jemison moved to Washington, D.C., to lobby full-time for the tribe. She took up residence at the E Street branch of the YWCA just as the IRA was moving toward final approval. As she voiced the concerns of Seneca leaders, Jemison found allies among other tribal leaders: representatives of several Oklahoma tribes, members of the Mission Indian Federation from California, and the Black Hills Treaty Council, representing tribes in North and South Dakota. Each group had its own set of complaints, but all agreed that the IRA ignored existing treaties and dangerously elevated the authority of the Indian

Office. After it failed to stop the passage of the new law, this loose coalition, buttressed by delegates from the nearby Navajo Reservation, met in Gallup, New Mexico, the following August to organize the American Indian Federation. They declared that this new national organization was being formed "to secure . . . the rights, privileges and responsibilities of free-born citizens and to maintain existing protections." One of the federation's first actions was to adopt a resolution calling on Congress to repeal the Indian Reorganization Act.[36]

Under its original provisions, the IRA applied to a reservation unless a majority of members voted to reject it in a special referendum. A small group voting yes in a community where most members abstained could therefore produce an official ratification. When the Indian Office scheduled the vote at New York's six federally recognized reservations for June 1935, Jemison and her allies swung into action, focusing particularly on this undemocratic provision. The Iroquois leadership cast the new law as an attempt to impose alien, government-approved tribal councils on their communities. She reminded Iroquois groups of Levi General's campaign against similar reforms in Canada a decade earlier, and she pointed out that a great many Cayugas, Oneidas, and Mohawks lived on the three Seneca reservations. If a new reservation-based government were voted in, she warned, non-Senecas could dominate their communities, diluting the authority of tribal members and undermining the power of traditional clan leaders. "If that is done," she declared, "our Seneca Nation will be entirely destroyed."[37]

Jemison and her allies condemned the impending "farce elections" on New York's reservations because they were being conducted by the Indian Office's authoritarian staff. "I ask you to keep in mind," she told the House Indian Affairs Committee in March 1935, "that when you speak of the Indians you are speaking of a subject people. . . ." She also pointed out that a recent attack on the "so-called American Indian Federation" published in the Indian Office's newsletter, *Indians at Work*, was nothing more than an official effort to silence Collier's critics. She rejected the article's claim that the new organization wanted nothing more than to remove "the federal bars that now safeguard Indian funds and lands from hungry whites." She charged that "Collier is pursuing the same old Bureau methods" of attacking his critics personally rather than engage them as equals. "Gentlemen, this is not a personal matter with any of us," she declared. "We are fighting for the constitutional rights of a whole race of people." Referring to the legislators sitting before her, Jemison added, "[T]his is the only tribunal where we can present our case and ask for relief." [38]

Jemison campaigned tirelessly to defeat the IRA in New York. Beginning in February 1935, she held strategy sessions in Buffalo and corresponded actively with allies across the region. She coordinated efforts on several reservations, organizing transportation to the polls and ensuring a strong turnout of elderly and traditional members of their communities. Collier responded by dispatching the anthropologist William Fenton and the Winnebago educator Henry Roe Cloud to New York to campaign on the law's behalf, but their efforts had little impact. Fenton (who had taken a job with the Indian Office to support his anthropology PhD field research) and his partner held meetings with Native people in several communities, but when the June vote was in, only 249 of the more than 3,000 eligible voters on the state's six reserves had voted in favor of adopting the new law; more than 1,500 had voted no. The rest stayed home. [39]

THE VOTE ON MONTANA's Crow Reservation followed a similar script except Collier had hoped that there his decadelong friendship with Robert Yellowtail would tip the scales in his favor. Although he was a lifelong Republican, Yellowtail had supported Roosevelt in the 1932 presidential election and urged the Crow superintendent to send a tribal delegation to the new president's inauguration the following March. When the superintendent refused, Yellowtail and two friends set off for Washington, D.C., by car. Yellowtail had met Collier when both had served on the 1923 Committee of One Hundred; he liked the man's brash style and hoped his reforms would buttress his own effort to expand the power of the Crow tribal council. Yellowtail and his friends were therefore pleased with Collier's appointment and were encouraged further a few months later, when the new administration acceded to their request and transferred their reservation superintendent, a crusty career man named James Hyde, to a post in South Dakota.[40]

But nothing prepared Yellowtail and his kinsmen for the news that arrived from Washington the following July: Commissioner Collier announced his intention to appoint the Crow troublemaker to the post of agency superintendent. "This is something I never dreamed of," the interim superintendent, Warren O'Hara, told the local press.[41] Several of Yellowtail's local political rivals expressed reservations. They were suspicious of the Indian Office's reasons for placing one of their own in such an important post. Collier responded to these protests by ordering a tribal referendum on the appointment, a vote that his appointee won by a wide margin. Yellowtail decided to ratify his standing by holding an elaborate inauguration ceremony at the agency headquarters. This unprecedented event took place on August 3, 1934, before a crowd of three thousand tribal members and local onlookers. Following a traditional parade featuring aging scouts, clan leaders, and the local high school band, Yellowtail delivered an inaugural address.

Speaking six weeks after the adoption of the Indian Reorganization

Act and flanked by the tribe's local attorneys, Yellowtail concentrated on the community's rights as Crows. "Friends," he began, "this is our home, this is our domain and this is our country. . . ." He observed the tribe had lived as "serfs" in recent years and that its "constitutional rights and other liberties were trampled under foot." Tribal leaders had combated this trend and fended off "bureaucratic dictatorship," he declared, but the community's future remained in doubt. He acknowledged that "a new deal has dawned for the American Indian," but he did not mention the IRA in his speech. Instead, he pledged to "add another flame to the torch of progress for the Crows" and to stand equally vigilant against disruptions from local whites and "reforms" dictated by officials in Washington, D.C. "This is your domain and therefore your business," he told his constituents. "You should be heard at all times on any and all phases of its administration."[42]

Yellowtail's unlikely appointment as agency superintendent did not alter the tribe's (or his own) skepticism regarding federal intentions. Despite his personal popularity and his grudging acceptance of the new law, the new Crow superintendent was unable to persuade his constituents to adopt the commissioner's program. As had been the case in New York, no amount of political patronage or idealistic rhetoric could budge the tribe from its faith in their treaties or its support for the tribal council it had established on its own domain.

The tribe's initial encounter with Collier had come in March 1934 at the Plains Indian Congress, called by the Indian Office to gauge support for Collier's reorganization proposal. After hearing the commissioner's presentation, the Crow delegation asked to be excluded from the law. Speaking on behalf of his colleagues, councilman Max Big Man told the Rapid City, South Dakota, assembly that the bill "takes away from us the spirit of independence so essential and so badly needed by the members of the Indian race." He added that he hoped the commissioner would "excuse us when we refuse."[43] While Big Man and the other Crows did not share Jemison's intense personal hostility to Collier and his administration, they agreed with her that the rights embedded in their treaties and the local councils they had devised in recent decades were a better source of political stability than the tribal body envisioned in the new law. The Indian Office scheduled the Crow referendum for May 18, 1935, nine months after Yellowtail's inauguration. In the campaign leading up to the vote, opponents of the new law repeated the arguments the tribal delegation had made first in Rapid City. Yellowtail campaigned on behalf of the bill, but his stump speeches focused on the economic benefits that would flow from future land acquisitions made possible by the new law rather than on the advantages to be gained from a reorganized tribal council. "We have demonstrated the fact that we have not been able to hang onto our lands," he told one rally. Adopting Collier's new program, he suggested, would empower the tribe to fix the problem.[44] His audiences remained skeptical. They were suspicious of any Indian Office reform and unconvinced that they needed a new council. This view was expressed most candidly by James Carpenter, one of Yellowtail's traveling companions to FDR's inauguration two years earlier, who called the new measure "the worst kind of law" because it "takes all [the Crows'] rights away giving them to the dictatorship of [the commissioner's] office." On the eve of the May 18 election, Yellowtail cabled his boss with a prediction of defeat: "Sentiment was crystallized beyond human endeavor to break. . . ." The next day, when 801 reservation ballots were counted, only 113 were marked in favor of accepting Collier's "reorganization."[45]

THE IRA's DEFEAT in New York and on the Crow Reservation revealed that Indian leaders in the 1930s had hardly been dwelling in silence. Opposition to the law was evident across the nation, particularly on large reservations. The most dramatic rejection of the new law came one month after the Crow ballot, when despite an energetic Indian Office campaign, 51 percent of the voters in the nation's largest tribe, the Navajos, voted against it. The largest Sioux reserves, Pine Ridge and Rosebud, voted narrowly to accept the new law in polling held in October 1934, but the opposition within those communities was so powerful that the adoption of new tribal constitutions was delayed for more than a year. The referendums on those documents, held in South Dakota at the end of 1935 and featuring campaign appearances by the commissioner himself, revealed that Collier's opponents numbered at least 40 percent of the electorate. As a consequence, despite its approval of a new constitution, each community was dogged for decades by political divisions and resistance to the new law.[46]

In addition to claiming that the IRA would undermine the force of existing treaties, critics of the new law used the controversy to vent their opposition to a wide array of Indian Office programs. These included the campaign to reduce the size of sheep and goat herds on the Navajo Reservation, efforts to promote centralized leadership at several Sioux agencies, and various initiatives aimed at promoting large-scale commercial development through leasing and mineral development. While the sources of opposition varied, community leaders at every agency where the balloting was close seemed to share Robert Yellowtail's dilemma: deciding between the promise of new federal subsidies and the fear of continuing Indian Office bullying and mismanagement. Every divided reservation contained political leaders who argued that existing councils and the promises embedded in treaties had more credibility than John Collier's glowing promises of a "new day" in government policy. During the New Deal years the Indian Office sponsored a total of 258 referendums on the IRA. Two-thirds of those voted to accept the new law, but the heavy negative votes among larger tribes like the Navajos and the Sioux meant that of the total ballots cast in all these elections, 40 percent were marked no. Clearly, there was no national Native consensus about the value of the Indian Reorganization Act or how best to defend a tribe's "rights."[47]

BECAUSE D'ARCY MCNICKLE had never been a tribal leader and no doubt also because by 1936 he had been living in New York City for nearly a decade, he shared few of the concerns voiced by IRA opponents at Crow or Pine Ridge. He had become deeply concerned about the future of tribal communities, but when he joined Collier's staff that year, the young author had few settled opinions on questions of national policy. Collier must have been delighted to have the articulate thirty-two-year-old on board. The Montanan was to be the only Native American working closely with him in Washington, D.C., during his tenure as commissioner.

McNickle's support for Collier's reforms established an enduring bond between the two men. The young author, who appears in pictures from this period as a slim, intense figure with dark hair and a neatly trimmed mustache, was captivated by the energy of Washington, D.C., at the high tide of the New Deal. Collier assigned him initially to the bureau's public relations department, where he wrote articles and reviews for the agency's house organ, *Indians at Work,* but he soon migrated to the organization division, the group responsible for shepherding tribes through the reorganization process. Over the next five years the novelist became one of his agency's principal representatives in the campaign to win ratification of the Indian Reorganization Act. At first, probably because of his inexperience, McNickle was sent to remote communities where Indians were poor, vulnerable, and eager for government assistance. He traveled to North Dakota to meet with the Mandans, Hidatsas, and Arikaras who shared the Fort Berthold reserve and to Montana, where he worked near Great Falls with landless Crees and Ojibwes who, like his grandparents, had been refugees from Canada. He traveled to Iowa to meet with the tiny Sac and Fox tribe and to Maine, where he discovered "a rather forlorn band of Algonquin-speaking Indians."[48]

Wherever he traveled, McNickle presented himself as a loyal defender of Collier's programs. Assigned to write an assessment of the IRA for *Indians at Work* in 1938, he betrayed no second thoughts. "In years past, the seasons came and went," McNickle wrote, but "this year, for some Indians, there is a difference." The difference, he declared, was the Indian Reorganization Act, under which "tribes have become organized . . . money has gone into tribal treasuries, land has been purchased, [and] students have secured loans to attend colleges." He did not mention the challenges launched by Jemison and other critics or the divisive campaigns for approval of the act that had taken place among the Navajos and Crows. He focused instead on communities where the government's efforts had met little organized resistance: Hopis, Blackfeet, Jicarilla Apaches, and his home community at Flathead, Montana. "Something has started," he observed, "and here is the general direction in which it moves."[49]

But McNickle was not simply a cheerleader. While he supported Collier's initiatives, his sudden immersion in the daily realities of tribal life quickly pushed him in a more practical direction. After little more than a year in Washington, he wrote a memo to his boss recommending that the Indian Office stop pressing tribes to accept the IRA and shift instead to technical assistance programs that would be implemented regardless of a reservation's governmental structure. He reported that the Indian Office leadership seemed unaware of the difficulties tribes faced once they adopted the new law. After a referendum was held, he noted, Washington lost interest, leaving tribal leaders saddled with new tasks but no new resources. The result, he noted, was a feeling of being "cast into the outer darkness. In selling the idea of reorganization," McNickle added, "we never did make clear enough that [the tribe] would be dealing with problems which . . . it must handle alone."[50]

Nothing came of this early memo, but McNickle returned to the idea of technical support for tribes the following year in the public assessment of the IRA he wrote for *Indians at Work*. "What has been done," he argued, "is only a fragment of the task remaining." The program "is not a simple matter of organizing tribes and lending money to them. They will need, for several years, as much encouragement and assistance as can be given them." He cited the need for housing, education, and subsidies for tribal operations as well as money for land purchases, police departments, and tribal courts. In his view, even if the new law could uncover a tribe's deep community, the immense task of repairing the effects of past assaults on tribal life and tribal resources remained unaddressed.[51] McNickle's growing doubts over Collier's highly publicized "renaissance of the Indians" were likely related to his personal struggles over the previous decade. While sharing enough of the commissioner's mind-set to write once that "the Indian has the quality of belonging to the earth," he had no illusions about the damage tribal governments had suffered at the hands of powerful economic interests and willful representatives and senators.[52] Having seen how completely historians and artists in the West had ignored or belittled the Indian presence, McNickle was attuned to the patronizing racial attitudes that pervaded Washington. He later recalled, "If one sees Indians as savages, or the often used euphemism 'children,' perhaps no other view and no other course of action are possible than to work for their extermination. . . . At the very heart of the Indian problem," he added, was "the need for land and [financial] credit." Outsiders who did not understand this, even those who rhapsodized over the beauty of Indian lifeways, condemned the tribes to a future of picturesque powerlessness—or worse.[53] Thus even D'Arcy McNickle, the one Indian John Collier could claim he had empowered to speak during the 1930s, imagined needs far beyond what the New Deal reformers had envisioned.[54]

Plucked from obscurity, McNickle soon became a national figure in Indian affairs despite the fact that he had no tribal constituents or previous links to traditional Native culture. He was a creature of Washington, D.C., and a protégé of John Collier's, but his rapid exposure to tribal communities in every part of the country quickly transformed him into a savvy expert, skilled at linking the needs of different communities and finding ways to obtain federal dollars for their needs. Thanks to the New Deal reforms that were bringing young men and women like him to prominence, McNickle did not serve briefly and disappear. Unlike Ely Parker, who lived out his days in the obscure offices of the New York Police Department, the former freelance writer continued in the Indian Office into the 1950s and remained a national figure for decades afterward. McNickle had seen the possibilities embedded in John Collier's reforms, and he set himself the task of building new tribal communities on the foundations of his boss's romantic vision.

ACTIVISTS DEBATE THE INDIAN FUTURE

The Collier era created a fundamental shift in the political atmosphere surrounding national Indian policy. By recognizing the authority of tribal governments, however limited their powers and resources, and shifting the United States's objective from civilizing Indians to developing their communities and resources, the New Deal Indian Office created an arena where the voices of new Indian activists would be heard. Now that tribes had governments, and government officials no longer blamed reservation poverty solely on Native backwardness, politicians could no longer dismiss Indian activists as irrelevant.

During the early years of the New Deal these activists were preoccupied with discussions of Washington's reforms, but as the Roosevelt administration drew to a close, a rising generation of Native leaders began to forge their own agenda. By the time Collier resigned from the Indian Office in January 1945, these leaders were prepared to articulate and sustain a national campaign on behalf of Indian participation in postwar discussions of the American Indian future.

In the late 1930s Alice Jemison was one of Native America's most outspoken voices. A relentless critic of Collier and the New Deal, the Seneca activist appeared regularly before congressional committees. She made her case to audiences beyond the capital through the *First American*, a national newsletter distributed first by the American Indian Federation and later, following her resignation from that group in 1939, by Jemison herself. Because she believed the IRA would reduce tribal governments to the status of Indian Office puppets, Jemison cast herself as an enemy of federal oppression and a defender of self-determination. Her campaign attracted support, not only from the American Indian Federation but also from other of the commissioner's

Indian critics. These included the Sioux leadership of the Black Hills Treaty Council and dissident traditionalists who had opposed the IRA at Dakota agencies such as Pine Ridge and Standing Rock as well as Indian Office critics at the Klamath reserve in Oregon and the Eastern Cherokee agency in North Carolina.[55] "The Wheeler-Howard Act provides only one form of government," Jemison told a gathering of the Black Hills Council in South Dakota in 1938, adding, "If [the commissioner] was going to give us self-government, he would let us set up a form of government we wanted to live under. He would give us the right to continue to live under our old tribal customs if we wanted to."[56]

As the years wore on and the New Deal continued, Jemison's protests grew more strident; she moved from challenging Collier's credentials and ideas to charging that he and his big-government supporters were un-American. Like many New Deal critics, she began to identify the Roosevelt administration as socialistic and anti-Christian. In the August 1937 issue of the *First American*, for example, Jemison charged that Collier had relied on "a constant, seditious stream of vituperation against the government of the United States, the courts and the white race. . . . Such appeals to the under privileged," she added, "are the tactics of communists who thrive and grow powerful, who capitalize on human misery. . . ."[57] Jemison seized on any evidence she believed supported her claims. She singled out the American Civil Liberties Union, for example, an organization Collier and several of his Indian Office colleagues supported, as notoriously soft on communism.

Largely indifferent to Indian issues but eager to embarrass the Roosevelt administration, the president's most virulent right-wing enemies quickly rallied behind Jemison. William Dudley Pelley, for example, the leader of the Silver Shirts of America, and John B. Trevor, the anti-Semitic founder of the American Coalition of Patriotic Societies, endorsed the American Indian Federation's anti-Collier platform and sought to enlist Jemison and her colleagues in their cause. In 1939 Trevor organized a conference to which Jemison submitted a long report, reprinted in the *First American*, detailing the federation's efforts to counter "the program of communism which is being promoted among the Indians by officials of the Indian Bureau."[58] Trevor's followers soon won the attention and support of American Nazi sympathizers. Jemison also accepted financial assistance from the anti-Semitic author James True, though she later claimed she did so only because the Indian Office had scared off her financial supporters, leaving her desperately short of cash.[59] Secretary of the Interior Harold Ickes and Collier made sure the press was aware of Jemison's right-wing connections. According to the secretary, the Seneca activist was "a dangerous agitator" who "constantly attacked the Indian Service." Collier presented an extended critique of Jemison in 1940 at a Senate hearing at which he charged that despite the fact that she had resigned from the American Indian Federation because of its extreme views, she was a fifth-column Nazi sympathizer.[60]

Jemison's ill-tempered attacks and extremist allies have prompted many to follow Ickes's and Collier's lead and dismiss her as a subversive crackpot. Her deep ties to the Seneca and Iroquois communities and her clear personal and philosophical connection to the legacy of Carlos Montezuma (together with the fact that she was later judged qualified for federal employment during World War II) argue against this simplistic view. A great many Indian activists shared Jemison's opposition to Collier's policies. They shared her determination to have treaties and traditional leaders, not federal guardians, define the relationship between Indian tribes and the United States. Her determination to defend the right of American Indian citizens to participate in tribal governments—whether they were organized in the Black Hills, Southern California, or New York State—was also consistent with the arguments of her friend and fellow Collier critic Thomas Sloan. Jemison's choice of non-Indian allies reflected very poor judgment, but her central concern for Indian rights (whether defined by treaties or by the rights of U.S. citizens) was the motivation for her activism throughout her career.

Jemison's primary focus remained on Indian issues. For example, in the summer of 1939 she devoted the bulk of the *First American* to an essay demanding the removal of Horatio Greenough's statue *The Rescue* from the east entrance of the U.S. Capitol. Her attack made no mention of the New Deal or John Collier. She wrote simply that the statue's depiction of the murder of a helpless young white woman by a muscular Native warrior was "most unjust to the Indian race. . . . It is conceded that Indians killed white men," Jemison added, "but where the Indians killed hundreds, the white men killed thousands. . . . Nor can the fact be overlooked that the white race were the invaders and the red race the defenders of their homelands which were being snatched from them."[61] These comments demonstrate the Seneca activist's fierce desire to bring Indian perspectives before the public. Her activism was not confined by the New Deal, and her agenda—protecting the autonomy and integrity of tribal governments—reached beyond John Collier and his reforms.

ROBERT YELLOWTAIL DID NOT join Jemison's attacks on John Collier, but his tenure as the superintendent of the Crow Reservation was also marked by a preoccupation with local community development and a growing dissatisfaction with the Indian Office. He embraced the possibilities offered by federal New Deal programs, but from his perspective, the test of each new venture would be the scale of benefits it would bring to his home reservation. During the Collier years Yellowtail presided over several federally funded projects: the construction of his reservation's first hospital, the acquisition of forty thousand acres of tribal grazing land, and stock purchases to build the herds of Crow ranchers. By the start of World War II the Crow tribe had expanded the size of the grazing territory it controlled sixfold. Beyond these economic development projects, scores of tribal members went to work on local construction projects funded by the Works Progress Administration and the special Indian Division of the Civilian Conservation Corps. Crow laborers built roads and reservoirs and participated in tribal logging and fire crews. Government dollars even supported the creation of a new dance hall and an Indian sewing cooperative.[62]

During his eleven-year tenure as agency superintendent Robert Yellowtail devoted almost as much attention to cultural activities as he did to economic enterprise. He ended the agency's opposition to peyote use and tolerated the reintroduction of the Sun Dance among the tribe. He also persuaded the National Park Service to donate excess buffalo from Yellowstone Park to the Crow tribe so they could reestablish a tribal herd in the Bighorn Mountains. The superintendent's tribesmen were thrilled that after nearly fifty years the shaggy beasts so important to their history and to their identity as plains hunters were back in Crow country. Most enduringly, Yellowtail transformed the annual agricultural fair that the Indian Office previously had insisted upon into a celebration of traditional Crow ways of life. Under Yellowtail, the Crow Fair took place in tourist season, August, instead of after the fall harvest, and it was widely promoted as a prominent stop on the region's powwow circuit. Each year hundreds of white tourists and Indian visitors crowded into the tribal campground on the banks of the Little Bighorn for a week of horse racing, dancing, and celebration. After the 1937 fair one local travel magazine reported that "the most spectacular event of each day was the parade led by 'Bobby' Yellowtail. . . . They proceeded in a single file," the magazine noted, "hundreds of Indians, each dressed differently, in a most magnificent array reminiscent of former days."[63]

By the end of Yellowtail's term of office in 1945 the question of which tribes had adopted the IRA and which had turned it down had become largely irrelevant. There emerged in every corner of the nation tribal members who, while not always as flamboyant and successful as Yellowtail, cast themselves as reservation leaders whom policy makers in Washington could neither patronize nor ignore. Despite their rejection of the Reorganization Act, the Crows prospered. Similarly, Collier's enemies on the Navajo Reservation became leaders of an active tribal council taken seriously by government and business leaders in both the Southwest and Washington, D.C. Where the new law was popular, such as among the Mescalero Apaches or the Montana Blackfeet, there emerged councils that commanded comparable influence. Even Jemison's Senecas, who had voted overwhelmingly against the IRA, gained strength and public prominence through a variety of New Deal community development efforts aimed at restoring tribal culture and daily life on New York's reservations.[64] Leaders there, as elsewhere in the country, had learned to separate their view of John Collier from their desire to participate in the next phase of Indian policy reform.

PROBABLY NO ONE GAVE this next phase more thought than Collier's ally D'Arcy McNickle. As the excitement surrounding the passage of the IRA faded and his own knowledge of the national scene deepened,

McNickle understood that future discussions of Indian affairs would hardly be affected by whether or not a tribe had adopted the IRA and embraced the commissioner's personal vision of the Indians' deep community. He also understood that for Indians, as for most Americans, the national effort to win World War II had created a new spirit of common purpose. During the war years more than forty thousand Native civilians had moved from reservations to cities and towns to work in war industries, while another twenty thousand men and women had served in integrated units in the armed forces.[65] "[F]oreign experience, the chance to observe other societies, the sharing of a comrade-in-arm relationship with servicemen and wage-earners of other ethnic and cultural origins, had an awakening effect," McNickle later wrote. "The anger which often followed upon the awakening was not directed at the reservation world . . . but at the institutions, the laws and regulations which impoverished Indian life."[66]

McNickle first noted this awakening in 1944, when on an official trip through the Southwest, he "held evening meetings with returned students and council members in the Hopi country, with the Navajos, the White River Apaches, and at Papago." At Papago (now Tohono O'odham), McNickle reported that the agency superintendent was so taken with the idea of bringing Indians together to discuss the postwar future that he "vacated his office and allowed us to conduct a meeting of Indian employees and any other Indians we could reach on short notice." When McNickle returned to headquarters, he discovered that many of his Native American coworkers in the Indian Office had been discussing the idea of creating an all-Indian group to advocate for Indian interests once the war ended. "Many people wanted an organization," he wrote in 1959, "but most were reluctant to start anything. They feared failure; they thought they might be criticized; it seemed too ambitious."[67]

After a series of meetings that stretched through the summer of 1944 and into the fall, McNickle's planning group decided to issue a call for a national organizing convention, to be held in Denver in mid-November.[68] The invitation, sent to tribal councils across the country, declared: "Indians are not charity patients of the Nation." It added: "Indians long ago bestowed great favors on the people of this Nation; these things need to be said over and over, and they need to be said by the Indian people speaking through their organization and their spokesmen."[69]

McNickle later recalled that he and his fellow organizer Charles Heacock, an Indian Office employee from the Rosebud reserve, arrived at the Cosmopolitan Hotel in Denver a day before the November convention was to begin. "[We] sat around that night and into the next morning," he later wrote, "wondering whether we should duck out of town."[70] Eighty-one delegates attended the convention. They included seven Indian Office employees from Chicago and Washington, eighteen other participants who identified themselves as Dakota or Lakota Sioux, and nineteen from Oklahoma tribes (most of whom, McNickle reported, had traveled together in the same reserved rail car). The remaining three dozen founders were from the Southwest, Utah, and the Great Lakes; no one appeared from the Navajo Reservation or the northwest coast.[71]

Despite its uneven turnout, the Denver meeting was a success. The delegates formally established the National Congress of American Indians (NCAI). The group would strive to become, as McNickle had hoped, the Indians' organization and spokesman. The Denver meeting also passed a series of resolutions establishing the organization's goal of becoming the political representative of all Native Americans. At the close of the gathering, the group elected officers. Napoleon Johnson, an Oklahoma Cherokee and a state judge, was named president.

With an eye to broadening its membership and preventing too close an association with the Indian Office, the founders also elected an executive council that included McNickle and Archie Phinney, a Nez Perce Indian Office employee, as well as reservation-based members from Montana, the Dakotas, and the Navajo Reservation. They also pledged to hold a convention each fall.[72]

A NEW DEBATE TAKES SHAPE

The NCAI's founding in November 1944 occurred on the eve of a series of momentous events. John Collier resigned from the Indian Office only a few weeks after the group's first convention. After his departure no comparable national figure emerged to assume the place of expert on Indian affairs. He left a space that could now be filled with new—Native—voices. Between the founding meeting and the second NCAI convention in late 1945, World War II ended, and the mass return of servicemen and defense workers envisioned by McNickle and other organizers began. Eager to assert themselves, many of these returning workers and veterans quickly joined the leadership of their reservation governments and embraced the goals of the NCAI.

On the eve of the group's third convention in Oklahoma City at the end of 1946, the Republican Party took control of Congress on a platform of reversing the policies of the New Deal. That event both marked a general repudiation of fourteen years of Democratic control (the GOP slogan that year was "Had Enough?") and created an occasion for John Collier's congressional critics to force a shift in national policy. The NCAI's leadership was eager to participate in the debates ahead. "[I]n moments of crisis Indian tribes and the Indian people are left without an effective champion," the NCAI president Napoleon

Johnson wrote on the eve of the 1946 convention. "Indian leadership should contribute to the formulation of federal policy. It should take the leading part in inquiring into the needs of Indians and of making those needs vocal."[73]

By 1947 the formulation of federal policy had become a congressional preoccupation. Driving this process was a group of outspoken New Deal critics, many of whom had provided the congressional audiences for Alice Jemison's attacks on the IRA a decade earlier. Others were new arrivals who had been carried into Washington on a tide of anti–New Deal sentiment. These conservative activists included Burton K. Wheeler, one of the IRA's original sponsors, who had been advocating repeal of the Reorganization Act since 1937, and Elmer Thomas, an Oklahoma Democrat who had succeeded Wheeler as the chairman of the Senate Indian Affairs Committee and who, in 1943, had proposed the abolition of the Indian Office. They were joined in 1940 by a newcomer, Hugh Butler from Nebraska, an outspoken enemy of Washington bureaucrats, and in 1946 by Arthur Watkins, a former judge and newspaperman from Utah.

Butler and Watkins quickly emerged as the Republican Party's principal spokesmen on Indian affairs. They proposed a program of termination that would involve both abandoning Collier's agenda of fostering tribal development and eventually severing all ties between tribes and the U.S. government. Advocates of termination called for state jurisdiction over tribes as well as the eventual dissolution of both reservations and the Indian Office. Terminationists did not call for a return to allotment or a new campaign to bring civilization to the tribes, but they shared the nineteenth-century reformers' vision of a future in which Indians would disappear as a distinctive group within the United States. In their view, Indians should cast aside tribalism in favor of freedom. In language that echoed the rhetoric of Henry Dawes and other Victorian reformers, they insisted that terminating the government's ties to tribes and treaties was necessary to set Native people free from federal authority. Watkins declared that "freeing" the Indians from the bureaucracy was "an ideal or universal truth, to which all men subscribe." In a widely circulated essay written in the 1950s he aligned himself with Abraham Lincoln's struggle to free the slaves. Without noting that Indians were eager to retain their treaties or that Native people were still barred from voting in his home state of Utah, the senator declared: "I see the following words emblazoned in letters of fire above the heads of the Indians—THESE PEOPLE SHALL BE FREE!"[74]

As had been the case in the 1930s, many Indians shared the Republican senators' low opinion of the Indian Office even though they were suspicious of the conservative politicians' motives and uncomfortable with their determination to end all federal protections for tribes. Jemison and many others endorsed the new call for integration. Napoleon Johnson, for example, told the NCAI's 1946 Oklahoma City convention: "We advocate the assimilation of the Indians into the general citizenship wherever and whenever such course is feasible." He added that the time had arrived "for the establishment of a planned program for the progressive liquidation of the United States Indian Service." Even Robert Yellowtail, the former agency superintendent, who had joined the NCAI in 1945, was sympathetic. Writing to a fellow NCAI member, the Choctaw attorney Ben Dwight, in the fall of 1946, Yellowtail warned darkly: "The Indian Bureau and its employees are not your friends. Mark that down. Their monthly checks are their chief concern. . . . Where," he asked of the recently retired officials, are "Collier and Ickes? Why don't they raise their voices for the Indian since their pay has stopped? I know them all," he added. "They are not our friends. The Indian Bureau should be abolished at the earliest date possible."[75]

Despite this rhetoric, none of the leaders who endorsed integration imagined a future without Indian tribes and Native organizations. They did not become terminationists. Yellowtail remained a fierce advocate of Indian unity: "[T]hings are done politically," he wrote in his letter to Dwight. He also argued that "it is necessary that the Indians become active and a potent factor in the politics of their respective homes and states."[76] Yellowtail, like Jemison, believed that treaties were the basis of the Indians' strongest claims on the federal government and could not be abandoned. As he explained in a speech to the NCAI's 1953 convention, "the United States by treaty . . . and [the] public pronouncements of its leaders and presidents have legally and morally committed their nation to a scrupulous respect of the rights, both legal and moral of the Indians. . . ."[77] He could not imagine that this commitment would be reversed. As the terminationists' assault on the New Deal gained strength, leaders as diverse as Yellowtail and Jemison resisted by defending a set of common principles: the enduring nature of treaty rights, the value of tribal autonomy for community well-being, and the importance of defending the rights of Indian citizens.

Alice Jemison had the opportunity to voice her opposition to termination in 1948, when Senators Butler and Watkins conducted a hearing on the Seneca reserve to gather comments on their proposal to extend New York State's legal jurisdiction over reservation communities, thereby abrogating the 1794 Canandaigua treaty between the United States and the Iroquois. As she had done a decade earlier in her testimony opposing Collier, Jemison devoted a large part of her allotted time to recounting the history of Iroquois treaty making. George Washington, she declared, "recognized us as human beings." By contrast, she argued, Butler's proposals "would violate every provision of our treaty for self-government. No Indian asked for the introduction of these bills," she added, referring to the senators' proposals. "We have kept our shares of the treaties, and we are here to ask that you keep yours." In the ensuing exchange Butler patronizingly noted that Jemison should "be proud of your lineage." She shot back: "Senator, all white people tell us that, but when it comes to helping us, listening to what we have to say, then they say, 'Well we will do what we please about it. We know better than you do.'"[78] Jemison tried to get Butler to promise not to pass any bills over Iroquois objections, but he demurred. "I can't give any assurances for the whole committee," he said.[79] Outspoken tribal opposition delayed Senate action on the bills for two years, but Butler and Watkins were finally successful in extending state jurisdiction over New York Indian reservations in 1950.

As Watkins and Butler gained the upper hand in the termination campaign, debate intensified among Native Americans about how to define a common position on the future place of tribes and indigenous people in the United States. Tribal leaders like Robert Yellowtail called for greater tribal autonomy within a framework of federal guardianship even as he joined Jemison and Napoleon Johnson in criticizing the embattled Indian Office. Like them, he attacked Washington's paternalism, but hc insisted that the hostility of local county and state governments and the weakness of reservation economies necessitated a continuation of federal guardianship for tribes. At the same time, supporters of the administration, like D'Arcy McNickle and many of his bureau colleagues, searched for a way to define the bureaucracy's mission without appearing simply to be worrying over their own paychecks.

In 1948 the NCAI leaders who supported the gradual elimination of the Indian Office proposed the "Indian Plan" at the group's annual convention. While the plan conceded that its *final* objective" was for the Indian to assume "his place in American society," it declared that the "withdrawal of the Indian Service must be determined locally as it cannot be fixed nationally."[80] In fact the Indian Plan was quite consistent with McNickle's 1937 proposal that the Indian Office concentrate on providing technical assistance to tribes. The plan's emphasis on economic development and federal partnerships with tribal governments also reflected a wider national discussion that had recently erupted following sensational reports of poverty on the Navajo reserve. NCAI leaders assisted by Representative Will Rogers, Jr., a California congressman and the son of the Cherokee humorist, urged Congress to adopt a long-range development program for the vast southwestern reservation. Rogers also criticized Arizona and New Mexico for not letting tribal members vote in state elections or claim Social Security benefits. As part of this effort, Rogers wrote an article for *Look* magazine entitled "Starvation Without Representation."[81]

Tribal leaders also spelled out their view of how and when the final elimination of the Indian Office might occur through the Governors Interstate Indian Council, a group organized in 1950 in response to congressional demands that states plan for the integration of tribal communities into their general populations. The interstate council operated on the assumption that reservations would eventually be incorporated into the surrounding states, but like the Indian Plan, it focused first on local development projects and argued that federal support must continue for an extended period. Several NCAI leaders, including President Napoleon Johnson and the Ojibwe attorney Edwin Rogers, participated in the council. They helped organize committees on law enforcement and other topics, but the gap between state and tribal expectations was soon tested by the conflicting timetables of tribal leaders and non-Indian officials. Congressional Republicans and their supporters opposed any commitment to extended federal assistance, while Indian advocates argued that programs such as the NCAI's Indian Plan could not succeed without it. As Ruth Muskrat Bronson, a longtime Indian Office social worker who had volunteered to act as the NCAI's executive director, observed in the fall of 1950, the tribes "need to be fed with the vitamins of a few successful experiences in self-determination. . . ."[82] From her perspective, self-determination was desirable, but a rapid cutoff of federal assistance was not. Johnson agreed. He told the group's 1951 gathering that the termination of federal services "cannot be done overnight"; it would only come "state by state and area by area."[83]

McNickle urged the public to view the debate over the future of the Indian Office from the perspective of Indian people. His principal contribution to this effort was a general history of Native Americans in the United States, *They Came Here First*, which he published in 1949. The book opened with an autobiographical vignette that illustrated how little outsiders understood about how Native people viewed the world. McNickle described a discussion between him and a Hopi tribal leader who had refused to cooperate with a new Indian Office directive. The anonymous Hopi man complained to the author that white people never asked permission to enter their lands; "they just moved in. They did not ask what our rules were," he added; "they wrote rules for us to follow. . . . How do you explain that?" McNickle recalled that he had been stumped. Moreover, he confessed, "nothing that had been written before by white men" could answer the Hopi elder's question.

McNickle realized that the only justification for the government's actions was the common assumption that Indians were a backward and defeated people who should simply follow the orders issued by their superiors in the Indian Office. He pointed out that the man confronting him on the Arizona mesa "was not [a] vanquished and vanishing American. Here was a living voice, and a competent voice, asking the white man to justify his works." McNickle argued that the American public should hear the insistence in the Hopi man's questions and respond to them in a spirit of equality and respect. He urged his white readers to learn more about Indian people and their history. He invited them to "visualize something of what it was like" for Indians in the past. "One ought to try," he added. "It was important."[84]

In an effort to further the goal of presenting a clear platform before the American public, McNickle urged his fellow NCAI members and other activists to avoid the political rancor of the 1930s and to unite around a set of common principles. Regardless of their internal differences, he believed Native leaders should recognize, as he wrote at the end of *They Came Here First*, that their political enemies were "the aggressively superior white men who would have no native people anywhere in the world, except as almsmen paying for their bread by praising their masters."[85] Like Yellowtail, McNickle was convinced that the differences among tribal leaders—over the scale of federal assistance, the future of the Indian Office, the power of treaty rights, or the meaning of U.S. citizenship—were far less important than their common belief that American Indians deserved to be recognized as occupying a permanent place within the society and government of the United States. Acting on this belief, he proposed in 1947 that all delegates to the NCAI convention sign a Treaty of Peace, Friendship and Mutual Assistance. He declared, "Never before has there been greater need for Indians to stand together against the forces that would deprive them of their rights, their liberties, and their lands." The treaty's conclusion invoked the spirit of the Iroquois Six Nations whose decisions, he declared, "have always in view not only the present but also the coming generations. . . ."[86]

The unity McNickle advocated was put to the test soon after Dwight Eisenhower's triumphal election in 1952. Republicans now controlled both the White House and Congress. Political pressure had already moved the Indian Office under President Truman's authoritarian appointee, Dillon Myer, a long way toward the Republicans' termination position. But as the Eighty-third Congress convened early in 1953, Senators Butler and Watkins prepared to press their agenda with new vigor. In the confirmation hearings for Glenn Emmons, President Eisenhower's nominee to head the Indian Office, Senator Watkins won a commitment from the former New Mexico banker to liquidate federal trusteeship over Indians "as rapidly as possible."[87] Watkins's committee then brought House Concurrent Resolution (HCR) 108 to the floor for a vote. HCR 108 committed Congress to ending the Indians' "status as wards" and named specific jurisdictions where the termination of federal services was to occur as quickly as possible. These included all the reserves in California, New York, Florida, and Texas as well as smaller agencies in several other states. The resolution ordered the Indian Office to come forward with plans for implementing these goals by January 1, 1954.

House Resolution 108 won final approval on August 1, 1953. Two weeks later Senator Watkins and his allies secured passage of Public Law 280, which unilaterally extended state civil and criminal jurisdiction over tribal communities in five states, including Wisconsin and Minnesota, and established procedures for similar extensions to occur in other states when requested. On the same day that it adopted Public Law 280, Congress voted positively on measures that lifted long-standing federal restrictions on the personal freedoms of Indians, including prohibitions on the sale of firearms and alcohol to Native people. The momentum for setting the Indians free suddenly seemed unstoppable. As Watkins and his allies prepared for the second session of the Eighty-third Congress that was to begin in January 1954, legislators moved to consider twenty termination bills that would affect all the tribes mentioned in HCR 108, plus other groups in Utah, southern Oregon, and Oklahoma.

REACHING CONSENSUS

By February 1954 the political activism sparked by John Collier's New Deal reforms suddenly appeared in the national spotlight. The National Congress of American Indians hosted 117 Native leaders from forty-three tribes at an emergency conference at the Raleigh Hotel in Washington, D.C. These delegates gathered to voice an "organized protest . . . against legislation which, if passed, would endanger the tribal existence of the American Indian people. . . ." The emergency conference adopted a Declaration of Indian Rights that drew together the themes and issues that had preoccupied Jemison, McNickle, Yellowtail, and other activists in the years since World War II. This manifesto moved beyond the general sentiments contained in the NCAI's treaty of peace to a set of specific goals. The emergency conference demanded recognition of the Indians' "rights of citizenship" as well as a "good faith" endorsement of treaty rights and recognition of America's continuing responsibilities to Indian people. "If the Federal Government will continue to deal with our tribal officials as it did with our ancestors," the declaration noted, "if it will deal with us as individuals . . . governing only by consent, we will be able to . . . discharge our full responsibilities as citizens, and yet remain faithful to the Indian way of life." The emergency conference marked an unprecedented moment of national unity. For the first time a group of representative Native leaders articulated a set of common principles and declared publicly that they would not be governed without their consent.[88]

The NCAI president, Joseph Garry, had issued invitations to the emergency conference on February 9, only three weeks before its proposed opening date, but the NCAI leadership had been discussing the idea of a national protest for months. The group's retiring president, W. W. Short, a Chickasaw from Oklahoma, had reported the previous November that he and several other NCAI officers worried about the quickening pace of the Republicans' termination campaign. Even relatively conservative tribal leaders were alarmed. "The Indians are up in the air," Short wrote, "as they are very much disturbed over the much talked about withdrawal program." Robert Yellowtail was more concerned. Writing to President Short from Montana shortly before the NCAI's fall 1953 convention, the Crow leader declared: "The Indians are at the cross roads of their destiny. They must now hang together, go to Washington together and there together fight the bad bills. . . . I will be there to do my part," he added, "and expect other Indian leaders to do the same." Yellowtail urged the NCAI president to use the upcoming meeting to "marshal our forces."[89]

Those who attended the 1953 NCAI annual meeting came ready to be mobilized. Even the Navajos, who continued to resist joining the NCAI, sent a delegation headed by their chairman, Sam Akeah. The delegates signaled their combative mood by electing forty-four-year-old Joseph Garry the organization's third president. A generation younger than his two Oklahoma predecessors, Garry was a World War II veteran from Coeur d'Alene, Idaho. Handsome, forceful, and articulate, he was a natural politician. He had served previously as the president of the Affiliated Tribes of the Northwest and was a firm advocate of both treaty rights and Robert Yellowtail's style of retail politics.[90]

In keeping with the annual meeting's energetic tone, Yellowtail spoke at the convention, telling his audience that he was drawing on "forty-four years of experience in the nation's capital." The Crows' elder statesman urged the group "to never let down your guards on behalf of your people." He emphasized the compatibility of treaty rights, federal support, and U.S. citizenship. "We are entitled," he declared, "by treaty, to the protection of the supreme law of the land, treaty law, and the Constitution of the United States." Yellowtail declared that the termination legislation then before Congress represented "a conspiracy" aimed "at the elimination of the Indian land base [and] separation of the Indian from all of his land holdings. . . . The job of the Indians everywhere," he concluded, "is to arrest and defeat these bills. . . . There is no time for bickering among the tribal leaders; it is instead time for the united action against the common enemy."[91]

The Washington emergency conference in February 1954 was a dramatic response to Yellowtail's invitation. More than one hundred delegates registered at the Raleigh Hotel. Dozens of tribes that could not send representatives sent official statements of support. Conference organizers claimed that also attending were more than thirty tribal emissaries who were not listed on the official register of 117 delegates, In addition, nineteen mainstream, non-Indian organizations were represented. These included the Boy Scouts of America, the National Council of Churches, Fisk University's Institute of Race Relations, and the American Friends Service Committee. Seven of the Indian delegates present, including D'Arcy McNickle and the former president Napoleon Johnson, had attended the organization's founding convention in 1944. They were joined by tribal representatives from

New York, Washington State, the Southwest, Oklahoma, and the Plains. Also present were Robert Yellowtail, Mrs. Henry Roe Cloud, the widow of the recently deceased educator who had campaigned for the IRA in the 1930s, and the NCAI's former executive director Ruth Muskrat Bronson.[92]

Notably absent was Alice Jemison, then living in suburban Herndon, Virginia. The Seneca activist never accepted the leadership of men like Yellowtail and McNickle, whom she dismissed as Collier protégés, while for their part, the NCAI leaders made little effort to draw their former critic into their united front. Nevertheless, Jemison was heard from. She testified at the congressional hearings on the proposed termination bills a few days before the emergency conference began. Watkins and his allies probably hoped she would provide some political cover for their cause, but as soon as she introduced herself, Jemison made it clear that she represented only herself. "I am here voluntarily," she said in her statement, "sort of a lone wolf howling."

Jemison's testimony was hardly supportive of the terminationists' agenda. She explained that she favored giving Indians more freedom, but she added: "I do not believe that the bills that are before this committee will accomplish that purpose. . . . I have been working in Indian affairs for more than twenty years," she told the committee; "let me please show you what is wrong with this legislation." In addition to specific suggestions, aimed primarily at preventing congressional meddling in Indian property rights, Jemison renewed her earlier proposal for a constitutional amendment to repeal Congress's power to regulate commerce with the Indian tribes. Such an amendment, she argued, would bolster Indian treaty rights by undercutting Congress's legislative power over the tribes. "Until the Constitution of the United States is amended," she told the legislators, "the property and the lives of tribal Indians will continue to be your responsibility." Jemison argued that treaties should be the sole basis for a tribe's relationship with the United States. Her appearance surely disappointed Watkins and his supporters; it generated no interest from the press.[93]

By contrast, the emergency conference was a high-profile hit. It had been timed to coincide with the joint hearings on the Republicans' termination proposals, and the city was full of angry tribal leaders prepared to speak directly to the threats before them. The NCAI gathering took full advantage of their presence. Fortunately as well, the venerable Indian Rights Association, whose patrician white leaders had lost considerable influence over policy making during the Collier years, agreed to subsidize the hiring of Jim Hayes, a public relations specialist, to help the NCAI broadcast its message as widely as possible. Hayes reported after the gathering that the emergency meeting had generated twenty-one editorials ("all sympathetic") and more than one hundred news stories written either by wire services or by local reporters. In his letter of thanks to the IRA leadership, Joseph Garry noted that the publicist "not only showed phenomenal skill in getting the press—in Washington and in Indian states—to print the Indians' position on issues, but he gave even greater help . . . by encouraging and aiding the Indian delegates who held individual sessions with reporters, press conferences, and private meetings with members of congress." With Hayes's help, Garry wrote, "even inarticulate Indian delegates became effectively vocal."[94]

The emergency meeting expressed support for both the Indian Office and a long-term federal commitment to tribal governments. While relationships among activists from different regions and tribes remained fluid and uncertain, it was now clear that the organization's effectively vocal members were speaking with one voice. The infrastructure for political activism had changed dramatically from the days of Gus Beaulieu and Thomas Sloan, when Indian advocates scrambled for an audience and counted their allies on the fingers of one hand. At the same time, in contrast with the early days of the New Deal, the reach of Indian leaders had been extended across the nation and into the highest levels of policy making. Still, the message Joseph Garry and other leaders delivered in 1954 was a familiar one; it would have been recognizable to their predecessors from Indian Territory, Nevada, Nebraska, or Minnesota.

The emergency conference occurred at a sensitive moment, when public interest in racial injustice was on the rise. The long era when white supremacy was simply accepted as an established fact and racial conflict was viewed as an unpleasant but inevitable feature of regional life in the South or the West was finally coming to an end. New Deal reformers had largely avoided racially sensitive issues (in fact much of Roosevelt's agenda had been enacted with support from his party's segregationist southern wing), but the rising activism of African Americans and the broad impact of World War II rendered that approach increasingly problematic. The postwar years produced two important symbolic events: Jackie Robinson's dramatic integration of professional baseball in 1947 and President Truman's order to integrate the armed forces one year later. At the time of the emergency conference even more momentous change was in the offing. Thurgood Marshall presented his oral arguments in the landmark case of *Brown v. Board of Education of Topeka, Kansas*, three months before the NCAI's delegates arrived at the Raleigh Hotel. When the justices announced their unanimous decision in the case on May 17, two months after the NCAI delegates had left town, the long reign of separate but equal suddenly came to an end.

For the Indian activists gathered at the Raleigh Hotel that February, the principal symbol of their new, united agenda was a forceful statement declaring that Native communities must henceforth be consulted in the development of legislation and Indian office policy. The assembly approved the text of a proposed congressional resolution it offered as a substitute for the general termination resolution passed by the Republican majority the previous summer. The NCAI resolution demanded that "any Indian tribe, band, or other identifiable group of Indians who may be directly affected by any legislation, shall be consulted prior to its drafting, particularly bills affecting rights and privileges guaranteed by Executive Orders, treaties or agreements."[95] This simple statement placing Indian consent at the center of future policy making captured the concerns of the Indian activists who had risen to prominence over the previous two decades.

The men and women who gathered for the emergency conference in 1954 were products of the New Deal. They may have differed earlier over the wisdom of John Collier's reforms, but they were now numerous enough and visible enough so that their declaration could not be ignored. While Alice Jemison was estranged from the NCAI leadership, she likely would have applauded their resolution's demand for consultation and respect for treaty rights. And while a political operator like Yellowtail and a cautious bureaucrat like McNickle had different upbringings and different agendas, they worked together to draft and promote the organization's declaration. The emergency conference did not stop the termination campaign, but the delegates' unanimous support for the NCAI's resolution damaged it considerably. Few in the Indian Office or in Congress could ignore the reality that most tribal leaders were now publicly opposed to the withdrawal of federal services and the elimination of legal protections for tribes.

By linking treaty rights and citizenship rights and demanding that tribes be consulted prior to the adoption of any new policies that might affect them, the delegates to the 1954 conference not only summarized the central beliefs of activists like Jemison, Yellowtail, and McNickle but also established the framework for national policy discussions to come. Federal officials would continue to bully and manipulate tribal leaders, but they could never again pretend that Native communities did not—or would not—exist as permanent, vocal members of American society. Speaking at a celebration of the fifteenth anniversary of the NCAI's founding in 1959, D'Arcy McNickle noted that while "a convention is not a good place to talk about ideas," powerful ideas had been central to the organization's success. The NCAI's ideas were particularly potent, he added, because they were products of a generation or more of struggle: "they came out of man's experience and out of his heart's desires." Recalling perhaps his personal struggles as a young author as well as the NCAI's struggle to forge a united position across the previous two decades, McNickle added: "Ideas born in this manner have a way of living, whatever forces may be ranged against them. An idea cannot be crushed like an eggshell."[96]

The ideas embodied in the 1954 conference resolution emerged out of the experiences of the men and women who framed them. They were born of the unprecedented range of political activism that had been made possible by the New Deal, and they were to live on in a new generation of Native leaders who would repeat the emergency conference's central themes in the decades to come. Acting in local Indian communities as well as within the federal bureaucracy and before Congress and the courts, activists in the late twentieth century demanded that Native people be consulted as citizens and recognized as representatives of communities with distinctive claims on the nation. After the 1954 conference, their views would no longer be "crushed like an eggshell." They instead became the explicit core of the activists' agenda as they pressed their case in the new millennium.

CHAPTER EIGHT

INDIAN AMERICAN OR AMERICAN INDIAN?

Vine Deloria, Jr., Sioux

When Vine Deloria, Jr., died in 2005, the *New York Times* announced that a "Champion of Indian Rights" had passed from the scene.[1] A man whose prominence had initially been due as much to accident as to talent, Deloria had become a central figure in most of the major confrontations and Indian policy debates of the late twentieth century. This unlikely leader, a bookish graduate of an eastern prep school and a Lutheran seminary, had become a bestselling author, an internationally recognized university professor, and the confidant of countless tribal leaders and government officials. Deloria began his public career in obscurity, but by the time of his death he was credited with shaping the legal and political environment Native Americans now occupied in the United States while inspiring and mentoring countless Native activists who were to carry his ideas on into the twenty-first century.

Deloria left his stamp on the shape of modern tribal governments as well as on academic debates over Native culture and public discussions of the Indians' place in the American political system. His wide-ranging activities—lobbying, lecturing, writing, and teaching—were often controversial. His career offers a unique window onto the tumultuous moment when the struggles of earlier activists converged to produce a stunning era of reform and cultural transformation. At the same time, his vision of both the possibilities and the limits of reconciliation between Indian America and the United States marks a fitting end to this narrative of political activism. In the end Deloria taught that the ultimate resolution of the centuries-long conflict between the continent's Native peoples and their American dispossessors—what D'Arcy McNickle called "the Indian war that never ends"—would be both uncertain and difficult to identify. He taught that if such a resolution were to be achieved, it would require great intellectual imagination, enormous powers of persuasion, and a generous portion of luck.

VINE DELORIA'S CAREER as an activist and thinker began in an unlikely and unpromising setting, the troubled 1964 convention of the National Congress of American Indians. Barely a decade after the organization had stood up to Arthur Watkins and his fellow terminationists and galvanized support for the right of Indians to maintain tribal governments and be consulted prior to the enactment of major reforms, the NCAI appeared politically adrift and on the verge of bankruptcy. The tribal politicians, lawyers, and activists who gathered that year in Sheridan, Wyoming, for the annual meeting were deeply divided over both tactics and goals. Beginning five years earlier, when Joe Garry stepped down from the NCAI presidency, regional tensions and personal rivalries had triggered a succession of bitterly fought elections. The San Carlos Apache leader Clarence Wesley had succeeded Garry in 1959, but in 1961, after two earlier unsuccessful attempts, Walter Wetzel from the Blackfeet reserve unseated Wesley and replaced the veteran executive director Helen Peterson, a principal organizer of the 1954 conference, with the Rosebud Sioux tribal chairman Robert Burnette. Wetzel set out to minimize the role of former leaders like Garry, Peterson, and D'Arcy McNickle and to cultivate the support of reservation-based figures like Burnette.

Wetzel's tactics further polarized the organization. He managed to beat back efforts to replace him as president but failed to reverse a decline in both membership and morale. When Burnette announced his resignation from the executive director post in the middle of 1964, no one clamored to succeed him.[2] The group's malaise also extended to its political agenda. As D'Arcy McNickle had noted in 1959, the NCAI's initial achievement had been conceptual and ideological: it had stalled the termination campaign by persuading the public that Native Americans had a right to maintain their tribal governments and that those governments should be a permanent feature of American life. A decade later tribal politicians had not made much progress defining the specific role these governments would play. The NCAI had saved the tribes from termination, but now what? Activists were unsure how to imagine modern tribal governments. Were they primarily local associations of needy people whose goal was to lobby Congress on behalf of their members? Certainly there were desperate needs in their communities for better schools, health care, and economic opportunities. Were tribes primarily in the business of generating federal dollars and improving living conditions? Or alternatively, should modern tribes be viewed as embryonic states, similar to Europe's newly free overseas colonies in Africa, Asia, and the Pacific?

Should American Indians pursue a broader, more ambitious agenda that would include some form of political independence and economic self-sufficiency? What was their principal desire? A better life in an increasingly affluent American nation or a fuller restoration of tribal institutions and the apparatus of Native sovereignty?

The troubled mood among the delegates at the Sheridan convention soon grew darker when they learned that the NCAI was broke. With the threat of termination receding and partisan bickering on the rise, several tribes had let their memberships lapse. The philanthropic groups that had been helpful in recent years were reconsidering their support. It appeared that much of the projected annual budget would have to be cut. President Wetzel's supporters managed to reelect him, but the annual meeting ended in an atmosphere of indecision. Several members pledged their help with fund-raising, but no one stepped forward to lead the effort.[3] Once the public meeting had ended, the executive council turned to the selection of a new executive director.

It was at this moment that Vine Deloria, Jr., stepped forward as a candidate. Previous executive directors had been prominent activists or tribal officials allied with the NCAI president. But in 1964 the choice was between two untested unknowns: Nelson Jose, an NCAI member from Gila River, Arizona, and Deloria, then a thirty-one-year-old former seminarian who was attending his first annual meeting.

Deloria was the weaker candidate. His knowledge of reservation life was limited to a childhood spent in Martin, South Dakota, on the edge of the Pine Ridge Sioux Reservation, where his father had served as an Episcopal priest. Deloria had grown up as part of a distinguished family of Sioux religious leaders, but he spoke only English and had few contacts of his own among tribal leaders. After a childhood spent in South Dakota and Iowa, he had come east to attend the Kent School, a prestigious New England boarding establishment affiliated with the Episcopal Church. He then enrolled at Iowa State University but, uncertain of his future path, soon left to join the Marines. Following his military service, he returned to Iowa State, from which he graduated with a degree in general science in 1958. While drawn to religious questions, the young graduate remained without clear career goals. He entered the Lutheran Theological Seminary in Rock Island, Illinois, but exhibited little of his father's missionary zeal. After he graduated from the seminary in 1963, he took a job with a nonprofit organization that provided scholarships to promising young Native Americans.

Deloria's Indian roots were unusual. The Delorias were enrolled as members of the Standing Rock Sioux tribe. His grandfather had been a mission priest at Standing Rock, but Vine junior had never lived there. Instead, he spent his early childhood near the Pine Ridge Reservation, watching his father, Vine senior, minister to the impoverished but proud descendants of Crazy Horse and Red Cloud. Deloria's father was a charismatic, bilingual preacher admired by parishioners and tribal leaders across the High Plains, but he too lacked a strong base on a single reservation. The Delorias' tribal origins were actually among the Yanktonais, a Sioux band whose homeland lay hundreds of miles east of Pine Ridge on the Missouri River.[4] So when he presented himself to the reservation politicians and hardened tribal leaders among the NCAI leadership, the young candidate had little to offer beyond his pedigree and wit.

Apparently uncertain how to proceed, the executive committee asked Deloria "to review his background" for them.[5] Everyone in the room certainly knew his father and namesake. Vine senior had appeared at the NCAI's sixth annual meeting in Rapid City in 1949 as well as the 1954 emergency conference in Washington, D.C. But no one appeared to know anything about the young man or his views.

Vine junior began with his educational résumé. He told them about his experience at the New England prep school and his two years in the Marines. He went on to describe his seminary training but assured the committee that he had not focused exclusively on religious topics there; he had "also studied anthropology."[6] Deloria had obviously prepared for this interview. While the record of his statements is thin, it is clear that he had come to Sheridan with the hope of leading the organization out of its present divisions and indecision. The meeting minutes indicate that "Mr. Deloria stated that he had given much thought as to whether one should assimilate or stand up and be counted as an Indian. He has chosen Indian life." The candidate pressed on: "Social scientists wish us to be Indian Americans[,] not American Indians." Asked to explain the distinction, he declared, "American Indians [are] a definite and separate group with roots in this country [and] a definite identity. Indian Americans would be an assimilated group."

The committee asked Deloria to expand on this theme. What did this distinction between Indian Americans and American Indians imply for the future of the beleaguered organization? Deloria was vague but assertive. "Indians have been on the defensive," he replied. "Let's propose legislation we want[,] not just fight legislation we do not want."[7] President Wetzel followed by asking if Deloria "stood for protection of treaties and against termination and state jurisdiction." The interview notes indicated only that "Mr. Deloria answered yes." The committee apparently had heard enough. Asking nothing of Mr. Jose, it proceeded to a ballot. There were eighteen votes for Deloria and five for Jose. On August 1, 1964, the NCAI not only had acquired a new employee but also, perhaps more than anyone present realized, had chosen a leader who would alter the course of Indian activism for the remainder of the twentieth century.

WHO SPEAKS FOR THE INDIANS?

Vine Deloria, Jr.'s Sheridan interview suggests that the new executive director had studied the issues that had divided tribal leaders in the decade since they had stood together to oppose termination. His analysis—that Indians must choose between identifying themselves as a definite and separate group (American Indians) or an assimilated group (Indian Americans)—captured a central dilemma that had lain dormant during the termination crisis but was becoming a pressing public concern. His call to action—to "propose legislation we want"—marked an important shift to a new era of assertiveness and political self-confidence.

Ever since the Eisenhower administration announced that it would not force termination on tribes without first gaining their approval, Indian leaders had wrestled with the question of how to define the tribal governments they now insisted should be a permanent feature of the American political system. Because poverty and social dislocation were such pressing realities, tribal leaders at first focused their attention on short-term needs. Years later, while recalling the attitude of Native lobbyists in the early 1960s, Deloria noted grimly that "the slogan of some of these people was, 'It doesn't matter what you get, but if you go to Washington, get something for somebody. If you can't get what you want, then take whatever they'll give you and we'll send another delegation later.'"[8]

At the national level leaders of the NCAI were more ambitious, but they remained uncertain about how to frame their long-term goals. The organization lobbied for assistance on the model of the State Department's aid to the developing world, but it spent little time defining the place of tribal governments in either the federal bureaucracy or national politics. D'Arcy McNickle, who had been advocating expanded technical assistance for tribes since the 1930s, couched this appeal in modern cold war terms, arguing that prosperous tribes could be models of American progress. He outlined this approach in a 1951 address in which he called for "a domestic Point 4 Program" modeled on President Truman's aid projects in underdeveloped countries overseas.[9]

Several western politicians, including Montana's Senator James Murray and the South Dakota congressman George McGovern, had been receptive to this appeal. Congressional support for tribal development only begged the question Deloria had made the focus of his interview. On the one hand, congressional leaders and some Indian advocates united around the call for a national community development initiative that would enable Indians to stand on their own two feet. These supporters of reservation development rallied behind John Kennedy's 1960 presidential campaign and hoped that a Democratic victory would produce a new era of federal largess. NCAI officials met with Robert F. Kennedy during the summer of 1960, and President Wesley attended the Democratic Party's nominating convention in Los Angeles. Following Kennedy's victory in November, the NCAI leadership was encouraged when the president-elect nominated Stewart Udall, a forty-year-old Arizona congressman with a good record of engagement with southwestern tribes, to be the secretary of the interior. To them, Udall's appointment signaled that tribal community development would be part of the incoming administration's energetic New Frontier.

Tribal leaders were also encouraged in January 1961, when the Fund for the Republic, a foundation established by the Ford Foundation, released "A Blueprint for Indian Citizens," a report that sketched out a road map for the new administration. The fund had charged a blue-ribbon commission that included the Cherokee chief W. W. Keeler, an oil company executive, to recommend what should be done to "facilitate [the Indians'] entry into the mainstream of American life."[10] Keeler and his colleagues concluded that federal programs should emphasize cooperation and technical assistance, but they avoided discussing tribal governments. They recommended a focus on "the Indian individual, the Indian family, and the Indian community. . . ."[11]

Still, the optimism surrounding Kennedy's victory and Udall's appointment did not end internal divisions over the future. At the end of 1960, just as momentum was building for a pragmatic program to help Indians gain "entry into the mainstream of American life," a separate group of activists came forward to advocate a broader, more Indian approach to the future. In the wake of John Kennedy's election, Sol Tax, an anthropologist at the University of Chicago who had been a confidant of McNickle's since his tenure at the Indian Office during World War II, suggested that the NCAI leadership sponsor a national gathering of Native community leaders to frame the Indian policy agenda for the incoming administration. Tax was an idealist, not a pragmatic politician. Over the course of his career he had developed the field of action anthropology, an approach to the discipline that emphasized the idea that the revival of cultural traditions could animate and consolidate community consensus. He did not support any particular policy goal, declaring instead his "fundamental faith . . . that the people involved are better able to solve their own problems . . . than anyone else."[12] With McNickle's help, Tax received the NCAI's endorsement, and in late 1960 he convened a working group that included the NCAI president Clarence Wesley, the executive director Helen Peterson, and McNickle to draft a preliminary statement of conference principles.

On the surface, Tax's approach seemed compatible with the Fund for the Republic's call for federal assistance and the ambitious plans of the New Frontier. But as plans for the NCAI-sponsored conference took shape, a number of the Indian community's elected leaders and their traditional allies among non-Indian reform groups began to worry that the meeting planned for Chicago in June 1961 would become a sounding board for extremists. Foremost among the non-Indian worriers was Oliver La Farge, the powerful president of the Association on American Indian Affairs, who maintained close ties to both the former commissioner John Collier and a wide network of Indian Office administrators. La Farge made it clear that he considered the Chicago conference organizers naive upstarts who threatened to upset the positive policy shifts he expected would soon occur under Kennedy and Udall. In a confidential letter to the association's executive director, La Farge rejected Tax's "woolly" ideas out of hand and predicted that the upcoming conference would "likely produce a great deal of discord as well as wild demands."[13]

Indian leaders who shared La Farge's pragmatic outlook were even more critical. Cherokee Chief Keeler met with the Inter-Tribal Council of the Five Civilized Tribes in January 1961 and warned that Professor Tax was manipulating Indian leaders in an effort to accomplish some dark, radical objective. A conservative cold war Republican, Keeler also suspected that the former New Dealer McNickle was a Communist. "I am not saying he is a communist," Keeler told the Inter-Tribal Council, "but I am saying that it worries me."[14] Several of Keeler's Oklahoma colleagues also expressed their reservations about Tax's politics and voiced their opposition to the anthropologist's plan to include urban, eastern, and nonrecognized tribes in the Chicago gathering. They argued that questionable Indians would dilute the conference's political influence and provoke terminationists in Congress.[15]

Despite these criticisms, McNickle and Tax remained committed to their inclusive approach. In February 1961 Tax announced the formation of an all-Indian conference steering committee. McNickle chaired the group. It included Helen Peterson, NCAI President Wesley, and a diverse group of Native leaders such as Judge Lacey Maynor, from the North Carolina Lumbees, and William Rickard, an outspoken Tuscarora activist from New York who was the son of Alice Jemison's first mentor, Clinton Rickard.[16] Using a mailing list that contained nearly five thousand names of individuals and Native organizations, the steering committee circulated a draft declaration of purpose to be discussed once the group assembled in Chicago in June. La Farge warned Tax that such freewheeling methods would enable radicals to take over and exploit the gathering, but the professor dismissed him with a curt note: "Why should we suppose that Indians will be tempted to bad rather than good ideas?"[17]

In June 467 delegates from 90 tribes and bands registered at the Chicago conference. Dozens, perhaps hundreds more Indians from the surrounding region crowded into the meeting hall to visit with friends and observe the proceedings. The presence of representatives from every region of the country alone made the meeting unprecedented, but the gathering also broke new ground in that it brought together a broad cross section of Native people: elected leaders of major federally recognized tribes, traditional community elders, urban Indians from organizations with mixed, multitribal memberships, and, perhaps most unexpected, two dozen American Indian college students who attended the conference as part of an NCAI-sponsored summer leadership workshop. Tax's critics—W. W. Keeler, the Rosebud leader Robert Burnette, and others—were also present, but despite their criticisms, the conference managed to maintain an air of unity. At its final session the group adopted a Declaration of Indian Purpose, an amended version of the document first circulated by the steering committee six months earlier.[18]

A forty-nine-page statement later published as a separate booklet, the declaration included recommendations for new approaches to economic development, health, education, housing, and the law. Thanks largely to Keeler and his Oklahoma allies, the statement opened with an "American Indian Pledge" that, among other things, denounced all "promoters of any alien form of government." After this nod to the loyalty of "Indian Americans," the document's tone shifted. The policy proposals were detailed and substantive, and contained specific recommendations that emphasized the need not only for greater federal assistance but also for greater tribal control over community institutions.

Despite the thoroughness of the Chicago declaration, its deeper significance lay in its tone and ambition. The document's concluding section ignored the language of assimilation and Indian uplift and offered instead a vision of tribal nationhood that had been absent in national policy discussions for nearly a century. "In the beginning," the statement read, "the people of the New World . . . were possessed of a continent and a way of life." Following the arrival of Europeans, it added, "every basic aspect of life has been transformed." As a consequence, it was essential that Native Americans preserve what remained: "With that continent gone, except for the few poor parcels they still retain, the basis of life is precariously held, but [Indians] mean to hold the scraps and parcels as earnestly as any small nation or ethnic group was ever determined to hold to identity and survival. . . . In short the Indians ask for assistance, technical and financial, for the time needed, however long that may be, to regain in the America of the space age some measure of the adjustment they enjoyed as the original possessors of their native land."[19] The Chicago declaration suggested that technical assistance and federal aid should be viewed from the perspective of "a small nation," rather than as charity designed to bring

American Indians into the national mainstream. Instead of a pragmatic program of uplift and assimilation, the statement envisioned the wholesale rehabilitation of Native communities to a status appropriate to the "original possessors of their native land."

La Verne Madigan, the Association on American Indian Affairs executive director, seemed to grasp this important shift when she debriefed La Farge at the close of the conference. Madigan believed the declaration was impractical and divisive, and she reported that she had pleaded with an editorial writer at the *New York Times* to downplay its anticolonial rhetoric. She told her boss that she had insisted that "it would be a disservice" if the Chicago statement were to win the newspaper's endorsement. Alas, the reporter had ignored her appeal, and his paper had run an editorial praising the gathering and its manifesto. Madigan closed her letter with a one-word declaration of her own: "Damn."[20]

Promoted as a platform for Indian unity, the Chicago conference widened the divide Deloria later identified in his 1964 interview with the NCAI. Critics of Tax's gathering encouraged federal support for the development of Native communities but said nothing about the formal status or historical significance of tribal governments. They avoided any discussion of cultural traditions or the history of colonial exploitation. Barely a month after the conference, for example, Secretary Udall released "A New Trail," a report written by an American Indian task force appointed earlier in the year. The group's recommendations echoed the Fund for the Republic report released six months earlier (perhaps in part because both groups recruited W. W. Keeler as their senior Native American adviser). Like the "Program for Indian Citizens," "A New Trail" promised that federal assistance would ensure that American Indians ultimately enjoyed "equal citizenship, maximum self-sufficiency, and full participation in American life."[21]

The divide deepened when just days after the release of Udall's task force report the Rosebud Sioux chairman Robert Burnette issued a general call for a special conference to be held in early August with the goal of "reorganizing the National Congress of American Indians." Few beyond Burnette's circle of allies attended the August meeting, but the energetic Sioux politician insisted that tribal leaders set aside the grandiose language of the Chicago declaration and focus instead on extracting larger appropriations from their friends in Congress. "We are in an era when the President created a favorable climate towards us as Indians," he wrote later in 1961. "Indian people have millions of friends who are waiting for us to tell them how they can best help. . . . We must select the best possible people to operate our National Organization [*sic*]." Burnette's appeal fueled a new campaign to unseat the NCAI leaders who had participated in planning the Chicago event. In an obvious swipe at McNickle and other leaders of mixed heritage, he declared that the Indians' representatives "must look Indian, act Indian and be Indian and still be able to contact and hold the attention of our friends." He added, "[T]he more one looks like an Indian the greater the chances are for success."[22] This divisive theme and Burnette's insistence that Indian leaders should "get something" for their communities resonated with other western leaders and carried Burnette and his allies to victory at the annual NCAI meeting later that year.[23]

Other divisions surfaced in the wake of the Chicago conference when a group of Native college students and recent college graduates gathered in Gallup, New Mexico. They were less interested in cultivating Burnette's "millions of friends" than in building what one of their leaders called "a greater Indian America." Most had attended both the Chicago gathering and the NCAI's summer leadership workshop in Colorado immediately following that event, and they were still angry at the Rosebud chairman and Keeler for leading the effort to water down the conference declaration and tack a pledge of loyalty to the United States onto its opening pages. As Clyde Warrior, a young Ponca from Oklahoma, later recalled, "It was sickening to see American Indians get up and just tell obvious lies about how well the federal government was treating them."[24] After three days of meetings the group established a new organization, the National Indian Youth Council (NIYC). Among the first targets of NIYC attacks was Secretary Udall's "A New Trail."

VINE DELORIA, JR.'s focus on Indian Americans and American Indians thus captured the essence of a debate that had divided both Native leaders and their white allies for more than three years. His predecessor as NCAI executive director, Robert Burnette, had happily supported the Association on American Indian Affairs and had been pleased with the administration's programs aimed at producing Indian Americans. His critics in the NIYC and elsewhere were not so enthusiastic. They argued that real community development was impossible without recognizing the historical, legal, and cultural issues that set American Indian communities apart from other racial and ethnic groups in the United States. As he entered this fractious arena, it was unclear which group would have more influence over the NCAI's young, untested leader.

With his thick glasses and biting wit, the NCAI's new executive director seemed far better prepared for an academic symposium than for legislative hearings or courtroom confrontations. He was inexperienced in the ways of government and knew little of Indian politics beyond what his father and friends had told him. He shared the genteel background of the sophisticated founders of the Society of

American Indians and the NCAI, groups that included his missionary grandfather and father. Like most of those earlier activists, Deloria sought to look beyond the demands of any one particular tribe or region.[25] Nevertheless, he demonstrated in his few minutes with the executive committee an uncanny ability to identify the central issues confronting (and dividing) Native activists and to propose a future course of action.

MR. DELORIA GOES TO WASHINGTON

Vine Deloria, Jr., went to Washington, D.C., at an extraordinary moment. Within weeks of his arrival Lyndon Johnson defeated Barry Goldwater in a landslide presidential election that placed Congress firmly in the hands of Democratic Party liberals. Johnson's followers quickly moved to pass a series of domestic reforms as a memorial to John F. Kennedy. Running in tandem with this rising political tide was a corresponding shift in public mood. In the same month that Deloria took up his new post, the Nobel Prize Committee announced that the 1964 Peace Prize would go to Martin Luther King, Jr., an African American whom southern segregationists had long demonized as a Communist rabble-rouser. As Deloria scrambled to pay the NCAI's bills and organize his legislative agenda, the newly reelected president announced that his administration was committed to ending poverty and racial discrimination in America through the creation of a Great Society.

Deloria quickly grasped the shifting contours of power in Lyndon Johnson's Washington. While generally aware, as Bob Burnette and other NCAI critics had argued, that Indians had many friends in the capital, he recognized a new opportunity within the federal bureaucracy. In August 1964 Congress had responded to President Johnson's call for a War on Poverty by creating the Office of Economic Opportunity (OEO), which in turn authorized a series of Community Action Programs (CAPs) to be initiated by grassroots leaders in poor communities across the nation. The CAPs were expected to cut through the federal bureaucracy by involving local aid recipients directly in government projects. Just as Deloria arrived in Washington, the OEO established an Indian Task Force and charged it with developing CAP projects on reservations across the country. Their efforts presented the NCAI's new executive director with an opportunity that had been unavailable since the end of treaty making a century earlier: tribes could acquire federal funds without first gaining the approval of the Bureau of Indian Affairs. In the spring of 1965 the OEO established an administrative Indian desk to manage its first initiatives and to develop new programs. Its director, a Lakota educator named Jim Wilson, quickly became one of Deloria's closest allies.[26]

From the outset the NCAI's new leader understood that the War on Poverty offered tribes more than federal dollars. In a 1974 essay, Deloria observed that while the Community Action Programs "did not solve the problem of poverty," they were "major factors in the development of the contemporary Indian scene." The new OEO enticed young, educated Indians to return to their tribes from cities and college campuses, triggering what Deloria called "a process of re-tribalization." He explained that the returnees were eager to link CAP programs to community traditions but were largely ignorant of their languages and customs. As he recalled, these young activists "made it a point to learn everything [they] could about the old tribal ways." At the same time, they "refused to accept the Bureau of Indian Affairs [practice of] continuing to make the decisions regarding the reservations." Deloria understood that the sixty-odd Community Action Programs that suddenly appeared in 1965 represented only a fraction of total federal spending in Indian communities, but he detected that the projects' direct connection to local people (and their independence from the Indian Office) had created a "serious generation gap" in communities, where entrepreneurial young Native activists were increasingly alienated from tribal politicians who had spent their lives working through the agency superintendent and other bureau officials.[27]

Deloria's sensitivity to the social and cultural dimensions of the policy changes taking place around him was not surprising. While he had not gone into detail in his interview with the executive committee in 1964, there was a firm basis for his claim that the NCAI should advocate for American Indians rather than for Indian Americans. Not only had his father and grandfather been deeply immersed in Sioux community life, but his father's sister Ella Deloria, often a member of his household while he was growing up, was an anthropologist who had devoted her life to the preservation of her tribe's language and traditions. He grew up a Christian missionary's son in a town on the border of the Pine Ridge Reservation, but the most compelling experiences of his youth had been his encounters with old tribal ways. "My earliest memories," he wrote in 1971, "are trips along dusty roads to . . . a small settlement in the heart of the reservation to attend dances. Ancient men . . . brought their costumes out of hiding and walked about the grounds gathering the honors they had earned half a century before." Throughout his career Deloria returned to these memories and the connection they represented between his modern persona and the traditions of his tribe. As he told an interviewer in 1980, "Maybe my generation is the last one that was affected by Indian values."[28]

Throughout his three-year tenure at NCAI, a time when CAPs were proliferating and the Indian Office seemed poised to support the development of tribal institutions, Deloria remained critical of programs that lumped Indians together with African Americans and other racial minorities because as he wrote in 1969, the equality demanded by civil rights advocates was too often "confused with sameness." This assumption, he explained, reflected the white majority's view that "legal equality and cultural conformity were identical." Insisting that Native communities needed land and political autonomy, Deloria rejected that proposition. "No movement can sustain itself, no people can continue, no government can function, and no religion can become a reality," he declared, "except it be bound to a land area of its own. . . . Peoplehood," he added, "is impossible without cultural independence."[29]

Deloria highlighted the distance between his view of Indian peoplehood and the attitudes of Keeler, Burnette, and other reservation politicians in testimony before the Senate Subcommittee on Constitutional Rights in the summer of 1965. Chaired by North Carolina's Sam Ervin, the committee was considering proposals to ensure that tribal governments followed constitutional principles and to protect Indian tribes from state encroachments on their authority. Despite his loyalty to the cause of segregation in the South, Ervin seemed genuinely interested in extending the constitutional protections in the Bill of Rights to Indians. When the senator called Deloria to testify, he might have expected the Indian leader to offer praise for his efforts. Instead, he heard a forceful critique and an extended lecture on the singular features of the Native Americans' legal status.

Speaking at the precise moment the Senate was moving toward final passage of the 1965 Voting Rights Act, a law that would soon enfranchise millions of African Americans in the segregated South, Deloria began by noting that he was testifying at a time when "this country is . . . groping for new forms of social understanding and participation." While sympathetic to the changes occurring around him, the

NCAI executive director rejected the idea of viewing Indians through the lens of the civil rights movement. He dismissed Senator Ervin's suggestion that Congress adopt a uniform criminal code for Indian tribes, pointing out that tribal governments were not backward institutions that federal administrators should reorganize or supervise. The point, he declared, was that tribes were not just another jurisdictional unit like a city or a rural county. They were something different; they had existed for centuries, and they were not going to disappear. "Tribes are not vestiges of the past," he declared, "but laboratories of the future." For this reason, he added, "we feel impelled to suggest that tribes be allowed maximum flexibility in developing their own economic, political, and human resources. . . ." Tribes should be able to train and develop their own lawyers and judges, for example, and to develop their own case law. He told Ervin, "I do not see ever any reason for assuming the disappearance of Indian tribes."[30]

Because tribal governments would continue into the future, Deloria argued, it was essential that Ervin's committee guarantee that state governments would be barred from extending their authority onto Indian land. The old terminationist approach, embodied in 1953's Public Law 280, was punitive and insulting, Deloria declared. Ideally, he added, "laws are passed to help us fulfill what we should be, not to punish us or regulate us." Reminding Ervin of the American Indian's long experience with exclusion and arbitrary rule, he declared: "All we basically ask is justice, the consent of the governed, [and] time to develop what we think should be developed in our own way. You cannot get a contribution to this society from Indians if you try to turn an Indian into a white man or anything else." The goal of federal policy, Deloria insisted, should not be uniformity but "an intersection of culture, societies, and judicial systems."[31]

As his first year at the NCAI drew to a close, Deloria sensed that the pace of change was accelerating. He expected the organization to have ninety member tribes by year's end, and he felt increasingly confident of the group's ability to lead a unified campaign for federal support. "We are witnessing fantastic changes in this country," he wrote in the NCAI's fall 1965 newsletter. "There [have] been more major programs in this year than in the previous twenty." The proliferation of Community Action Programs and the rise of grassroots activism seemed to the executive director to signal a confirmation of his view that policy should focus on developing tribal communities rather than simply looking for ways to extract money from the federal bureaucracy. In this new atmosphere, he wrote, "tribes need a great deal of help in forming programs [and] learning how to use existing government agencies. . . ."[32] He was also increasingly determined that outsiders should not set the Indians' policy agenda for them: "It is time that Indians . . . gave new directions to American social thought and development."[33]

As he settled into his new position, Deloria also allowed his sense of humor to come forward. Satire and humorous jabs at his opponents connected him to his Indian constituents and allowed him to stress the human values and unique experiences that set Native people apart from other Americans. For decades most Indian activists had phrased their communications with non-Indians and one another in earnest, serious phrases. Irony and humor had appeared occasionally in public, but they had rarely been used in serious political discourse. That pattern was broken in November 1965, when the association's newsletter (written entirely by the executive director) included "From the Archives," a feature that reported that the diary of Chief Knock Knock had been discovered "deep in the NCAI files." The diary revealed that Chief Knock Knock had received "some strange visitors" on October 12,

1492. "It was pretty hot," Knock Knock wrote, "and we were all down at the beach swimming when this boat pulled up." On October 17 he wrote: "They are still here." The diary ended with this entry for November 24: "They finally left this morning. . . . I hated to see them go. They were so happy thinking they had found India and so delighted with the coffee and tobacco that they acted like children. But they were quite a pest on the other hand. They kept wanting us to try on clothes. . . . We are having a big Thanksgiving Day dinner now that they have departed."[34] Deloria probably dashed off these columns to relieve tension and fill the blank spaces in his newsletter, but the nature of his humor—poking fun at white icons (Custer was a regular target) and reversing conventional historical narratives (a Thanksgiving dinner to celebrate Columbus's departure)—fitted neatly with his provocative political positions. The message of these columns was consistent and clear: Indians are not the same as other Americans.

A surge in memberships, a rise in federal funding for tribally sponsored projects, and Deloria's tireless lobbying ensured his reappointment as executive director at the NCAI conventions in 1965 and 1966. The 1965 convention was a particular triumph. He had managed to pay off some of the organization's debts and keep its Washington office open, but his greatest coup was securing the presence of the OEO director Sargent Shriver at the annual meeting. As the head of the agency responsible for Community Action Programs, Shriver received a hero's welcome in the Scottsdale, Arizona, meeting hall. "By God, it took ten minutes to get on the podium," Deloria later recalled. "All these people wanted to show him pictures of their [CAP] projects or talk to him. Everybody was just shaking hands with him." When Shriver finally addressed the crowd, he told them exactly what they (and Deloria) wanted to hear. "The whole basis of the poverty program is self-determination," Shriver declared, "the right of the people . . . to find their own way."[35] The NCAI's embrace of Shriver's new philosophy was made complete at the same meeting when the convention replaced Burnette's ally and NCAI president Walter Wetzel with Wendell Chino, a Mescalero Apache leader who had risen to prominence by demanding tribal control over reservation timberland.

The NCAI continued to struggle financially for the remainder of Deloria's tenure, but by the end of 1965 it had stabilized sufficiently to act on his 1964 proposal that the group "propose legislation we want." At a meeting of the executive committee in El Paso, Texas, in March 1966, Deloria observed that traditionally the NCAI had confined itself to testifying on major bills that came before Congress, most of which had been proposed by the administration. Now, he noted, "the focus of activity has changed. . . . Since 1960 there have been major laws passed giving tribes eligibility for development programs. . . ." With the OEO's philosophy of funding community projects independent of the Indian Office now spreading to other agencies, tribal governments and other local organizations had the opportunity to mount their own legislative agendas. Deloria believed the moment had arrived for a comprehensive set of suggestions to widen federal support for direct aid to community-based institutions. He argued that "the emphasis of the NCAI should be redirected to help with reservation community development programs. . . ."[36]

The executive committee welcomed Deloria's recommendation, but the ambitious planning was suddenly interrupted by the news that while the NCAI's leaders were meeting in El Paso, Secretary Udall had proposed that Congress transfer supervision of all Indian CAP programs from Shriver's OEO to the Bureau of Indian Affairs. The Indian leaders were aghast, and their fear of Indian Office maneuvering was confirmed when they learned that the interior secretary had also announced that he would host an emergency closed-door planning conference in Santa Fe to flesh out his initiative. Deloria sprang into action. He called on all tribal leaders to gather in New Mexico at the same time as Udall's conference and to demand to be heard. By the time Udall's conference began a few weeks' later, more than two hundred representatives from sixty-two tribes had gathered a few blocks from the meeting site.

Udall and his aides first refused to admit the tribal leaders to their meeting, but after the *New York Times* and other national newspapers reported the contradictions in their position, they were forced to relent. As Deloria told one reporter on the scene, it was ironic that "the people whose future they're planning" had been shut out. Badly outmaneuvered, the secretary agreed to allow the NCAI to send observers to his conference and to submit its recommendations to a committee of tribal leaders before sending them on to Congress. The *New York Times* noted that while Deloria welcomed Udall's concessions, he had not retreated from his position that any new programs "should be administered by the Indians themselves. . . ." "We want the right to plan and program for ourselves," Deloria declared the next day, adding, "If we start seeing the old bureaucrats show up on the reservations again . . . no dice."[37]

Deloria's confrontation with Secretary Udall did not resolve the tension between tribal leaders and the federal bureaucracy, but it did put government officials on notice that the politics of policy making had changed. Not only were the tribes largely united in their determination to set their own priorities, but the non-Indian missionary and reform groups that had been so influential in the past were no longer in the government's corner. A few weeks after his return from New Mexico, Deloria wrote that "one cannot help but recognize in the events of Santa Fe . . . a real turning point in the relations of tribes, the NCAI and non-Indian interest groups." He noted that the reform organizations typically involved in Indian affairs—the churches, the Indian Rights Association, and the American Friends Service Committee—had refused Udall's invitation to be observers at the conference so long as the NCAI leadership was barred. "Human relations are now coming full circle," Deloria wrote. "In the last century it was a favorite government practice to send in the missionaries to soften up the tribes with religion before treaties were signed." At Santa Fe, he added, "we saw for the first time . . . a total rejection of this role." Instead, "the principle of self-determination . . . became the guideline for the friends of the Indians and the role of the wise protector of the 'little red children' became a thing of the past."[38]

IN HIS REMAINING TIME in Washington, D.C., Deloria pressed this theme with the tribes as well as with the Indian Office. At the fall 1966 NCAI convention, for example, he reminded the assembled delegates that if they agreed that self-government required more than mere consultation by federal officials, they should be prepared to assume the burden of reclaiming their independent status. "The time is now here when Indians will have to put up or shut up about the right to self-government," he declared. "Many tribes are afraid of the Bureau," he wrote. "They don't take any initiative . . . and they let the Bureau do things to them rather than speak up." Tribes must be willing to act independently and "compete with corporations in the business and social world. . . . The reason we have anything," he reminded the membership, "is that one hundred years ago we had people who would at least stand up for themselves and on occasion stood together." At present, he argued, there were only two choices: "stand up and be responsible or—form a National Congress of FORMER American Indians."[39]

Deloria's sharper tone and his insistence that Native leaders "put up or shut up" were not solely the product of his successful confrontation with Udall. Despite his official position as the administrator of a mainstream organization largely made up of recognized tribal governments, the young activist had developed a close relationship with the leaders of the National Indian Youth Council, the organization of disaffected young activists that had formed in the wake of the 1961 Chicago conference. His closest friendship was with Clyde Warrior, one of the group's founders, who had grown increasingly impatient with NIYC's focus on education and community organization. Soon after taking office in the fall of 1964, Deloria had invited Warrior to advise him on policy matters. During 1965 the young Ponca joined Hank Adams and other Native activists in Washington State to organize fish-ins to challenge the local authorities, claim that they, not the tribes, had the authority to regulate fishing in the Columbia River. The local tribes argued that the nineteenth-century treaties guaranteeing their right to fish in their "usual and customary places" preceded the creation of the state and continued in force. (Modeled on civil disobedience protests in the South, fish-ins featured tribal members intentionally violating state fish and game laws and then challenging their arrests in federal court.) By 1966 Warrior, Adams, and their young colleagues were insisting that tribes move toward greater autonomy by developing programs with local resources rather than government antipoverty funds. These activists "attempted to use shock treatment to get people to stand up for themselves," Deloria later wrote.[40]

EVENTS TAKING PLACE simultaneously within the African American activist community strengthened Warrior's influence and sharpened Deloria's vision. When the civil rights leader Stokely Carmichael issued his famous call for greater Black Power in the summer of 1966, the NCAI executive director saw the potential of this slogan for Indian politics. He wrote in 1970 that Black Power "never received the careful and impartial reading it deserved." He insisted Carmichael's appeal was not a call for racial violence. Instead, the African American leader "spoke to a longing within other racial minorities to express the dignity and sovereignty of their own communities." The slogan encapsulated Deloria's disdain for leaders who cowered before powerful legislators or the White House, accepting paternalistic treatment so long as it came wrapped in federal dollars.[41]

For Deloria, "The concept of power meant that the group could demand recognition in society as a group." Still smarting from Secretary Udall's attempt to exclude him from the Santa Fe conference, Deloria observed that "so long as groups are visible and vocal but have no status . . . within the political system, there is no conceivable way that the present system can be relevant to them." The Indians' special status, he believed, derived from their indigenous cultural traditions and their unique treaty relationship with the federal government.[42] So long as Indians retained their cultures and their treaties, he argued, "Red Power will win. . . . We are no longer fighting for physical survival," he declared at the end of his time in Washington. "We are fighting for ideological survival." In the years to come he turned repeatedly to this theme, reminding his readers that Indian cultures and the tribes' special relationship with the federal government were essential elements of their "basic sovereignty."[43]

DELORIA AND THE RISE OF RED POWER

Deloria resigned from the NCAI in the fall of 1967 and entered law school at the University of Colorado. "It was apparent to me," he wrote a few years later, "that the Indian revolution was well underway and that someone had better get a legal education so that we could have our own program for defense of Indian treaty rights."[44] While this statement is plausible, the executive director was no doubt also aware of the Johnson administration's rapidly declining political fortunes as well as of shifts in his own views. A few years after leaving the NCAI, Deloria wrote that in his final months in office he had undergone a "radical change in thinking." Washington was no longer attractive to him; non-Indian experts had "wormed their way back into power" at government agencies and universities, he reported. Meanwhile "reservation people . . . were making steady progress. . . . [Y]ounger Indian leaders . . . began working at the local level to build community movements from the ground up." For Deloria, no doubt influenced by NIYC activists such as Clyde Warrior and Hank Adams, "the Indian revolution" suggested he turn away from Washington lobbying and join the effort to revive the fortunes, both cultural and legal, of Indian communities.

Possessed of enormous energy and creative talent, Deloria did not let law school interfere with his activism. He spent much of 1967 and 1968 assembling a series of commentaries on Indian affairs, which Macmillan and Company published with significant fanfare in October 1969 as *Custer Died for Your Sins: An Indian Manifesto.* Drawing heavily on experiences in Washington, D.C., Deloria treated readers to chapters on racial stereotypes, treaties, missionaries, anthropologists, and the Bureau of Indian Affairs. "Indians are like the weather," Deloria wrote in the book's opening paragraph, "everyone knows all about the weather but none can change it." Biting wit drove home a serious argument: that what America's majority population knew about Indian life was not only wrong but invented and phony. "One of the finest things about being an Indian," Deloria wrote in the opening chapter, "is that people are always interested in you and your 'plight.' Other groups have difficulties," he added; "we Indians have had a plight." The reason for this habit was the imaginary Native world created by scholars, artists, and politicians. "Experts paint us as they would like us to be," he observed, adding, "To be an Indian in modern American society is in a very real sense to be unreal and ahistorical."[45]

Deloria called on his readers to reject the long-standing popular belief that Indians were essentially backward and incompetent and to replace their romantic images with a hard-eyed look at the reality of modern Native life. He argued that even anthropologists, long the self-proclaimed champions of Native culture, were too preoccupied with their own abstract theories to understand real Indians. As a consequence, they taught that "Indians are a folk people, whites are an urban people, and never the twain shall meet." The result of this fiction, the former executive director wrote, were habits of mind that produced "intellectual stagnation." By expecting that *real* Indians should conform to a specific list of backward traits and live as "folk people," anthropologists, and their missionary colleagues, convinced themselves that helping Indians required changing or even eradicating their cultures. As a consequence, Deloria declared, the Indians' friends were really "forerunners of destruction."[46]

By contrast, the tribal revitalization movement that began in the 1960s rested on a rejection of the assumption that Native culture was destined to disappear. The eagerness of Native groups to organize under the Office of Economic Opportunity, the rise of a new generation of leaders on reservations as well as in cities, and the forgotten tribal homelands of the eastern United States were evidence, Deloria argued, that "[t]he famed melting pot, that great sociological theory devised to explain the dispersion of the European immigrant into

American society, had cracks in it." Deloria's book celebrated those cracks and called on readers to support the "retribalizing" process. That effort, Deloria wrote, would nurture tribal groups that were "stronger and more democratic." While criticizing the romanticism of others, Deloria showed that he was not immune to idealistic optimism. Referring to the cultural revivals going on among Indians across the nation, he observed, "The potential for development is unlimited. . . ."[47]

Custer Died for Your Sins stirred strong emotions among both reviewers and the public when it appeared in the fall of 1969. John Greenway, a senior anthropologist at the University of Colorado, angrily dismissed Deloria's book as a "meaningless bleat" whose title had been "lifted from the men's room in the New York subway." At the other extreme, the popular environmental writer Edward Abbey announced in the *New York Times* that Deloria had presented a compelling case for American Indians "with much humor. . . . Genocide is used a little too easily and carelessly these days," Abbey wrote, "but in the case of the American Indians . . . the term may not be inapplicable." The *Times's* chief cultural critic, John Leonard, devoted a second column to Deloria, declaring that his book's clever blend of "ghastly facts" and engaging personal style was impossible to dismiss. The author's words, Leonard added, "frighten therapeutically."[48]

THE COINCIDENCES OF TIMING in Vine Deloria, Jr.'s early career were remarkable. He appeared at the 1964 NCAI convention at a moment of political paralysis and financial peril, but he came to Washington, D.C., just as new federal dollars were beginning to revitalize long-neglected reservation communities. His tenure as the organization's executive director coincided with the height of Lyndon Johnson's War on Poverty. ("The skies opened and the money poured down," he later recalled.[49]) Equally fortuitous, *Custer Died for Your Sins* arrived in bookstores just as the public's support for the Vietnam War was reaching a low point and only weeks before a group of Indian college students and relocated city dwellers occupied the former federal penitentiary on Alcatraz Island in San Francisco Bay and demanded that the site be handed over to them for use as a Native American cultural center. The landing of the Indians of All Tribes on Alcatraz during the night of November 19, 1969, was a symbolic event that soon created a very real political confrontation. By occupying this famous former prison, just a short boat ride from a vibrant urban metropolis and international tourist destination, the college students and local activists who made up the Indians of All Tribes suddenly became global celebrities. While to many the occupation seemed little more than the latest act in a decadelong succession of guerrilla theater productions, to others, it confirmed the Sioux author's declaration that "urban Indians have become the cutting edge of the new Indian nationalism. . . . [T]hey are asserting themselves as a power to be reckoned with."[50]

As Hollywood celebrities and the international press descended on Alcatraz, sales of *Custer* surged. A few days after the landing, a Thanksgiving feast drew hundreds of supporters to the island, where they celebrated its liberation with powwow drums and rock music.[51] Though these events amplified his fame, Deloria grew skeptical. He admired the dedication of the urban activists, but he believed they were naive. Unlike the protesters at the Columbia River fish-ins, the Indians of All Tribes were unprepared for serious negotiations with federal officials. Their counterculture vibe and polyglot urban roots communicated a vague pan-Indian identity that threatened to shift attention away from reservations, treaties, and the tribes' cultural traditions. Deloria worried that the rock bands and movie stars assembled at Alcatraz would trivialize the Indian cause. He told a Los Angeles reporter a few months into the occupation, for example, that while he supported the Alcatraz "militancy," he also knew that "[i]f you're out front shouting all the time, you can't be in the background doing what has to be done to change policy."[52]

Six months after the initial landing, Deloria's fears seemed to have been realized: negotiations with federal authorities reached a stalemate, the occupiers began fighting with one another, and the public's attention shifted elsewhere. Despite the uncertain outcome of the Alcatraz takeover, a chain reaction of similar protests over the following year carried the protesters' demands to communities across the United States. In March a group of local activists and Alcatraz veterans took control of Fort Lawton near Seattle, demanding the army base be transformed into an Indian arts center. Their success attracted wide attention in the Northwest and spurred similar actions in other cities as well as new support for the ongoing fish-ins. In subsequent months angry crowds occupied Bureau of Indian Affairs offices in Chicago, Cleveland, and Minneapolis, while Mohawks in New York claimed jurisdiction over islands in the St. Lawrence River and a new organization based in Minneapolis, the American Indian Movement, threatened to occupy Mount Rushmore and Plymouth Rock. The following year advocates for Chicago's impoverished Indian community occupied a former Nike missile site on the city's lakefront to dramatize their claims, while a group of college students took over another abandoned military post near Davis, California, and pledged to remain until the government turned it over to them for use as a Native American university. Everywhere, it seemed, the angry words in *Custer Died for Your Sins* were taking human form. As Edward Abbey had observed in his review of Deloria's book, "Even the Indians are turning against us now. Red Power. All the chickens coming home to roost."[53]

IN THE FALL OF 1972 a broad coalition of urban and reservation-based leaders called for a national protest in Washington, D.C. Called the Trail of Broken Treaties, the demonstration would consist of a collective journey to the U.S. capital, where a series of demands would be presented to the president on the eve of the presidential election. The operation was loosely organized and poorly funded. When the vanguard of the group reached the Bureau of Indian Affairs headquarters on November 2, they sought a hearing with federal officials as well as assistance with housing the hundreds of unexpected followers who were now crowding into the building. Ordered to leave by nervous security guards, the entire group suddenly barricaded the doors and declared the site a Native American embassy.[54]

The occupation of the BIA lasted only a few days, but it catapulted to national fame the activists who took center stage during the crisis, leaders of the American Indian Movement, particularly Russell Means, an Oglala Sioux who had been raised in California, and Dennis Banks, an Ojibwe who had helped found the organization in Minneapolis. Three months later these telegenic men solidified their leadership when they led a group of AIM members and tribal elders into the village of Wounded Knee, South Dakota, on the Pine Ridge Reservation, and occupied it in the name of the Oglala Nation. Acting on behalf of traditionalists who had opposed the tribal leaders elected under the Indian Reorganization Act since the 1930s, the protesters declared themselves heirs to the Sioux tribe's nineteenth-century chiefs. They pledged to remain in their freshly dug bunkers until the tribe's elders and chiefs had been restored to power. After a nine-week standoff, during which two Native American protesters were killed and one FBI agent was severely wounded, negotiations involving

Nixon administration officials, AIM leaders, and various intermediaries (including Deloria's close friend Hank Adams) produced a face-saving agreement. The protesters agreed to disperse, and the White House promised to investigate complaints against the elected tribal government.

The proliferation of these occupations and protests left Deloria in a quandary. On the one hand, they thrust him more firmly into the public eye. The former executive director was quick to use the many platforms now available to him to underscore the unique and compelling nature of the Indians' demands. "Every tool we have for gathering information and finding our way has been designed for a world of assimilation and integration," he told a group of scholars at the Smithsonian Institution in 1970. On the other hand, the Indian protests demonstrated that Americans "have left the comfortable land of assimilation and been thrust into the outer darkness of ethnicity." Deloria explained that these events proved that the integrationist dreams outlined a decade earlier in documents like the Fund for the Republic's "Blueprint for Indian Citizens" had been illusory. He urged his audiences to face this new reality. "We can use the American political arena to allow one group to oppress another," he declared, "or we can use it as a forum, an arena in which the problems of our society and perhaps the world can finally be resolved."[55] What this resolution would look like, however, Deloria could not yet say.

As he traveled the country in 1970 and 1971, Deloria pointed out the many connections he saw between the Indians' quest for peoplehood and the black nationalist and Mexican American desire to "build viable communities with political and economic power." In *We Talk, You Listen*, a collection of essays published in late 1970, the young lawyer insisted that recent protests mounted by all three groups revealed a common longing for solidarity and the recognition of their collective rights. Referring to blacks, Mexican Americans, and Indians, he wrote, using capital letters to emphasize his point, that the public should realize "that IN NO CASE DID THESE GROUPS ENTER THE CONSTITUTIONAL FRAMEWORK AS INDIVIDUALS. . . . We have seen over the past century," he added, "the utter inability of American society to absorb these groups."[56]

But even as he praised the militant protesters for demonstrating that "white society is breaking down all around us," Deloria grew critical of their leaders and their tactics.[57] For example, while he admired Richard Oakes, the charismatic young Mohawk who had initiated the Alcatraz occupation, Deloria wrote that the former college student "overestimate[d] his impact" and "failed to recognize the necessity of prolonged negotiations" in any serious confrontation with federal officials. Similarly, Deloria argued that the Trail of Broken Treaties organizers "wasted their time enhancing their images as glamorous Indian leaders" instead of attending to the tedious details associated with housing and feeding the hundreds of men, women, and children who had followed them to the capital. The chaos of the BIA sit-in, together with the destruction of furniture, office files, and artwork that had occurred there, had been a public relations disaster. "Until the 'occupation' of the BIA," Deloria wrote, "we had an almost perfect media image." Similarly, he pronounced the scene of swarming television crews at Wounded Knee a "high tragedy and . . . grotesque comedy." He noted that the Pine Ridge occupation had brought forward a "bizarre parade of characters: Ralph Abernathy, the National Council of Churches, Angela Davis and assorted hippies and well-wishers who have made a valiant effort to turn the confrontation into the last rock festival and clan gathering of the New Left." Watching these events, he complained, had been "torture."[58]

The Wounded Knee occupation was especially painful for Deloria because he knew the blood-soaked prairie surrounding Wounded Knee village well; visiting it as a boy, he wrote, had been "the most memorable event of my early childhood. . . . Many times over the years," he recalled, "my father would point out survivors of the massacre, and people on the reservation always went out of their way to help them."[59] He was also moved by the Sioux traditionalists whose complaints against the Indian Reorganization Act government on the reservation had inspired the takeover. He believed their demand that the United States live up to its treaties was completely justified. "The courts," he wrote, "have done a veritable St. Vitus dance to keep from enforcing [the treaty's] provisions. . . ." He also wrote approvingly of the occupation's charismatic leader, Russell Means, saying at one point that he "may be the greatest Lakota of this century."[60] But Deloria rejected the occupiers' spontaneous, sometimes violent tactics, and he despaired over how exactly they would govern the reservation with a group of aging elders. He urged his friend Hank Adams and other intermediaries to negotiate a quick solution to the armed standoff and called on government officials to hold hearings to air the group's complaints. But even these modest pleas fell on dead ears, and Deloria grew deeply discouraged. "How do we believe in the system any longer?" he wrote in the midst of the crisis. "What does this nation want us to do?" His answer: "You live in trembling rage and burn your emotional batteries down."[61]

The crisis confronted Deloria with the realization that despite his lectures, skillful lobbying, and bestselling books, the problem he had identified four years earlier remained: contemporary Indians were invisible to the American public unless they struck a familiar pose as bare-chested warriors or glassy-eyed mystics. "American Indians," he wrote, "are prohibited from having a modern identity." Protesters in braids and dark glasses attracted the attention of Ralph Abernathy and received visits from White House emissaries, while serious leaders were ignored in favor of non-Indian experts and Hollywood celebrities. Deloria had had it: "We seek responsible spokesmen and the first movie star that comes along gets prime television time to expound his or her theories on how bad things are with the Indians. . . . [Y]ou gag halfway through the show," he complained, "and search for a late movie."[62]

Deloria avoided confessional writing; he attacked his enemies rather than reflecting on his private feelings. But as the surreal events of the early 1970s multiplied—from the angry, spontaneous takeovers of parks and monuments to bizarre incidents like the appearance of an actress, in buckskin, who claimed Apache heritage at the 1973 Oscar ceremony—they prompted Deloria to question his commitment to activism and writing.[63] He had completed law school but was as uninterested in a conventional legal career as he had been in the mainstream ministry. He tried teaching but found the experience "unsatisfying."[64] He had no interest in returning to Washington, D.C. He had a growing family to support and was about to turn forty.

Deloria had a perceptive take on the events he witnessed during his years in law school, but he was uncertain about which group to support or what path to pursue. Native leaders needed "a philosophy of Indian affairs," he noted in 1971; "no real progress has been made in developing new concepts since the Indian Reorganization Act."[65] In a remarkably revealing essay published in an obscure religious journal at the end of 1972, Deloria sketched out his response to the personal and professional uncertainty he felt at the beginning of the 1970s. *Katallagete: Be Reconciled* was a religious journal published by a group of liberal southerners that included James Holloway of Berea College and the novelist Walker Percy. Deloria's reflections appeared in an issue devoted to vocations. He described his own search for meaningful work. He recalled that he had entered the seminary searching for a calling that would enable him to guide others through life but had soon discovered that church doctrines were "virtually useless" for that purpose. The intellectual atmosphere had "provided an incredible variety of food for thought," but theology, he concluded, was "at once too general to be useful and too specific to be meaningful in the novel events of the 1960s and beyond." Looking elsewhere, he had discovered the law, hoping that statutes and judicial decisions would provide "answers to immediate problems and a . . . sense of orientation in the situation man finds himself in. . . ." That system also fell short. "Law was even less related to life than theology," he wrote. The seminary offered a broad framework for living but little in the way of daily guidance. Alternatively, the law simply offered a means of "balancing of relative powers," nothing more.[66]

Deloria proposed that even though religion and the law originated from separate needs—on the one hand, to articulate basic beliefs, and on the other, to regulate human behavior—each should be "experiential" if it was to remain relevant to human experience. He had long dismissed rigid theologies that sought to eradicate Indian paganism or politicians who insisted that Native people conform to civilized rules and standards. Ideally, he wrote, religion and the law should avoid such rigidity and be complementary "components of a constantly shifting value scheme of both individuals and societies." Deloria presented himself as the embodiment of this pragmatic experimental framework, someone who could combine American Indian cultural values with a coherent agenda to inspire his daily actions. He could speak for culture and common sense. In short, he concluded, meaningful work for him was a "desperate balancing act of a sense of justice . . . and a continual confrontation of the immediate situation. . . ."[67]

This existential pose perfectly matched the Sioux author's growing unease with both government policy and the rhetorical appeal of Red Power. At the end of the *Katallagete* essay, he described himself as a participant in "an Indian tribal situation that fluctuates between memories of an exotic past and a precarious future defined in derogation of that past." Deloria added that maintaining his Indian identity "involve[d] a certain tension between a willingness to share its happiness and grief and the personal demand to be its severest critic and most disloyal member." This was a tall order, he conceded, but he reminded his readers that Indians had always believed that "living cannot be postponed." Crazy Horse, he noted, had embodied that self-confident view when he rode into battle shouting, "It is a good day to die." Calling on that warrior's legacy, Deloria concluded that the "question of man's life and identity is to let the bastards know you've been there and that it is always a good day to die. We are therefore able to live."[68]

TWO FOUNDATIONAL TEXTS

In the wake of his confessional *Katallegete* essay, Deloria published two books, one that spelled out the spiritual beliefs that underlay the Native traditions of the continent and another that sketched the outlines of practical reforms that would resolve the Indians' two-century-long political struggle with the United States. The first, *God Is Red*, published in the fall of 1973, described his view of the fundamental values that united American Indians and separated them from other citizens.[69] The second, *Behind the Trail of Broken Treaties*, which appeared ten months later, summarized Deloria's view of the Red Power phenomenon and outlined the principal political adjustments that could ensure the long-term viability of the nation's tribes.[70] The two books distilled the Sioux activist's thinking at this pivotal moment in his life. They also reflected his growing involvement in the world of ideas and announced his new persona as a Native philosopher, critic, and guide.

God Is Red contained much of the humor and general commentary that had characterized Deloria's earlier writing. Its opening chapters reviewed the proliferation of Indian protests during the previous few years and repeated Deloria's dismay at their poor leadership and disappointing achievements. He argued, for example, that the BIA takeover had brought attention to little more than "broken treaties and broken urinals," while the public's rising interest in Native issues (an interest that had fueled sales of his own books) only demonstrated "that there exists in the minds of non-Indian Americans a vision of what they would like Indians to be." While "anthologies blossom like weeds in an untended garden," he wrote, looters continued to desecrate Indian burial grounds and federal courts continued to ignore tribal fishing rights. "The impasse seems to be constant," he observed; "Indians are unable to get non-Indians to accept them as contemporary beings."[71]

The problem, Deloria argued, was not political hostility or even racism; it was a profound cultural and spiritual breakdown that had triggered a "desperate" effort among non-Indians "to flee the abstract and find authenticity." In this chaotic atmosphere, "the stoic and heroic red man . . . seemed to hold the key to survival. . . ." Indians too were victims of this fantasy. Activists posing as warriors ended up "dancing for liberal dollars," he wrote, while "tribal officials with a heady sense of power demanded and received lucrative government contracts . . . and by taking the federal funds forever surrendered their rights to criticize the Bureau of Indian Affairs." Viewing the aftermath of Alcatraz, Wounded Knee, and other recent confrontations, Deloria not only believed little had been accomplished but also argued that these events revealed an emptiness in the hearts of many young activists. For the former seminarian, this state of affairs amounted to a "religious crisis" that compelled all Americans to reexamine and identify their basic cultural values.[72]

The "fundamental difference" between American Indian and Western European traditions, Deloria argued, was that Native people "hold their lands—places—as having the highest possible meaning," while the American majority oriented itself around time, a concept that viewed history as a "steady progression of basically good events." The problems the American public faced in the early 1970s were triggered by recent events; they had not been "good." The civil rights promise had gone up in flames. America's vaunted power had been defeated in Vietnam. Indians had spurned the idea of assimilating into the majority culture. Western faith in continuous progress had been defeated by the realities of resistance and geography. The world turned out not to be a happy global village; it was "a series of non-homogenous pockets of identity" spread across the globe. Deloria urged his readers to recognize and adjust to this new environment by shifting their focus away from the arc of "progress" and embracing instead the Native reverence for place. He predicted that personal growth would flow from "a particular experience at a particular place" rather than from achieving a distant and abstract goal. Reoriented to place, "religion thus becomes a present examination of community needs and values, not a progression of conceptual advances."[73]

Deloria spent the bulk of *God Is Red* elaborating on the differences between Western European cultures based on time and Native American cultures based on space, but the message of his title—"for this land, God is Red"—carried a warning that Indian people would never belong to American society until both they and the non-Indian majority recognized the implications of his argument. Both groups must abandon the unrealistic goals of complete assimilation, on the one hand, and the revival of a romantic past, on the other, he declared. Americans should turn instead to reconciliation through the application of traditional Native values to the complexities of the modern world. "Within the traditions, beliefs and customs of the American Indian people are the guidelines for mankind's future," he wrote. "It is this spirit of the continent . . . that shines through the Indian anthologies and glimmers in the Indian communities in grotesque and tortured forms."[74]

BY CONTRAST, *Behind the Trail of Broken Treaties* had a straightforward political purpose. Deloria wrote it in the wake of the Wounded Knee occupation while he was applying his legal training to the defense of several American Indian Movement leaders facing federal conspiracy charges. The book sought to make intelligible one of the most radical, and widely dismissed, demands of the Wounded Knee occupiers: that the United States should resume making treaties with Indian tribes. His goal, Deloria wrote, was to demonstrate that this proposal was "far from a stupid or ill-considered proposal."[75] The book followed the organizational pattern of *God Is Red*: four stinging chapters that commented sarcastically on recent events, followed by short essays containing the author's core conceptual argument. Like *God Is Red*, *Behind the Trail* identified a crisis in American life, though here the crisis was legal, not spiritual.

According to Deloria, the hasty occupation of Wounded Knee

village in early 1973 introduced a new element to Indian protests: "revered medicine men and several well-known holy men" joined the militants, along with "representatives of the Iroquois League." Their presence, and the elders' "declaration of independence" and call for the reinstatement of old treaties, "marked a historic watershed in the relations of American Indians and the Western European peoples. . . . In their declaration of independence," Deloria wrote, "the Oglala Sioux spoke to the world about freedom for all aboriginal peoples. . . ." The fact that these claims were made before a global audience not only animated other tribes but enlivened fellow critics of colonialism across the globe. As bizarre as it may have seemed to have Angela Davis and other media figures parading before television cameras on the windswept prairies of South Dakota, the point had been made: American Indians were now being presented and understood as a distinct and separate people. As one Indian participant later observed, we "had become the VC [Vietcong] in our own homeland."[76]

Even as he underscored the international dimensions of American Indian treaty rights claims, Deloria argued that the demands raised at Wounded Knee should still be addressed within the framework of U.S. law. He insisted that reactivating Indian treaties was practical. Indian communities were no less deserving of recognition than the small nations of the Pacific or Central America or (repeating William Potter Ross's argument from a century earlier) European principalities such as San Marino or the Vatican. The Sioux author also noted that these international examples demonstrated that tiny countries could survive without being self-sufficient. Any state, he wrote, was "perfectly free to contract with a neighbor for the transfer of certain governmental functions without prejudice to its status." Deloria believed that this flexible outlook could inspire a new round of treaty negotiations that would produce formal agreements outlining the powers, rights, and responsibilities of both the tribes and the American nation.[77]

Behind the Trail of Broken Treaties also warned that ignoring international standards of conduct would earn the United States "continued protest and discontent" in the global community. Deloria reminded readers that Israel's recent emergence onto the world stage represented "a dramatic vindication of the validity of traditional historic claims to specific territory as the sovereign heritage of a specific people." The current crisis in Indian affairs should be viewed as an opportunity to reverse the nation's colonial legacy. "Action by Congress . . . to define Indian tribes as smaller nations under the protection of the United States," he argued, "would . . . eliminate the errors of the past and bring to a close the nebulous period of history which has plagued us since the days of [the] discovery of the New World."[78]

THE PUBLICATION OF *God Is Red* and *Behind the Trail of Broken Treaties* capped an extraordinary decade in Deloria's life and, at least for him, marked the moment when Native activists were to abandon forever the idea of becoming Indian Americans. Despite his insistent optimism about the possibility of negotiating a new relationship between Indian tribes and the central government, the two books challenged activists of all stripes to face both cultural and constitutional realities and devise a new generation of solutions. "It is not enough," he declared in an essay published in 1974, "that some Indians are clever enough to get appointed to high places or that others [are] . . . skillful politicians. . . . [F]uture generations of Indians will judge this generation from a different perspective. . . . We must not let this chance slip away from us by hoping that in the confusion we can get something for ourselves."[79]

THE PROFESSOR

Events in the 1970s largely vindicated Deloria's analysis. High-profile confrontations ended after 1975, but a series of shifts in both federal policy making and the nation's cultural life confirmed a dramatic change in relations between Indians and the American majority. While the federal government shied away from restarting wholesale treaty negotiations with tribes, Congress adopted a number of initiatives that promised tribal leaders would never again be locked out of decision making. Not only were commissioners of Indian affairs now routinely Native Americans, but a self-determination statute passed in 1975 empowered tribes to contract with federal agencies to take over the delivery of government services in their own communities. Funded by these contracts, reservation governments gradually organized their own school systems, housing projects, health centers, and other agencies to address law enforcement, environmental protection, and economic development.

This expansion of tribal government was accompanied by an extraordinary rise in the number of American Indian professionals, particularly lawyers. Law schools encouraged this trend through the proliferation of courses on federal Indian law and the creation of special programs such as the University of New Mexico's American Indian Law Center. In 1970 private foundation grants supported the creation of the Native American Rights Fund, a public interest law firm modeled on the NAACP Legal Defense Fund. By the middle of the decade these investments had begun to pay off: eastern Indians won legal recognition and financial compensation for nineteenth-century land seizures, judges and politicians increasingly accepted the expanded powers of tribal governments over local affairs, Congress affirmed

the rights of Indians to religious freedom, and the federal courts vindicated long-standing claims to fishing rights in the Pacific Northwest
and on the Great Lakes.[80]

Running parallel to the growing effectiveness of Indians in policy
making and the law was a rising presence of Indians in American
higher education. Academic disciplines that had long viewed Indians
as marginal actors or passive subjects of research—literature, history,
sociology, and anthropology—responded to criticism from activists
like Deloria by focusing resources on contemporary issues as well as on
the task of training a new generation of Native scholars. Public protests
also inspired the creation of interdisciplinary American Indian studies
programs at research universities such as UCLA (1969), the University
of Minnesota (1969), and the University of California, Berkeley (1972).

Deloria taught in the College of Ethnic Studies at Western Washington University immediately after receiving his law degree in 1970,
but his first foray into academia ended unhappily after two years.
Despite his delight at being close to the treaty rights activists pressing
their claims in nearby Puget Sound, Deloria found his new duties a
poor fit for his wide-ranging, irreverent intellect. Throughout his career
he found universities oddly obsessed with credentials, stodgy disciplines, and outdated rules.

Deloria returned to Colorado in 1972 and spent the next six years as
a freelance writer, lecturer, and consultant. He lectured on college
campuses, lobbied Congress when called upon, and taught short
courses as a visiting professor. He continued to publish essays and
books, but the extraordinary one-book-per-year output he had maintained for the five years following the publication of *Custer* now slowed
considerably.[81]

By the middle 1970s additional Indian studies programs had appeared, spawning academic journals and producing students who ea-

gerly sought careers with tribes or in urban Indian communities. One of these new journals, the *American Indian Quarterly*, reviewed *God Is Red* in its maiden issue.[82] Despite inadequate funding, inconsistent leadership, and the predictable carping of academic critics, these university programs, which had grown to number more than one hundred by century's end, not only provided a ready venue for iconoclastic Native authors like Deloria but also produced a growing stream of scholarship on social, cultural, and legal issues that kept an American Indian perspective on events before the public.[83]

This evolving political, legal, and cultural landscape encouraged both Native activists and their white allies to reflect upon the deeper meaning of the issues protesters had raised at Alcatraz and Wounded Knee. Deloria welcomed this ferment, believing it had produced a "growth to maturity," but he was not so sure what that maturity would produce.[84] Reviewing the encouraging trends in law and policy making in the spring of 1978, for example, he noted that even though Indians had made "substantial progress," Natives and non-Natives still lacked a "theoretical conception of the contemporary status of Indians." He believed such a conception was essential because "without ideological guidelines," tribes would likely return to their old habit of simply lobbying for more of whatever federal dollars they were currently receiving. Without leaders who held to a firm cultural identity and clear set of cultural values, American Indians could expect nothing more than "continuous movement to and fro, between the poles of sovereignty and wardship. . . . How much better the future would be," he wrote, "was the unanswered question."[85]

Shortly after Deloria wondered aloud about the Indian community's future prospects, the University of Arizona invited him to become a professor of law and political science at its Tucson campus. By assuming the position of a tenured professor, the Sioux author would now be able to address the "unanswered question" of the Native American future in an atmosphere of economic and political security. Deloria was not the first Native American to hold a senior position at a major research university, but he was certainly the first Indian political activist to assume such a post. He was also the first Native scholar to have senior American Indian colleagues who, also protected by tenure and the rules of academic freedom, could write and speak alongside him without fear of retribution. At Arizona, Deloria focused the bulk of his intellectual energy on the two broad themes he had identified in *Behind the Trail of Broken Treaties* and *God Is Red:* spiritual renewal and political reforms that embraced the sovereignty of Native peoples within the United States. He explored these twin themes in several books and a steady stream of essays published in legal, religious, and popular journals.[86] His legal writings appeared during a time of extraordinary litigiousness, when tribes and their adversaries tested the limits of the Indians' ambition for power and political recognition. This activity produced a torrent of decisions in the federal courts. While Native advocates celebrated their victories in cases upholding treaty rights, reservation exemptions from state taxation, aboriginal land titles in eastern states, tribal jurisdiction over membership rolls, and other important issues, Deloria continued to remind his colleagues that the surging field now called federal Indian law was being shaped by white judges who had never denied Congress's power to void treaties and who had never declared a federal statute affecting Indians to be unconstitutional.

Deloria clearly understood that the nation's founding had erased American Indians from the social contract that defined the United States as a nation. Excluded from the phrase "We the people" in the preamble to the U.S. Constitution, Indians had therefore never been in a position to consent to be governed by the nation's institutions.

Nor, Deloria added, could that document "provide any significant guidance or protection" for them.[87]

Deloria argued that simply extending the rights of U.S. citizenship to Native people could not repair their original exclusion from the American nation. This was so, he wrote, because Indians by definition were members of tribes. So long as the Indians' institutions were ignored, so were they. Consultation, a term that had become popular among congressional policy makers in the 1970s, was no substitute for recognition of a tribe's sovereign status. According to Deloria, a requirement to consult with tribes "merely means that you try to talk the Indians into what you want to do. Following that meeting," he added, "you proceed to do what you want to do anyway." The only solution, he told a congressional hearing in December 1987, would be a series of negotiated agreements with Indian tribes that would establish the constitutional basis for their relationship with the United States: "What we need is a federal statute saying that there must be Indian consent before any program of the federal government can be operated on a reservation."[88]

As he witnessed the proliferation of legal decisions involving Indian tribes, Deloria worried that the expanding cadre of Indian law experts was itself creating a barrier to the recognition of tribal sovereignty. In an essay in the *Arizona Law Review*, he charged that like lawyers everywhere, the Indians' current advocates, however well intentioned, dwelled in a world of rules and doctrine rather than justice and humanity. As a consequence, Deloria worried that the new generation of Native practitioners had "thrown caution to the winds and produced a massive amount of new literature which pretends that a few popular concepts can be used to explain a very complicated, very diverse body of data." These concepts (jurisdiction, tribal sovereignty, water rights, congressional supremacy, among others) in turn had created a self-contained legal universe in which lawyers played the role of enlightened priests. "What is missing in Indian law," he pointed out with his characteristic wit, "are the Indians." Legal rules and categories flattened complex human predicaments into cases whose outcomes, the lawyers argued, should be determined by the application of rules. The ultimate result of these developments, Deloria argued, was an ironic state of affairs where a field initially conceived to aid Native people had become "an oppressive and obtuse thing. . . . Consequently, there is no need to discuss justice; there is only the requirement of understanding law."[89]

Just as national leaders in Washington, D.C., should come to terms with tribal governments through the negotiation of new treaties, so, Deloria argued, should lawyers and judges free themselves from the rules and doctrines that defined federal Indian law. In 1989, for example, Deloria cited the recent case of *Oliphant v. Suquamish Indian Tribe,* a conflict that arose on the tiny Port Madison Reservation of western Washington, where most of the land had been acquired by non-Indian purchasers over the course of the twentieth century and where only fifty Indians reportedly maintained a tribal government in the midst of nearly three thousand non-Indian neighbors. Despite these disparities, the tribe's attorneys had insisted that federal courts apply the doctrine of tribal sovereignty to the situation, thereby empowering a tiny group to exercise criminal jurisdiction over thousands of nonmembers. Deloria reported he had not been surprised when the tribe's solid doctrinal argument had failed in the Supreme Court. "Surely here," he wrote, "was an instance of a doctrine run amok." In the face of such cases, he urged tribal leaders to negotiate binding agreements with their counterparts in county and state governments rather than force them into litigation. Deloria was aware that many of his legal colleagues would be hurt by his sharply worded essay, but he insisted that negotiations had proved successful in the return of Taos Pueblo's sacred Blue Lake to tribal ownership, the settlement of a century-long dispute over Native land claims in Alaska, and the struggle of several New England tribes to win recognition for their reservation governments.[90]

Deloria also believed that tribes should set aside fixed rules and doctrines when seeking to repair the spiritual damage that had been done to them over the centuries. It was fruitless for Native groups to seek a return to precontact tribal life, he argued. "Almost all Indian tribes have been forcibly removed from their ancestral homelands and subjected to cultural and religious indignities. . . ." This process, he noted in 1985, "result[ed] in the destruction of ceremonial life and much of the cultural structure which has made ceremony and ritual significant." Searching world history for a parallel to the Indians' predicament, the former seminarian pointed to the ancient Hebrews. Their suffering, he argued, had prepared the Israelites to move from a "parochial, tribal religion" toward a broader, more universal conception of their place in the world. "Their exile did not drive them back to their original beliefs, but instead propelled them forward so that they could reimagine themselves as an exemplary society." While admitting that the comparison was not exact (and acknowledging that he was promulgating a distinctly Christian view of Jewish history), Deloria urged other Indians to discern "the same kind of message and mission that inspired the Hebrew prophets" in "the chaos of their shattered lives."[91]

From this broad historical perspective, the challenge for tribes was to organize their communities around the most universal aspects of their cultural beliefs. The most important of these, he wrote in the religious journal *Church and Society*, were that "all things are alive and all things are related." (He commented wryly that these two ideas "might be the only general propositions with which all Indians could agree.") To animate this faith, Indian communities should pursue the ideal of peoplehood, a term he had first used in *Custer Died for Your Sins*. For Deloria, the term referred to a group's shared history as well as its commonly shared social obligations, spiritual beliefs, and sacred places. Tribal elders such as the men and women Deloria had met on his childhood visits to Wounded Knee embodied the peoplehood ideal, he wrote. He was aware that tribal leaders convinced of the uniqueness of their own traditions and beliefs would be skeptical of his universalistic rhetoric, but he stuck to his guns. He insisted that Native thinkers should reach for ways to integrate and synthesize indigenous wisdom. "How we accomplish the task of bringing experience, belief, and institutional behavior into line with each other," Deloria wrote, "may well determine whether or not we survive as a people."[92]

During his years at Arizona, Deloria clarified the link between his view of politics and his vision of modern tribal values. He insisted that reviving treaty making and reinvigorating tribal spiritual life were two interlinked aspects of the contemporary struggle to achieve a viable state of modern American Indian peoplehood. Tribes should therefore keep both in mind by, for example, bringing elders into tribal government or infusing reservation courts with traditional Native concepts of justice. "Indian affairs has thus moved beyond political institutions into an arena primarily cultural, religious, and sociological," Deloria observed in 1984. It was essential, he wrote, that tribal leaders engaged in political questions should also take into account "the profound cultural and emotional energies that are influencing Indians today." At the end of the 1980s he was still at it. He told one interviewer, "I am trying to shift the progressive people from defense to offense."[93]

AN AMBIGUOUS LEGACY

Vine Deloria, Jr., moved to the University of Colorado in 1990 and taught there until he retired in 2000. During this last phase of his career he continued the publishing pattern he had established at Arizona: he produced books for general readers with startling regularity while placing specialized essays in journals and editing collections of essays and historical documents.[94] He told an interviewer in 1998 that he now wrote for students, activists, and "educated Indians," adding, "I have hit the glass ceiling that minority writers eventually hit when American white intellectuals no longer pay attention to them."[95] Despite his declining public profile, his preoccupations (and sense of humor) remained unchanged. There was no shortage of new targets for his scorn. "American Indians finally have it made," he wrote in 1995, as tribally owned casinos spread across the nation. "Indeed," he added, "some tribal chairmen are now well heeled Republicans worried about gun control, moral fiber, and prayer in the schools." In the introduction to *The World We Used to Live In*, published a year after his death, Deloria observed that it was now possible for suburban Americans to find "sweat lodges conducted for $50, peyote meetings for $1500. . . . The consumer society," he added, "is . . . consuming everything in its path."[96]

In a world where Indian Americans seemed to have found considerable success, Deloria remained critical of leaders who pursued economic goals alone. He insisted that however wealthy a tribe might become, it was essential to explore and revitalize the central elements of its American Indian identities. These views had emerged during the first decade of his public career, but they grew sharper, and harsher, during his years in Boulder. He charged, for example, that the growing cadre of Native scholars in American universities had been so captivated by academia that they had entered "an intellectual fantasy world where ideology rules over common sense."[97] "Too many people think being Indian is a state of mind," he declared in 1998, noting that prominent men and women presented themselves as Native but then added that they were also anthropologists or lawyers. "What's going on here?" he asked. "People are trading their personal identity as an Indian for a professional identity and in effect siding with their profession." This practice, he warned (in reference to the Supreme Court justice whose conservatism put him at odds with his fellow African Americans), "is simply creating a generation of Clarence Thomases."[98]

"Every Indian tribe has a spiritual heritage that distinguishes them from all other peoples," Deloria declared near the end of his life. Because that unique heritage had been produced by both historical experience and religious faith, tribal identities required personal engagement, not suburban sweat lodges or superficial "walk-through" ceremonies. "We cannot 'revive' a religion," he declared. "What we can do is respect religious traditions and allow them to take us forward into the future."[99]

Deloria spent the last years of his career preaching this vision. His loyalty to tribal traditions put him at odds with mainstream thinkers, particularly when he attacked the idea that his ancestors had migrated to America across the Bering Strait. But Deloria took pleasure in their scorn because, he insisted, it proved that they were taking Indian ideas seriously. His goal, he declared, was simply to "provoke discussion." He reported happily in 1998: "I think I am winning."[100]

While Deloria persuaded few scientists that tribal origin stories were scientifically correct, his passionate calls for spiritual renewal and his withering attacks on racial stereotypes and academic paternalism won him considerable support. His insistence that tribal governments define their own identities and political agendas was welcomed by a rising generation of leaders who declared that their sovereign powers entitled them to do far more than simply administer social service programs designed in Washington, D.C. Deloria's urgent appeal to Native communities to take seriously the pursuit of peoplehood was picked up by writers, artists, and commentators across the continent. By the end of the century his ideas had come to define the American Indian's cultural and political identity in the United States.[101]

SHORTLY BEFORE his death Vine Deloria, Jr., wrote that the power of tribal ceremonies and other cultural traditions should "be applied to our daily lives to enrich our well-being and enhance our understanding of life."[102] It is significant that in the end Deloria appealed for cultural renewal rather than a major new statute or federal policy. Working and writing in an era when American Indians suddenly enjoyed steady, albeit limited, access to government decision makers, cultural institutions, and the media, he continued to believe that Native communities could survive and their unique values could flourish within a modern industrial democracy. His optimism was rooted in the conviction, impressed upon him from childhood, that American Indians need not bow before federal power or the teachings of Western civilization.

Deloria was a worrier and a skeptic. He worried that as beneficiaries of the civil rights and social welfare advances of the 1960s, modern Indians would defer to the American nation-state and settle for a future as detribalized Indian Americans. At the same time, he was skeptical about the struggles of idealistic young Native people to reconstruct an idyllic version of their tribal cultures. From his first emergence into public life in 1964, Deloria had argued that American

Indians should take advantage of every benefit they could derive from their status as citizens of the United States but that they should also never doubt the power that flowed from an indigenous heritage whose roots were far older than the nation's constitution or its laws and whose wisdom could not be contained in a single ceremony or shaman's aphorism. From the 1970s onward he advocated an open-ended process of both cultural renewal and legal reform. He accepted the contradictions and ambiguity that were inherent in his agenda, and he continued to criticize the activists around him, refusing to provide them with a simple blueprint for the future.

Vine Deloria, Jr.'s constant dissatisfaction with government policy and judicial decision making, as well as his persistent skepticism regarding contemporary cultural practices, often frustrated his colleagues and alienated his political allies. He understood his prescriptions were not always precise or realistic. He also knew that he frequently disappointed former allies who were confused by his barbs and scathing critiques. He seemed perpetually dissatisfied. His steady reply was that American Indians should look beyond short-term victories. Native people should think of themselves as heirs to an immense heritage that propelled them, steadily and creatively, toward the twin goals of protecting and revitalizing Indian peoplehood. Only this constant striving could reinvigorate the nation's tribes, reignite their values, and truly restore the social and political bonds that had sustained them over the centuries. His legacy was ambiguous because he sought more than a new legal decision or the appointment of American Indians to high offices. His goal was nothing less than the continued survival of Indian people—and an Indian country—within the boundaries of the United States.

THIS INDIAN COUNTRY

The activists portrayed in this book represent one thread in the long and complex history of Native Americans. These lawyers, lobbyists, writers, and politicians, together with the many other activists who remained unmentioned in my narrative, chose to oppose the aggressions of the United States with words and ideas rather than violence. Many of these people admired the warriors and military strategists who had opposed the Americans at different times and places, but during their lifetimes they put their faith in a future in which Indians and non-Indians would share the North American continent rather than fight over it. Rooted in a practical assessment of their individual predicaments as well as in humanistic tribal traditions that placed personal relationships at the center of community life, these activists struggled to persuade the invading newcomers to find peaceful solutions to their differences over land, resources, and rights. They insisted that the United States and the Indian country could be one. By the year 2000 it seemed that they had successfully made their case.

The 2000 presidential election was among the most contentious in American history. The November 7 voting, which occurred after months of campaigning and a series of rancorous candidate debates, produced a tiny popular-vote majority for the Democrat Al Gore and a deadlock in the electoral college. The victor was decided in Florida, where a close vote and disputes over recount procedures delayed a final decision on who would receive the state's twenty-five electoral votes and thereby become the next president. Weeks of maneuvering and tension culminated on December 12, when the U.S. Supreme Court intervened to stop a statewide recount of ballots in Florida, effectively awarding the election to the Republican, George W. Bush. No presidential election had ended in as much confusion since 1876, when former Confederates and former Unionists battled up to inauguration day over who would next occupy the White House.

The tensions surrounding the 2000 election could not compare with 1876. Then, only eleven years after Appomattox, talk of rebellion and revenge circulated throughout the country. The atmosphere in 2000 was more subdued, but Republicans and Democrats had spent months insisting that their opponents represented a deeply misguided approach to the future. The previous summer their conventions had produced platforms that attacked the opposing parties' approaches to health care, taxation, reproductive rights, and environmental protection. Even the platform prologues sounded in different keys. The incumbent Democrats pronounced the election season a time of "prosperity, progress and peace" while the Republicans condemned Bill Clinton's presidency as "a time of drift."

In the midst of this divisiveness, however, one policy area was immune to partisan bickering: American Indian affairs. On this topic the major parties agreed. The Republicans pledged to "uphold the unique government to government relationship between the tribes and the United States" while the Democrats declared that the "sovereignty of the American Indians . . . and a strong affirmation of the government to government relationship are basic to our approach to tribal governments." Nuances certainly were evident—Republicans stressed a desire for "economic self-sufficiency" among tribes while Democrats promised federal assistance to aid "Indians who live in terrible poverty"—but each party assured the public that it was better prepared to protect the interests and autonomy of tribes and the civil rights of Indian people.[1]

Throughout a bitter campaign in which each side searched for wedge issues that might divide the opposition (and at a time when Indian voters held the balance of power in Montana and New Mexico), this remarkable consensus over Indian policy held firm. There was a brief moment during the summer preceding the election when Democratic activists seized on a statement candidate Bush had made suggesting he would favor states over tribes when the two groups came into dispute. Vice President Gore's supporters used the statement to question the sincerity of Governor Bush's support for tribal sovereignty. The attacks quickly ended, however, once Governor Bush met with a group of tribal leaders and promised that his administration would "strengthen Indian self-determination by respecting tribal sovereignty." He added, "I believe the federal government should allow tribes greater control over their lives, land and destiny."[2]

One should hesitate before making too much of this convergence of party platforms and campaign statements. After all, election-year promises are an uncertain indicator of future performance. As president, George W. Bush revealed himself to be an uncertain supporter of tribal claims to sovereign power. On the other hand, considering the many issues that divided Republicans and Democrats in 2000, their agreement on Indian policy, even at the level of campaign rhetoric, was remarkable. Their agreement would have seemed even more surprising to the Founding Fathers who had ignored leaders like Joseph Brant and Alexander McGillivray when making peace with Great Britain in 1782. It would have amazed them that Native people remained significant enough to be mentioned in a presidential campaign two centuries later and, even more remarkable, that candidates for federal office would vie with each other to be the leading champion of government-to-government relationships with the tribes.

Similarly, if the white settlers who had illegally crossed the boundaries into Indian Territory or the Minnesota homesteaders who had trespassed onto the Mille Lacs Reservation had been brought back to life in 2000, they would have been aghast. National political parties now *guaranteed* the right of tribes to hold communal land and participate actively in national policy debates. They would likely have asked, "Hasn't the West been won? Didn't the expansion of the United States across the continent represent the triumph of civilization over savagery?" What, they might wonder, had forced the nation's leaders to surrender so completely to the legal and political claims of the continent's indigenous people?

By November 2000 there was a national consensus in the United States on the future of American Indians and their governments. Indians would be citizens. Their tribes would function as local governments, enjoying most of the privileges granted them in treaties with the United States and negotiating with federal authorities over their status within the nation's political institutions. The clarity of this consensus is more than a historical surprise. It is also a reminder that the modern government-to-government relationship between tribes and federal authorities did not emerge from some domestic political reform of the Progressive Era or the New Deal but from the work of American Indian political activists. This consensus was pressed on the American majority by eloquent, insistent Native people, and it was articulated with increasing rigor and clarity through decades of argument, suffering, and struggle.

It would be foolish to claim that in 2000 the enemies of tribal sovereignty had been banished from the United States or that faith in Indian backwardness had been eradicated. It would be incorrect also to assume that all was well in Indian America. Anti-Indian groups calling for the abrogation of treaties and the abolition of reservations continued to function, particularly among non-Indians living near tribes that were enforcing their treaty rights to fish, water, and other resources. Problems caused by poverty, poor health care, inadequate housing, and shoddy schools continued to afflict Native communities more frequently than most other groups. The socioeconomic gaps separating Indians and other Americans, while narrowing, certainly remained. Dispossession inflicted deep and enduring wounds on the indigenous people who survived what the historian Francis Jennings called the invasion of America, and the consequences of that invasion for Indians and non-Indians alike remain. Scars produced by those wounds remain as well. Still, the place Native Americans occupied in 2000—both in major party platforms and within the United States itself—tell us that profound changes had taken place since the time of the nation's founding.

According to the 2000 federal census, American Indians lived in every county in the United States. More than half their number made their homes in cities, and all exercised the constitutional rights of American citizens. While Indian tribes operate autonomously in many respects—policing their highways, regulating business life, and operating schools, colleges, and social services—these very activities bring them into intimate contact with their non-Native neighbors. Successful gaming operations employ thousands of people, the majority of them not tribal members. Police departments rely on cooperative agreements with authorities in surrounding counties in order to function efficiently. Tribal schools are effective in large part because they educate children in accordance with state and national curriculum standards. Tribal colleges earn accreditation from the same bodies that certify the quality of educational institutions operated by states and local governments.

In these ways, by 2000 the activists had carried the day. The United States had become an *Indian* country. Tribes and Native culture were no longer external to the United States. "They" were now "our" neighbors, employers, customers, and fellow citizens. It was no longer possible to define Native Americans, as the Supreme Court had less than a century earlier, as people who were "simple, uninformed, and inferior. . . ."[3]

TODAY ACTIVISTS continue to animate discussions of the Indian future, but the cast of characters has expanded to include environmentalists, corporate leaders, physicians, bankers, actors, and astronauts. The community of activists is large and diverse, with Native women forming an ever-growing portion of the whole, but it continues to be united in its support for treaty rights, tribal autonomy, and the rights of American Indian citizens to live life as they choose. These goals remain important despite the fact that the nation's Native and non-Native populations have become increasingly intertwined. Tribes with significant business operations and groups that control water and other vital resources routinely collaborate with partners, investors, and local governments. Native and non-Native communities frequently fall into contentious disputes, but the resolution of these conflicts is more likely to come in settlements reached in face-to-face negotiation than in a judge's decision announced after prolonged and expensive litigation.

Even universities, often the most hidebound and inflexible of institutions, have incorporated dozens of interdisciplinary programs in American Indian studies into their curriculums, moving far beyond the tentative beachheads established by Vine Deloria, Jr., and his pioneering colleagues a generation ago.

The fact that Indian families and communities have scattered across the American landscape and that Native people appear regularly in the nation's party platforms, voting booths, and courts does not adequately measure the significance of the transformation produced by the activists profiled in this book. Beginning in the early nineteenth century, Indian people relentlessly drew upon the American government's political ideas and institutions in order to establish themselves as communities deserving protection from arbitrary power. These activists cared little about gaining entry to the American cultural mainstream; their campaign was for something other than assimilation into the society pressing on their borders.

Instead, they sought legal visibility and human recognition. James McDonald, for example, believed that once federal authorities grasped the Choctaw's legal claims and basic humanity, relations between his tribe and the United States could be managed through negotiation and a common adherence to the rule of law. William Potter Ross pressed for recognition of his tribe's national institutions and civilized behavior and wondered aloud why a powerful continental power like the United States could not accept a loyal but autonomous political community within its borders. In a similar vein, Sarah Winnemucca demanded to know why an idealistic, religious people could not recognize the wrongs they had inflicted on Native people like her and the members of her family while they pursued their national destiny in the American West.

The Indian activists' struggle to win recognition from federal authorities accelerated in the twentieth century as their numbers and resources grew. Benefiting in unexpected ways from the American education that had often been forced upon them, community leaders found new tools in the legal and political arenas and new allies among officials of other tribes and sympathetic non-Indians. By the end of World War II a group of sophisticated leaders had emerged to solidify this support for tribal autonomy and to insist on the human rights of Indian citizens who deserved to be allowed to live in communities of their own choosing. The National Congress of American Indians was only the most prominent of many Native groups that honed and promoted this message. They insisted that the federal government was obligated to honor treaty commitments, no matter how long those agreements had been neglected or ignored, and that tribal leaders were legitimate representatives of governments who had the right to participate fully in all policy decisions affecting them. Undergirding these specific claims was the explicit demand that Indian people be allowed to live as freely as other Americans and to organize their own communities without interference from missionaries, reformers, or federal officials.

But even as their cause was finding success, Indian activists reminded both their communities and the decision makers in Congress and the Indian Office that their goals could not be contained by a simple legislative agenda or a single set of political talking points. An intellectual like Vine Deloria, Jr., could point out that despite the hundreds of legitimate local complaints they brought to legislatures, courts, and the American public, their ultimate goal was far larger and more complex than any individual dispute. They should not seek one victory, he argued—citizenship, compensation for unlawful seizures, or the right to organize tribal governments—but all of them and more. Indians had insisted from the start that U.S. leaders recognize that their "empire for liberty" had taken root on Native soil and that the new country they celebrated every Fourth of July also encompassed and contained an enduring set of indigenous communities that deserved recognition as a distinguishing feature of the American nation. As Deloria so powerfully reminded his students and readers, the presence of Indian people and the legacy of their dispossession compelled Americans to reimagine themselves by developing a reverence for placc and a deeper relationship with other living beings on the planet. The continent's unique history, he argued, should inspire a unique cultural and political identity. America was not simply the headquarters of a successful commercial enterprise; it could also be the seat of an exemplary society.

Almost from the start, Indian activists had wanted American officials and legislators—and all their citizens—to appreciate that the nation could represent much more than a beautiful territory that had been wrested from the grasp of its original inhabitants. By recognizing and defending the rights of Native people to occupy and maintain their own homelands within the national landscape, American leaders could finally embrace the humanity of Native people and the undeniable truth that Indians did not exist "out there" or "back then," but instead, that they were, and had always been, fellow travelers on the American journey. Discovering the legacy of American Indian activism, then, opens a doorway to the discovery of a new place: *this Indian country*.

Acknowledgments

This book began more than a decade ago as an informal lecture at the University of Illinois and it has taken shape in conversation with the people in Champaign/Urbana who in the years since have been my students and valued colleagues. Chief among the latter are the three department chairs who have nurtured and defended our special culture and values over the past decade: James Barrett, Peter Fritzsche, and Antoinette Burton. Two early chapters benefited from the extraordinary barrage of advice and criticism that comes to anyone presenting his or her work to the department's History Workshop, and nearly every other later one received a separate, careful reading from one or more of the following Illinois colleagues: James Barrett, Antoinette Burton, Tony Clark, Matthew Gilbert, Dan Hamilton, LeAnne Howe, Harry Liebersohn, and Robert Parker. To that list must be added Robert Warrior, who arrived on campus to direct the Program in American Indian Studies just as my manuscript was in need of the extra scrutiny and advice that he provided.

As I struggled to select the subjects for each chapter and to frame the project's argument, I received valuable feedback from colleagues at institutions where I was invited to speak or participate in ongoing seminars. These included Joel Beinen and Richard White at Stanford University; Linda Kerber at the University of Iowa; Jean O'Brien,

Brenda Child, and David Wilkins at the University of Minnesota; the late David Weber at the Clements Center for Southwest Studies at Southern Methodist University; Phil Deloria and Gregory Evans Dowd at the University of Michigan; and former Illinois Chancellor Richard Herman, who invited me to deliver the Chancellor's Center for Advanced Study Special Lecture in 2007.

While ideas are cheap, turning them into a book like this has required a substantial investment of research support that enabled me to travel to distant libraries and archives and to enjoy extended periods of uninterrupted research and writing. Early support came from a Mellon Foundation Humanities Fellowship. In November 2005 I was privileged to receive a scholarly residency at the Rockefeller Foundation's Bellagio Center in northern Italy. The month of quiet isolation at Bellagio provided crucial time not only to think, organize material, and begin writing but also to imagine a project worthy of the extraordinary community that shared the time there with me. This challenging and stimulating interdisciplinary group included Darius and Cathy Brubeck, Tom De Wall, Honor Moore, Raul and Elizabeth Pangalangan, David Rousseve, Ellen Spiro, Sandy Levinson, Sushma Joshi, and the center's gracious director, Pilar Palacio. A faculty fellowship from the National Endowment for the Humanities during the 2007–08 academic year provided precious months during which I was able to write a substantial portion of the book, and a semester's release from teaching made possible by my university's Center for Advanced Study in 2009 allowed me to complete a draft of the entire manuscript.

Thanks to research support provided by the University of Illinois, I was also able to enlist several graduate students to assemble documents and other research materials necessary for so wide-ranging a book project. These included Michael Sherfy, Troy Smith, Jennifer Guiliano, Brian Ingrassia, and Michael Hughes. I am grateful for their hard work and steady support. The project also benefited from the extraordinary generosity of librarians and archivists in Champaign/Urbana (particularly the university's history librarian, Mary Stuart) and at my second scholarly home, Chicago's Newberry Library. The staff at the latter institution was particularly accommodating to a former employee. I am grateful for the support provided by David Spadafora, president and librarian; James Grossman, former vice president for research and education; Diane Dillon of the Office of Research and Education; Robert Karrow, curator of special collections; and the dozens of reading room assistants and reference specialists who guided me as I assembled this story. Most important among those is John Aubrey, Ayer librarian, who has been a valued colleague and guide for more than three decades. I am also grateful to the archivists and librarians who accommodated me during visits to the Gilcrease Museum in Tulsa, Oklahoma, the Western History Collections at the University of Oklahoma, the National Archives, the Library of Congress, and the National Museum of the American Indian (NMAI). Jennifer O'Neil, archivist at the NMAI, was particularly helpful during my exploration of the papers of the National Congress of American Indians. I also appreciate the efforts of Maeve Herbert Glass who generously volunteered to locate images for me in the Princeton University Library. Finally, my discussion of the Ojibwe community at Mille Lacs and its heroic efforts in the U.S. Court of Claims was helped immensely by the access to primary documents related to the era and the case provided to me by the tribe's attorney, Marc D. Slonim, of Ziontz, Chestnut, Varnell, Berley and Slonim of Seattle, Washington.

I tell entering graduate students that the first thing an aspiring historian should do is "Make friends; you will need them." The friends who advised, corrected, and encouraged me during this project (in addition to those already mentioned) include Colin Calloway, Claudio

Saunt, Patrick Wolfe, Paul Rosier, Harvey Markowitz, Theda Perdue, R. David Edmunds, David Wilkins, David Beck, and Peter Nabokov. Two others—Alexandra "Sasha" Harmon at the University of Washington and Christian McMillen at the University of Virginia—deserve special thanks for reading and offering trenchant criticisms of the entire manuscript. Finally, I am grateful to James Merrell, who encouraged me to write a "big book" about American Indian political activists, and to Laura Stickney and Scott Moyers, my editors at Penguin Press, who have prodded me to enliven my prose. They and the tireless Emily Graff shepherded the project through the many steps leading to final publication. In addition, Rolly Woodyatt supplied expert proofreading. Despite all this terrific advice, I alone am responsible for the final product, including any errors it might contain.

My wife, Holly, has listened to the ideas embedded in this book for many years. She has never failed to identify the false notes and windy asides. She has always had a keen eye for the central story. If the story here makes sense and seems important, it is because Holly has long been my guide in the task of separating the significant from the insignificant, a skill she brings to our life together every day. This book is dedicated to our four sons in gratitude for the many years when they have been my favorite audience, my best fans, and my loving companions; my peeps. Thanks, boys.

NOTES

INTRODUCTION

1. *Tee-Hit Ton Indians v. U.S.*, 348 U.S. 272 (1955), 289.

CHAPTER ONE

1. Richard Morris, *The Peacemakers: The Great Powers and American Independence* (New York: Harper, 1965). Leonard J. Sadosky places this moment in the broader history of diplomacy both in and about North America in *Revolutionary Negotiations: Indians, Empires and Diplomats in the Founding of America* (Charlottesville: University of Virginia Press, 2009). For a popular recounting of these events, see also Thomas Fleming, *The Perils of Peace. America's Struggle for Survival After Yorktown* (New York: HarperCollins, 2007).
2. J. Leitch Wright, *Britain and the American Frontier, 1783–1815* (Athens: University of Georgia Press, 1975), 2.
3. Colin G. Calloway, *The Revolution in Indian Country: Crisis and Diversity in Native American Communities* (New York: Cambridge University Press, 1995), 3.
4. Speech of Major Walls to the Shawnees, July 7, 1783, Frederick Haldimand Papers, 21779:117, Reel 54. See also Colin G. Calloway, "Suspicion and Self Interest: The British Indian Alliance and the Peace of Paris," *Historian* v. 48, n. 1 (November 1985), 41–60, especially 49–52.
5. Brant used this expression in a letter to the British Indian agent John Johnson at the end of 1781. See Isabel Thompson Kelsay, *Joseph Brant (1743–1807): A Man of Two Worlds* (Syracuse: Syracuse University Press, 1984), 336.
6. Assembly and Brant quoted in Alan Taylor, *The Divided Ground* (New York: Knopf, 2006), 113; Declaration of Joseph Brant included with Allan McLean (Fort Niagara commander) to Frederick Haldimand, May 18, 1783, Frederick Haldimand Papers, 21756:138–40, Reel 39.
7. Quoted in Kelsay, *Joseph Brant*, 340.
8. Marvin L. Brown, Jr., trans., *Baroness von Riedesel and the American Revolution: Journal and Correspondence of a Tour of Duty, 1776–1783* (Chapel Hill: University

of North Carolina Press, 1965), 122. For a description of the Indians' victories in the West after Yorktown, see Timothy D. Willig, *Restoring the Chain of Friendship: British Policy and the Indians of the Great Lakes, 1783–1815* (Lincoln: University of Nebraska Press, 2008), 14.

9. Quoted in Kelsay, *Brant*, 339.

10. Frederick Haldimand to Lord North, November 27, 1783, 21717: 178, Reel 21. See also Robert Berkhofer, "Barrier to Settlement: British Indian Policy in the Old Northwest, 1783–1794," in *The Frontier in American Development*, ed. David M. Ellis (Ithaca: Cornell University Press, 1969), 249–76.

11. Declaration of Joseph Brant.

12. Edward J. Cashin, *Lachlan McGillivray, Indian Trader* (Athens: University of Georgia Press, 1992), 71–72, 262–63.

13. Thomas Brown to Lord Sidney, May 20, 1784, Frederick Haldimand Papers, Folder 29, Gilcrease Institute.

14. Quoted in Calloway, *The Revolution in Indian Country*, 276.

15. McGillivray to O'Neill, March 10, 1783; O'Neill to Ezpeleta, October 19, 1873, in John Walton Caughey, *McGillivray of the Creeks* (Columbia: University of South Carolina Press, 2007), 61, 62, 63.

16. Louis Sadosky discusses the political background to this diplomatic maneuver in *Revolutionary Negotiations*, 93–118, though his discussion of the Paris maneuvering is quite brief: 116–18. For an English perspective on the European context for the peace negotiations, see Brendan Simms, *Three Victories and a Defeat: The Rise and Fall of the First British Empire* (New York: Penguin, 2007).

17. For a discussion of the size of the Loyalist group, see Wright, *Britain and the American Frontier*, 4–5.

18. John Jay, one of the American representatives at the peace negotiations in Paris, rejected any compensation for Loyalist "cut throats." Morris, *The Peacemakers*, 369.

19. Robert Rhodes Crout, "In Search of a Just and Lasting Peace: The Treaty of 1783, Louis XVI, Vergennes, and the Regeneration of the Realm," *International History Review*, v. 5, n. 3 (1983), 374.

20. Vergennes to Gerard, March 29, 1778, *Revolutionary Diplomatic Correspondence*, ed. Francis Wharton (Washington, D.C.: Government Printing Office, 1889), v. II, 524.

21. American Memorial to Spain, March 8, 1778; Duke de Grimaldi to Congress, March 8, 1778; Arthur Lee to Grimaldi, March 17, 1778; Benjamin Franklin to Conde de Aranda (Spanish ambassador to Paris), April 17, 1777, in *Revolutionary Diplomatic Correspondence*, v. II, 282, 290, 304.

22. See John Fisher, *Commercial Relations Between Spain and Spanish America in the Era of Free Trade, 1778–1796* (Liverpool: Centre for Latin American Studies, University of Liverpool, 1985), 9–15, 46, 47.

For more on the eighteenth-century Spanish Empire, see Jeremy Adelman, *Sovereignty and Revolution in the Iberian Atlantic* (Princeton: Princeton University Press, 2006), 33–47; and Stanley J. Stein and Barbara H. Stein, *Apogee of Empire: Spain and New Spain in the Age of Charles III, 1759–1789* (Baltimore: Johns Hopkins University Press, 2003), 19.

23. Fisher, *Commercial Relations*, 9.

24. Quoted in David J. Weber, *The Spanish Frontier in North America* (New Haven: Yale University Press, 1992), 267. For more on Spanish motives in their alliance with the Americans, see Jane M. Berry, "The Indian Policy of Spain in the Southwest, 1783–1795," *Mississippi Valley Historical Review*, v. 3, n. 4 (March 1917), 463. Spain's strategic concerns only increased in 1780, when the two-year Tupac Amaru revolt began in highland Peru and Bolivia. See Adelman, *Sovereignty*, 50. The Spanish ambassador in Paris, who was intimately involved with the American peace negotiators in 1782, later wrote his superiors that his government had been mistaken in joining a war that was "opposed to our own interests." Quoted in Stein and Stein, *Apogee of Empire*, 346.

25. John Adams to Congress, June 2, 1780, *Revolutionary Diplomatic Correspondence*, v. III, 782–83.

26. Vincent T. Harlow, *The Founding of the Second British Empire, 1763–1793* (London: Longmans, Green and Co., 1952), v. I, 5.

27. See Fleming, *Perils of Peace*, 134–53; North is quoted on p. 100.

28. Montmorin to Vergennes, March 30, 1782, *Revolutionary Diplomatic Correspondence*, v. 288.

29. Journals of the Continental Congress v. 16, 115.

30. Ibid.

31. Ibid., 116.

32. Robert Livingston to Benjamin Franklin, January 7, 1782, *Papers of Benjamin Franklin*, ed. Ellen Cohen (New Haven: Yale University Press, 2001), v. 36, 390, 394.

33. Shelburne to Franklin, April 6, 1782, *Revolutionary Diplomatic Correspondence*, v. 536.

34. *The Papers of Benjamin Franklin* (New Haven: Yale University Press, 2003), v. 37, 184–90.

35. Franklin to John Jay, April 24, 1782, *Franklin Papers*, v. 7, 206–7.

36. Ibid., v. 37, 186.

37. Harlow, *Founding of the Second British Empire*, 316–19.

38. *John Jay: The Winning of the Peace: Unpublished Papers, 1708–1784*, ed. Richard B. Morris (New York: Harper & Row, 1980), 238.

39. "Boundary Discussions Between Jay and Aranda," reprinted in ibid., 270, 272.

40. Ibid., 274.

41. See ibid., 275–76.

42. Rayneval to Jay, September 6, 1782; ibid., 229–30. The Rayneval memorandum is reprinted here, 330–33. See also Bemis, "The Rayneval Memo," 15–92.

43. Quoted in Morris, *The Peacemakers*, 367.

44. Haldimand to John Johnson, April 12, 1784, 21723-65-66, Reel 23, Haldimand Papers. Haldimand's support for Brant is clear in a letter to John Johnson, dated March 23, 1784, Frederick Haldimand Papers, Folder 28, Gilcrease Institute. For a description of Brant's extensive travels during 1784 and 1785, see Kelsay, *Joseph Brant*, 352–78.

45. Brant's 1785–86 visit to England is described in Kelsay, *Joseph Brant*, 379–393; Sydney's letter is quoted on page 392. This visit may have been the last time Brant could present himself as a spokesperson for all the crown's Indian allies. Soon after his return to Canada, an attack by Kentucky militia on Shawnee villages in Ohio caused the local confederacy to relocate its headquarters at Brownstown, near Detroit. By 1787 British commanders were dealing directly with these western tribes, bypassing Brant. See Willig, *Restoring*, 18–30.

46. Because of the American-Spanish alliance, the Mississippi had been open to American shipping during the war. See Arthur Preston Whitaker, *The Spanish American Frontier, 1783–1795* (Boston: Houghton Mifflin, 1927), 8, 10–12, 68–69.

47. McGillivray to O'Neil, January 1, 1784, in Caughey, *McGillivray of the Creeks*, 64–66. See O'Neil to Miró, February 17, 1784, ibid., 71.

48. The text of the treaty is reprinted in Caughey, *McGillivray of the Creeks*, 75–76, and Miró's appointment letter, dated June 7, 1784, is at page 77. McGillivray's central role in immediate postwar politics along the southern frontier is discussed in Eliga H. Gould, "Entangled Histories, Entangled Worlds: The English-Speaking Atlantic as a Spanish Periphery," *American Historical Review*, v. 112, n. 3 (June 2007), 778–79.

49. The bloody massacre of Christian Delawares in Ohio in the spring of 1783 was a harbinger of the bloodshed and invasion American settlers were soon to unleash on the Indian communities on their borders. For a discussion of this event and its significance, see Peter Silver, *Our Savage Neighbors: How Indian War Transformed Early America* (New York: Norton, 2008), 263–91.

50. Haldimand to John Johnson, April 12, 1784.

CHAPTER TWO

1. For the American defeat in Ohio, see Wiley Sword, *President Washington's Indian War: The Struggle for the Old Northwest, 1790–1795* (Norman: University of Oklahoma Press, 1985). Despite the high-profile ceremonies accompanying it, the Treaty of New York was controversial in Creek country. See Claudio Saunt, *A New Order of Things: Property, Power and the Transformation of the Creek Indians, 1733–1816* (New York: Cambridge University Press, 1999). An excellent overview of this complex landscape can be found in David Andrew Nichols, *Red Gentlemen and White Savages: Indians, Federalists and the Search for Order on the American Frontier* (Charlottesville: University of Virginia Press, 2008).

2. The frontier dwellers' animosity is well described in Peter Silver, *Our Savage Neighbors: How Indian War Transformed Early America* (New York: Norton, 2007).

3. Jefferson quoted in Anthony F. C. Wallace, *Thomas Jefferson and the Indians: The Tragic Fate of the First Americans* (Cambridge: Harvard University Press, 1999), 78. For an overview of the Americans' motives for the conciliatory diplomacy of the 1790s, see Leonard J. Sadosky, *Revolutionary Negotiations: Indians, Empires, and Diplomats in the Founding of America* (Charlottesville: University of Virginia Press, 2009), 157–63. For an overview of Indian policy in the early years of the American Republic, see also Reginald Horsman, "The Indian Policy of an 'Empire of Liberty,'" in *Native Americans in the Early Republic,* ed. Frederick E. Hoxie, Ronald Hoffman, and Peter J. Albert (Charlottesville: University of Virginia Press, 1999), 37–53.

4. For a discussion of intermarriage between white traders and Indian women, see Theda Perdue, "A Sprightly Lover Is the Most Prevailing Missionary: Intermarriage Between Europeans and Indians in the Eighteenth Century South," in *Light on the Path: The Anthropology and History of the Southeastern Indians*, ed. Thomas J. Pluckhahn and Robbie Etheridge (Tuscaloosa: University of Alabama Press, 2006), 165–78. For McLean, see Francis P. Weisenburger, *The Life of John McLean: A Politician on the U.S. Supreme Court*, Ohio State University Studies, Contributions in History and Political Science, no. 15 (Columbus: Ohio State University Press, 1937).

5. James McDonald to Thomas L. McKenney, April 25, 1826, Letters Received by the Office of Indian Affairs, 1824–1881 (hereafter LR-OIA), Reel 169.

6. Greg O'Brien estimates that there were fifteen to twenty thousand Choctaws living in three communities in what is now Mississippi at the close of the American Revolution. See Greg O'Brien, ed., *Pre-removal Choctaw History: Exploring New Paths* (Norman: University of Oklahoma Press, 2008), 126. Theda Perdue and Michael Green estimate the Cherokee population at the time of removal to have been "approximately 17,000." See *The Cherokee Nation and the Trail of Tears* (New York: Penguin, 2007), 119.

7. For a description of Choctaw and southeastern Indian diplomacy and treaty making in the late eighteenth century, see Charles A. Weeks, *Paths to a Middle Ground: The Diplomacy of Natchez, Boufouka, Nogales and San Fernando de las Barrancas, 1791–1795* (Tuscaloosa: University of Alabama Press, 2005), especially chapter 3, "Forging Diplomatic Paths," 25–44. The events at Hopewell have also been described by Greg O'Brien in "The Conqueror Meets the Unconquered: Negotiating Cultural Boundaries on the Post-revolutionary Southern Frontier," *Pre-removal Choctaw History*, 148–82; and David Nichols, *Red Gentlemen and White Savages*, 50–52.

8. Weeks, *Paths to a Middle Ground*, 118, 123.

9. For an overview of late-eighteenth-century diplomacy in the Southeast from the perspective of the Spanish Empire, see David J. Weber, *Bárbaros: Spaniards and*

Their Savages in the Age of Enlightenment (New Haven: Yale University Press, 2005), 214–17. In 1787 Taboca visited Philadelphia, where he met George Washington and other American leaders. See O'Brien, *Pre-removal Choctaw History*, 169. See also Galloway, "The Chief Who Is Your Father," 272.

10. See O'Brien, *Pre-removal Choctaw History*, 58, for a description of the closing ceremony. See also "Choctaw Negotiations with the United States at Hopewell, South Carolina, 1785–1786, Journal Kept by General Joseph Martin. . . ," in O'Brien, *Pre-removal Choctaw History*, 243.

11. Treaty with the Choctaw, January 3, 1785, 7 Stat., 21.

12. "Report on the Northwestern Indians, June 15, 1789," in *Documents of United States Indian Policy*, 3rd ed., ed. Francis Paul Prucha (Lincoln: University of Nebraska Press, 2000), 12.

13. North Callahan, *Henry Knox: General Washington's General* (New York: Rinehart, 1958), 330–35. See also Whitaker, *The Spanish-American Frontier*, 138; and Nichols, *Red Gentlemen and White Savages*, 106–12, 118–24.

14. Article IV, Treaty of Greenville, 7 Stat 49, August 3, 1795. The retreat of British forces in Ohio had been made clear to the region's Indian leaders the previous summer, when the crown refused to resupply their forces after they had been driven from the field at the battle of Fallen Timbers. For a summary of the Greenville negotiations, see Nichols, *Red Gentlemen and White Savages*, 171–76.

15. While the Louisiana Purchase had a dramatic impact on western settlement, tensions in the region had eased considerably eight years earlier, when the United States and Spain negotiated the Treaty of San Lorenzo. That agreement ended the dispute over West Florida's northern boundary and guaranteed Americans the right to "deposit" their goods in New Orleans.

16. See Jefferson to the Senate of the United States, January 15, 1808; and Treaty of Limits Between the United States of America and the Choctaw Nation of Indians, November 16, 1805. *American State Papers* (Washington, D.C.: Gale and Seator, 1832), 748–49 (hereafter *ASP*). The complex story behind this agreement is told in Anna Lewis, *Chief Pushmataha, American Patriot* (New York: Exposition Press, 1959), 51–56. On Jefferson's departure from his predecessors on the issue of Indian land tenure, see Nichols, *Red Gentlemen and White Savages*, 191–202.

17. Thomas L. McKenney, *Memoirs: Official and Personal* (New York: Paine and Burgess, 1846), 110. See Herman J. Viola, *Thomas L. McKenney: Architect of America's Early Indian Policy, 1816–1830* (Chicago: Swallow Press, 1974), 40–41.

18. Quoted in Viola, *Thomas L. McKenney*, 41.

19. Ibid., 44.

20. John C. Calhoun to Henry Clay, *Niles Weekly Register* (hereafter *NWR*), January 22, 1820.

21. Viola, *Thomas L. McKenney*, 44, 45; McKenney, *Memoirs*, 110–11. For more on Carnahan, see Frederick Webb Hodge, "Indtroduction," in Thomas L.

McKenney and James Hall, *Indian Tribes of North America* (Edinburgh: J. Grant, 1933–34).

22. McKenney, *Memoirs*, 115–16. It is difficult to credit all the details of McKenney's retrospective account of McDonald's Washington years. I have relied on Herman Viola's analysis of McKenney's account and have tried to use McDonald's own words whenever possible rather than statements attributed to him by self-interested third parties. It is also clear that McDonald did not "qualify for the bar" when he left Ohio in 1823; he returned there four years later to complete his studies.

23. McKenney, *Memoirs*, 112–13. Emphasis in original.

24. James McDonald to John C. Calhoun, October, 13, 1823, in W. Edwin Hemphill, ed., *The Papers of John C. Calhoun* (Columbia: University of South Carolina Press, 1975), VII, 309–10.

25. The war leader Mushulatubbe apparently always kept a portrait of Andrew Jackson on a wall in his home. See James Taylor Carson, *Searching for the Bright Path: The Mississippi Choctaws from Prehistory to Removal* (Lincoln: University of Nebraska Press, 1999), 117. A detailed account of Chief Pushmataha's confrontation with Tecumseh is included in Lewis, *Chief Pushmataha: American Patriot*, 62–68.

26. Greg O'Brien has an excellent discussion of the process by which traders entered the Choctaw world in chapter 5 ("Trading for Power") of *Choctaws in a Revolutionary Age*; see especially 88–92. For an estimate of the size of the mixed-heritage population and for Durant, see Samuel J. Wells, "The Role of Mixed-Bloods in Mississippi Choctaw History," in *After Removal: The Choctaw in Mississippi*, ed. Samuel J. Wells and Roseanna Tubby (Jackson: University Press of Mississippi, 1986), 49, 47. For a description of the onset of cattle raising in the 1820s, see James Taylor Carson, "Native Americans, the Market Revolution and Culture Change: The Choctaw Cattle Economy, 1690–1830," *Agricultural History*, v. 71, n.1 (1997), 1–18.

27. See Carson, *Searching for the Bright Path*, 82; Carson's larger discussion of traders and their new business interests is on pp. 80–83.

28. Andrew Jackson to John McKee, April 22, 1819, *ASP*, v. II, 229. The Choctaws had made one minor land sale to the United States in 1816. See Treaty of October 24, 1816, 7 Stat 152.

29. See Ruth Tenison West, "Pushmataha's Travels," *Chronicles of Oklahoma*, v. 37, n. 2 (1959), 162–74. See also Daniel Usner, *American Indians in the Lower Mississippi Valley: Social and Cultural Histories* (Lincoln: University of Nebraska Press, 1999), 99, 107, 108. The historian James Taylor Carson has noted that some chiefs may have been interested in moving west to avoid the Christian missionaries who were gaining influence in the tribe. See Carson, *Searching for the Bright Path*, 89.

30. In General Council of the Choctaw Nation, August 12, 1819, in *ASP*, v. II, 230.

31. For an overview of Jackson's relations with American Indians by a modern admirer, see Robert V. Remini, *Andrew Jackson and His Indian Wars* (New York: Penguin, 2001).

32. There are a variety of spellings of these leaders' (and their district's) names. See Peter James Hudson, "A Story of Choctaw Chiefs," *Chronicles of Oklahoma*, v. 17, n. 1 (1939), 7.

33. Andrew Jackson to Choctaw Chiefs, October 10, 1820, *ASP*, v. II, 231, 236, 236–37.

34. Ibid., 234.

35. Ibid., 240–41.

36. See Treaty with the Choctaws, October 18, 1820, 7 Stat, 210; ibid., 243.

37. Ibid., 243.

38. *NWR*, March 17, 1821; March 8, 1823.

39. Ibid., April 17, 1824. For extended discussions of the Georgia situation, see ibid., November 30, 1822; December 21, 1822; and May 21, 1823.

40. Ibid., April 17, 1824.

41. Statement of the Choctaw delegation, November 8, 1824, U.S. Bureau of Indian Affairs, Documents Relating to the Negotiation of Ratified and Unratified Treaties with Various Tribes of Indians, Reel 1 (hereafter cited as Documents).

42. See Clara Sue Kidwell, *Choctaws and Missionaries in Mississippi* (Norman: University of Oklahoma Press, 1995), 93, for a discussion of the delegation. McDonald transcribed letters from tribal leaders to relatives back home. See Mooshulatubbee to Peter Pitchlynn, October 10, 1824, Peter Pitchlynn Papers, University of Oklahoma.

43. James McDonald to Peter Pitchlynn, November 6, 1824, Pitchlynn Papers, Gilcrease Museum.

44. Good general descriptions of the 1824 negotiations are in Viola, *Thomas L. McKenney*, 127–32; and Kidwell, *Choctaws and Missionaries*, 92–96. The delegation's refusal to discuss Mississippi land sales is in its letter to the secretary of war, November 12, 1824, Documents, Reel 1. Pushmataha's comment is quoted in Viola, *Thomas L. McKenney*, 128.

45. David Folsom and James McDonald to Calhoun, November 20, 1824, *ASP*, cited in Viola, *Thomas L. McKenney*, 128. Documents, Reel 1.

46. Choctaw delegation to Calhoun, November 22, 1824. Documents, Reel 1. McKenney's pleas to McDonald are described in Viola, *Thomas L. McKenney*, 129.

47. See Choctaw Delegation to Calhoun, January 3, 1825, Documents, Reel 1; and Article Seven, Treaty of January 20, 1825; 7 Stat 234.

48. On war claims, see James McDonald to Calhoun, January 20, 1825, Letters Received, Office of Indian Affairs, Reel 169 (hereafter cited as LR-OIA). McDonald wrote in part, "The Choctaws have for a long while been waiting for their pay: it was due them ten years ago. . . ."

49. The Creeks soon learned that William McIntosh, the leader who negotiated the Indian Springs treaty, had been bribed.
50. The Creek treaty was signed in February 1825 but later repudiated by federal authorities. William McIntosh, the Creek leader who negotiated the agreement, was executed by his fellow tribesmen on April 30, 1825. See Andrew K. Frank, *Creeks and Southerners: Biculturalism on the Early American Frontier* (Lincoln: University of Nebraska Press, 2005), 95–98. The legal historian Stuart Banner emphasizes the long-standing and widespread public support for removal in the early nineteenth century in *How the Indians Lost Their Land: Land and Power on the Frontier* (Cambridge: Harvard University Press, 2005), chapter 6.
51. Choctaw delegation to Congress, February 18, 1825, reprinted in McKenney, *Memoirs*, 120–22.
52. James McDonald to Thomas L. McKenney, April 25, 1826; LR-OIA, Reel 169.
53. James McDonald to Thomas McKenney, April 27, 1826, LR-OIA, Reel 16. (There are two letters from McDonald to McKenney dated on this date. The first focused on education; the second on tribal politics.) See also Carson, *Searching for the Bright Path*, 89.
54. James McDonald to Peter Pitchlynn, March 3, 1827, Pitchlynn Papers, Gilcrease Museum.
55. James McDonald to Peter Pitchlynn, May 5, 1827, Pitchlynn Papers, Gilcrease Museum. Pitchlynn's relation to Mushulatubbe is mentioned in Carson, *Searching for the Bright Path*, 124.
56. George Harkin to Peter Pitchlynn, December 12, 1827, Pitchlynn Papers, Gilcrease Museum.
57. Rowena McClinton, ed., *The Moravian Springplace Mission to the Cherokees* (Lincoln: University of Nebraska Press, 2007), v. 1, 21, 31–32, 38.
58. Stephen Warren, *The Shawnees and Their Neighbors, 1795–1830* (Urbana: University of Illinois Press, 2005), 49–59, 64.
59. Thomas L. McKenney, "Statement shewing the number of Indian schools, where established, by whom, the number of teachers, the number of pupils, and the amount annually allowed and paid to each by the government, with remarks as to their condition," Department of War, Office of Indian Affairs, December 2, 1825. Ayer Collection, Newberry Library.
60. James McDonald to Thomas McKenney, April 27, 1825, LR-OIA, Reel 169.
61. Historians have been to quick to characterize these divisions as racial, with "mixed bloods" favoring one agenda and "full bloods" favoring another. The historian James Taylor Carson has argued effectively that all the major political groups within the tribe contained people with a variety of racial backgrounds. See Carson, *Searching for the Bright Path*, 87–88.
62. See Kidwell, *Choctaws and Missionaries*, 112. See also Carson, *Searching for the Bright Path*, 97–102. The Choctaw constitution, like the Cherokee constitution of 1828, also empowered men at the expense of traditional female clan elders.

This subject, which deserves far more study, is discussed in Theda Perdue, *Cherokee Women: Gender and Culture Change* (Lincoln: University of Nebraska Press, 1998), as well as in an insightful study of one family, Tiya Miles, *The House on Diamond Hill* (Chapel Hill: University of North Carolina Press, 2010).

63. For more on the shifts in Cherokee political culture (and their national significance), see Cynthia Cumfer, *Separate Peoples, One Land: The Minds of Cherokees, Blacks, and Whites on the Tennessee Frontier* (Chapel Hill: University of North Carolina Press, 2007), 101–24; and Cynthia Cumfer, "Local Origins of National Indian Policy: Cherokee and Tennessean Ideas About Sovereignty and Nationhood, 1790–1811," *Journal of the Early Republic*, v. 23, n. 1 (Spring, 2003), 21–46.

64. See Mary Elizabeth Young, *Redskins, Ruffleshirts and Rednecks: Indian Allotments in Alabama and Mississippi, 1830–1860* (Norman: University of Oklahoma Press, 2002), 14–15.

65. *NWR*, October 28, 1828; Garrison, *The Legal Ideology of Removal*, 104–05.

66. Carson, *Searching for the Bright Path*, 116.

67. *NWR*, May 15, 1830, 216.

68. James McDonald to Peter Pitchlynn, March 21, 1830, Peter Pitchlynn Papers, Gilcrease Museum.

69. James McDonald to Thomas McKenney, March 22, 1830, LR-OIA Reel 169.

70. James McDonald to Peter Pitchlynn, November 2, 1830, Pitchlynn Papers, Gilcrease Museum.

71. See H. S. Halbert, "The Story of the Treaty of Dancing Rabbit Creek," *Mississippi Historical Society Publications*, v. 4 (1902), 385. This account identifies the speaker as "Killihota." Could that have been McDonald's Choctaw name?

72. For a description of the proceedings, see Carson, *Searching for the Bright Path*, 120–25. Grant Foreman also described these tribal divisions in his classic *Indian Removal* (Norman: University of Oklahoma Press, 1932), 22–30.

73. Cyrus Kingsbury to Jeremiah Evarts, October 11, 1830, American Board of Commissioners for Foreign Missions Correspondence, Microfilm A467, Lamont Library, Harvard University, Reel 758, 3–32. The 1830 treaty is at: 7 Stat 333; Section 14 outlined the provisions for the distribution of land in Mississippi. I am grateful to Dawn Peterson for bringing Kingsbury's letter to my attention.

74. Ibid.

75. *National Gazette*, August 14, 1830, reprinting a speech delivered by McDonald on July 5. Thanks to Jeff Giambrone for bringing this document to my attention. The issue of relations among states, tribes, and the federal government during this period is discussed from an original, comparative perspective in Lisa Ford, *Settler Sovereignty: Jurisdiction and Indigenous People in America and Australia, 1788–1836* (Cambridge: Harvard University Press, 2010).

76. James McDonald to John C. Calhoun, November 9, 1824, LR-OIA, Reel 169.

77. The hidden irony in McDonald's appeal to Calhoun was that his complaint arose from the theft of one of his mother's slaves. The young lawyer was arguing

for recognition in state court so that he could defend his "right" to his human property. His appeal also carried the hidden request that the state of Mississippi treat Indians the same as white people in matters of the law; this was no small demand in the era of removal.

78. Andrew Jackson, "First Annual Message to Congress," December 8, 1829, in Prucha, *Documents of United States Indian Policy*, 47–48.

79. John Ross, George Lowrey, Major Ridge, and Elijah Hicks to John C. Calhoun, February 11, 1824, in *The Papers of Chief John Ross*, ed. Gary Moulton (Norman: University of Oklahoma Press, 1984), 65.

80. Quoted in *NWR*, December 19, 1829; March 14, 1829.

81. James McDonald to Peter Pitchlynn, Pitchlynn Papers, University of Oklahoma.

82. James McDonald to Peter Pitchlynn, July 1, 1828, Pitchlynn Papers, University of Oklahoma. In this letter McDonald also confessed that he "deserved the disgusting appellation" of a "drunkard."

83. James McDonald to Peter Pitchlynn, January 17, 1829, Pitchlynn Papers, Gilcrease Museum.

84. The state's action was reported in *NWR*, February 13, 1830, 410.

85. James McDonald to Peter Pitchlynn, March 28, 1831, Peter Pitchlynn Papers, Western Heritage Collection, University of Oklahoma.

86. James McDonald to Alexander McKee, March 30, 1831, Peter Pitchlynn Papers, Western Heritage Collection, University of Oklahoma.

87. Thomas McKenney wrote in his memoirs that McDonald killed himself after a white woman rejected his marriage proposal, but no other evidence exists to confirm that claim. McDonald battled alcoholism during his career, and this may have also been a factor. See McKenney, *Memoirs*, 116, 119. McDonald's own letters reveal a man who struggled with the disease but who also enjoyed extended periods of sobriety. See James McDonald to Peter Pitchlynn, July 1, 1828, Pitchlynn Papers, Western History Collection, University of Oklahoma.

88. Henry Vose to Peter Pitchlynn, September 31 [*sic*], 1831, Peter Pitchlynn Papers, Western History Collection, University of Oklahoma.

89. Ibid.

CHAPTER THREE

1. Speech of William Potter Ross, delivered at Vinita, Indian Territory, September 11, 1874. William Potter Ross Collection, Oklahoma University, Box 1. See also Charles Bruc, *The Republic of San Marino* (Cambridge: Riverside Press, 1880), 147–149.

2. Ibid.

3. "Biography of Hon. William P. Ross," in William P. Ross, *The Life and Times of Hon. William P. Ross* (Fort Smith, Ark.: Weldon and Williams Printers, 1893), n.p.

4. For a brief survey of Ross's life, see John Bartlett Meserve, "Chief William Potter Ross," *Chronicles of Oklahoma*, v. 15, n. 1 (March 1937), 21–29.

5. "Biography of Hon. William P. Ross,"., n.p.

6. Ross was an early editor and one of the publishers of the *Indian Journal*, published in Muskogee, Creek Nation, beginning in 1876; an editor of the *Weekly Chieftain*, published in Vinita, from 1883 to 1884; and a founder of the *Indian Arrow*, also published in Vinita, beginning in 1888. See Daniel Littlefield and James Pairns, *American Indian and Alaska Native Newspapers and Periodicals* (Westport: Greenwood Press, 1983), v. I, 189–91, 39–91, 76–77.

7. Treaty with the Choctaws, 1830, 7 Stat 333.

8. A minority of each relocated tribe had traveled to Indian Territory prior to the forced removals, but these "old settler" groups generally did not play a major role in the representation of these tribes to outsiders. The tribes relocated from northern states and territories followed a similar pattern, and many interacted with tribal leaders in Indian Territory. For a comprehensive review of their history, see John P. Bowes, *Exiles and Pioneers: Eastern Indians in the Trans-Mississippi West* (New York: Cambridge University Press, 2007).

9. Tim Alan Garrison, *The Legal Ideology of Removal* (Athens: University of Georgia Press, 2002), 103–04.

10. William P. Ross to John Ross, April 3, 1838, *Papers of Chief John Ross*, ed. Gary E. Moulton (Norman: University of Oklahoma Press, 1984), v. I, 621.

11. Treaty of August 6, 1846, 9 Stat 871.

12. Article Five, Treaty of December 29, 1835, 7 Stat 478.

13. *U.S. v. Rogers*, 45 U.S. 567, 572, 573 (1846).

14. The Cherokees had been represented by several prominent Whig lawyers in their challenges to the state of Georgia before the U.S. Supreme Court prior to their removal, but they did not end the practice of seeking legal assistance once they were resettled in the West. John Ross secured the services of the Washington attorney Waddy Thompson during the negotiation of the 1846 treaty and contracted with his firm to pursue the tribe's claims against the United States for damages suffered during removal. See John Ross to Waddy Thompson, June 2, 1846, *Papers of Chief John Ross*, v. II, 309.

15. See Grant Foreman, *Advancing the Frontier, 1830–186* (Norman: University of Oklahoma Press, 1933), 131–38.

16. A. M. Gibson provides an overview of this situation in the opening pages of "An Indian Territory United Nations," *Chronicles of Oklahoma*, v. 39, n. 4 (1962), 398–413.

17. Quoted in Foreman, *Advancing the Frontier*, 213. For descriptions of the council, see ibid., 205–14, and Boes, *Exiles and Pioneers*, 141–46.

18. Reverend William H. Goode quoted in Boes, *Exiles and Pioneers*, 145.

19. *Cherokee Advocate*, May 22, 1845. Gibson annotated and reprinted the entire *Advocate* coverage of the council in "An Indian Territory United Nations," cited above.

20. Gibson, "An Indian Territory United Nations," 405–6, 412.

21. Ibid., 411. The Creek leader's reference to an Indian-run territorial government was also a clear retort to the missionary-sponsored proposals then circulating in Congress to create a U.S.-style territorial government across the region. That idea, which would have replaced tribal governments with a territorial regime regulated by Congress, had been roundly rejected by tribal leaders. See Gibson, *Advancing the Frontier*, ch. 13 ("Attempt to Form an Indian Confederacy").

22. William Potter Ross and David Vann to John Ross, November 18, 1850, *Papers of Chief John Ross*, v. II, 342. For a brief summary of Ross's service to the Cherokee Nation, see ibid., 735.

23. William McLoughlin, *After the Trail of Tears: The Cherokees Struggle for Sovereignty, 1839–1880* (Chapel Hill: University of North Carolina Press, 1993), 63.

24. Ibid., 130–31, 144.

25. William P. Ross, Thomas Pegg, Lewis Downing, and John Spears to John Ross, March 15, 1861; see McLoughlin, *After the Trail of Tears*, 172–74.

26. Ibid., 187. It is also notable that the Cherokee treaty with the Confederates was negotiated in tandem with similar agreements involving the Osages, Shawnees, and Senecas, frequent participants in prewar intertribal councils. See Annie H. Abel, *The American Indian as Slaveholder and Secessionist* (Cleveland: Arthur H. Clark Co, 1915), 237–38.

27. Commissioner Albert Pike claimed that he wrote the declaration. See Emmet Starr, *Starr's History of the Cherokee Indians* (Fayetteville: Indian Heritage Association, 1967; originally published in 1922), 158.

28. William P. Ross to John Ross, January 11, 1864, *Papers of Chief John Ross*, v. II, 552.

29. Quoted in McLoughlin, *After the Trail of Tears*, 211–12.

30. See Andrew Denson, *Demanding the Cherokee Nation: Indian Autonomy and American Culture, 1830–1900* (Lincoln: University of Nebraska Press, 2004), 82.

31. Ross, *Life and Times*, 10.

32. Ibid., 2.

33. Ross, *Life and Times*, 56, 58. Interestingly, the Confederate Cherokees also emphasized the theme of unity. When they met with federal officials, they promoted the agreements they had recently reached with western tribes. See Anna Lewis, "Camp Napoleon," *Chronicles of Oklahoma*, v. 9, no. 4 (December, 1931), 359–64; and Paul Kelton, "William Penn Adair: Cherokee Slaveholder and Indian Freedom Advocate," *Chronicles of Oklahoma*, v. 77, n. 1 (1999), 32–34.

34. David Lavere, *Contrary Neighbors: Southern Plains Indians and Removed Indians in Indian Territory* (Norman: University of Oklahoma Press, 2000), 26–27.

35. While Ross did not sign the 1866 treaty, he was apparently named to the delegation that traveled to Washington, D.C. See Morris L. Wardell, *A Political History of the Cherokee Nation, 1838–1907* (Norman: University of Oklahoma Press, 1938), 208.

36. Ross, *Life and Times*, 17.

37. Treaty with the Cherokee, July 19, 1866, 14 Stat., 799.

38. See McLoughlin, *After the Trail of Tears*, 231–32; H. Craig Miner, *The Corporation and the Indian: Tribal Sovereignty and Industrial Civilization in Indian Territory, 1865–1907* (Norman: University of Oklahoma Press, 1989), 22. The Union Pacific's initial offer (which proposed a line from Kansas to Fort Smith) is contained in R. M. McBratney and John J. Cox to John Ross et al., June, 1866, Folder 170, Box 6, Ballenger Collection, Newberry Library.

39. Quoted in James Pairns, *Elias Cornelius Boudinot: A Life on the Cherokee Border* (Lincoln: University of Nebraska Press, 2006), 88.

40. Quoted in ibid., 101. While the former Confederates Johnson and Pike originally represented Boudinot and Watie in federal district court, the Cherokee Nation secured the services of the former Union general Benjamin F. Butler for its appeal to the Supreme Court. Despite his past differences with his fellow attorneys, Butler made a parallel argument. "The United States have never claimed to exercise general jurisdiction independent of treaty provisions," he told the Court. The nation had always "legislated in subordination to those [treaty] provisions." See ibid., 101.

41. The Cherokee Tobacco, 78 U.S. 616 (1870).

42. "Letter of the Cherokee Delegation of Indians," Senate Miscellaneous Document 154, 41st Congress, 2nd Session, Serial 1408.

43. See "A Copy of the Proceedings of the Council of Indian Tribes Held at Ocmulgee, in December, 1870," *Senate Executive Document 26*, 41st Congress, 3rd Session, Serial 1440. Andrew Denson includes an excellent description of this gathering in *Demanding the Cherokee Nation*, 121–47.

44. Serial 1440, 8–12. The invitation to western tribes is reprinted on page 21.

45. Ibid., 6.

46. Denson, *Demanding*, 129.

47. Grant Foreman, "General Sherman in Okmulgee," Foreman Papers, Oklahoma Historical Society.

48. In March 1871 Congress approved a resolution declaring that no further treaties would be negotiated with Indian tribes. While the legislation acknowledged that all existing treaties would remain in force (and the Indian Office would continue to negotiate "agreements" with tribes), this action underscored how disenchanted white politicians had become with the American government's traditional method of dealing with Indian tribes. See Francis Paul Prucha, *The Great Father: The United States Government and the American Indians* (Lincoln: University of Nebraska Press, 1984), 527–33.

49. "Argument Delivered February 1, 1872," in Ross, *Life and Times*, 12.

50. Ibid., 21.

51. "Argument Delivered March 5, 1872," Ross, *Life and Times*, 35, 44.

52. Ibid., 30, 33.

53. Ibid., 37.

54. See William Potter Ross Collection, statements of November 28, 1873, February 21, 1874, March 28, 1874, and February 3, 1877. Box 1.

55. Ibid. October 17, 1874.

56. Ibid.

57. For the meeting with Grant, see "To the Honorable National Council of the Cherokee Nation" (n.d. 1876?), Cherokee Nation Papers, Federal Relations, Box 71, Oklahoma Historical Society. See also articles in *Cherokee Advocate*, February 3, 1877, McAlester, *Star Vindicator*, October 20, 1877, William Potter Ross Collection, University of Oklahoma, Box 1. On Ross's later career, see McLoughlin, *After the Trail of Tears*, 289–314, 344, 365.

58. "The Raven," *Cherokee Advocate*, March 7, 1874, Box 1, William Potter Ross Collection, University of Oklahoma.

CHAPTER FOUR

1. Sally Zanjani's biography *Sarah Winnemucca* (Lincoln: University of Nebraska Press, 2001) contains an excellent narrative of the activist's early life. See especially 3–41.

2. Ibid., 47–49.

3. Ibid., 56–67; Gae Whitney Canfield, *Sarah Winnemucca of the Northern Paiutes* (Norman: University of Oklahoma Press, 1983), 21–28.

4. Zanjani, *Sarah Winnemucca*, 72–77. Canfield, *Sarah Winnemucca*, 36–43.

5. Zanjani, *Sarah Winnemucca*, 78, 82.

6. Quoted ibid., 106.

7. Ibid., 90–99, 126–27, 128–31. Canfield, *Sarah Winnemucca*, 76–77.

8. Zanjani, *Sarah Winnemucca*, 134–38.

9. Zanjani, *Sarah Winnemucca*, 128–201; Canfield, *Sarah Winnemucca*, 109–61.

10. Sarah Winnemucca Hopkins, *Life Among the Piutes* (Boston: Cupples, Upham and Co., 1883), 5, 6.

11. "Editor's Preface," Hopkins, *Life Among the Piutes*, 2; Zanjani, *Sarah Winnemucca*, 336–39.

12. Zanjani, *Sarah Winnemucca*, 37.

13. Ibid., 34. For a full and insightful discussion of this theme in Winnemucca's writings, see Rosemarie Stremlau, "Rape Narratives on the Northern Paiute Frontier," in Dee Garceau-Hagen, ed., *Portraits of Women in the American West* (New York: Routledge, 2005), 37–60, especially 48, 52. For the story of frontier violence in California, see Robert Heizer, *The Destruction of the California Indians* (Lincoln: University of Nebraska Press, 1993).

14. Hopkins, *Life Among the Piutes*, 71–72.

15. Ibid., 139.

16. Ibid., 41, 43.

17. Ibid., 87.

18. Ibid., 209. See also Zanjani, *Sarah Winnemucca*, 193, on Wilbur.

19. Zanjani, *Sarah Winnemucca*, 45, 50, 53.

20. Hopkins, *Life Among the Piutes*, 107.

21. Ibid., 115, 116.

22. Ibid., 207.

23. Elizabeth Peabody to Edwin Munroe Bacon, n.d. 1883, *Letters of Elizabeth Palmer Peabody, American Renaissance Woman*, ed. Bruce A. Ronda (Middletown, Conn.: Wesleyan University Press, 1984), 415.

24. The petition was reprinted as part of an appendix to Hopkins, *Life Among the Piutes*, 247.

25. Luke Lea, Annual Report of the Commissioner of Indian Affairs, 1850, quoted in Francis Paul Prucha, ed., *Documents*, 81.

26. For modern biographies of these leaders, see Angie Debo, *Geronimo: The Man, His Time, His Place* (Norman: University of Oklahoma Press, 1989); Kingsley M. Bray, *Crazy Horse: A Lakota Life* (Norman: University of Oklahoma Press, 2006).

27. Francis A. Walker, *Annual Report of the Commissioner of Indian Affairs*, 1872, quoted in Prucha, *Documents*, 139–40.

28. Ibid., 140.

29. John Wesley Powell to Henry Teller, March 23, 1880, quoted in Frederick E. Hoxie, *A Final Promise: The Campaign to Assimilate the Indians, 1880–1920* (Lincoln: University of Nebraska Press, 1984), 24. For a discussion of the broad cultural appeal of the assimilation campaign for U.S. leaders in the 1870s, see ibid., 1–40.

30. See, for example, Jeanne Boydston, *Home and Work: Housework, Wages and the Ideology of Labor in the Early Republic* (New York: Oxford University Press, 1990); Gail Bederman, *Manliness and Civilization: A Cultural History of Gender and Race in the United States, 1880–1917* (Chicago: University of Chicago Press, 1997); Anne McClintock, *Imperial Leather: Race, Gender and Sexuality in the Colonial Contest* (New York: Routledge, 1995); Mary P. Ryan, *Empire of the Mother: American Writing About Domesticity, 1830–1860* (New York: Haworth Press, 1982).

31. This theme is central in Jane E. Simonsen, *Making Home Work: Domesticity and Native American Assimilation in the American West, 1860–1919* (Chapel Hill: University of North Carolina Press, 2006).

32. Quoted in Robert Winston Murdock, *The Reformers and the American Indian* (Columbia: University of Missouri Press, 1971), 16. The early linkage of woman reformers and Indian issues is explored by Alisse Portnoy, *Their Right to Speak: Women's Activism in the Indian and Slave Debates* (Cambridge: Harvard University Press, 2005).

33. For a description of this process, see Peggy Pascoe, *Relations of Rescue: The Search for Female Moral Authority in the American West, 1874–1939* (New York: Oxford University Press, 1990).

34. See Slobhan Senier, *Voices of Indian Assimilation and Resistance: Helen Hunt Jackson, Sarah Winnemucca, and Victoria Howard* (Norman: University of Oklahoma Press, 2003), 41.

35. "Letter from Sarah Winnemucca, April 4, 1870," reprinted in Helen Hunt Jackson, *A Century of Dishonor: A Sketch of the United States Government's Dealings with Some of the Indian Tribes* (Boston: Roberts Brothers, 1886; originally published in 1881), 396.

36. Hopkins, *Life Among the Piutes*, 243.

37. "Editor's Preface," ibid.

38. Quoted in Zanjani, *Sarah Winnemucca*, 248; report from Virginia City, Nevada, reprinted in *Chicago Tribune*, September 27, 1884.

39. C. C. Painter, "A Visit to the Mission Indians of Southern California and Other Western Tribes" (Indian Rights Association: Philadelphia, 1886), 18.

40. O. O. Howard, *My Life and Experiences Among Our Hostile Indians* (Hartford: A. D. Worthington, 1907), 420.

41. Zanjani, *Sarah Winnemucca*, 256–59.

42. See Senier, *Voices of American Indian Assimilation and Resistance*, 89, 93–95. See also Gretchen M. Bataille and Kathleen Mullen Sands, *American Indian Women: Telling Their Lives* (Lincoln: University of Nebraska Press, 1984), 21. The exception to this literature is an essay by the anthropologist Catherine Fowler, "Sarah Winnemucca, Northern Paiute, 1844–1891," *American Indian Intellectuals*, ed. Margot Liberty (Pittsburgh: West Publishing, 1978).

43. The *Virginia City Appeal* story was reprinted in the *New York Times*, July 29, 1873. Agent Rinehart to Commissioner of Indian Affairs, March 20, 1880, Office of Indian Affairs, Special Case #268. This "Special Case" file contains numerous affidavits charging Winnemucca with immorality. Zanjani discusses these accusations in *Sarah Winnemucca*, 206–7.

44. See Special Case #268, Wilbur to Commissioner of Indian Affairs, October 27, 1881. Wilbur repeated his charge a month later; see ibid., November 21, 1881.

45. See Special Case #268, Nevada Agency to Commissioner of Indian Affairs, January 31, 1885 (encloses December 1884 report on Winnemucca's behavior). For the Indian Office decision on relocating the Paiutes, see Report of the Secretary of the Interior, House Executive Document 1, Part 5, v. 1, 46th Congress, 3rd Session (1881), Serial 1959, 26–27. For the Interior Department's recommendation to close the Malheur agency, see Senate Executive Document 121, 47th Congress, 1st Session (1882).

46. See Zanjani, *Sarah Winnemucca*, 252, 281–83. Hopkins lived three more years. He came back to her after her return to Nevada and stole from her again, but she remained loyal and mourned him when he died.

47. Virginia City report reprinted in *Chicago Tribune*, September 27, 1844.

48. *San Francisco Alta California*, February 11, 1885. Zanjani believes that this event was Winnemucca's last public appearance. See Zanjani, *Sarah Winnemucca*, 262.

49. *San Francisco Alta California*, December 4, 1879.

50. See Zanjani, *Sarah Winnemucca*, 265–83.

51. Elizabeth Palmer Peabody, *Sarah Winnemucca's Practical Solution to the Indian Problem: A Letter to Dr. Lyman Abbott of the Christian Union* (Cambridge: John Wilson and Son, 1886), 3.

52. Painter, "A Visit to the Mission Indians of Southern California and Other Western Tribes," 18. According to Winnemucca's most recent biographer, Sarah Zanjani, the finances of the Lovelock school were "one of the murkier episodes" in her career. See *Sarah Winnemucca*, 276.

53. For Standing Bear's tour, see Hoxie, *A Final Promise*, chapter 1; for Red Cloud, see *New York Times* June 7, 1870, for Joseph, see "An Indian's View of Indian Affairs," *North American Review*, v. 128 (April 1879), 412–33.

54. The care with which the guest list at Mohonk was created is discussed in Larry Burgess, "The Lake Mohonk Conferences on the Indian, 1883–1916" (PhD dissertation, Claremont Graduate School, 1972), 19–21. The first Indians to address the group included Sherman Coolidge, an Episcopal priest. See ibid., 91.

55. While my historical narrative differs in emphasis from Kevin Bruyneel's discussion of Native American resistance to American expansion, it has benefited from his description of the late nineteenth century as an era of "American colonial imposition" and his assessment that American Indian activists of this era, whatever their differences, were "compelled . . . to counter" the expansion of U.S. authority. See Bruyneel, *The Third Space of Sovereignty: The Post-colonial Politics of U.S.-Indigenous Politics* (Minneapolis: University of Minnesota Press, 2007), 93, 94.

56. Francis La Flesche, *The Middle Five*, quoted in Frederick Hoxie, *Talking Back to Civilization: Indian Voices from the Progressive Era* (New York: Palgrave Macmillan, 2001), 43.

57. Charles Eastman, *From the Deep Woods to Civilization* (Boston: Little Brown, 1916), quoted in Hoxie, *Talking Back*, 76. A recent study of Charles Eastman's career as a writer and activist takes special note of his caution, noting that he worried about the "retribution" of government officials could deliver to educated Indians like him. See David Martinez, *Dakota Philosopher: Charles Eastman and American Indian Thought* (St. Paul: Minnesota Historical Society Press, 2009), 86.

58. It is not known how many copies of Winnemucca's book were printed in 1883. Today 153 libraries report on WorldCat that they own a copy of a first edition of *Life Among the Piutes*. Guessing that perhaps one in ten or one in twenty copies might have survived into the mid-twentieth century, when her book was considered worth saving, it seems reasonable to estimate that two thousand copies of the book might have been printed.

59. Filed with the Office of Indian Affairs archives, this letter has been reproduced at least twice, most recently in Bernd C. Peyer, *American Indian Nonfiction: An Anthology of Writings, 1760s–1930s* (Norman: University of Oklahoma Press, 2007), 276.

60. Ely Parker to Harriet Maxwell Converse, n.d. [1885], Ayer Manuscript 674, Folder 5, Newberry Library. All subsequent quotations in this sections are from that document. An edited version of the letter is reprinted in Peyer, *American Indian Nonfiction*, 268–69. While the letter is undated, Parker refers to the Indian Rights Association (founded in December 1882) and refers to the rising popularity of forced allotment, a policy adopted with the passage of the Dawes Act in February 1887. The letter was apparently written after the first date and before the second. For a more sanguine view of Parker's career, see C. Joseph Genetin-Pilawa, "Ely Parker and the Contentious Peace Policy," *Western Historical Quarterly*, v. 41, n. 2 (Summer 2010), 196–217.

CHAPTER FIVE

1. *Annual Report of the Secretary of Interior, 1880*, House Executive Document 1, Part 5, 46th Congress, 3rd Session (Serial 1959), 4. The Indian Office was (and remains) a division of the Department of Interior.
2. For two famous examples, see Angie Debo, *Geronimo: The Man, His Time, His Place* (Norman: University of Oklahoma Press, 1989); Robert M. Utley, *The Lance and the Shield: The Life and Times of Sitting Bull* (New York: Henry Holt, 1993). Sitting Bull both resisted militarily and later fled to Canada. He was killed during the government's crackdown on the Ghost Dance movement in 1890.
3. See James Mooney, *The Ghost Dance Religion and the Sioux Outbreak of 1890* (Washington, D.C.: Government Printing Office, 1893); Michael Hittman, *Wovoka and the Ghost Dance* (Lincoln: University of Nebraska Press, 1990); Susan A. Miller, *Coacoochee's Bones: A Seminole Saga* (Lawrence: University Press of Kansas, 2003). Sitting Bull offered his followers both military and spiritual resistance. See Robert M. Utley, *Lance and the Shield*.
4. See Melissa Meyer, *The White Earth Tragedy: Ethnicity and Dispossession at a Minnesota Anishinaabe Reservation, 1889–1920* (Lincoln: University of Nebraska Press, 1994).
5. Article Two, Treaty with the Chippewas of the Mississippi, 1867. 16 Stat. 719.
6. "Chippewa Indians in Minnesota," House Executive Document 247, 51st Congress, 1st Session, March 6, 1890, 22.
7. Ibid., 166. Spellings of this man's name vary.
8. Ibid., 171.
9. Article Two, Treaty with the Chippewas, 10 Stat. 1165.
10. Treaty with the Chippewa of the Mississippi and the Pillager and Lake Winnibigoshish Bands, 1863. 12 Stat. 1249. Shobaushkung was in Washington, D.C., to sign the 1867 treaty that established the White Earth Reservation but expressed no interest in moving there.
11. "Chippewa Indians in Minnesota," 174.

12. "Report of Interview Between Commissioner of Indian Affairs and Delegation of Mille Lacs Chippewas, February 23, 25, 1875. Letters Received, Bureau of Indian Affairs, National Archives Microfilm (NAM), 234, Reel 162, Frames 320–329; 59–70.

13. "Chippewa Indians of Minnesota," 168.

14. Ibid., 173.

15. Ibid., 46.

16. Ibid., 174.

17. Ibid., 10.

18. Nathan Richardson to Herbert Welsh, February 12, 1890, Letters Received, Office of Indian Affairs (LROIA), 6199-1890. For more on Richardson, see Mary Warner, *A Big Hearted Paleface Man: Nathan Richardson and the History of Morrison County, Minnesota* (Little Falls: Morrison County Historical Society, 2006), 102–5.

19. Ibid.

20. Ibid.

21. Decisions of the Department of the Interior and General Land Office in Cases Relating to the Public Lands, v. XIII (Washington, D.C.: Government Printing Office, 1892), 234. Secretary Noble's decision was later challenged by the Northern Pacific Railroad (which would have gained a right-of-way had Mille Lacs been deemed a reservation), but the matter was ultimately settled by a special resolution passed at the behest of the Minnesota congressional delegation. See 28 Stat 576. It is interesting as well that Nathan Richardson, the Mille Lacs band's local defender, was a former business partner of Henry Rice's. Richardson fell silent on the Mille Lacs land dispute after he registered his initial protests. See Warner, *A Big Hearted Paleface Man*, 29.

22. Henry Rice to Commissioner of Indian Affairs, February 19, 1891, LROIA 7049-1891.

23. Darwin Hall to Commissioner of Indian Affairs, October 24, 1891, LROIA 38714-1891.

24. Waweacomsek et al. to The Great Father, October 10, 1894, LROIA 48382-1894. The letter was reprinted in the *Princeton* (Minn.) *Union*, December 6, 1894. Richardson wrote separately to the president endorsing the petition but not claiming to have written it. Nathan Richardson to Grover Cleveland, December 21, 1894, LROIA 50831-1894.

25. Gus Beaulieu to Secretary of Interior, March 5, 1895, LROIA 10795-1895.

26. Mille Lacs Chiefs to Grover Cleveland, June 9, 1895, LROIA 28660-1895.

27. James M. McClurken, "The 1837 Treaty of St. Peters Preserving the Rights of the Mille Lacs Ojibwa to Hunt, Fish and Gather: The Effect of Treaties and Agreements Since 1855," in *Fish in the Lakes, Wild Rice and Game in Abundance: Testimony on Behalf of Mille Lacs Ojibwe Hunting and Fishing Rights*, ed. James M. McClurken (East Lansing: Michigan State University Press, 2000), 416.

28. *Princeton Union*, July 1, 1897.

29. Commissioner of Indian Affairs to Secretary Interior, March 17, 1898. Records Group 233, House of Representatives, 57th Congress, HR55A-F15.4, National Archives.

30. Joint Resolution 40, 55th Congress, 2nd Session. 30 U.S. Stat. 745.

31. Gus Beaulieu to Secretary of Interior, March 3, 1898, LROIA, 11122-1898. Bliss's statement is in Senate Report 1007, 55th Congress, 2nd Session, 4.

32. Senate Document 446, "Mille Lacs Band of Chippewa Indians," 5th Congress, 1st Session, June 7, 1900, Serial 3878, 2, 3. On Beaulieu's lobbying of Nelson, see *Princeton Union*, March 8, 15, 1900.

33. James McLaughlin to Commissioner of Indian Affairs, September 10, 1902, CF-White Earth 46578-09, 175.2, Part 2, Records Group 75, National Archives.

34. "Contest, Homestead Entry, Indian Occupation, *Ma-Gee-See v. Johnson*," July 5, 1900, LROIA 40374-1901.

35. Chief Negwenaby to Commissioner of Indian Affairs, May 27, 1901, LROIA 28575-1901; GoGee to Commissioner of Indian Affairs, June 6, 1901, LROIA 30901-1901; D. H. Robbins to Commissioner of Indian Affairs, June 7, 1901, LROIA 31221-1901; Samuel Brosius, "The Urgent Case of the Mille Lacs Indians" (Philadelphia: Indian Rights Association, October 1901), 1.

36. Samuel Brosius to Commissioner of Indian Affairs, November 8, 1901, LROIA 63359-1901.

37. House Report 1784, 57th Congress, 1st Session, "Mille Lacs Chippewa Indians of Minnesota."

38. "Proceedings of Mille Lacs Council, August 30, 1902," 3, enclosed with Commissioner of Indian Affairs to Secretary of Interior, n.d., LROIA, CCF White Earth, 46578-1909, 175.2, Part 1. McLaughlin's comments are surprising, coming from a veteran Indian Office official who spent his career moving "around the country" working "for other people."

39. Ibid., 29, 31.

40. Ibid. Aindusogeeshig added later, "I have visited Washington five different times. . . . I don't think we have done anything else but work for the Indians, to secure for them the right to have land allotted to them here." Ibid., 59.

41. Ibid., 44, 46, 49, 51.

42. Ibid., 65, 66. See also "Agreement Between the U.S. and Mille Lacs Indians," August 30, 1902; and "Council Proceedings of Mille Lacs Indians, August 30, 1902," both enclosed with LROIA, CCF White Earth, 46578-1909, Part 1.

43. Simon Michelet to Commissioner of Indian Affairs, June 1, 1904, LROIA 37014-1904; and C. F. Hauke to Daniel B. Henderson, April 4, 1913, LROIA, CCF White Earth, Land Records-Mille Lacs Removals.

44. See W. Roger Buffalohead, *Against the Tide of American History: The Story of the Mille Lacs Anishinabe* (Cass Lake: Minnesota Chippewa Tribe, 1985), 68. A report to the agent at White Earth in 1909 reported "about nine Indian villages" on the reservation, "in all about three hundred Indians." See D. F. Porter to John R. Howard, December 4, 1908, LROIA, CCF-White Earth 74787-08.

45. Nineteenth-century treaties frequently settled grievances against the tribes by directing part of the promised funds to settle the tribes (largely unaudited) debts to local traders and business partners.

46. See H. D. Rosenthal, *Their Day in Court: A History of the Indian Claims Commission* (New York: Garland, 1990), 100–12. Congress wanted to bar Confederate-sympathizing tribes from bringing their complaints to court. Rosenthal also argues that Congress feared that the courts would be swamped with complaints from tribes. Ironically, as Congress closed the court to Indians, it was opened to whites who claimed they had suffered from "depredations" inflicted by Native violence. By 1890 nearly eight thousand "depredation claims" had been filed with the Indian Office in preparation for court hearings. See Prucha, *The Great Father*, 720.

47. Article Twelve, Treaty with the Choctaw and Chickasaw, 1855, 11 Stat. 611. For an overview of the Choctaw claim, see Clara Sue Kidwell, *The Choctaws in Oklahoma: From Tribe to Nation, 1855–1970* (Norman: University of Oklahoma Press, 2007), 121–36.

48. Kidwell traces these "Byzantine" disputes in ibid.

49. See Rosenthal, *Their Day in Court*, 24. For a listing of tribal claims adjudicated before the court, see appendix I.

50. Perhaps the most famous example from the first twenty years of the twentieth century involved the Sioux and the Black Hills. Significantly, the movement to bring this claim began in the 1890s, just after the Choctaws had won their case. The historian Jeffery Ostler notes that more than one hundred meetings that were focused on winning compensation for the loss of the tribe's sacred land took place on the various Sioux reservations during that decade. See Ostler, *The Lakotas and the Black Hills* (New York: Viking, 2010), 128–29.

51. Quoted in *Otoe and Missouria Tribes of Indians v. U.S.* 52 Ct. Cls. 424, 428.

52. See Rosenthal, *Their Day in Court*, appendix I. The jurisdictional acts authorizing each suit are quoted in each decision.

53. After World War I Henderson also represented tribes in the Pacific Northwest. See *Coos (or Kowes) Bay, Lower Umpqua (Kalawatset) & Sinslaw Indian Tribes v. United States*, 306 U.S. 653; *United States v. Klamath & Moadoc Tribes*, 304 U.S. 119.

54. 35 U.S. Statutes 619. The Mille Lacs complaint is in Docket 30447, Record Group 205, National Archives, Washington, D.C. (hereafter Docket 30447).

55. On Wahweyaycumig's removal, see J. Adam Bede to Commissioner of Indian Affairs, May 23, 1904, LROIA 34762-1904 (Bede reports only "one chief and a family of seven" had moved to White Earth). On complaint against Beaulieu, see Steward and Brewer (attorneys representing Meegeesee and others at Mille Lacs) to Commissioner of Indian Affairs, March 8, 1905, LROIA 19255-1905.

56. Chauncey E. Richardson, "In the matter of the services of attorneys . . ." October 17, 1916, U.S. Court of Claims, Docket 30447, Box 5144, Records Group 123,

National Archives, Washington, D.C. Beaulieu confirmed this activity in a separate deposition, "Affidavit of Gus H. Beaulieu," November, 1916, Claims Docket 30447, Box 2151, RG 123. NA.

57. See "Son of State's First Senator Dies," *St. Paul Dispatch*, December 22, 1944, 3. The third principal in the firm, Frederick D. Price, was the son of the former senator Henry Rice. I am grateful to the historian Bruce White for closing the circle on this small mystery by locating Frederick Rice's obituary for me.

58. Chauncey Richardson, "In the matter of the services of attorneys . . ." 4, quoting a letter dated November 25, 1908. For "my lawyer" comment, see Beaulieu to J. R. Howard, July 9, 1909, LROIA, CCF-White Earth 58921-09, 150.

59. See "Minutes of a Council of the Mille Lacs Band of Chippewa Indians, Held at Elbow Lake on the White Earth Reservation," December 15, 1908; "Minutes of a Council of the Non-removal Mille Lacs Band of Chippewa Indians, Held at Onamia . . ." January 23, 1909; "Memorandum of Agreement . . . 8th day of February, 1909 . . ." All included with Docket 30447, Box 123, Record Group 123, NA.

60. James Garfield to the President, February 15, 1909, LROIA, CCF-White Earth 11208-1909, 308.1.

61. See affidavit, "Mr. Houghton's Work," November 2, 1916, in Docket 30447, Box 2152, RG 123. Clapp had been involved in White Earth land disputes at least since 1907 and had often worked alongside Gus Beaulieu. For Clapp at White Earth, see Harvey S. Clapp to Commissioner of Indian Affairs, April 9, 1907, LROIA, CCF- White Earth 81251-07, 150.

62. Deposition of Naygwonaybe, August 4, 1909, Docket 30447, RG123.

63. See Chauncey Richardson to Commissioner of Indian Affairs, August 25, 1909; LROIA, CCF-White Earth 69493-09, 123; and Chief Clerk to C. E. Richardson, September 1909, LROIA, CCF White Earth 69493-09, 123.

64. J. Adam Bede to Commissioner of Indian Affairs, February 28, 1908; Acting Commissioner of Indian Affairs to Bede, March 3, 1908. Both letters filed as LROIA, CCF-White Earth 14465-08, 123.

65. Darwin Hall to J. R. Howard, September 13, 1910, LROIA, CCF White Earth 68171-10, 175.2. Hall also reported in November that the band had held "their 'Grand Medicine' ceremonies" at Mille Lacs; adding "it occupies their entire attention and thought. . . ." Hall to Commissioner of Indian Affairs, November 1, 1910, LROIA, CCF-White Earth 88006-10, 032.

66. State of Minnesota, County of Mille Lacs, Seventh Judicial District, "Mille Lacs Investment and Improvement Company, a Corporation vs. Chief Wadena, John Pewash, John Schwab, et al.," Civil Case 2248, Minnesota Historical Society. The case file includes the complaint, the defendants' response, a report on the court's decision, and the order to the sheriff.

67. *Princeton Union*, May 11, 1911.

68. This added detail was not included in the local press but is a part of the description in the tribe's history. Buffalohead, *Against the Tide of History*, 73.

69. *Princeton Union*, May 11, 1911.
70. *Mille Lacs Band of Chippewa Indians v. United States*, 46 Ct. Cls. 464. A loyal Republican and close friend of Speaker of the House Joseph Cannon's, Booth also presided over the claims case brought by the deposed Hawaiian monarch Liliuokalani in 1910. He later was named chief judge of the court. See Neil Thomas Proto, *The Rights of My People: Liliuokalani's Enduring Battle with the United States, 1893–1917* (New York: Algora, 2009), 4, 165–66.
71. Ibid., 461, 475, 478.
72. The tortured history of the Mille Lacs case following the band's initial victory is described in the affidavit filed by Frederick Houghton, titled "Mr. Houghton's Work," dated November 2, 1916, with Docket 30447, Box 2152, RG 123, National Archives.
73. Buffalohead, *Against the Tide of History*, 76; see also 72–75. For a summary of events following the band's victory in the Court of Claims, see James McClurken, "The Effects of Treaties and Agreements Since 1855," in *Fish in the Lakes, Wild Rice and Game in Abundance*, 439–41.
74. See Prucha, *The Great Father*, 1018.
75. In 1946 Congress established the Indian Claims Commission, which operated until 1978. The commission received 370 petitions from 176 tribes and ultimately awarded $657 million to plaintiffs. When the commission ceased operation in 1978, its caseload was transferred to the U.S. Court of Claims. See Prucha, *The Great Father*, 1021; and Paul Rosier, *Serving Their Country: American Indian Politics and Patriotism in the Twentieth Century* (Cambridge: Harvard University Press, 2009), 312.

CHAPTER SIX

1. *Quarterly Journal of the Society of American Indians*, v. 1, n. 1 (1913), 3, 7.
2. The commissioner of Indian affairs who was in office when Thomas Sloan graduated from a government boarding school voiced the rationale for this educational program. "The logic of events demands the absorption of the Indians into our national life," Thomas Jefferson Morgan wrote in 1889. "Each Indian must be treated like a man, be allowed a man's rights and privileges, and be held to the performance of a man's obligations." For more on this philosophy of inclusion, see Frederick Hoxie, *A Final Promise: The Campaign to Assimilate the Indians, 1880–1920* (Lincoln: University of Nebraska Press, 1984), 1–39. Morgan was quoted in Francis Paul Prucha, ed., *Documents of United States Indian Policy*, 3rd ed. (Lincoln: University of Nebraska Press, 2000), 179.
3. Montezuma had worked as the school's physician from July 1893 to January 1896, and Eastman had served as a recruiter and outing agent (an official who placed students with white families during school vacations) from November 1899 to September 1900. During Eastman's time at Carlisle, his wife, Elaine Goodale

Eastman, edited the school's newspaper, the *Red Man*. See Raymond Wilson, *Ohiyesa: Charles Eastman, Santee Sioux* (Urbana: University of Illinois Press), 1983, 105–06; and Peter Iverson, *Carlos Montezuma and the Changing World of American Indians* (Albuquerque: University of New Mexico Press, 1982), 25. For more on Eastman and Pratt, see David J. Carlson, *Sovereign Selves: American Indian Autobiography and the Law* (Urbana: University of Illinois Press, 2006), 147, 150–51.

4. Thomas Sloan, Henry Standing Bear, Charles Eastman, Laura Cornelius, Carlos Montezuma, and Charles Dagenett to Richard Pratt, April 4, 1911, *Society of American Indian Papers* (hereafter *SAI Papers*).

5. Richard Pratt to Carlos Montezuma, April 14, 1911, Papers of Carlos Montezuma, Scholarly Resources Edition (hereafter PCMSR).

6. Richard Pratt to Thomas Sloan, Henry Standing Bear, Charles Eastman, Laura Cornelius, Carlos Montezuma, Charles Dagenett, April 13, 1911, PCMSR.

7. *Quarterly Journal of the Society of American Indians*, v. 1, n. 1 (1913), 6. Emphasis in original.

8. The idea that Indians could be citizens and still serve their communities was a basic assumption among the new organization's founders. For an overview of this point of view based largely on literary sources, see Joel Pfister, *Individuality Incorporated: Indians and the Multicultural Modern* (Durham: Duke University Press, 2004) and Lucy Maddox, *Citizen Indians: Native American Intellectuals, Race and Reform* (Ithaca: Cornell University Press, 2006).

9. Thomas Sloan to Arthur Parker, October 31, 1911, *SAI Papers*.

10. For a summary of the era's debates over national citizenship, see Heather Cox Richardson, "North and West of Reconstruction: Studies in Political Economy," in *Reconstructions: New Perspectives on the Postbellum United States*, ed. Thomas J. Brown (New York: Oxford University Press, 2006), 66–90. The impact of the Civil War on conceptions of the American nation-state are outlined in Morton Keller, *Affairs of State* (Cambridge: Harvard University Press, 1977) and Robert Wiebe, *The Search for Order, 1877–1920* (New York: Farrar, Straus, 1966).

11. While this narrative avoids political labels that often flatten the differences among actors, it has benefited from the analysis of the citizenship issue by the political scientist Kevin Bruyneel, *The Third Space of Sovereignty: The Post-colonial Politics of U.S.-Indigenous Relations* (Minneapolis: University of Minnesota Press, 2007), 97, 102–7, 120. While Bruyneel does not mention Thomas Sloan, the Omaha lawyer seems to fit his view that "indigenous people who engaged the debate over U.S. citizenship sought . . . to redefine the boundary location of indigenous political identity. . . ." (97).

12. Indian activists were optimistic about citizenship despite the Supreme Court's decision in *Elk v. Wilkins* that declared they were not eligible for protection under the Fourteenth Amendment. See 112 U.S. 94.

13. See *Sloan v. U.S.*, 95 F 193, July 1, 1899, 194.

14. Sloan's birth in St. Louis is mentioned in an undated newspaper clipping, probably from 1921, included with a collection of his writings in PCMSR, Reel 5. Sloan first lived on the Nemaha Reservation in southeastern Nebraska, a federal reservation available to homesteaders from the Omaha, Iowa, and Otoe tribes. Nemaha was established under terms of a treaty negotiated by William Clark with a group of Missouri tribes. See 7 Stat. 328. Sloan's ancestry is described in the circuit court decision in *Sloan v. United States* (1899). See 95 F. 193. Margaret (born 1820) and Thomas (born 1863) Sloan are listed in the 1891 Omaha Tribal Census. See M595, Indian Census Rolls, 1885–1940, Reel 32. Sloan and his grandmother moved to the Omaha reserve north of the city of Omaha in 1880, when the future lawyer was seventeen. An exhaustive congressional hearing on the claims of Michael Barada's descendants to membership in the Omaha tribe in 1930 includes an affidavit from Sloan (then living in San Diego) and an elaborate family tree that indicated that Sloan (who had long been accepted as a tribal member) had no children. See "Enrollment of Certain Persons with the Omaha Tribe of Indians," Hearings Before the Committee on Indian Affairs, House of Representatives on H.R. 10457, 7st Congress, 3rd Session (Washington, D.C.: Government Printing Office, 1931). Sloan's affidavit is at 54–55.

15. Sloan's early career as a herder is described in Joan T. Mark, *A Stranger in Her Native Land* (Lincoln: University of Nebraska Press, 1988), 315, 317. The "troublemaker" reference is in Sloan's testimony on S.2755 before the Senate Committee on Indian Affairs, February 27, 1934, 132; his recounting of his imprisonment is in a hearing on "Indian Conditions and Affairs on H.R. 7781," February 11, 1935, 528. These years are also described in a profile published in the Society of American Indians magazine in 1920: Leicester Knickerbacker Davis, "Thomas L. Sloan— American Indian," *American Indian Magazine*, v. 7, n. 4 (August 1920), 39–40.

16. Sloan later claimed that he was sent to Hampton "in order to get me away from the reservation" and that he decided to become a lawyer while he was incarcerated. See testimony of February 27, 1934, 132; and testimony of February 11, 1935, 528. He repeated this story in a commencement address at Carlisle, delivered in April 1912, and reprinted in the school magazine. See "The Indian's Protection and His Place as an American," *Red Man*, v. 4 (May 1912), 398–403.

17. Annual Report of the U.S. Secretary of Interior, 1887, Serial 2542, 1035. For more on Sloan at Hampton, see Donal F. Lindsey, *Indians at Hampton Institute, 1877– 1923* (Urbana: University of Illinois Press, 1995), 128, 230.

18. *Standing Bear v. Crook*, in Prucha, *Documents*, 150.

19. Quoted in Hoxie, *A Final Promise*, 8. Standing Bear's companions on his lecture tour were Susette and Francis La Flesche. The siblings became prominent Indian spokespeople in the 1880s and 1890s.

20. For a fuller description of the Standing Bear tour and the events leading up to the passage of the Omaha allotment act, see ibid., 25–39.

21. *Elk v. Wilkins* (November 3, 1884), in Prucha, *Documents*, 165–66.

22. Quoted in Hoxie, *A Final Promise*, 76.

23. Quoted in Judith A. Boughter, *Betraying the Omaha Nation, 1790–1916* (Norman: University of Oklahoma Press, 1998), 113.

24. Arthur Tinker to Secretary of the Interior, December 22, 1890, Reports of Inspection of the Field Jurisdictions of the Office of Indian Affairs, Omaha and Winnebago Agency (RIFJ, Omaha), National Archives Microfilm 1070, Reel 32.

25. For a report on Sloan and his recent admission to the bar, see Senate Executive Document 31, 52 Congress, 1 Session, Serial 2892, "Report on Returned Hampton Students," 27.

26. "Supplemental Hearing . . . on H.R. 25663, January 27, 1913, 25.

27. *Sloan v. U.S.*, 95 F 193, July 1, 1899, 194, 196, 197.

28. *Sloan v.U.S.*, 118 F 183, October 31, 1902, 285,286, 288, 293, 294.

29. *Sloan v. U.S.* 193 U.S. 614, April 4, 1904.

30. Inspector McCormick to Secretary of Interior, June 20, 1894, RIFJ, Omaha, Reel 32.

31. James McLaughlin to Secretary of Interior, June 19, 1895, RIFJ, Omaha, Reel 32. The reference to Senator Thurston is in Arthur Tinker to Secretary of Interior, March 10, 1899, RIFJ, Omaha, Reel 32.

32. The Flournoy controversy is described in Boughter, *Betraying the Omaha Nation*, 146–53. While Boughter provides a useful summary of the case, she was critical of Sloan. Unfortunately, in reaching her judgment, she seems to have ignored both Inspector McLaughlin's laudatory reports on Beck and Sloan and the Omaha lawyer's later career as an Indian advocate.

33. *U.S. v. Flournoy Livestock and Real Estate Co.*, 69 F 886, October 8, 1895, 891–92. The Supreme Court's dismissal of Flournoy's appeal can be found at *Flournoy Livestock and Real Estate Company v. Beck*, 163 U.S. 686, October 23, 1895. The final appeals court disposition of the case is: *U.S. v. Flournoy Livestock and Real Estate Co.*, 71 F 576, January 7, 1896.

34. Arthur Tinker to Secretary of Interior, March 10, 1899, RIFJ, Omaha, Reel 32.

35. Samuel Brosius to Matthew Sniffen, February 14, 1909, Indian Rights Association Papers (hereafter IRA Papers), Reel 21.

36. See *U.S. v. Rickert* quoted in Hoxie, *A Final Promise*, 218.

37. The *Heff* decision and its consequences are discussed in Hoxie, *A Final Promise*, 219–21. Justice Harlan dissented in the case, but he did not file a dissenting opinion.

38. *U.S. v. Thurston County* et al., 140 F 456, September 14, 1905, 458, 459.

39. For a discussion of Lone Wolf and its aftermath, see Hoxie, *A Final Promise*, 154–59. An extended discussion of the legal history of increased federal authority over Indians, noncitizens, and racial minorities during the turn of the twentieth century can be found in Sarah H. Cleveland, "Powers Inherent in Sovereignty: Indians, Aliens, Territories, and the Nineteenth Century Origins of Plenary Power over Foreign Affairs," *Texas Law Review*, v. 81, n.1 (November 2002),

1–284. Cleveland, an expert in international law, argues that racial ideology and perceived threats from outside its borders caused U.S. jurists to uphold expanded power for federal agencies engaged with foreign, Indian, and territorial affairs at the same time that it struck down the extension of such powers in the domestic arena.

40. *U.S. v. Thurston Co.* et al., 143 F 287, March 21, 1906, 289.

41. *Rainbow et al. v. Young*, Sheriff, 161 F 835, June 8, 1908, 837. The court also addressed the question of whether or not the agent's actions could be subject to judicial review: "[W]e think it is intended there shall be none." Ibid., 838.

42. *Hallowell v. United States*, 209 U.S. 101, decided March 23, 1908; see syllabus for quotation.

43. *U.S. v. Celestine*, 215 U.S. 278, December 13, 1909, 290–91; emphasis mine. See also *U.S. v. Sutton* 215 U.S. 291. Interestingly no lawyers appeared on behalf of the Indian defendants in either case. The government's attorneys evidently made their arguments without opposition. It would seem that the Indian Office was seeking to establish a legally sanctioned policy with these decisions.

44. *Marchie Tiger v. Western Investment Co.*, 221 U.S. 286, May 15, 1911. See Lawyer's Edition Headnotes.

45. Ibid., 316.

46. *Hallowell v. United States*, 221 U.S. 317, May 15, 1911, 324.

47. Thomas Sloan to Richard Henry Pratt, August 24, 1909, Richard Henry Pratt Papers, Box 8, Folder 283, Yale University (hereafter Pratt Papers). See also *Washington Herald*, March 7, 1909, 7. See also Samuel Brosius to Thomas Sloan, February 14, 1909, IRA Papers, Reel 21.

48. Quoted in. D. Anthony Tyeeme Clarle, "At the Headwaters of a Twentieth-century Indian Political Agenda: Rethinking the Origins of the Society of American Indians," in Daniel M. Cobb and Loretta Fowler, eds., *Beyond Red Power: New Perspectives on American Indian Politics and Activism* (Santa Fe: School of Advanced Research 2007), 79.

49. "The Indian of Tomorrow," n.d., National Woman's Christian Temperance Union, Reel 5, PCMSR.

50. Quoted in Hoxie, *A Final Promise*, 163.

51. In February 1918 Thomas Sloan testified against a bill that would have banned peyote. Supporting him were the Smithsonian anthropologist James Mooney and the SAI member (and fellow Omaha) Francis La Flesche. Among those in favor of the ban were Charles Eastman and Richard Pratt. See "Peyote Hearings Before a Subcommittee of the Committee on Indian Affairs on H.R. 2614" (Washington, D.C.: Government Printing Office, 1918).

52. The discussion of Coolidge is in Sloan to Arthur Parker, November 11, 1911, *SAI Papers*. For more a sympathetic view of Parker's career and role in the SAI, see Joy Porter, *To Be Indian: The Life of Iroquois-Seneca Arthur Caswell Parker* (Norman: University of Oklahoma Press, 2001), 91–142.

53. Sloan to Parker, February 19, 1912, and ibid., March 16, 1912, *SAI Papers*.

54. Parker to Sloan, November 20, 1911, *SAI Papers*.

55. Parker to Sloan, January 22, 1912, *SAI Papers*.

56. Dennison Wheelock to Richard Henry Pratt, December 20, 1912, Folder 323, Pratt Papers.

57. "The Indian's Protection and His Place as an American," 399; Sloan to Fayette McKenzie, March 31, 1916; Sloan to Parker, May 6, 1916, *SAI Papers*.

58. Sloan to Parker, April 17, 1916, *SAI Papers*.

59. See, for example, "Indian Appropriation Bill . . . Hearing Before the Committee on Indian Affairs of the United States Senate . . . on H.R. 26874," 62nd Congress, 3rd Session, 55–57, January 17, 1913. Senator Robert La Follette's papers also contain a file of correspondence with Crow tribal leaders seeking to stop the allotment of their reservation. The file contains a 1911 letter in which Sloan offered to represent the tribe in Washington, D.C. See Thomas Sloan to Commissioner of Indian Affairs, n.d. but stamped "August 23, 1911," Robert La Follette Papers, Library of Congress, Box 122, Indian Affairs, Crow. In aletter to Sloan dated August 24, the acting secretary of interior denied Sloan's request.

60. See *U.S. v. Chase*, 245 U.S. 89, November 5, 1917.

61. For Sloan's report on his investigation of the Yankton agency, see "Hearings Before the Joint Commission . . ." January 21 and March 9, 1914, 63rd Congress, 2nd Session, Part 5, 508–24. The creation of the Joint Commission is described in Hoxie, *A Final Promise*, 178–79.

62. "Hearings Before the Committee on Indian Affairs, United States Senate . . . on H.R. 21050," 63rd Congress, 3rd Session, v. 2, 33.

63. Ibid., 64–66. See also Paul C. Rosier, *Rebirth of the Blackfeet Nation, 1912–1954* (Lincoln: University of Nebraska Press, 2001), 15–18. Sloan's work at Blackfeet earned the praise of the Indian Rights Association. See Samuel Brosius to Sloan, March 11, 1915, IRA Papers.

64. "Granting Indians Rights to Select Agents and Superintendents. Hearing . . . on S.3904," 64th Congress, 1st Session, March 9, 1916, 39–41.

65. "Leasing of Crow Indian Lands. Hearing Before a Subcommittee of the Committee on Indian Affairs . . . on S.2890," 66th Congress, 1st Session, 16.

66. "Army Reorganization. Hearing Before the Committee on Military Affairs on H.R. 8287," 66th Congress, 1st & 2nd Congress, v. 2, 2224–26.

67. "Hearings on H.R. 21150," 57.

68. "Army Reorganization Hearing," 2228.

69. *Wassaja*, v. 2, n . 9 (December 1917), 1, 2. Eastman's name was added to the list of sponsors in January 1918, in v. 2, n.10. A collection of *Wassaja* is included in PCMSR.

70. *American Indian Magazine*, v. 6, n. 3 (Autumn 1918), 139. Montezuma's address was reprinted the following year in v. 7, n. 1 (Spring 1919), 11. The society's magazine changed its name from *Quarterly Journal* in 1916.

71. *Wassaja*, v. 3, n. 8 (November, 1918), 2.

72. Ibid., 3.

73. "Editorial Comment," *American Indian Magazine*, v. 6, n. 4 (Winter 1919), 161–62.

74. Charles Eastman, "The Indian's Plea for Freedom," *American Indian Magazine*, v. 6, n. 4 (Winter 1919), 163.

75. *Wassaja*, v. 4, n. 11 (February 1920), 2; excerpts from Sloan's speech were published in *American Indian Magazine*, v. 7, n. 3 (Fall 1919), 162; the election is described in ibid., 179.

76. "Thomas L. Sloan," reprinted in *American Indian Magazine*, v. 7, n. 3 (Fall 1919), 143.

77. Richard Pratt to Sloan, February 23, 1920, Series II, *SAI Papers*. Privately, Pratt expressed reservations about Sloan's association with anthropologists and his tolerance for the use of peyote in religious ceremonies.

78. Thomas Sloan to Hubert Work, March 10, 1923, Series II, SAI Papers.

79. The description of Sloan's physique is in "Thomas L. Sloan," 40. The charges of "slandering" are in Thomas Sloan to Richard Pratt, June 5, 1920; the meeting with Harding is described in Sloan to Pratt, June 29, 1920. Both letters in Box 8, Folder 283, Pratt Papers, Yale University.

80. The anti-Sloan correspondence was attached to a general circular from SAI member P. H. Kennerly to L. V. McWhorter, May 11, 1921, *SAI Papers*. Carter's letter, included in this packet, was dated September 20, 1920. For Parker, see Parker, *To Be Indian*, 136. For Roe Cloud's position, see Joel Phister, *The Yale Indian: The Education of Henry Roe Cloud* (Durham: Duke University Press, 2009), 205, n. 188.

81. Hazel Hertzberg, *The Search for an American Indian Identity: Modern Pan Indian Movements* (Syracuse: Syracuse University Press, 1971), 193, 194, 197.

82. Pratt preferred Wheelock. See Richard Pratt to Rose La Flesche, March 25, 1921, Folder 409, Pratt Papers, Yale University.

83. Foreword to G. E. E. Lindquist, *The Red Man in the United States* (New York: George H. Doran, 1923), vi. The commissioner conceded that many tribal traditions were "beautiful . . . but many are benighted and sometimes degrading. . . ." Burke was to act on his principles in 1921, when he issued his famous "dance order," banning dances that involved "acts of self-torture, immoral relations between the sexes, the sacrificial destruction of clothing or other useful articles, the reckless giving away of property, the use of injurious drugs or intoxicants, and frequent or prolonged periods of celebration. . . ." See Francis Paul Prucha, *The Great Father: The United States Government and the Indian* (Lincoln: University of Nebraska Press, 1984), 801.

84. An apparently complete list of invitees was published in the *New York Times*, May 12, 1923.

85. See Prucha, *The Great Father*, 807–8.

86. The committee's resolutions were published in January 1924. See "The Indian Problem," House Document 149, 68 Congress, 1 Session, 1–4.

87. Sloan to Secretary of Interior, December 14, 1923, *SAI Papers*; Sloan to Richard Pratt, March 4, 1924, Box 8, Folder 283, Pratt Papers, Yale University.

88. Oswald Garrison Villard, "For the Indians' Sake," *Nation* (December 26, 1923), 734.

89. John Collier, "The Red Slaves of Oklahoma" *Sunset* (March 1924), 96.

90. Sloan to Richard Pratt, March 4, 1924.

91. For the persistence of non-Indian interest in romantic views of Indians and the dilemma this produced for Indian activists, see Michelle Wick Patterson, "'Real' Indian Songs: The Society of American Indians and the Use of Native American Culture as a Means of Reform," *American Indian Quarterly*, v. 26, n. 1 (Winter 2002), 44–66.

92. Elizabeth Shepley Sergeant, "The Red Man's Burden," *New Republic* (January 16, 1924), 199.

93. "Appraisal of Tribal Property of Indians," Hearings Before the Senate Committee on Indian Affairs on H.R. 13835, February 16, 1923, 25.

94. Ibid., 15.

95. Ibid.

96. For a comprehensive description of the passage of the Indian Citizenship Act, see Gary C. Stein, "The Indian Citizenship Act of 1924," *New Mexico Historical Review*, v. 47, n. 3 (1972), 257–74. See also Bruyneel, *The Third Space of Sovereignty*, 97–121.

97. In the 1920s and 1930s Sloan lobbied on behalf of the Blackfeet, the Montana Salish, the Omaha and Winnebago tribes from his native Nebraska, the Washington Yakimas, and Mission Indian communities in Southern California. He also maintained regular contact with delegations representing Oregon Klamaths, Creeks from Oklahoma, and the Minnesota Ojibwes. He traced many of his ties to these groups to contacts among Hampton alumni as well as to his years of activism with the Society of American Indians. By 1928 Sloan had moved to Southern California, where he represented Indian allottees he had first met in Washington and developed new contacts with western tribes. Over the next decade he filed suits on behalf of Indians at Palm Springs and was involved with reformers and tribal activists in California, Washington, and Oregon. See *St. Marie et al. v. United States*, 24 F. Supp, 237, July 23, 1938; 108 F. 2nd 876, January 3, 1940 (appeals court) and 311 U.S. 652, October 14, 1940. For Sloan's activities in California, see *Los Angeles Times*, September 29, 1929 ("Thomas Sloan, Attorney, Guest of Wigwam Club of America"), ibid., July 7, 1937 ("Palm Springs Indians Win Champion in Land Sale Row"), and ibid., June 20, 1938 (letter from Thomas Sloan "representing Indians of California"). Sloan described his first contact with California Indians (which occurred in 1922) in a 1937 congressional hearing. See "Hearings Before the Committee on

Indian Affairs on S. 1651," U.S. Senate, 75th Congress, 1st Session, March, 1936, 129.

98. "Indian Conditions and Affairs," Hearings . . . on H.R. 7781, February 11, 1935, 531.

99. Thomas Sloan to Matthew Sniffen, March 27, 1940, IRA Mss.

100. For a description of the politics surrounding the passage of the American Indian Civil Rights Act, see Prucha, *The Great Father*, 1106–8.

CHAPTER SEVEN

1. For a description of Collier's early supporters, see Lawrence Kelly, *The Assault on Assimilation: John Collier and the Origins of Indian Policy Reform* (Albuquerque: University of New Mexico Press, 1983), chapter 8.

2. Robert Yellowtail to John Collier, June 6, 1932, Papers of John Collier, Reel Four, File 177. For a listing of Collier's correspondents, see *The John Collier Papers, 1922–1968: A Guide to the Microfilm Edition*, ed. Andrew M. Patterson and Maureen Brodoff (Sanford, N.C.: Microfilming Corporation of America, 1980), 7–12. In their introduction to Collier's correspondence from the years 1922 to 1933, the editors write, "This series pertains almost exclusively to Indian matters. . . . Correspondents include prominent lawyers (Louis Hanna, Richard Hanna), United States Senators (Lynn Frazier), Congressmen (James A. Frear), authors (Mabel Dodge Luhan, Elizabeth Shepley Sergeant) and others who devoted their energies to Indian causes." The editors do not mention Indian correspondents. Collier does not appear to have corresponded during this period with Charles Eastman, Thomas Sloan, Fred Lookout, or even Chee Dodge, the Navajo leader who later became an important ally.

3. John Collier, *From Every Zenith* (Thousand Oaks, Ca.: Sage Books, 1963), 4.

4. Ibid., 126, 119, 123.

5. For a biographical profile of Yellowtail, see Frederick E. Hoxie and Tim Bernardis, "Robert Yellowtail, Crow," in *The New Warriors: Native American Leaders Since 1900*, ed. R. David Edmunds (Lincoln: University of Nebraska Press, 2001), 55–77.

6. Quoted in Frederick E. Hoxie, *Parading Through History: The Making of the Crow Nation in America, 1880–1935* (New York: Cambridge University Press, 1995), 328.

7. Quoted in ibid., 258.

8. "Address by Robert Yellowtail in Defense of the Rights of the Crow Indians, and the Indian Generally Before the Senate Committee on Indian Affairs, September 9, 1919," U.S. Senate Report 219, 66th Congress, 1st Session, Serial 7590 (Washington, D.C.: Government Printing Office, 1919).

9. Yellowtail's draft "plank" for the national parties was enclosed in his letter to John Collier, dated May 25, 1932. Papers of John Collier, Reel 4, File 177.

10. "To the Indians of Montana," enclosed with Yellowtail to Collier, May 25, ibid.

11. For Sloan and his Coahuilla clients, see Van H. Garner, *The Broken Ring: The Destruction of California Indians* (Tucson: Westernlore Books, 1982), 127–40.

12. *U.S. v. Boylan*, 265 F 165 (1920), 170, 174.

13. Laurence M. Hauptman, *The Iroquois and the New Deal* (Syracuse: Syracuse University Press, 1981), 11–13.

14. For General's remarkable campaign, see *Deskaheh: Iroquois Statesman and Patriot*, Six Nation Indian Museum Series (1970).

15. For Rickard and his views on Levi General, see Clinton Rickard, *Fighting Tuscarora: The Autobiography of Chief Clinton Rickard*, ed. Barbara Graymont (Syracuse: Syracuse University Press, 1973), 59–77. For more on Rickard, see Kevin Bruyneel, *The Third Space of Sovereignty; The Post-colonial Politics of U.S.-Indigenous Relations* (Minneapolis: University of Minnesota Press, 2007), 112–19.

16. The Seneca activists are described in *The Six Nations*, v. 3, n. 1 (January 1929), 11. For the heirship case, see *Woodin v. Seeley*, 252 N.Y.S. 818, decided August 27, 1931.

17. Laurence Hauptman, *Seven Generations of Iroquois Leadership* (Syracuse: Syracuse University Press, 2008), 69–72.

18. Joseph W. Latimer, *Our Indian Bureau System* (New York: n.p. 1923), 9. I am grateful to Jamie Singson for bringing Latimer's pamphlet to my attention. For a biographical sketch of Latimer, see John W. Larner, ed., *The Papers of Carlos Montezuma, M.D., Including the Papers of Maria Keller Montezuma Moore and Joseph W. Latimer* (Washington, D.C.: Scholarly Resources, 1983), 9–10. For Latimer's support for tribal governments, see Elmer Rusco, *A Fateful Time: The Background and Legislative History of the Indian Reorganization Act* (Reno: University of Nevada Press, 2000), 90.

19. "Six Nations Cite Grievances Against Government Bureau," *Buffalo Evening News*, February 4, 1933. Jemison, who had worked for the Census Bureau in 1930, was likely drawing here on personal observation.

20. Alice Lee Jemison, "Indians Want Some Voice in Selecting Commissioner," *Buffalo Evening News*, April 20, 1933.

21. Alice Jemison, "Indian Affairs, Denial of Hearing on New Commissioner Is Protested," *New York Times*, May 25, 1933, 18.

22. For details of McNickle's life, see Dorothy R. Parker, *Singing an Indian Song: A Biography of D'Arcy McNickle* (Lincoln: University of Nebraska Press, 1992).

23. From "Going to School," in Birgit Hans, ed., *D'Arcy McNickle: The Hawk Is Hungry and Other Stories* (Tucson: University of Arizona Press, 1992), 112.

24. "Meat for God," in ibid., 25–26, 33, 34.

25. McNickle to Collier, draft, May 4, 1934, quoted in Parker, *Singing an Indian Song*, 35, 67.

26. Representative William Hastings quoted in Kenneth Philp, *John Collier's Crusade for Indian Reform* (Tucson: University of Arizona Press, 1977), 158.

27. The best recent analysis of the final bill and its relation to Collier's original proposal is in Rusco, *A Fateful Time*, 255–81. Roosevelt is quoted on pp. 239–40. Collier repeated his (and the president's) prediction that failure to pass his bill would lead to the "extinction" of American Indians in a radio address delivered on May 7, 1934. See File 74-13, Association on American Indian Affairs Papers.

28. *From Every Zenith*, 200, 203. For a summary of Collier's accomplishments in office, see Philp, *John Collier's Crusade*, chapters 6, 7, 8.

29. Quoted in Hauptman, *Iroquois and the New Deal*, 44.

30. Jemison's column in the *Buffalo Evening News* for April 21, 1934, was read into the record at a Senate hearing in 1940. See "Wheeler Howard Act—Exempt Certain Indians," U.S. Senate Hearings on S.2103, 76th Congress, 3rd Session, 168.

31. "Indian Conditions and Affairs," Hearings Before the Subcommittee on General Bills of the Committee on Indian Affairs, House of Representatives, on H.R. 7781, February 11, 1935, 37.

32. Ibid., 36, 38. Free passage across the border had long been a central concern of Seneca leaders as well as Levi General and Clinton Rickard.

33. Ibid., 41.

34. Ibid., 483.

35. Ibid., 499.

36. Jemison's activities in 1934 are described in Laurence M. Hauptman, "The Modern Mother of the Nation," in *Sisters: Native American Women's Lives*, ed. Theda Perdue (New York: Oxford University Press, 2001), 179. The American Indian Federation's founding and the August resolution are described in the *First American*, the federation's newsletter (ed. Jemison), v. 1, n. 1, 6, 13. A June 15, 1934, letter from Jemison to New York Congressman Alfred Beiter expressing opposition to the new law was written from the YWCA. See "Indian Conditions and Affairs," 40. For a discussion of the AIF, see also Hauptman, *Iroquois and the New Deal*, 47–51.

37. "Indian Conditions and Affairs," 32.

38. Ibid., 498, 484, 485, 501.

39. The referendum results are summarized in Hauptman, *Iroquois and the New Deal*, 57; Fenton and Roe Cloud's role is described in ibid., 65–68.

40. This discussion of Yellowtail's activities in the 1930s is taken largely from Hoxie, *Parading Through History*, chapter 11.

41. Quoted in ibid., 326. See the telegram appointing Yellowtail: John Collier to Robert Yellowtail, July 31, 1934, John Collier Papers, Reel 18.

42. Quoted in Hoxie, *Parading Through History*, 334–35.

43. Vine Deloria, Jr., *The Indian Reorganization Act: Congresses and Bills* (Norman: University of Oklahoma Press, 2002), 69.

44. Quoted in Hoxie, *Parading Through History*, 341. The IRA allowed for the transfer of public land to tribal control and for modest purchases but did not address

the millions of acres lost by allottees to non-Indian farmers and ranchers. Crow tribal members understood that the new law would do little to repair the devastating land losses of the previous half century.

45. James Carpenter to Robert Lowie, February 26, 1935, and Robert Yellowtail to Commissioner of Indian Affairs, May 17, 1935; both quotations and the referendum results quoted in Hoxie, *Parading Through History*, 341.

46. For a history of the ratification and constitution-writing process at Rosebud and Pine Ridge, see Thomas Biolsi, *Organizing the Lakota: The Political Economy of the Pine Ridge and Rosebud Reservations* (Tucson: University of Arizona Press, 1992).

47. See Vine Deloria, Jr., and Clifford Lytle, *The Nations Within: The Past and Future of American Indian Sovereignty* (New York: Pantheon, 1984), 172.

48. See Parker, *Singing an Indian Song*, 71–72 and D'Arcy McNickle, "In Maine," *Indians at Work* (October 1, 1937), 15–18. McNickle's travels can also be deduced from his comments in a speech to the Missouri Archaeological Society. See D'Arcy McNickle, "The Indian Today," *Missouri Archaeologist*, v. 5, n. 2 (September 1939), 1–10.

49. D'Arcy McNickle, "Four Years of Indian Reorganization," *Indians at Work*, v. 5, n. 11 (July 1938), 4–11.

50. McNickle to Collier, June 30, 1937, quoted in Parker, *Singing an Indian Song*, 74.

51. McNickle, "Four Years of Indian Reorganization," 11.

52. McNickle, "The Indian Today," 10.

53. Harold E. Fey and D'Arcy McNickle, *Indians and Other Americans: Two Ways of Life Meet* (New York: Harper and Brothers, 1959), 146–47.

54. The evolution of McNickle's view of himself as an Indian advocate was also evident in his decision in 1939 to sign on to a separate statement issued by Indian delegates at a U.S.-Canadian conference on Indian policy. See Donald Smith, "Now We Talk—You Listen," *Rotunda* (Fall 1990), 48–52.

55. For her ties to the Black Hills group, see "Survey of Conditions of Indians in the United States," Senate Committee on Indian Affairs, Pursuant to S. Res. 79 (70th Congress) and Subsequent Continuing Resolution, 21441; for others, see ibid., 21553.

56. Jemison speech, July 27, 1938, quoted in Hauptman, *Iroquois and the New Deal*, 50.

57. *First American* (August 14, 1937), 2.

58. Ibid. (February 21, 1939), 1.

59. See Hauptman, *Iroquois and the New Deal*, 51–52.

60. Harold Ickes, *The Secret Diaries of Harold Ickes* (New York: Simon and Schuster, 1953), 507. Collier's charges were made in a hearing on a bill to repeal the Wheeler-Howard Act. See "Wheeler Howard Act—Exempt Certain Indians," House Committee on Indian Affairs (76th Congress, 3rd Session), Hearings on S. 2103, 69. The commissioner, who testified while the Nazi invasion of France

was unfolding, charged that Jemison's activities were "something deadly serious," 91.

61. *First American* (July 1, 1939), 2. The statue was ultimately removed in 1958.

62. See Hoxie and Bernardis, "Robert Yellowtail," 69–70, and Constance Poten, "Robert Yellowtail, the New Warrior," *Montana: The Magazine of Western History*, v. 39, n. 3 (1989), 38–39.

63. G. E. Barrett, "Crow Indians Hold Second Annual Tribal Fair," *Scenic Trails* (October 1937), 10.

64. See Hauptman, *Iroquois and the New Deal*, 136–63.

65. See Kenneth R. Philp, *Termination Revisited: American Indians on the Trail to Self-determination, 1933–1953* (Lincoln: University of Nebraska Press, 1999), 11–12.

66. D'Arcy McNickle, *They Came Here First: The Epic of the American Indian* (New York: Octagon Books, 1975; originally published in 1949), 262.

67. D'Arcy McNickle to Helen Peterson, August 13, 1959, NCAI Papers, Box 1.

68. The Bureau of Indian Affairs moved to Chicago during the war to free up office space in Washington, D.C., for the war effort. McNickle's planning for the first NCAI meeting thus took place at the BIA's temporary headquarters in the Midwest. McNickle described the process in his August 13, 1959 letter cited above.

69. "To Tribal Councils and Indian Leaders," October 16, 1944, NCAI Papers, Box 1.

70. McNickle to Peterson, August 13, 1959.

71. "Register of Delegates at the National Convention of American Indians Held in Denver, Colorado, November 15–18, 1944," NCAI Papers, Box 1.

72. Thomas W. Cowger, *The National Congress of American Indians: The Founding Years* (Lincoln: University of Nebraska Press, 1999), 44.

73. Napoleon Johnson, "The National Congress of American Indians," typescript of article published in *American Indian Magazine* (Summer 1946). NCAI Papers, Folder 27, Box 65. In February 1945 Dan Madrano, the newly elected secretary of the NCAI, testified in the confirmation hearing of William Brophy, who had been named by Roosevelt to succeed Collier. Madrano urged Congress to delay confirming Brophy and to consider appointing a Native American. See "Nomination of William A. Brophy to Be Commissioner of Indian Affairs," Hearings Before the Committee on Indian Affairs, U.S. Senate, February 26, 27, 28 and March 1, 1945.

74. Quoted in Prucha, *The Great Father*, 1015–16. See also Philp, *Termination Revisited*.

75. Robert Yellowtail to Ben Dwight, September 27, 1946. "Correspondence, Outgoing," Box 1, NCAI Papers.

76. Ibid.

77. Address by Robert Yellowtail, December 7, 1953, "Speeches," Box 4, NCAI Papers.

78. "New York Indians," Hearings Before the Subcommittee of the Committee on Interior and Insular Affairs, U.S. Senate, 80th Congress, 2nd Session, on S. 1683, S. 1686, and S. 1687, 23, 24, 26. See also Laurence M. Hauptman, *The Iroquois Struggle for Survival: World War II to Red Power* (Syracuse: Syracuse University Press, 1986), 48–64.

79. "New York Indians," 27.

80. "Resolution No. 15, The Indian Plan," "Proceedings, 1948," Box 2, NCAI Papers.

81. See Kenneth R. Philp, *Termination Revisited: American Indians on the Trail to Self-Determination, 1933–1953* (Lincoln: University of Nebraska Press, 1999), 60. Congressman Rogers's efforts helped prompt the Truman administration to propose spending $90 million for rehabilitation there.

82. Ruth Bronson to Harold Ickes, September 14, 1950[?], Series 8, Folder 1, Box 10, NCAI Papers.

83. "N. B. Johnson Urged 'Progressive Liquidation' of Indian Service," *Havre* (Mont.) *News*, December 11, 1951 in File 108-16, Governor's Interstate Council Clippings, Association on American Indian Affairs Papers.

84. McNickle, *They Came Here First*, 8–9.

85. Ibid., 300.

86. "Convention Proceedings, 1947," Box 1, NCAI Papers.

87. Prucha, *The Great Father*, 1043–44. See also Philp, *Termination Revisited*, 170–75 and passim, for a view of the termination campaign that downplays the role of Watkins, Butler, and other congressional critics.

88. Letter of invitation, February 9, 1954, and "A Declaration of Indian Rights," in "Résumé of the Emergency Conference of American Indians on Legislation," "Emergency Conference Bulletin," Box 257, NCAI Papers.

89. W. W. Short to Ruth Bronson, November 3, 1953, and Robert Yellowtail to Short, November 13, 1953, both in "General Correspondence, 1953," Box 4, NCAI Papers.

90. Garry was elected to the Idaho legislature in 1956.

91. "Address delivered to the National Congress of American Indians at Hotel Westward Ho, Phoenix, Arizona, December 7, 1953, by Robert Yellowtail, a Crow Indian," "Speeches, 1953," Box 4, NCAI Papers.

92. See "Indian Registrations," "Emergency Conference Bulletin," Box 257, NCAI. Yellowtail was not listed as a registered delegate to the conference, but he is referred to in the "Emergency Conference Bulletin" and was likely present.

93. "Termination of Federal Supervision over Certain Tribes of Indians," Joint Hearings Before the Subcommittees of the Committees on Interior and Insular Affairs on S.2745 and H.R. 7320, 83rd Congress, 2nd Session, Part Four, 342, 345, 347. Hauptman notes that Jemison's self-published newsletter, which she revived in the 1950s and published irregularly, declared that termination would leave Indians "suspended in a twilight zone of political nonentity." See Hauptman, *Iroquois Struggle for Survival*, 63.

94. Jim Hayes to Lawrence Lindley, March 29, 1954; Joseph Garry and Helen Peterson to Jonathan M. Steere, April 6, 1954, "Emergency Conference, Hayes Correspondence," Box 257, NCAI Papers. The conference featured appearances by Commissioner of Indian Affairs Glenn Emmons, Congressmen Carl Albert and Ed Emondson of Oklahoma, and Roger Baldwin, the founder of the American Civil Liberties Union. None of the prominent terminationist legislators appeared.
95. "Emergency Conference Bulletin," Box 257, NCAI Papers.
96. D'Arcy McNickle, "The Role of the National Congress of American Indians," 15th Anniversary Booklet, "D'Arcy McNickle Correspondence," Box 66, NCAI Papers.

CHAPTER EIGHT

1. *New York Times*, November 15, 2005.
2. Burnette wrote in his memoirs that he had told members of the executive committee in January 1964 that he would step down as executive director in July. See Robert Burnette, *The Tortured Americans* (New York: Prentice-Hall, 1971), 83.
3. For the bleak financial news, see "Convention Materials, 1964," Box 13, NCAI Papers, 6.
4. Deloria later claimed that he happened on the Sheridan meeting by accident and that he was "more a pawn" in the battle between the organization's factions than a serious candidate. See Vine Deloria, Jr., *Custer Died for Your Sins: An Indian Manifesto* (New York: Avon, 1969), 264–65. For more on the extraordinary history of the Delorias, see Vine Deloria, Jr., *Singing for a Spirit* (Santa Fe: Clear Light Publishers, 1999), 6–87.
5. "Convention Materials, 1964," 7.
6. Ibid.
7. Ibid., 8.
8. October 19, 2001, interview, quoted in Daniel Cobb, *Native Activism in Cold War America: The Struggle for Sovereignty* (Lawrence: University Press of Kansas, 2008), 118–19.
9. Quoted in ibid., 8. See also, D'Arcy McNickle, "Process or Compulsion: The Search for a Policy of Administration in Indian Affairs," *America Indigena*, v. 17, n. 3 (July 1957), 269. The connection between Point Four and Indian policy is also described in Paul Rosier, *Serving Their Country: American Indian Politics and Patriotism in the Twentieth Century* (Cambridge: Harvard University Press, 2009), 138–43, 191–201, though Rosier does not note McNickle's support for tribal development in the 1930s.
10. "A Program for Indian Citizens" (Albuquerque: Commission on the Rights, Liberties and Responsibilities of the American Indian, January 1961), iii. See Papers of the Association on American Indian Affairs (hereafter PAAIA), File 107 18, Fund for the Republic.

11. Ibid., 1, 4.

12. Nancy Oestreich Lurie, "The Voice of the American Indian: Report on the American Indian Chicago Conference," *Current Anthropology*, v. 2, n. 5 (December 1961), 481.

13. Oliver La Farge to LaVerne Madigan, December 16, 1960, PAAIA, File 59-6, American Indian Chicago Conference.

14. Quoted in Cobb, *Native Activism*, 38 ff. 18, 225.

15. The Association on American Indian Affairs executive director LaVerne Madigan reported to Oliver La Farge in April that the Rosebud tribal chairman Robert Burnette expressed fear of congressional termination sentiment at a meeting to discuss the Chicago conference. See Madigan to La Farge, April 6, 1961, PAAIA, File 59-7, American Indian Chicago Conference.

16. While William Rickard was not listed in the press release announcing the formation of the steering committee, he was present at the committee's preconference meetings, and he took an active role in the June conference. Apparently he was added to the group after the original announcement. See press release, February 15, 1961, PAAIA, File 59-6, American Indian Chicago Conference and "American Indian Chicago Conference Progress Report No. 3, March 16, 1961," 2 (photo of Rickard with steering committee), PAAIA, File 59-7, American Indian Chicago Conference. Rickard was also an associate of Wallace "Mad Bear" Anderson, a Tuscarora activist who had campaigned against the seizure of tribal lands for reservoirs in upstate New York and had traveled with a Seminole delegation to Havana, Cuba, in 1959 to seek the assistance of the country's revolutionary leader Fidel Castro. For a summary of his activities, see Rosier, *Serving Their Country*, 227–28.

17. Sol Tax to Oliver La Farge, January 20, 1961, PAAIA, File 59-6, American Indian Chicago Conference.

18. The final declaration and list of attendees were published as *Declaration of Indian Purpose: The Voice of the American Indian* (Chicago: University of Chicago, 1961).

19. Lurie, "The Voice of the American Indian," 497, 498.

20. LaVerne Madigan to Oliver La Farge, June 29, 1961, PAAIA, File 59-7, American Indian Chicago Conference.

21. See Cobb, *Native Activism*, 61–62, and George Pierre Castile, *To Show Heart: Native American Self-determination and Federal Indian Policy, 1960–1975* (Tucson: University of Arizona Press, 1998), 8–10. Bending to political pressure, the task force also noted that tribal development could lead to the termination of tribes, an outcome that could occur "with maximum benefit for all concerned."

22. "Notice of Meeting" and "Presentation," Burnette Proposal, Box 54, NCAI Papers.

23. "Presentation," ibid. See also Thomas W. Cowger, *The National Congress of American Indians: The Founding Years* (Lincoln: University of Nebraska Press, 1999), 141–44. Cowger notes that the Chicago conference "proved to be the

downfall of [the] NCAI leadership that had boldly led [the] NCAI through termination," 142.

24. Clyde Warrior quoted in Cobb, *Native Activism*, 53–54.

25. Deloria's grandfather Philip (Tipi Sapa) had been an early member of the society. See Deloria, *Singing for a Spirit*, 71.

26. See Castile, *To Show Heart*, 29–42; Cobb, *Native Activism*, 102–24. Three members of the OEO Indian Task Force were veterans of the 1961 Chicago Conference: Helen Maynor Schierbeck (Lumbee), Forest Gerrard (Blackfeet), and B. Frank Belvin (Choctaw).

27. Vine Deloria, Jr., *The Indian Affair* (New York: Friendship Press, 1974), 32, 33, 34, 33. For an overview of the size and nature of CAP projects, see Francis Paul Prucha, *The Great Father*, 1094, 1095.

28. Vine Deloria, Jr., "This Country Was Better Off When the Indians Were Running It," in *Red Power: The American Indian's Fight for Freedom*, ed. Alvin M. Josephy, Joane Nagel, and Troy Johnson (Lincoln: University of Nebraska Press, 1991, 1999), 30; originally published in the *New York Times*, March 8, 1970); quoted in Studs Terkel, *American Dreams, Lost and Found* (New York: Pantheon, 1980), 48.

29. Deloria, *Custer Died for Your Sins*, 180, 179, 180.

30. "Constitutional Rights of the American Indian," Hearings Before the Subcommittee on Constitutional Rights of the Committee on the Judiciary," U.S. Senate, June 24, 1965, 194, 195, 199.

31. Ibid., 196, 200, 201.

32. *NCAI Newsletter* (November 1965), 10.

33. Ibid. (Summer 1965), 2.

34. Ibid. (November 1965), 11.

35. Both quotations are in Cobb, *Native Activism*, 122.

36. Program, 23rd Annual Convention of the National Congress of American Indians, "Executive Committee Meeting," March 24–25, El Paso, Texas, 2. NCAI Papers, "NCAI Reports to 1966 Convention," Executive Director, Box 14.

37. "Indian Bureau Parley Rebuffs Tribes," *New York Times*, April 14, 1966, 29; ibid., "Two Indian Demands Granted by Udall," April 15, 1966, 20; "Indian Bureau Hails Udall Plan," ibid., April 16, 1966, 81. For a summary of the Santa Fe confrontation, see Cobb, *Native Activism*, 130–33.

38. *NCAI Newsletter* (Spring 1966), n.p. This issue also reported on another "lost document," a supposed report from Minnesota Chippewas, dated 1516. They described having found "the tracks of a Green Giant" and disclosed that "the HoHoHoing has kept them awake for nights on end."

39. *NCAI Newsletter*, Convention Issue (1966), n.p.

40. Deloria, *Custer Died for Your Sins*, 184, 270.

41. Vine Deloria, Jr., *We Talk, You Listen: New Tribes, New Turf* (Lincoln: University of Nebraska Press, 2007; originally published in 1970), 101, 100.

42. Ibid., 112.

43. Stan Steiner, *The New Indians* (New York: Harper & Row, 1968), ix; Deloria, *We Talk*, 113. Steiner's quotation of Deloria was not dated, but from its context it was clearly a statement made between the emergence of Black Power in mid-1966 and the executive director's departure from Washington, D.C., in 1967.

44. Deloria, "The Country Was Better Off When the Indians Were Running It," 36.

45. Deloria, *Custer Died for Your Sins*, 9, 10. The promotion of Deloria's book included the advance appearance of his scathing chapter on anthropologists in *Playboy* magazine.

46. Ibid., 87, 88, 103. Significantly, Deloria singled out Oliver La Farge for special scorn. He described this well-connected "friend of the Indian," who had supported John Collier and opposed the NCAI leadership's involvement in the 1961 Chicago conference, as a "skillful manipulator of Indian people" who "dealt primarily with Uncle Tomahawks who would say anything to stay on the good side of him." Ibid., 206.

47. Ibid., 240, 260.

48. John Greenway, "Books This Week," *Chicago Tribune*, October 7, 1969, 18; Edward Abbey, "Custer Died for Your Sins," *New York Times*, November 9, 1969, Book Review, 46; John Leonard, "Red Powerlessness," *New York Times*, November 18, 1969, 45. See also "Authors and Editors," *Publishers Weekly*, v. 196, n. 22 (December 1, 1969), 7. Abbey was probably referring to Arthur Kopit's *Indians*, a controversial play (which compared U.S. Indian policy to the war in Vietnam) that had recently opened in New York. Interestingly, one of Stewart Udall's anthropologist aides, James Officer, called *Custer* a "significant statement" despite its "invective." See *Arizona and the West*, v. 12, n. 3 (Autumn 1970), 292, 293.

49. Deloria, *Custer Died for Your Sins*, 209.

50. For a summary of the Alcatraz occupation, see Castile, *To Show Heart*, 112–15; Deloria, *Custer Died for Your Sins*, 243–44. The definitive study of Alcatraz and its aftermath is Paul Chaat Smith and Robert Allen Warrior, *Like a Hurricane: The Indian Movement from Alcatraz to Wounded Knee* (New York: New Press, 1996).

51. Smith and Warrior, *Like a Hurricane*, 22–23.

52. "Arrows for the White Man Fill Sioux Author's Quiver," *Los Angeles Times*, March 12, 1970, H1, 16.

53. *New York Times*, November 9, 1969, Book Review, 46. For a summary of protests and occupation in the wake of the Alcatraz takeover, see Smith and Warrior, *Like a Hurricane*, 87–93. For Chicago, see James LaGrand, *Indian Metropolis: Native Americans in Chicago, 1945–1975* (Urbana: University of Illinois Press, 2002), 240–43. Kevin Bruyneel places Custer in the context of anticolonialism and postcolonial theory in *The Third Space of Sovereignty: The Post-colonial Politics of U.S.-Indigenous Relations* (Minneapolis: University of Minnesota Press, 2007), 134–69.

54. This necessarily brief summary of the 1972 occupation focuses on Deloria's reaction to the crisis and says little about the important role many leaders played. For a fuller description, see Smith and Warrior, *Like a Hurricane*, 149–78.

55. Vine Deloria, Jr., "The New Exodus," *Civil Rights Digest*, v. 4, n. 2 (Spring 1971), 39, 44. This essay was a written version of his address at the Smithsonian Institution on November 18, 1970. See *Washington Post*, November 17, 1970, B1.

56. Deloria, *We Talk*, 105, 145–46, 208–9.

57. Deloria made the comments in an interview published in the tribal newspaper *Akwesasne Notes* (Early Winter 1973), 43.

58. Vine Deloria, Jr., *Behind the Trail of Broken Treaties: An Indian Declaration of Independence* (Austin: University of Texas Press, 1985; originally published in 1974), 39, 54; Vine Deloria, Jr., "The Indian World Today," *American Indian Culture Center Journal*, UCLA (Winter 1973), 4; Vine Deloria, Jr., "Bury Our Hopes at Wounded Knee," *Los Angeles Times*, April 1, 1973, VI, 1. Deloria also criticized the AIM leaders at Wounded Knee for having failed to provide a coherent strategy for their followers. See *Los Angeles Times*, May 5, 1973, A1, 18. He declared, "One of AIM's problems is they come and stay too long."

59. Deloria, "The Country Was a Lot Better Off," 31.

60. "Russell Means: A New Indian Hope," quoted in Smith and Warrior, *Like a Hurricane*, 273.

61. Deloria, "Bury Our Hopes at Wounded Knee," VI, 1, 7.

62. Ibid., 7.

63. Actress Maria Cruz, dressed as an Apache named Sacheen Littlefeather, accepted Marlon Brando's Best Actor award and made a brief statement in support of the Wounded Knee protesters. See Smith and Warrior, *Like a Hurricane*, 235–36.

64. Vine Deloria, Jr., *Integrated Education*, v. 12, n. 3 (May–June 1974), 25.

65. Vine Deloria, Jr., ed., *Of Utmost Good Faith* (San Francisco: Straight Arrow Books, 1971), 4.

66. Vine Deloria, Jr., "It's a Good Day to Die," *Katallagete: Be Reconciled*, v. 4, n. 2, 3 (Fall–Winter 1972), 63–64.

67. Ibid., 64, 65.

68. Ibid., 65.

69. Vine Deloria, Jr., *God Is Red* (New York: Grosset & Dunlap, 1973). Journalist Stan Steiner was the first to report Deloria's using the slogan in Steiner, *The New Indians*, 108.

70. Anthropologist Raymond DeMallie presented a similar view of Deloria's two-sided approach to Indian affairs in an obituary published in the *American Anthropologist* after the Sioux activist's death. See Raymond J. DeMallie, "Vine Deloria, Jr. (1933–2005)," *American Anthropologist*, v. 108, n. 4 (2006), 932–35.

71. Deloria, *God Is Red*, 38, 50, 53, 56. *God Is Red* seems to have gone to press while the Wounded Knee occupation was still taking place.

72. Ibid., 64, 65, 73, 67. The linkage between Deloria's view of sacred lands and his childhood experiences in South Dakota was made plain in his introduction to the 1994 edition of *God Is Red*. There he wrote that the stories his father told him about the sacred landscape of Sioux country taught him that "the Sioux people cherished their lands and treated them as if they were people who shared a common history with humans." See *God Is Red* (Golden, Colo.: Fulcrum, 1994), 1.

73. Ibid., 75, 76, 77, 80, 83.

74. Ibid., 301, 300. Deloria devoted several pages in *God Is Red* to a defense of the astronomer Immanuel Velikovsky, who argued that both Venus and Mars had passed close to Earth in ancient times, causing worldwide catastrophes. Deloria drew on Velikovsky's arguments to defend the historical accuracy of ancient myths and legends. Writing just as Velikovsky was being discredited by Carl Sagan and other luminaries, Deloria no doubt hurt his case by relying on the controversial scientist. He was drawn to controversial scientific ideas throughout his career. He always enjoyed provoking self-important scholars and challenging their most precious assumptions.

75. Deloria, *Behind the Trail of Broken Treaties*, x.

76. Ibid., 75, 80, 81; Guy Dull Knife, Jr., quoted in Rosier, *Serving Their Country*, 265.

77. Deloria, *Behind the Trail of Broken Treaties*, 172, 255. Deloria invoked San Marino several times in his discussion of small states; see ibid., 163–86.

78. Deloria, ibid., 247, 183, 252.

79. Vine Deloria, Jr., "The Next Three Years: A Time for Change," *Indian Historian*, v. 7, n. 2 (Spring 1974), 27. In addition to publishing *Custer Died for Your Sins; We Talk, You Listen; God Is Red*; and *Behind the Trail of Broken Treaties*, Deloria wrote *The Indian Affair* (New York: Friendship Press, 1974), an overview of Indian issues, for Friendship Press, an arm of the National Council of Churches.

80. For an overview of these events, see R. David Edmunds, Frederick E. Hoxie, and Neal Salisbury, *The People: A History of Native America* (Boston: Houghton Mifflin, 2007), 435–44.

81. Vine Deloria, Jr., *Indians of the Pacific Northwest* (New York: Doubleday, 1977), *The Metaphysics of Modern Existence* (New York: Harper & Row, 1979).

82. Donald Worcester, "God Is Red," *American Indian Quarterly*, v. 1, n. 1 (Spring 1974), 87–88.

83. See Spintz Stiles Harrison, "Everything You Wanted to Know About American Indian Studies but Were Afraid to Ask: Assessing Indian Studies as an Academic Discipline" (PhD dissertation, University of Arizona, 2006), 63–65.

84. Vine Deloria, Jr., "Activism, 1950–1980," in *Handbook of North American Indians: Indians in Contemporary Society*, ed. Garrick Bailey (Washington, D.C.: Government Printing Office, 2008), v. 2, 44.

85. Vine Deloria, Jr., "Legislation and Litigation Concerning American Indians," *Annals of the American Academy of Political and Social Science*, v. 436, n. 1 (March 1978), 96.

86. Following his move to Arizona, Deloria also began a collaboration with Clifford Lytle, a constitutional scholar who was a colleague in the political science department. Lytle and Deloria published two major monographs, *American Indians, American Justice* (Austin: University of Texas Press, 1983) and *The Nations Within: The Past and Future of American Indian Sovereignty* (New York: Pantheon, 1983). During his early years at Arizona, Deloria also organized the publication of two volumes of essays on federal Indian policy: Sandra L. Cadwalader and Vine Deloria, Jr., eds., *The Aggressions of Civilization: Federal Indian Policy Since the 1880s* (Philadelphia: Temple University Press, 1984) and Vine Deloria, Jr., ed., *American Indian Policy in the Twentieth Century* (Norman: University of Oklahoma Press, 1985). Finally, he spent considerable time on a book exploring the relationship between the psychology of C. G. Jung and the traditions of the Sioux. Unfinished at the time of Deloria's death, the book was eventually published as *C. G. Jung and the Sioux Traditions: Dreams, Visions, Nature and the Primitive*, ed. Jerome S. Bernstein and Philip J. Deloria (New Orleans: Spring Journal, 2009).

87. Vine Deloria, Jr., "Minorities and the Social Contract," *Georgia Law Review*, v. 20, n. 4 (Summer 1986), 925, 919.

88. Testimony reprinted in *Northeast Indian Quarterly*, v. 4, n. 4 (Winter 1987), 59. Original testimony in "Hearings Before the Select Committee on Indian Affairs on S. Con. Res. 76," 100th Congress, 1st Session, December 2, 1987, 22–27.

89. Vine Deloria, Jr., "Reflections on Federal Indian Law," *Arizona Law Review*, v. 31 (1989), 203, 204, 205, 213, 219–20.

90. Ibid., 215, 217, 219.

91. Vine Deloria, Jr., "Out of Chaos," *Parabola*, v. 10, n. 2 (May 1985), 15, 17, 20–21.

92. Deloria and Lytle, *The Nations Within*, 243, 264; Robert Allen Warrior, "Vine Deloria Jr.," *Progressive*, v. 54 (April, 1990), 27.

93. Vine Deloria, Jr., "American Indians and the Moral Community" and "Law and Theology III: The Theme," *Church and Society* v. 79, n. 1 (September–October 1988), 29, 30, 13.

94. Deloria's single-author books from his years at Colorado were *Red Earth, White Lies: Native Americans and the Myth of Scientific Fact* (New York: Scribner, 1995); *Evolution, Creationism and Other Modern Myths* (Golden, Colo.: Fulcrum, 2002), and *The World We Used to Live In: Remembering the Powers of the Medicine Men* (Golden, Colo.: Fulcrum, 2006). Deloria also cowrote one book with his former student David Wilkins, *Tribes, Treaties and Constitutional Tribulations* (Austin: University of Texas Press, 1999), and edited three others. The first of these was a reissue of Sarah Olden's *The People of Tipi Sapa*, a religious book about his grandfather published first in 1918: *Singing for a Spirit: A Portrait of the Dakota Sioux* (Santa Fe: Clearlight, 1999). The second was *Exiled in the Land of the Free: Democracy, Indian Nations and the U.S. Constitution* (Santa Fe: Clearlight, 1992), a collaboration with several Iroquois experts and scholars. The third was the

record of John Collier's Indian congresses, held in 1934, prior to the passage of the Indian Reorganization Act: *The Indian Reorganization Act: Congresses and Bills* (Norman: University of Oklahoma Press, 2002). A final edited collection was coedited with the anthropologist Raymond J. DeMallie, *Documents of American Indian Diplomacy: Treaties, Agreements and Conventions, 1775–1979* (Norman: University of Oklahoma Press, 1999).

95. Vine Deloria, Jr., "Thinking in Public," *American Literary History*, v. 10, n. 1 (Spring 1998), 24.

96. Deloria, *Red Earth, White Lies*, 13; Deloria, *The World We Used to Live In*, xvii.

97. Vine Deloria, Jr., "Intellectual Self Determination and Sovereignty: Looking at the Windmills in Our Minds," *Wicazo Sa Review*, v. 13, n. 1 (Spring 1998), 27; Deloria, and Wilkins, *Tribes, Treaties*, ix.

98. Deloria, "Intellectual Self-determination," 31.

99. Deloria, *The World We Used to Live In*, xxiii; Vine Deloria, Jr., "Is Religion Possible? An Evaluation of Present Efforts to Revive Traditional Tribal Religions," *Wicazo Sa Review*, v. 8, n. 1 (Spring 1992), 39. In this 1992 essay Deloria also described a project that preoccupied him for much of his time at the University of Colorado, gathering tribal elders together to hear their stories and their teachings for contemporary Indians. See ibid., 38.

100. Vine Deloria, Jr., "Response to David Brumble," *American Literary History*, v. 10, n. 2 (Summer 1998), 349.

101. For a summary of how extensively Deloria's ideas were incorporated into Indian policy and academic discourse, see David Wilkins, "Forging a Political, Educational and Cultural Agenda for Indian Country," in *Destroying Dogma: Vine Deloria, Jr. and His Influence on American Society*, ed. Steve Pavlik and David R. Wildcat (Golden, Colo.: Fulcrum, 2006), 157–96.

102. Deloria, *The World We Used to Live In*, 214.

AFTERWORD

1. The Republican and Democratic platforms are available at the American Presidency Project, www.presidency.ucsb.edu/showplatforms.php.

2. "Bush Pledges to Uphold Sovereignty," *Indian Country Today* (August 30, 2000); see also Valerie Tailman, "Politics and Indian Country in 2000," *Indian Country Today* (October 11, 2000).

3. *United States v. Sandoval*, 231 U.S. 28 (1913).

INDEX

THE PENGUIN HISTORY OF AMERICAN LIFE

Founding Editor: Arthur M. Schlesinger, Jr.

Board Members:

Other available titles in the series: